HOUSING PROVISION AND BOTTOM-UP APP

Housing Provision and Bottom-up Approaches

Family case studies from Africa, Asia and South America

Edited by
ADENRELE AWOTONA
Southern University and A & M College
Baton Rouge, Louisiana, USA

Routledge
Taylor & Francis Group

LONDON AND NEW YORK

First published 1999 by Ashgate Publishing

Reissued 2018 by Routledge
2 Park Square, Milton Park, Abingdon, Oxon OX14 4RN
711 Third Avenue, New York, NY 10017, USA

Routledge is an imprint of the Taylor & Francis Group, an informa business

Publisher's Note
The publisher has gone to great lengths to ensure the quality of this reprint but points out that some imperfections in the original copies may be apparent.

Disclaimer
The publisher has made every effort to trace copyright holders and welcomes correspondence from those they have been unable to contact.

A Library of Congress record exists under LC control number: 98073753

ISBN 13: 978-1-138-32182-3 (hbk)
ISBN 13: 978-1-138-32188-5 (pbk)
ISBN 13: 978-0-429-45239-0 (ebk)

Contents

v

List of charts

List of figures

List of plates

List of tables

Notes on contributors

Iris Aravot is a Senior Lecturer in the Faculty of Architecture and Town Planning, Technion, I.I.T., Haifa, Israel and Head of the Centre for Architectural Research and Development. She gained her DSc in 1987 for the thesis *Toward a Theory of Architectural Knowledge*, and has also studied philosophy at Haifa University. A recipient of numerous awards at the Technion, Dr. Aravot has been a member of staff since 1979. She has published numerous articles in both Hebrew and English and her major fields of research and teaching are: Urban design; Housing, and Philosophy of architecture. She is also a partner of Aravot Ltd., a practice in urban design.

Ben C. Arimah is on the Faculty of the Centre for Urban and Regional Planning, University of Ibadan, Nigeria and is a policy analyst at the Development Policy Centre in Ibadan. He obtained his PhD from the University of Ibadan in 1990. His areas of specialisation include housing and urban economics and environmental management. He has published many articles in *Land Economics, Urban Studies, Environment and Planning, Netherlands Journal of Housing and the Built Environment, Journal of Environmental Management, Journal of Real Estate and Construction,* and *OPEC Review* amongst many others. At the time of writing this chapter, he was visiting Shelter-Afrique in Nairobi, Kenya on a research fellowship.

Adenrele Awotona, who was educated at the Universities of Newcastle and Cambridge, is currently a Professor of Architecture at Southern University in Baton Rouge in the United States of America. He was formerly the Director of the Centre for Architectural Research and Development Overseas (CARDO) and the

Director of Postgraduate Studies in Architecture, both at the University of Newcastle upon Tyne, England. He has been a principal investigator (or co-investigator) on major research projects funded by national and international agencies including the United Nations Centre for Human Settlements (UNCHS), the United Nations Development Programme (UNDP), the Department for International Development (DFID) of the British Government, and the European Union.

Professor Awotona has been on research assignments to various parts of North America (*United States of America and Canada*), South America, The Caribbean, Europe, The Middle East, Asia (including *India, Turkey, Singapore and the People's Republic of China*), the South Pacific and various countries in Africa (including *Egypt, Ghana, Nigeria and South Africa*). Similarly, he has been invited to advise on curriculum development in Universities internationally. Furthermore, he has extensive experience in graduate supervision, particularly doctoral dissertations. He has also been an External examiner for 231 higher degree dissertations and theses (MA, MSc, PhD and DPhil) in several universities world-wide.

Professor Awotona has published three edited books and 127 research papers. He is a referee for a number of international academic journals and is at present a Member of the International Advisory Board of the *Third World Planning Review* (Liverpool University Press, UK). Similarly, he has been listed in a number of *International Who's Who in Education.*

Magda Behloul graduated from Algiers' School of Architecture in 1986, obtained her PhD at Sheffield University in 1991 and is currently lecturing at the Department of Architecture in Huddersfield University where she is in charge of the International component of the architecture course which provides students with the opportunity to carrying out design projects in Non-European Cultures.

Dr. Behloul has contributed to various international Housing and Development conferences, and has published numerous papers. She organised the 13th Inter-Schools Conference on Development at Huddersfield University in March 1996. She is a member of the International Association for People-Environment Studies and a referee for *Habitat International*. Current research interests are: Housing design in North Africa and the Middle East; Appropriate building materials; Contemporary architecture in the Arab world; Post-occupancy evaluation of buildings; and Environment and Behaviour.

Souheil El-Masri graduated from the Faculty of Architecture of Beirut Arab University in 1981, after which he practised architecture for five years during which he designed a wide range of projects in Lebanon and the Middle East. He holds MPhil (1988) and PhD (1992) degrees from the University of Newcastle upon Tyne, England, both focusing on Post-war Settlement Reconstruction with special reference to Lebanon. As a Guest Member of Staff at the Centre for Architectural Research and Development Overseas, University of Newcastle. he initiated a network and research activities in the field of disaster and human settlements and co-edited a *Reconstruction After Disaster* newsletter. In 1994, Dr El-Masri joined the Department of Civil and Architectural Engineering at the University of Bahrain, where he is now Assistant Professor. He has delivered papers at many international conferences and published extensively in the area of reconstruction after disaster.

Hala Kardash graduated as an architect in 1983 from Cairo University, Egypt. Subsequently she gained a Diploma in Architectural Design in 1986 from the same university. Before and after gaining a PhD in Architecture from the University of Newcastle upon Tyne, England, in 1993 Dr Kardash was a research assistant for the General Organisation for Housing, Planning and Building Research in Cairo. Dr Kardash now lives in the United States of America where she works part-time as a home-based architect. Her publications deal mainly with the issues of users transformations of public housing and the evaluation of self-help projects.

Ying Liu was born in Dalian, the People's Republic of China, in 1962. She received the BSc degree in architecture in 1984 from Dalian University, and a diploma of advanced study in architectural design in 1987 from Tsinghua University, Beijing. From 1987 to 1993, she worked in the Department of Civil Engineering, Dalian University as an assistant lecturer and later as a lecturer. She has recently obtained an MPhil degree in architecture at the University of Newcastle Upon Tyne, UK. Her current research interests include architectural design for the development of traditional housing settlements, vernacular architecture in Asia, socio-cultural influences in design, and principles of architectural design.

Amos Rapoport is Distinguished Professor in the School of Architecture and Urban Planning at the University of Wisconsin-Milwaukee. He teaches Vernacular Design, Behavioural Factors in Housing, Behavioural Factors in Urban Design and Design for Developing Countries.
  He is one of the founders of the new field of Environment-Behaviour Studies. His work has focused mainly on the role of cultural variables, cross-cultural studies, and theory development and synthesis. He is the editor or co-editor of four books and several monographs and the author of approximately 200 papers, five books and several monographs. His work has been translated into many languages.

David Sanderson was educated in architecture with a Masters degree in Development Practices. His project experience since 1992 has been in countries in

Central and South America, the Caribbean, Africa, Asia, Eastern Europe and the Former Soviet Union. He has carried out consultancy, research and training projects for the Department for International Development (DFID), the European Commission Humanitarian Office (ECHO), the World Bank (DEI Section), the British Council and Tear Fund. He is also the author/contributor to several articles and publications regarding development and risk reduction.

As Project Manager for the Oxford Centre for Disaster Studies, Mr Sanderson is currently working on a two year research project into urban risk reduction in India for the DFID's Technology Development and Research (TDR) programme.

Abubaker M. Shawesh obtained his PhD (1996) from the Centre for Architectural Research and Development Overseas, University of Newcastle upon Tyne with a thesis on the investigation of traditional and contemporary housing design and socio-cultural values in Libya. Prior to this Dr Shawesh was involved in the management and construction of buildings in Libya. He has now returned to Libya to work at the University of Al-Fateh, Tripoli.

Andrew Spiegel is a Senior Lecturer in the Department of Social Anthropology at the University of Cape Town and has published widely on rural and urban poverty, household formation, and migration patterns in Southern Africa. He is continuing to work with Vanessa Watson and Peter Wilkinson on the issues raised by their joint research enterprise of which their contribution to this book is part.

Ola Uduku is a lecturer in Architecture at the School of Architecture and Building Engineering at the University of Liverpool. She has research interests in social infrastructure provision in urban areas in sub Saharan Africa and amongst ethnic minorities in inner city areas in Europe. She also has an interest in school design in Africa.

Dr Uduku was formerly the Smuts Research Fellow at the African Studies Centre, University of Cambridge, and remains a Research Associate of the Centre for African Studies at the University of Cape Town. In 1995 she co-hosted the *Learning Spaces Development in Southern Africa* at the School of Education at the University of Durban, and has worked with Dr Awotona on the DFID sponsored Cape Town regeneration project. Currently she is working on a book on school design in Africa and a research project on social infrastructure provision in Granby Toxteth Liverpool.

Vanessa Watson is an Associate Professor in the School of Architecture and Planning at the University of Cape Town. She has published work on South African urbanisation and housing policy, amongst other topics. She is continuing to work with Andrew Spiegel and Peter Wilkinson on the issues raised by their joint research enterprise of which their contribution to this book is part.

Peter Wilkinson is an Associate Professor in the Department of Social Anthropology at the University of Cape Town and Director of the Urban Problems Research Unit. He has published work on the historical and contemporary dynamics of housing policy formation in South Africa. He is continuing to work with Andrew Spiegel and Vanessa Watson on the issues raised by their joint research enterprise of which their contribution to this book is part.

Preface

ADENRELE AWOTONA

It has been estimated that between 1990 and 2030, the world population will enlarge by 3.7 billion people, 90 per cent of which will take place in Africa, Asia and South America, mainly in urban areas (Wichman, 1995, p.1). By 2030, urban populations in these continents will be twice the size of rural populations. However, due to wide spread poverty, a recent study by the United Nations Centre for Human Settlements (1996, pp.114-122), has shown that 'at least 600 million urban dwellers in Africa, Asia and Latin America live in "life- and health-threatening" homes and neighbourhoods because of poor housing and living conditions and the lack of adequate provision for safe, sufficient water supplies and provision for sanitation, drainage, the removal of garbage, and health care'. The study also noted that out of the one billion 'poor people' (those whose incomes and consumption levels fall below nationally defined poverty levels), two-thirds are in Asia and over a fifth in sub-Saharan Africa. Similarly, *The Guardian* (1996) has revealed that there are 11 million homeless people in the world; that one person in three is homeless or in severely sub-standard housing in Africa, Asia and South America; that a third of the population in most cities in these three continents are squatters; that 37 million people have been driven from their homes by violence or armed conflict, and 80 per cent of these are women and children; that more than one billion people have no clean water or sanitation; and, that 25,000 people die each day from water-borne disease. A paper by the United Nations Economic and Social Commission for Asia and the Pacific Division of Industry, Human Settlements and Environment notes that (1991, p.45):

The growth of slums, squatter settlements and informal subdivisions (in Asia and the Pacific) is symptomatic of rapid urban population growth. Some of the sprawling low-income settlements, with marginal or no access to basic urban services, like Dharavi in Bombay and Orangi-Baldia in Karachi, house as many as a million people. Estimates show that between 20 and 40 per cent of the population in South Asian and Southeast Asian mega-cities live in sub-standard housing. Homelessness is a major problem in Bombay and Calcutta. It is estimated that as many as 200,000 people in Bombay live on streets. Some have been there for as long as 10 years. Urban poverty has increased in other countries as well. In the Republic of Korea, Pakistan and Myanmar, the percentage of population living below the poverty line is higher in urban areas than in rural areas.

A recent study by the UNCHS (1996, p.199) reveals that only 56 per cent of dwellings in low-income countries (such as Nigeria and China) have water connections to their plots. It also shows that the number of persons per room in low-income countries is 2.47. The figures are 2.24 for low-mid income countries (e.g. Algeria, Malaysia and South Africa), 1.03 for mid-high income countries (such as Israel) and 0.66 for high income countries (such as UK, USA and Japan). Furthermore in Nigeria, for instance, a national integrated survey conducted by the Federal Office of Statistics between April 1991 and March 1992, results of which were published in 1993, reveal that in rural areas only 11 per cent of the households have access to piped water supplies, 42 per cent have pit latrines, 52 per cent have no formal toilets and use the bush or dunghills, while only 19 per cent have electricity (Awotona, 1996, pp.45-46). The same study shows that in urban areas, more than 87 per cent still live in single rooms or a combination of single rooms, while about 75 per cent continue to use pit latrines. In Ghana, it has been estimated that there is a deficit of 83,000 toilets, 57,000 bathrooms and 46,000 kitchens in the Accra Metropolitan Area alone (Government of Ghana, 1990, p.5).

Furthermore, between 30 per cent and 60 per cent of the dwelling units in most cities of Africa, Asia and South America are 'illegal' in that either they contravene land ownership laws or they contravene official building and planning laws or codes. Many contravene both sets of laws (UNCHS (Habitat), 1996, p.199). In low-income countries, 64 per cent of the total housing stock is 'illegal' while only 13 per cent is public housing; 33 per cent of the dwelling units are owned by the occupants. In the low-mid income countries, the corresponding figures are 36 per cent, 11 per cent and 52 per cent. In the high income countries, the figures are 0 per cent, 13 per cent and 51 per cent respectively.

The governments of most countries in Africa, Asia and South America have, however, failed to tackle the housing problem in a coherent way, largely due to inadequate budgetary allocation to this sector. For instance, government expenditure per person on water supply, sanitation, drainage, garbage collection, roads and electricity are (UNCHS (Habitat), 1996, p.200) US$16.6 in cities in sub-

Saharan Africa, US$15.0 in South Asia, US$72.5 in East Asia, and US$48.4 in Latin America and the Caribbean. The figure is US$656.0 in West Europe, North America and Australasia. Indeed, it has been assessed that in most African countries, for example, 'public housing projects account for less than five per cent of total housing production' (Tipple, 1994, p.590). For example, the inability of the public sector in South Africa to provide housing for the overwhelming majority of the homeless poor is borne out by the results of recent surveys (People's Dialogue Report, 1995, p.24; The South African Homeless People's Federation, 1995, pp.12-13). These reveal that in 35 informal settlements, the Government has failed to build a single house since 27 April 1994. Table 1 shows that the private sector has built 38 four-roomed houses at an average cost (top structure only) of R25,000 (R7.36=£1.00 Sterling as at 12 June 1997), and 30 two-roomed houses at an average cost of R12,000. During that same period, the people themselves actually built 9,581 shacks.

Table 1   **Housing delivery from April 1994 to April 1995 in 35 poor communities in South Africa**

City/Region	East Rand	North-West	Cape Town	George	Total
No. of informal Settlements	14	4	7	10	35
Public housing (Built by the Government)	0	0	0	0	0
Private Sector					
• 4-room	23	5	-	10	38
(average cost)	(R15,500)	(R60,000)		(R26,000)	(R24,000)
• 2-room	20	0	0	10	30
(average cost)	(R8,000)*			(R15,000)	(R10,333)
People's sector					
• Shacks built by the people	1,859	1,205	3,877	2,640	9,581
• Shacks demolished	166	0	0	5	171
Government allocated plots	0	0	0	120	120
Plots invaded (by the poor)	0	0	0	191	191

* R7.36=£1.00 Sterling as at 12 June 1997
Source: People's Dialogue Report (1995, p.24)

Thus, the rapidly increasing gap between supply and demand has led to the proliferation of informal settlements and the growth of shanty towns, offering precarious and dismal conditions to their residents (e.g. substandard shelter, overcrowding, high vulnerability to disasters, and inadequate water supplies, sanitation, electricity, refuse collection, etc.). Governmental, or top-down, responses to these problems have ranged from the non-existent to the irrational destruction of slums, through to the construction of 'symbolic' housing schemes. In addition to limited resources, such responses have been driven by the perceived low priority of housing, the belief that housing demand should be met by the private sector or, perhaps most significantly, the inappropriate use of Western approaches to town planning and housing. Indeed, by the 1980s, it had become transparently obvious that 'governments could not maintain a role as direct producers of housing, and that this role must necessarily be performed by the formal or informal private sector' (World Bank, 1993, p.19). The Lieutenant Governor of Pondicherry in India, Dr Singh (1991, pp.10-11), has observed, in his critique of the role of government in housing production as follows:

> In my opinion, the government should not get involved in actually producing housing and I have a feeling that most people would agree with me... We have a Housing Board in Pondicherry, but I am not too happy with its performance. We have received a number of complaints about the poor quality of the houses produced by the Board... There is also the question of efficiency. There seems to be no co-ordination between various stages in the production process. Often, there are long and unconscionable delays in construction and almost every project ultimately involves cost over-runs.
>
> Government Bodies and Corporations have become massive bureaucracies and their functioning is no different from that of a Government Department. Such Bodies were created in the hope that they would have freedom of action, be able to take expeditious decisions, and have an efficient and productive work force. On all points, the reality belies the expectations.

Consequently, Dr Singh concluded that 'rather than constructing housing of questionable quality with which no one is happy, it may be better to discontinue such agencies and leave the process of housing to the individual consumer'.

In contrast to the inability of government to supply housing units which meet the needs of the mass of the people directly, both quantitatively and qualitatively, the people themselves have initiated and acquired shelter by using their own networks, resources and ingenuity. These initiatives are commonly referred to as informal, incremental, unauthorised, unconventional, popular or bottom-up approaches. They are usually characterised by family/household and community involvement, the use of local resources, incremental building, and the adoption of appropriate standards and technology.

Against this background, the purpose of this book is to provide a clear understanding of the physical and non-physical structures in bottom-up housing approaches through the use of in-depth case studies from Africa, Asia and South America. Physical structures include design aspects, materials, infrastructure, and construction methods and stages. Non-physical structures include finance sources, participation and decision-making processes. All these elements present a challenging task for academics, researchers, policy makers and non-governmental organisations when intervening in bottom-up housing approaches.

Structure of the book

This book, which is aimed primarily at all those who are concerned with housing provision for the majority of the people in a way that responds to their social, cultural and economic circumstances, consists of four sections. Section I is an overview of conceptual issues. Sections II through IV are composed of case studies and fieldwork experiences from Africa, Asia (including the Middle East), and South America, respectively.

In Chapter 1 (Section I), Rapoport proposes a conceptual analysis of family/housing relations which he had derived from a model of culture/built environment relations. He examines various aspects of the family, households, culture and housing, intrinsic and extrinsic aspects of housing/family relations, and the meaning of 'housing'. Having explained the extraordinary variety of dwellings and their contexts in terms of the latent aspects of activity systems and lifestyles, he then uses a number of examples from around the world to illustrate some of the points made. In conclusion, Rapoport notes that 'housing not only reflects social and cultural change but also leads to it: Housing which is inappropriate, and hence inhibiting (or merely not supportive), may lead to undesirable changes in family structure, behaviour and other aspects of culture'.

Section II consists of six chapters. The first of these, Chapter 2 by Arimah, proposes that user modification can be seen as a bottom-up approach which seeks to rectify some of the physical shortcomings associated with the direct construction of public housing. Empirical data are presented to illustrate the degree and nature of user modifications in Satellite Town, a middle income housing estate in Lagos, Nigeria. The study shows that user modifications are relatively widespread in the civil servants' section of the estate and that these transformations are likely to continue in the future, since they serve many useful functions. The chapter concludes by recommending that policy makers in Nigeria should 'move away from the narrow conception of housing which simply entails provision of core shelter' and concentrate efforts on creating liveable environments that are in 'consonance with the culture and socio-economic characteristics of the intended beneficiaries. This will to some extent stem the tide of user modifications and prevent the occurrence of some of the problems associated with these modifications in public housing estates'. In Chapter 3, Kardash examines the transformation introduced by the users on a core housing scheme in the Tenth of Ramadan City, a newly built settlement near Cairo, Egypt. In this public estate, the users managed to increase considerably, their habitable space by building extensions to the initially provided core houses. The study shows that this was achieved in the absence of any form of organisational, financial or technical help from any formal authority. Ignoring the officially produced prototype plans, the users defied the laws and regulations in order to create a more responsive environment to their needs, expectations and hopes. In Chapter 4, Behloul investigates users' perception of their housing environment in Algiers. In response to the acute housing shortage in Algeria, large mass public housing programmes were launched from the late 1970s. The rapidity with which these housing estates were constructed, however, resulted in certain qualitative aspects of dwelling design being either overlooked or ill considered. Based on the research findings, the chapter ends with a number of recommendations which are applicable to the programming, design and the management of future mass housing estates in Algeria. In a similar vein, Chapter 5, by Shawesh and Awotona, reports the findings of research into the attitudes of Libyan families to their traditional and contemporary houses. These are based on case studies from the ancient city of Ghadames. The study shows that contemporary ('Western') housing layout and design fail to adapt to the social life needs of the Libyan households, hence their high degree of dissatisfaction with them, in contrast to their very positive attitudes towards their traditional forms of settlements, neighbourhood and dwellings. In Chapter 6, Spiegel, Watson and Wilkinson use case study material to support their view that the current South African national housing policy framework is likely to produce only a very limited set of housing options for the majority of African households. After examining some of the obstacles to effective housing delivery in the present policy, they conclude that, to be more effectual 'South African housing policy needs to be formulated in ways that are accommodative of the diverse situations of the people to whom it is directed, and sensitive towards their experiences and understanding of urban living'. In Chapter 7, Uduku's central argument is that 'even in totalitarian states, there are often avenues for community action through non-conventional ideas and methods' to call official attention to, and demand authoritative intervention in alleviating, their desperate housing circumstances. She uses the 'direct action, bottom-up' approach of the former residents of District Six in Cape Town, South Africa, as a case study.

Section III (chapters 8 to 10) consists of three case studies from Asia. In Chapter 8, Aravot examines how two neighbourhoods in Israel, which were built in the fifties as humble housing solutions for new immigrants, have come to be currently enjoying 'an upsurge of spontaneous revitalisation on private initiative'. The study presents a detailed analysis of their physical characteristics and some conclusions about possible adaptation of these to future housing development. In Chapter 9, El-Masri uses the family case study method to carry out an in-depth investigation into the survival and shelter provision strategies of three families from one of the war-damaged villages in Lebanon. It starts by discussing top-down and grass-roots approaches to reconstruction, stressing the need for partnerships between victims and intervenors. The chapter ends by emphasising consequential issues of interventions in disaster prone areas. In Chapter 10, Liu and Awotona present traditional courtyard houses, which are closely related to the social, cultural and political lives of the mass of the Chinese people, as bottom-up housing supply. In order to explain their popularisation and continuance, various forms of the courtyard houses in different parts of China and in different historical periods are explored for analysis and comparison. The layout, spatial organisation and the functions of typical courtyard houses, with their socio-cultural meaning, are also probed in detail.

Section IV (chapter 11), is a case study from South America by Sanderson. It seeks to identify and discuss the conditions faced by families living in some of the most vulnerable areas of Lima in Peru. It also stresses some of the strategies that were employed by these families to mitigate the risks faced.

In conclusion, it can be said that the key message that emerges from all the case studies in this book is the necessity and efficacy of putting a premium on the people themselves, on local political leadership and on local institutions, to identify, participate in setting the priorities of, co-ordinate, negotiate and to implement, actions that would enhance both their housing and economic circumstances. But in order for this approach to succeed, the active participation of the public, private and non-governmental partners as well as other civil society organisations at all levels must be sought. This is to 'ensure legal security of tenure, protection from discrimination and equal access to affordable adequate housing for all persons and their families' (United Nations Conference on Human Settlements (Habitat II), 1996, p.2).

Acknowledgement

I would like to express my thanks to Mrs Julie Elliott, my research secretary at the University of Newcastle upon Tyne, England, for her assistance in the preparation of this book.

Bibliography

Awotona, A. (1996), 'A review of housing research in West Africa.' *Third World Planning Review*, Vol. 18, No. 1, pp.45-58.

Government of Ghana. (1990), *Housing needs assessment study*. Executive summary and recommendations, Final Report, Vol. III, April, Housing and Urban Development Associates: Kumasi, Ghana.

People's Dialogue Report. (1994), *Utshani Buyakluluma*. April, Johannesburg.

People's Dialogue Report. (1995), *Utshani Buyakhuluma*. October, Johannesburg.

Singh, H.S. (1991), 'Sustainable development and urban human settlements', in Bandhu, D. (ed) *International workshop on human settlements for sustainable development - proceedings*, Indian Environmental Society: Delhi, pp.3-19.

The Guardian. (1996), 'Guardian Education', *The Guardian*, 15 October, London,

The South African Homeless People's Federation. (1995), *You see a monument - We see the way to build a million houses*. 7 June, The South African Homeless People's Federation Proposals for a People-centred housing policy:

Tipple, A.G. (1994), 'The need for new urban housing in sub-Saharan Africa: problem or opportunity.' *African Affairs*, Vol. 93, pp.587-608.

UNCHS (Habitat). (1996), *An urbanizing world: global report on human settlements, 1996*, Oxford University Press: Oxford.

United Nations Conference on Human Settlements (Habitat II). (1996), 'The Istanbul declaration on human settlements', Istanbul, Turkey, 14 June,

United Nations Economic and Social Commission for Asia and the Pacific Division of Industry, H.S.a.E. (1991), 'Towards environmentally sound and sustainable cities', in Bandhu, D. (ed) *International workshop on human settlements for sustainable development - proceedings*, Indian Environmental Society: Delhi, India, pp.43-47.

Wichman, R. (1995), 'The link between poverty, environment and development.' *Habitat II: Countdown to Istanbul*, Vol. 1, No. 5, November, pp.1, 3-4.

World Bank. (1993), *Housing: enabling markets to work*. A World Bank Policy Paper, Washington, DC.

Section I

An overview of some conceptual issues

1   On the relationships between family and housing

AMOS RAPOPORT

Introduction

The relationship between family and housing can be discussed either in terms of process or by looking at housing as product, or by looking at both. This book in general emphasises **process**, whereas this chapter deals primarily with product, with dwellings as artefacts which are also consumer goods. In any case, this product is always the goal of any process and some aspects of process are discussed briefly. The model of family/housing relations which is proposed is **general**, being derived from a model of culture/built environment relations which, in turn, leads to an approach to culture-specific design.

In principle this model and the approach are applicable anywhere (as any model or approach should be). It follows that examples can be used from anywhere, including countries such as the US, UK, Australia and the like in addition to a variety of developing countries, although the latter are of primary interest in the present context. This ability provides a major advantage because it makes available a much larger and more diverse body of evidence, making generalisation possible (Rapoport, 1990b; 1990e). It also allows for stronger generalisations, which are broadly applicable, any differences being due to the specifics of any given case which include various aspects of the family and the meaning of 'housing', both of which are discussed below. The generalisations often also suggest which specifics to look for and allow for mutual learning.

This approach can also serve as a point of entry to broader issues of environment-behaviour relations (EBR). The main intention of this chapter, therefore, is to present **a general** approach to the topic.

Following the conceptual part of the chapter a number of examples from different locales in both developed and developing countries are used to illustrate some of the points made. The primary concern, however, is with the approach rather than examples or case studies. This is for two reasons. First, because there is an almost endless supply of examples since family and housing are **always** related in some way. Second, this book itself contains many case studies with references to many more.

Culture and housing

The starting point for looking at how family and kinship relate to housing is the more general relationship between culture and housing, because family and kinship are an important aspect of culture. Looking at family/housing relationships is therefore tantamount to trying to link housing and culture (or an aspect of culture). However, as I have argued elsewhere, at that level of abstraction and generality housing (or any environment) and culture cannot be related or studied. As a result I have suggested that the concept of culture needs to be dismantled (or unpacked) and have over the past 20 years refined and elaborated a way of doing that which I find very useful and broadly applicable, although many anthropologists would not accept it (e.g. Cooper and Rodam, 1995, p.124).

I will not review the general argument, nor the various intermediate versions of the model, but present the current version which will be used as the framework for looking more specifically at family and kinship[1]. (See Figure 1.1)

The purpose of this dismantling is to operationalise the concept of 'culture.' In addressing the view that 'culture' is too abstract, the dismantling along the vertical axis distinguishes between 'cultural' and 'social' variables, rather that using the frequently encountered reference to 'socio-cultural' variables. On this view, 'cultural' refers to an **ideational** concept, a blueprint for the social variables which are then seen as referring to more concrete manifestations of culture and are potentially observable. Among these are family and kinship structures and associated variables such as roles, status, social networks etc.

It needs to be emphasised that 'culture' is a **theoretical construct,** i.e. it exists by definition and is a conceptual shorthand (and proposed explanation) for particular conjunctions of a great variety of human phenomena. No one has ever seen or will ever see or observe culture, only its manifestations, effects or products. One is thus making inferences about an unobservable entity and one that is extremely broad -too broad to be useful. The dismantling along the horizontal axis addresses this issue and some of these expressions of culture are also relevant to this chapter, most specifically lifestyle and activity systems (and possibly values and images) all of which often characterise families and will, in fact, be used (e.g. Rapoport, 1977; 1990f; 1993; 1994; in press-c).

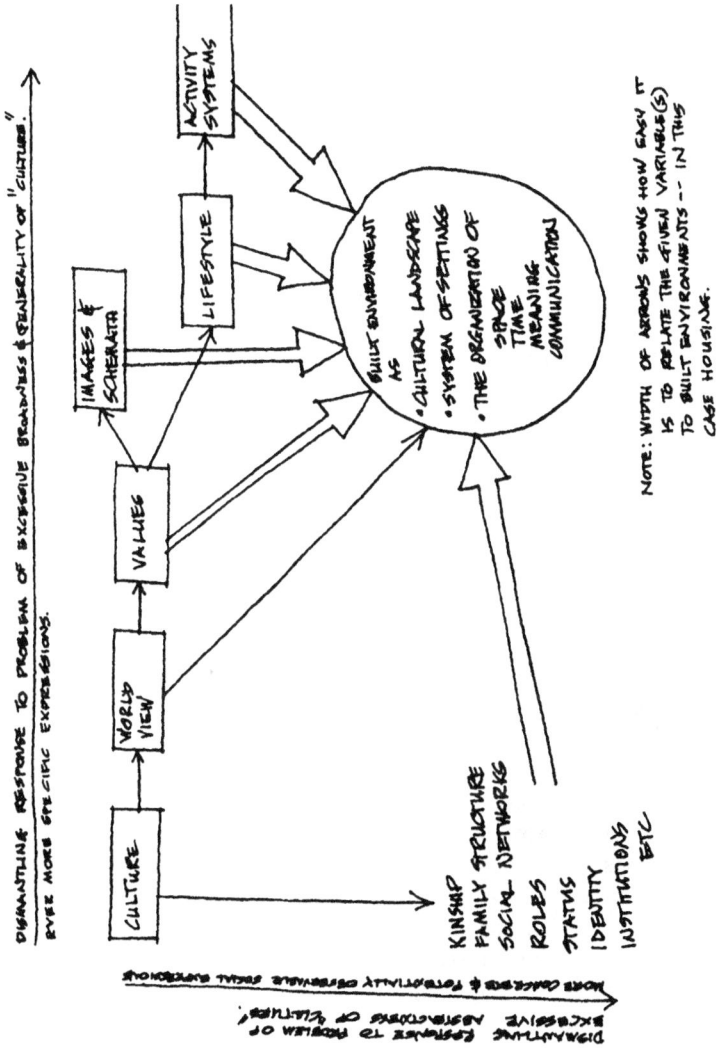

Figure 1.1 Model of culture/built environment relations

Source: Based on Rapoport (1993, Fig1, p.16; in press a, Fig.3)

Note that although in traditional situations the cognitive cultural model of housing is extremely strong, being based on widely shared cultural norms (e.g. Rapoport, 1989) such models are also found in other situations. In all cases, however, this model is modified, to a greater or lesser extent, by the decisions of household members (Blanton, 1996; Netting et al., 1984; Wilk, 1989; Wilk and Ashmore, 1988). Also, in traditional situations many although certainly not all of the attributes of tradition relate to family and kinship and greatly influence the form and use of housing (e.g. Cornell, 1997; Rapoport, 1989; Stahl, 1991) as they also do in other cases, although possibly to a lesser extent (e.g. Franck and Ahrentzen, 1991).

Dismantling is also necessary for 'environment' and other concepts, such as 'vernacular' and 'traditional,' but these are not relevant here (e.g. Rapoport, 1989; 1990a). It is essential to operationalise and define the term 'housing.'

What is 'housing?'

I have argued elsewhere that one cannot use the particular artefact called 'house' in studying EBR generally and in cross-cultural studies specifically. I suggested that dwellings are best understood as those systems of setting within which systems of activities (including their latent aspects) take place. It is thus necessary explicitly to list and describe the activities in question and to discover or identify the extent of the system of settings involved (Rapoport, 1969; 1977; 1990c; 1990f; 1993; 1994). I have also suggested that the process is similar to that of 'progressive contextualisation' (Vayda, 1983).

It can also be shown that what happens or does not happen in certain settings influences the use of other settings (e.g. Rapoport, 1986; 1990f). This can be influenced by values and norms, and hence rules, sex roles, lifestyle, etc., but how the system of settings is used also depends on the spatial relationships between nuclear families and relatives and other kin, as well as the nature of social networks. This means that the subsystem of settings which constitutes the dwelling discussed above must be seen in the context of an even more extensive system of settings - the block, neighbourhood or ward, settlement or even system of settlements. In order to discuss 'housing,' therefore, and to compare it across different cultures and periods, it is necessary to go well beyond the individual 'house' and also to discover and identify the larger system within which the dwelling is embedded. This is the way 'housing' is conceptualised in this chapter.

This means that the relations between the family and housing (as a product) goes beyond the dwelling to the larger environment. This system of settings is then expressed as the cultural landscape, with specific ambience (Rapoport, 1992a; 1992b), the components of which various groups evaluate differently in their search for environmental quality. It then follows that the system of settings is characterised by a certain environmental quality describable as a profile which is also part of 'housing' (Rapoport, 1985; 1995 Ch.30, pp.471-488).

This is important not only in order to conceptualise 'housing' adequately. It also plays a role in the choices people make about how and where to live. In doing so, people make trade-offs between the dwelling and the neighbourhood and among different aspects of environmental quality. These choices and the degree of emphasis on components of environmental quality vary with lifestyle, activity systems and such aspects of family as its size and composition, provisions for the elderly, presence of children, work patterns, etc. They also vary over time, depending on various circumstances. A striking example not related to family is the case of the recency of arrival in the city of migrants in developing countries, where environmental quality is unimportant at the beginning but very important after 15 years (Sastrosasmita and Nurul Amin, 1990). In the very different context of the US, with the growth of two working parent families, children's settings within the dwelling have become replaced or supplemented by other settings such as child care centres, after school programs, etc. (New York Times, 1993). The role of shopping malls and other settings also needs to be considered (Rapoport, 1986). They are all important in the choices made and depend on the definition of housing used in this chapter.

Intrinsic and extrinsic aspects of housing/family relations

In order to analyse and hence to understand housing, and in order to design it better, one needs to consider family/housing relations among other factors. One needs to bear in mind that not only do family and kinship forms, organisations and arrangements influence housing, but that housing forms also influence and change family life (e.g. Gasparini, 1973). This is because planning and design decisions can have unforeseen consequences on many aspects of culture, including family and kinship (Rapoport, 1977; 1980; 1983; 1985). These may even lead to the destruction of cultures (e.g. Jaulin, 1971; Rapoport, 1978a). This one can consider to be the intrinsic importance of the topic. Such an analysis, however, also has extrinsic value, providing one useful point of entry into more general EBR questions.

This is also the case with the ability to use examples from both developed and developing countries due to broader and stronger generalisations which also allow for mutual learning and for back and forth movement among examples. This also represents an extrinsic aspect of considering developing countries. As I have argued elsewhere (Rapoport, 1983) developing countries as well as vernacular design (Rapoport, 1990a) generally provide an extremely useful point of entry for the study of EBR more generally. This is because phenomena, being more extreme, are much starker and clearer: one can think of them in terms of black and white rather than shades of grey. This makes it easier to identify EBR phenomena and mechanisms. By analogy to biomedical research one can think of developing countries as **model systems**. Once having identified patterns, processes, relationships and mechanisms in developing countries these can be sought also in developed countries. One reason for this is what I have called the higher criticality in developing countries, so that the effects of environment on behaviour, particularly the negative effects, are much greater. The constraints of money, space, information, materials and equipment, power etc. are also much stronger limiting choice, exacerbating criticality and making culture/housing congruence more difficult although more important.

To give just two general examples: the need of culture- or group- specific design is seen much more clearly in developing countries, although it applies universally; and culture change, which is universal, is seen much more clearly in the case of developing countries because it is more rapid, leading to more extreme situations, rapidly changing roles, family structures and relationships, institutions, etc. In fact, an extremely important aspect of culture change is family change which is both influenced by and influences the former. Moreover, culture change best describes development from an environment-behaviour studies (EBS) and planning/design perspective (Rapoport, 1983). One finds clear and strong examples of synthesis/syncretism in images, fashions, roles, structures, housing, etc. which also occur, but more subtly, in developed countries.

Thus in both developed and, especially, developing countries one can list some general reasons for the importance of family/housing relations which summarise the above discussion:

1. Housing, like all environments, should respond to human wants and needs, and family and kinship play an important role in establishing these.
2. Housing needs to be supportive generally, and especially in developing countries where resources and social programs are scarce (Rapoport, 1969; 1980; 1983).
3. Rapid culture change in developing countries is highly stressful (Rapoport, 1978b; 1983). This leads to high criticality, and supportiveness becomes more important as it does for certain groups in developed countries (e.g. Badura, 1986; Gaunt, 1997).
4. The lack of resources, government social programs, etc., make family and other social support networks and mutual help more important and, in turn, require appropriate housing.
5. The very survival of cultures may depend on the form of housing capable of supporting the culture core (Rapoport, 1983). This applies not only to supportiveness of existing cultural patterns, but also making possible the transmission of culture across generations through enculturation which is

influenced both by housing and its use directly, and by the possibility of contact with elders (e.g. Rapoport, 1978c; Sebba, 1991).

Families and households

With this background discussion completed, we reach the central part of this chapter - the approach or framework for looking at family/housing relationships. Before doing so, however, the use of the terms 'family' and 'kinship' need to be re-examined. Increasingly, in studies addressing this topic the term (or concept) of *household* is used. This is defined as a group of people who co-reside in a dwelling or residential compound and who, to some degree, share householding activities and decision-making (Blanton, 1996 p.5; Wilk, 1989; Wilk and Ashmore, 1988). This also corresponds to what has been called a 'task oriented residence unit' (Netting et al., 1984, p.xx).

The term 'household' and its cognates are more inclusive and may, therefore, offer a useful starting point for describing certain residential patterns, although it has been pointed out that it is difficult to define 'household' for purposes of cross-cultural comparison as, incidentally, it is to define 'family' (Stephens, 1963) as will be discussed later. The important attribute in all these terms is, however, always **the co-resident group**.

Stahl (1991) writing in French refers to the 'domestic group' (= household) and also suggests using 'extended domestic group' rather than 'extended family' and discusses the possible variations, their occurrence in many parts of Europe, and the corresponding dwellings. He points out that, as far as he knows, there have been no comparative studies of these dwellings and looks at a number of them especially, but not exclusively, in Albania, where they have survived best to see whether any commonalties emerge. He develops a taxonomy wherein one finds development from single houses to double, then quadruple, to compounds all related to the extended residential group. The changes can occur either through 'agglutination' or through subdivision of the original internal space (what I have called 'additive' and 'subtractive' (Rapoport, 1969)). In all cases the domestic group changes continually due to births, deaths, marriages and separations so that the dwelling needs to be able to evolve, i.e. to be open-ended enough to allow for the frequent remodelling, demolitions and rebuilding. Under such circumstances, still common in developing countries, houses that do no allow for this do not work (e.g. Osmont, 1986; Schwerdtfeger, 1982). In effect, there is what can be called a 'development cycle' of modifications relating to the changing nature of the co-resident group (Banning and Byrd, 1987). The point is also made that the boundaries of the domestic group are difficult to determine (especially in this latter case 10,000 years ago) since the house as a spatial unit does not adequately reflect the residential unit. This is, as already discussed, because it does not include the whole system of settings (Bourdier and Minh-Ha, 1996, esp. p.152; Rapoport, 1969; 1977; 1990f; 1993; 1994).

These more inclusive terms, such as 'household,' 'co-residence group' and 'domestic group' have another advantage - one can see how and when they change to family groups when dependents are no longer included (Cornell, 1997). In that case, referring to Japan, the point is made that social organisation cannot be read directly from house form: there is 'loose fit' (Rapoport, 1990f) a point which will be discussed later. Household size and composition change more easily than dwellings. Thus house-form is not very useful for identifying short-term, small household changes (the decisions of household members discussed earlier). House-form can, however, be very useful at capturing broad, long-term changes in culture core elements, what earlier was called the cultural cognitive model. These core elements include family, and Cornell (1997) shows how temporal change of the family and dwelling evolved together in early modern Japan. Both the 'traditional' family and house are the outcomes of a process of change, not static features of a uniform past. Moreover, not only does the household become limited to family as already mentioned but the family itself becomes simplified to the stem family, eliminating collateral relatives, whereas the house becomes internally more differentiated (Kent, 1991; Rapoport, 1990f).

The utility of this set of concepts seems clear, in spite of the difficulty of defining them. What comprises the 'household' and its 'activities and decision making' (Blanton, 1996, p.5) will vary in each case. Moreover the pooling of resources is not crucial to all definitions of households. Thus two or more families with separate budgets can form a household as long as they are co-resident and share at least some household activities, not necessarily including child rearing.

The crucial aspect in all of these discussions of the household is co-residence within the same dwellings, which may be a residential compound, what Wilk (1989) calls the 'household cluster' (for more detail see Blanton, 1996, pp.6-7) and Stahl (1991) the 'extended domestic group'. In essence, one is concerned with a version of a general question I find useful (who does what, where, when, including/excluding whom and why)—in this case: Who lives where, when, including/excluding whom and why. Asking that one can go beyond co-residence in a single dwelling or compound and identify at least six patterns:

1. Scattered regionally without settlements as among the Maya (Fedick, 1989) possibly with ceremonial or other meeting places linked by ritual or other movement (Rapoport, 1977; 1990b; 1990d; 1990f). This kind of pattern, if not considered, can lead to difficulties in planning and design (Doshi, 1969; Rapoport, 1977; 1984; 1993).
2. Scattered among settlements (either permanent or nomadic). Contacts and social links can occur at special institutions such as markets (Mahdjoubi and Awotona, 1997; Skinner, 1972) churches or workplaces (Ablon, 1971) and

many others (Rapoport 1977,1983, 1986, 1990a). They thus occur through movement, which may include pilgrimages, as in India, and others. In that sense 1 and 2 are variants on a common theme.

3. Scattered in one settlement either among non-kin or the whole settlement can be one extended family or clan as has been the case in China, (Knapp, 1992), Korea (Han, 1991), the Caucasus (Stahl, 1991) and elsewhere.
4. Clustered in a particular neighbourhood or ward, with or without special institutions, as in China (Knapp, 1992), sub-Saharan Africa (Hardie, 1980; Hull, 1976; Schwerdtfeger, 1982), North Africa (Mahdjoubi and Awotona, 1997), the Middle East (Shami, 1989) and elsewhere (Rapoport, 1977; Rapoport, 1984; Rapoport, 1993).
5. In a compound consisting of houses for conjugal families (or wives and children in polygamous situation) (Bourdier and Minh-Ha, 1996; Rapoport, 1969; in press-a, esp. figs. 4 and 5 and references; Schwerdtfeger, 1982).
6. In a single dwelling, i.e. under one roof.

This can diagrammed as in Figure 1.2.

Although contact will be maintained in all these cases, they will clearly be very different in nature, frequency, location etc.

The above discussion begins to deal with family and kinship more than households. However, starting with a consideration of the nature of the household rather than the family is still useful because of the many changes undergone by the family, especially since World War II. It has become less stable (due to divorce), smaller, characterised by changing roles and changing economic and larger societal contexts etc. It is, of course, the case that frequently, although not always, the household is indeed the family which is almost a human universal (Stephens, 1963). However, the changes mentioned above have led to a proliferation of family and also household types, in addition to the many types previously known. The study of kinship and family has been a major preoccupation of cultural anthropology for a long time, and is thus a very complex and specialised topic with a voluminous literature. But a brief discussion may be helpful.

One can start with the conjugal or nuclear family which is sometimes called the simple family or household. One can then perform a mental experiment. Subtracting one parent leads to the single parent family or household (Franck and Ahrentzen, 1991). Adding various other individuals to the household may involve unrelated dependents: servants, farms workers - in medieval times apprentices etc. In the case of families they most commonly but not always are married offspring of the senior generation(s). These can then be described as complex families, which include the stem, lineal and extended forms with a range of variations. One can also find quasi-extended families which do not reside together but are close enough for frequent meetings, strong links and mutual aid (to be discussed in more detail later). There are also polygamous and, much less common, polyandrous

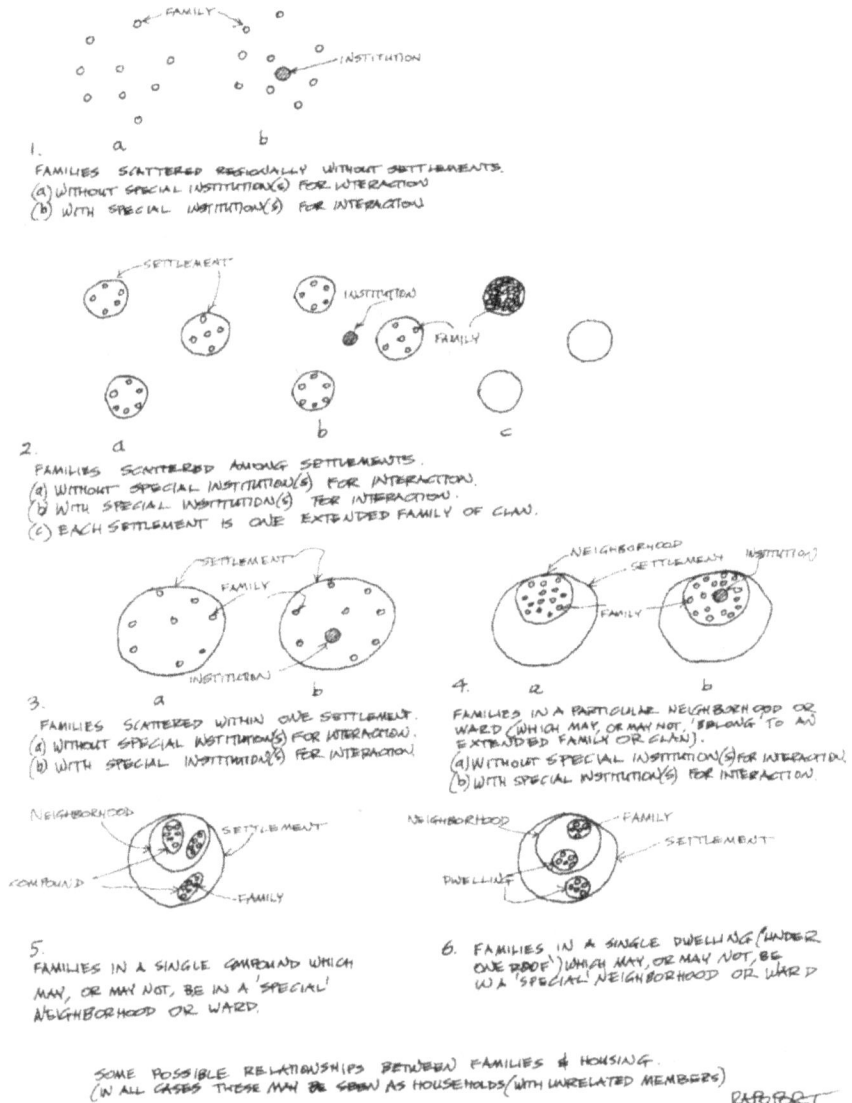

1.
FAMILIES SCATTERED REGIONALLY WITHOUT SETTLEMENTS.
(a) WITHOUT SPECIAL INSTITUTION(S) FOR INTERACTION
(b) WITH SPECIAL INSTITUTION(S) FOR INTERACTION

2.
FAMILIES SCATTERED AMONG SETTLEMENTS.
(a) WITHOUT SPECIAL INSTITUTION(S) FOR INTERACTION.
(b) WITH SPECIAL INSTITUTION(S) FOR INTERACTION.
(c) EACH SETTLEMENT IS ONE EXTENDED FAMILY OR CLAN.

3.
FAMILIES SCATTERED WITHIN ONE SETTLEMENT.
(a) WITHOUT SPECIAL INSTITUTION(S) FOR INTERACTION.
(b) WITH SPECIAL INSTITUTION(S) FOR INTERACTION

4.
FAMILIES IN A PARTICULAR NEIGHBORHOOD OR
WARD (WHICH MAY, OR MAY NOT, BELONG TO AN
EXTENDED FAMILY OR CLAN).
(a) WITHOUT SPECIAL INSTITUTION(S) FOR INTERACTION.
(b) WITH SPECIAL INSTITUTION(S) FOR INTERACTION

5.
FAMILIES IN A SINGLE COMPOUND WHICH
MAY, OR MAY NOT, BE IN A 'SPECIAL'
NEIGHBORHOOD OR WARD.

6. FAMILIES IN A SINGLE DWELLING (UNDER
ONE ROOF) WHICH MAY, OR MAY NOT, BE
IN A 'SPECIAL' NEIGHBORHOOD OR WARD

SOME POSSIBLE RELATIONSHIPS BETWEEN FAMILIES & HOUSING.
(IN ALL CASES THESE MAY BE SEEN AS HOUSEHOLDS (WITH UNRELATED MEMBERS)
RAPOPORT

Figure 1.2 Some possible relationships between families and housing

forms. All can be understood as households, but those can also include unrelated adults sharing responsibility for children, different or same sex partnerships, various co-housing arrangements, unrelated single people living in the same dwelling (Hole and Taylor, 1978). There are also multifamily dwellings comprising tenants or lodgers, and other types. In all cases, of course, the contextual systems of settings play an important role.

It can thus be seen that in many cases 'family' and 'household' can be used interchangeably but that the use of 'household' as a starting point seems to present clear advantages so that, for example, Awotona and Briggs (1997) suggest using the *household* as the unit for planning policy and design in developing countries and, I would add, also in developed countries.

Family/housing relations—a conceptual analysis

I have now discussed the relationship between household and family, defined 'housing' as used in this chapter and dismantled the concept of culture. In the latter case I suggested that its various components and expressions, including family and kinship, are more useful in studying culture-environment relations and designing appropriate, culture-specific housing. However, to link family and housing this process needs to continue, so that one explicitly considers which specific aspects of the family can be linked to which specific aspects of housing and, if possible, through which mechanisms. This is made even more important by the difficulty of defining 'family' precisely, especially for cross-cultural analysis (Stahl, 1991; Stephens, 1963). Despite the complexity of this concept discussed earlier, it is possible to list some of the more specific relevant attributes of the family (within the context of the household) as a starting point, without claiming that it is more than an example of the types of variables that need to be considered. Among them would be:

1. The size of the household.
2. The composition of the household.
3. If the household is the family, then the nature of the family (e.g. nuclear, polygamous, stem, extended etc.).
4. The size of the family (related to 1 above) which raises two points. The first, that smaller families (and households) increase settlement size since certain settings, such as kitchens, bathrooms, parking etc., are still needed. The second is the debate (as in Australia, for example) whether existing housing is now too large given smaller family size, or whether wants and higher standards need to be considered. (Troy, 1995).
5. The nature of the ties, links and relationships among family members and how members are defined, e.g. how far 'family' extends.

6. Given 5, the nature of social networks, who is included or excluded, their spatial and temporal organisation and whether they are intensive or extensive.
7. Given 5 and 6, relations to other kin and how these are defined (Rapoport, 1975; 1977; 1978b).
8. The roles of various family members by age, status, gender etc. (Franck and Ahrentzen, 1991; Shokeid, 1971).
9. The economic relationship within the family, especially when it is a unit of production as well as a unit of consumption, and the resulting particular activity systems including their latent aspects.
10. The supportive role of the family both regarding behaviour and 'social security' and mutual help.
11. The nature of residence, of which there are two dominant types. In the first, neo-local strategy, offspring establish themselves as early as possible in separate nuclear households in their own dwelling with or without the help of parents[2]. In the second, household continuity strategy, the goal is to maintain the social integrity of the household over multiple generations, by encouraging married offspring to remain in the parental dwelling or compounds. This can be achieved by males or females remaining with their fathers/mothers involving the movement of spouses: patrilocality or matrilocality. Other variations are possible, so that the specifics of each case need to be considered.
12. The nature of the relationships with ancestors who, although not 'physically present' may greatly influence activity systems and dwellings use, e.g. through family altars and festivals linked to them as in China and Taiwan (Chua, 1988; Zich, 1997, p.105) or Japan (Cornell, 1997). In Guatemala also as in many other places 'ancestors are remembered as part of the family that have never gone away, so communication between the living and the dead is very important' (Rohter, 1997). This often makes the cemetery very important, in that case and in many other cultures, because it plays a major role in the system of settings (Rapoport, 1983; 1990d).
13. Related to 12, the importance of ritual within the family and dwelling as opposed to their occurrence in other, more public settings, such as sacred buildings, cemeteries etc. (Byrd, 1994; Cornell, 1997; Rapoport, 1990d).
14. Related to 13, the importance of specific rules about purity, allowable interaction and hence privacy etc. (Chua, 1988).
15. Relations with the elderly and their roles within the family/household.
16. Relations with children and their roles also related to privacy.
17. Gender relations also related to privacy, and the use of public/private domains.
18. Need for dowries, especially where there is a need to provide housing as in the Greek islands (Rapoport, 1969)[3].
19. Inheritance patterns.

20. Land tenure patterns (Payne, 1997, pp.38 and 66; Tipple, 1987) which may make possible or impossible certain forms of housing supportive of family and kinship patterns (Rapoport, 1980).
21. Changes in the various aspects of the family listed above and the rate of such change.

As already pointed out, this list is not meant to be either complete or exhaustive, and a more systematic literature search or the co-operation of experts in the fields would probably reveal more and also modify (or eliminate) some of the above. The list is thus meant to show the **types** of more specific aspects of the family due to further dismantling, that will need to be considered in order to be able to relate family to housing; the specifics will also vary from case to case.

A similar process also needs to be carried out with regard to housing. For example:

1. Which are the settings that comprise the dwelling.
2. Which are the activities that occur in these settings, how do they occur and what do they mean i.e. who does what, where, when, including or excluding whom (and why).
3. Hence the size of the dwelling.
4. The size of the lot. Large lots have a number of advantages in addition to the disadvantages usually emphasised. They allow for large households with tenants or lodgers as well as kin, extended families, which is very common and important in sub-Saharan Africa and elsewhere (Correa, 1978; Tipple, 1977). In Milwaukee, during the 19th century, the development of the 'Polish flat,' a semi-basement slid under a house after raising it (Kenny, in press), as well as units at the back of the lot, again depended on lot size which allowed for both alternatives to be used simultaneously. Lot size also influences open-endedness, with larger lots providing an advantage (Rapoport, 1980).
5. The organisation of the settings, i.e. the dwelling which both reflects and constrains the organisation of communication and hence privacy, household and family structure and relations etc.
6. Hence the nature of privacy in the sense of controlling unwanted interaction, and the mechanisms employed (Rapoport, 1977, pp. 201-207 and 289-298). Note that in the case of nomads this is accomplished by moving away, changing location within the camp, changing the direction of entries, erection of 'spite fences' etc. (Rapoport, 1978d). These become difficult, if not impossible, among settled people and new mechanisms are needed as well as maximum open-endedness. One also finds both changes in dwellings and great mobility among them in some settled villages with men's houses far more constant. For example, in Vanuatu such movements symbolise complex family, kinship and residential patterns and meanings (Rapoport, 1978d;

Rodman, 1985a; 1985b)). This pattern of a stable community with unstable, i.e. mobile, households is also found in Kutse, Bostwana where the population is, admittedly, nomadic. In that case, since everyone is related in some way, it is friendship among kin and even non-kin that structures the community, site organisation and sharing partnerships. Friendship, in fact, activates some kinship relationships while leaving other, equally close, kin relationships dormant. People live near, and share with kin who are genealogically more distant than other kin who live further away. Like friendship, sharing networks **also vary in time**, some being very brief, others enduring (Kent, 1995).

7. The number and nature of transitions between the public and private realms and the rules that operate in them (Rapoport, 1977).

8. The nature of the aggregate of all the relevant settings, i.e. the nature of the larger units: compounds, streets, wards, neighbourhoods, settlements or systems of settlements, institutions etc.

9. Related to 8 the nature of the linkages and separations between the system comprising the dwelling and the larger system of settings, their location and their nature.

10. The meaning of 'housing' regarding identity, status etc. and which elements communicate these: size, materials, location, type, semi-fixed elements etc. (Blanton, 1996; Duncan, 1981; 1985; Rapoport, 1981; 1988; 1990d).

11. The need for and nature of open-endedness needed to respond to changing family and kinship patterns, trajectories and transitions which replace 'stage in life-cycle'. As already pointed out, changes can be additive or subtractive (Banning and Byrd, 1987; Brown, 1996; Byrd, 1994; Carp, 1987; Rapoport, 1969; 1995 Ch.33).

The specific attributes discussed, and others, can also be derived from more general considerations. Since housing is a type of built environment one can use the conceptualisation of the latter as the organisation of space, time, meaning and communication. For example, space can be understood as being male or female; for young or old; for the initiated or uninitiated; private/public; pure/impure; sacred/profane etc., accompanied by rules which turn space into settings. Time plays a role in terms of how much discretionary time is available to various family members, how they use it, where they spend it and with whom etc. Communication is significant in terms of who communicates with whom, where, when, under what circumstances, why and how: face to face, by walking or driving, by telephone, via computer etc. Meaning is significant both in terms of what family, as such, means and what housing means to the family, in terms of identity, status, honour etc. (Duncan, 1981; 1985; Rapoport, 1981; 1990d). An even more general approach is to begin by using a version of what I have called the three basic questions of EBS (Rapoport, 1977; 1990b; 1990f).

1. One human characteristic (among others) seems to be almost universal - the propensity to form social units among which, and possibly the most important, are family and kinship (Stephens, 1963). How can these units be characterised, i.e. what are their attributes?
2. Housing both reflects and influences family and kinship structures and relationships and can be supportive or inhibiting. The family/housing relationship may be reflected spatially, though co-residence or proximity within the neighbourhood, ward or settlement, or can be 'aspatial' (to be discussed later) (Ferguson, 1996; Rapoport, in press-b).
3. The third question deals with the mechanisms that link people and environments and in this case leads to a consideration of the mechanisms that link the two sets of variables discussed above. Among the mechanisms some may be general, such as supportiveness or inhibition in the case of family patterns, rules and lifestyle (to be discussed below). There are also more specific mechanisms such as the meaning of housing (communicating identity, status, etc.) or the role of housing in enculturating children by passing on rules, appropriate behaviour, language, myths, cultural knowledge etc. (Rapoport, 1978c; Sebba, 1991). Another mechanism is open-endedness, allowing housing to respond to changes in family which often tend to be continuous and ongoing.

Returning to supportiveness, it should be noted that in the case of some groups but not others neighbouring networks can replace kin networks (Rapoport, 1977 esp. Ch.5). In either case one is dealing with intermediate structures or institutions that mediate between people and their cultural, social, economic and other contexts, and which become more important as criticality goes up e.g. among immigrants, in conditions of rapid culture change, as in developing countries, and among groups with reduced competence (Badura, 1986). Among such mediating structures or institutions, family and kinship, while not the only ones, are very important and, for example, have always helped migrants adjust more easily (Yans-McLaughlin, 1977). The survival of such institutions and the modulation of rates of change often depend on the design of a supportive physical environment, above all housing as defined here (Rapoport, 1977; 1983; 1985).

It is important to emphasise that the family/housing relationship is loose rather than tight so that there is no direct one-to-one relation between social and spatial organisation, and houses and households are not necessarily identical (Byrd, 1994; Cornell, 1997; Ferguson, 1996; Kent, 1995; Netting et al., 1984; Rapoport, in press-a). As just one example, the *Hakka* dwelling, Fujian, China houses a kin-group of up to several hundred people (Laude, 1992) whereas the very similar form of the European apartment house houses unrelated people (Rapoport, in press-a).

I have now outlined and sketched the framework and approach, which is not in final form and could be greatly elaborated and developed. It might be useful to illustrate some of these points by brief reference to a few examples from diverse locales, cultures and periods. Note that in most cases different numbers of the different variables act and interact at the same time through multiple mechanisms. It is thus impossible at this time systematically to relate specific housing characteristics to specific household and family characteristics by means of specific mechanisms. The examples are thus intended to illustrate multiple interactions leading to the great variety of dwelling and settlement forms which, I have previously argued, are one of the most important problems to be explained.

Discussion—and some examples

I have previously explained the extraordinary variety of dwellings and their contexts in terms of the latent aspects of activity systems and lifestyles. It is clear from Figure 1.1, however, that together with other variables, family and kinship and related social variables play a significant role. We have thus seen that family and house form co-evolved although the relationship always remains loose rather than tight (Byrd, 1994; Cornell, 1997; Ferguson, 1996; Kent, 1995; Netting et al., 1984; Rapoport, in press-a).

In the emergence of Neolithic villages in Southwest Asia, in itself the development of a new housing/settlement type, one finds two parallel and interrelated organisational trends over time: a more restricted social network for sharing production and consumption activities i.e. smaller households and the concomitant development of more formal institutionalised mechanisms for integrating the community as a whole i.e. new important settings within the larger system (Byrd, 1994). One result is an increased distinction between private and public, with restricted visibility and access into dwelling interiors, more compartmentalisation of interior spaces (Kent, 1991; Rapoport, 1990f; Sancar and Koop, 1995). Another result is the development of non-domestic, larger buildings which are the settings for more formal and institutionalised mechanisms for integrating the community, for supra-household decision-making and ceremonial activities (Byrd, 1994; Rapoport, in press-b Fig. 4).

Another example of the importance of family form is the very different form dwellings of the Mofou and Moundang in the Cameroons, which are for monogamous and polygamous families respectively (Rapoport, 1969 Fig. 3.5, p.56). This also partly accounts for the great variety of dwelling forms in a relatively small country such as Senegal (Bourdier and Minh-Ha, 1996; Oyediran, 1994 on Northern Nigeria; Schwerdtfeger, 1982). In all these cases family kinship patterns among other variables play an important role. This is also the case in contemporary urban situations such as Ismaïlia, Egypt where the dwellings of polygamous households are quite different to those of monogamous ones, with each wife having her own 'suite' and only sharing an entrance and/or a court (Bourdier and Minh-Ha, 1996; Elgohary and Hanson, 1997). The need for open-endedness is quite clear and is made even clearer by the fact that some households may also include lodgers which is a major component of many sub-Saharan dwellings and compounds (Benna, 1997; personal observations). Note that the latter can create problems of privacy particularly when space and physical barriers are lacking. The potential problems depend partly on the number and location of settings used, i.e. the larger context (Rapoport, 1975; 1977; 1986; 1990f). Such problems are also often solved through the use of behavioural norms and rules which become easier the more homogeneous the household members and the stronger their social relations (El-Sherif, 1977) - and, clearly, family and kinship are the strongest so that in Hong Kong, and China generally, one finds that the same number of people in the same space has quite different effects when they are kin or non-kin (Rapoport, 1975; 1977; 1978b; 1985). That, in turn, clearly depends on how 'kin' are defined.

Such definition varies cross-culturally, not only between China and Western countries but also between Mexico and the US (Stea, 1995). The Mexican culture core, unlike material culture, has proved remarkably resilient, and primary among Mexican values is the family which often eclipses all other values (Rapoport, 1983). Stea (1995) argues that personal identity apart from family identity is meaningless (Duncan, 1981; 1985; Rapoport, 1981) and that the whole society reflects family so that the continuing strength of the family remains the pivot of life. The family is self-sufficient, and social life involves being with relatives, and children essentially only play with siblings and cousins. Mexicans need few friends because they have many relatives, and that depends on **how kinship is defined**. In the US or Northern Europe 'family' means the nuclear family of four or five members; in Mexico and also in other parts of Latin America *familia* means something very different and consists of hundreds of members. It extends beyond grandparents, uncles, aunts and cousins and this happens not only through the system of *compadrazgo*, whereby godparents are incorporated into the *familia* at each of many ceremonies, but also in other ways. In any case, the result is an enormous conglomerate which is an 'insurance umbrella'. In rural areas members of such extended families live close to one another and often constitute entire neighbourhoods. In urban contexts, however, although nuclear families seem to predominate, and urban dwellings do not show other links, the extended family continues to thrive. In effect, the linkages in this matrifocal world have been spatially lengthened but not markedly strained, and ties of the nuclear family dwellings to other *familia*-related dwellings is in general still infinitely stronger than to neighbours, and this influences public/private relationships including the upkeep of public domains, or lack of it. As in other cases to be discussed, the dwelling is clearly female territory, the kitchen exclusively so and, also as elsewhere, men do not use the house but in the provinces, the street and the cantina and in middle-class Mexico City, often the office. In the domestic sphere the male-dominated social hierarchy and territory do not coincide (Stea, 1995 pp.188-192).

This particular pattern continues even after immigration to the US. One example is the unexpected defeat in Hispanic areas of Proposition M on rent control, although it was widely expected to win there. The best explanation is in terms of lifestyle (Rapoport, 1985) which also matches Stea's (1995) argument: the proposition defined family as nuclear only, ignoring the importance of the extended family (Los Angeles Times, 1983). The same pattern is the best explanation for the recent finding that Hispanic families in the US use child-care centres much less than other ethnic groups because of a cultural preference for family, or at least family-like, care. They prefer asking relatives, or use family day-care at home; the important thing is to keep children in a warm and family-like atmosphere (Chira, 1994).

In comparing different housing site layouts in Arizona it was also found that they were very different for Hispanics and Anglos: the differences clearly had to do with layouts allowing for family and kin clustering and higher levels of social interaction (Wheeler, 1977). It was also found that the use of domestic space - and time - among Mexican immigrants in the US resembled those found in rural Mexico (Pader, 1993) where the development of the multi-room courtyard complex is intimately related to the closely knit extended family, a characteristic also of many other traditional folk societies (West, 1974 p.113). The sharing of spaces, including bedrooms, and lack of physical barriers changed with acculturation, as family norms, rules, values and roles changed, especially among offspring, leading to conflicts with parents (Pader, 1993). There was also similar space use - sharing of bedrooms and other settings - among Hispanics and Navaho in Arizona, as opposed to Anglos in similar suburban houses (Kent, 1984), a pattern Graeme Hardie and I also found among the Tswana in South Africa, and which is also found among Australian Aborigines (to be discussed later).

In examining only house organisation in East Asia rather than the dwelling and its larger context, Zgusta (1991) shows that much can be attributed to male/female dichotomy or distinctions - clearly an aspect of family organisation. This shows how central these distinctions are to the great variety of forms which become comprehensible as variations on a single theme. It also shows how important meaning is as a mechanism linking house form to gender relations in the family. As already pointed out, the link between women and dwellings has generally, if not universally, been stronger and more intimate. Dwellings are typically women's domain, whereas public space has tended to be dominated by men, although this changes as roles and family structures change. This applies in sub-Saharan Africa (Bourdier and Minh-Ha, 1996; Rapoport, 1969), North Africa (Mahdjoubi and Awotona, 1997), Latin America (Stea, 1995), Britain (Madigan and Munro, 1991; Wilmott, 1963; Young and Wilmott, 1962), the USA (Suttles, 1968) and elsewhere (Rapoport, 1977 esp. Ch.5). In all those cases particular institutions - men's houses, as in New Guinea, North India, etc., coffee shops, tea houses, pubs, taverns etc.) often become men's domains more than do their dwellings (Rapoport, 1977; 1983; 1984; 1986; 1990b; 1990f).

The use of such institutions depends on their accessibility and is thus related to their location, to settlement size, and organisation and mobility, and two patterns can be identified (see Figure 1.3).

The two may be equivalent when cars are available but not when pedestrian movement is required, i.e. it is related to the effort involved. The 'aspatial' form with centrally located institutions for social interaction may thus work better in developed countries where mobility is greater, cars, telephones and computers being widely available and where mutual help is less needed, or for specific groups - a topic to be discussed below.

This discussion reinforces the point made that the conceptualisation of housing used in this chapter is essential. For example, in Bethnal Green (East London) households were nuclear families with neo-local residence. However, married daughters settled near their mothers who were able to manipulate landlords and contact was maintained by frequent daily visits among the women. This became impossible after the move to Dagenham and, at least for this group at the time, telephones and cars were neither widely available nor able to substitute, so that contacts with kin became less frequent, and scheduling became necessary, although still possible at critical times; also lacking in the new environment were the men's institutions - the pubs (Wilmott, 1963; Young and Wilmott, 1962). On the other hand in Adelaide (Australia) telephones and cars were able to maintain regular family and kinship links even though the households were widely dispersed, although, as in Dagenham, scheduling was necessary (Martin, 1967).

These two patterns can be found even in a single city. Thus, in Los Angeles, Samoans were widely dispersed but used cars, work-places and other institutions such as churches to maintain strong links and to co-operate with and help each other (Ablon, 1971). They retained a traditional social system with traditional units and affective ties modified for the city. The main social units were extended families and churches, and the overlapping bonds based on kinship, church and ethnicity-linked occupations, where mutual help in job-finding led to clustering, created a strong community. At the same time the Samoans tried to live as close to each other as possible - several minutes by car (Ablon, 1971). Clearly planning and design to facilitate some clustering would be helpful and desirable (Rapoport, 1977; 1980; 1980/81; in press-b). In the case of Los Angeles, a similar pattern also applied to Serbs, where the church played a similar role in linking dispersed household (personal observation). On the other hand, other immigrant groups in Los Angeles e.g. Hispanic and Asian, tended to cluster much more closely; similar

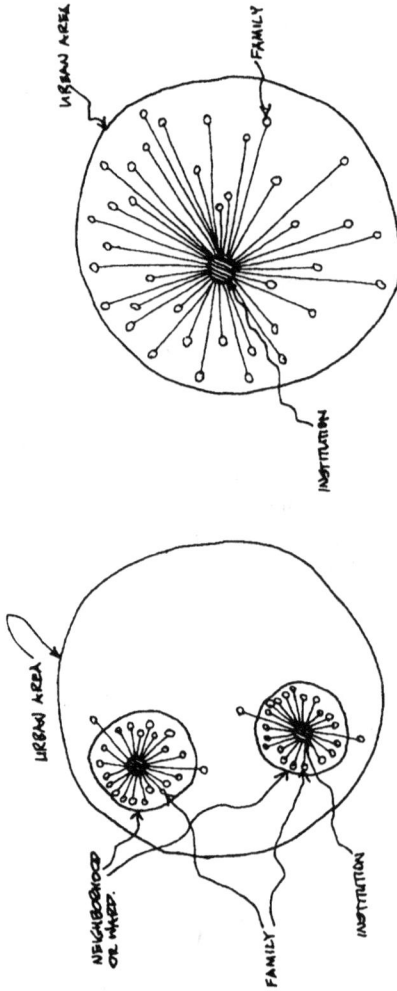

Figure 1.3   Clustered and unclustered families in urban areas and their relationship to institutions
Source: Based on Rapoport (in press c, Fig. 4)

differences are also found among different groups in Australian cities (Rapoport, 1977). These examples, and the discussion above about Britain, the US and elsewhere, suggests that kin-clusters are still desired, at least by some groups (Gaunt, 1997).

Note that such clustering has major implications for the survival of languages and cultures (Ehrlich, 1971; Rapoport, 1977, esp. Ch.5; 1983; Rosser and Harris, 1965). It should also be noted that spatial and temporal patterns of family and kinship relations vary not only among groups, but with stage in lifecycle, definitions of kinship and family and their meaning etc.

In the case of a Jordanian village one finds clusters of dwellings of families related by kinship. As the village grew, families tried to stay together, and the number of houses grew, leading to ever greater density to the extent that with one exception there are no streets among the houses, and people move directly from house to house (Shami, 1989, pp.464-465). This pattern of direct movement among houses is also found in Yazd, Iran (Rapoport, 1987, Fig.3, p.165). Similarly, expansion to include ever more family within a dwelling is also found in China and in Senegal where compounds house large extended families (Bourdier and Minh-Ha, 1996). Compounds are extremely flexible and open-ended, and able to accommodate changing family sizes, organisations and relationships and house types over hundreds of years (Schwerdtfeger, 1982).

It is also the case that changing residential patterns are not always as abrupt as believed. Thus, for example, urbanisation in India, although it changed residence patterns from patrilocal to other forms, does not necessarily lead to completely neo-local residence patterns (Vatuk, 1971; Vatuk, 1972). There is gradual change, synthesis and syncretism, with some patterns retained and others given up or changed (Brazao-Teixeira, 1990; Laslett and Wall, 1972; Rapoport, 1983; 1990b, Ch.4). Thus, among other aspects, clustering continues, although possibly in a weaker form, on the basis of various forms of homogeneity such as caste, religion, class, place of origin, language, lifestyle and even kinship and family (Rapoport, 1977; 1980; 1980/81; in press-b).

Even in Sweden, where family structure and residence patterns changed early and radically, and despite decreasing household size, urbanisation, increased mobility and female employment, nuclear families are not isolated from family and kin. Frequent contacts with close relatives remain important and this is reflected in what has been called the 'family circle' (Gaunt, 1997). This corresponds to the extended family and needs to be recognised in planning and design. The family circle does not have to live under one roof and is a group formed by genetically related people and their families, core groupings within kinship networks which, in turn, form a system of interrelated family circles. The importance of the family circle, while great, varied for different groups. It was more important for the working class (Rapoport, 1977, Ch.3 and 5 and references; 1985). Members of the family circle in that case lived as close together as possible, and considering the neighbourhood as part of housing is essential. Although being in the same neighbourhood was very important for working class women, it was hardly at all important for male professionals, with working class men and professional women somewhere in-between. The conclusion is thus that even in Sweden it is still necessary to consider opportunities and obstacles for extended families (Gaunt, 1997). This is also the case in Japan and possibly elsewhere (Morgan and Hiroshima, 1983; Rapoport, 1980; 1983; 1985; in press-b). Similar patterns underlie the development of 'granny flats' in Australia (Rapoport, 1985) made possible by large lots, as discussed earlier, and also development of design criteria for adding second units to single-family ranch houses in Canada, due to a rise in reconstituted extended families, non-related households and households with one or more home-based worker (Despres and Murphy, 1997)[4].

Note that in all these European, Australian and North American examples people do not necessarily wish to live under one roof and share with households outside the nuclear family; in fact this is often seen rather negatively (Baumgartner, 1988; Pruchno and et al., 1993). They do, however, want to live closer to elderly parents, adult children etc. Given the group differences found in developed countries, and the greater importance of supportive social networks there for people with reduced competence due to age, illness etc., i.e. in terms of criticality (Frick, 1986, Part B, pp.49-92, and Part C, pp.93-149; and esp. Badura, 1986), I would argue that the much higher criticality in developing countries makes such concerns, needs and wants far more important. Social networks, social ties, mutual help and support etc. can be based on ethnicity, place of origin, religion, caste, language, occupation etc. (Rapoport, 1977), but family and kinship are, in principle, both the strongest and most supportive. There is thus need for carefully thought through solutions and high degrees of open-endedness (Rapoport, 1980; 1983; 1995, Ch.33, pp.529-562).

In Zuni Pueblos neolocality has replaced matrilocality, but the maternal lineage is still critical socially, regarding rituals etc. Thus the basic social organisation has been maintained to a much greater extent than the more fluid settlement system (Ferguson, 1996, p.46) - an example of the 'loose fit' between housing and family discussed earlier (Rapoport, 1990f). In traditional Pueblos, kin and clan relations were related to spatial organisation, so that related families (mothers and daughters) lived in adjacent houses (Wilmott, 1963, regarding Bethnal Green; Young and Wilmott, 1962). However, there was no spatial localisation of clans, and these were dispersed throughout the settlement; their social solidarity did not derive from their spatial location (Ferguson, 1996, p.80). This is another example of the two patterns: spatial clustering and the absence of spatial clustering discussed earlier (Rapoport, in press-b).

In effect two cases are possible. In one there is correspondence between socially labelled groups and space, in the other there is no such correspondence and social groups are 'scattered'. It is also possible to find both simultaneously as in the case of Zuni Pueblos and all societies exhibit a mix of both patterns in their relation between social and spatial arrangements - one territorial, the other not, so that Zuni households are simultaneously spatial and transpatial groups (Ferguson, 1996, pp.115, 140, 170; Figure 1.3 above; Rapoport, in press-b, Fig.4).

It should be added that, as already discussed, certain institutions may act as places of interaction and maintain strong social and kinship links. These include the churches, workplaces, pubs etc. mentioned above and, in the case of the Zuni Kivas, medicine fraternities and priesthoods and, later, also churches (Ferguson, 1996). Non-fixed features such as ceremonies, dances and other gatherings, some occurring in plazas and Kivas also play a role. In this connection, as Zuni dwellings are increasingly for family households, rather than having at least some relation to larger social groups such as lineages and clans, and as these have changed from relatively large economic groups to smaller family units, they have also become more aspatial. The extended families of earlier households at Zuni Pueblos with their close ties to their farming, grazing and other economic activities are gradually being replaced by smaller social units, such as nuclear family households. Privacy in the use of space has increased as the need to invest in joint economic pursuits has decreased (Ferguson, 1996, p.147; Netting et al., 1984; Wilk, 1989; Wilk and Ashmore, 1988). In some US suburbs this has gone much further, leading to a new culture of 'moral minimalism' not only among families but **within** the family, where individuals dominate and lead almost independent lives, even avoiding sharing possessions and houses are divided into numerous private spaces, avoiding the shared use of the dwelling (Baumgartner, 1988). Privatisation occurs both among families and within the family, the resulting 'moral minimalism' means minimal social cohesion, weak ties, social atomisation and autonomy, avoiding trouble and confrontation. Public settings are greatly reduced with implications for housing as I have defined it. Both domestic life and family bonds are greatly weakened: there is high privacy, little communication and lack of mutual support and aid via social networks (Baumgartner, 1988). It is significant that in the same town, patterns are very different for the working class, particularly young people (Badura, 1986; Gaunt, 1997).

It is also worth pointing out that with the development and growth of computers, and hence home-based work, both family and housing (dwelling **and** neighbourhood) patterns are changing and will continue to change (Ahrentzen, 1989; Rapoport, in press-b).

In the case of the Zuni things have not yet gone that far, and families maintain their links with each other and larger social groups through meetings in the dwellings of their clan and lineage matriarchs during feasts and other ritual occasions with implications for the design of such dwellings. Clan groups also build *Shalako* houses annually to host religious rituals, and those houses then become dwellings for an individual household (Ferguson, 1996, p.140) (cf. the temporary Hogans built by Navaho for ceremonies).

However, as the Zuni moved to the suburbs, a form of clustering based on directionalism continued, so that their location was congruent with the (nuclear) family's original placement and corresponded to the section of town which they originally occupied. Such directionalism was also found among Australian Aborigines in multi-tribe camps (Rapoport, 1977), with Irish immigrants to London (Young, 1973), with rural immigrants to Cairo (Abu-Lughod, 1969) and elsewhere. When Tswana towns, which were mobile, moved, the kin-based wards arranged themselves in the same relationship to the centre as in the previous town, i.e. the directional patterns persisted (Hardie, 1980).

Household, family and kinship not only vary cross-culturally (albeit with constancies if not universals (Barkow et al., 1992; Fox, 1980; Stephens, 1963)). Like other phenomena they also change over time. As the Cambridge Population group has shown, such changes, as is often the case, can also best be considered in terms of constancy and change. Some elements remain unchanged, so that historical precedents are directly relevant albeit at some level of abstraction; some elements undergo change, but some lessons from the past are possible, for example, in terms of constant processes; other elements disappear, and it is then useful to ask why they have disappeared and what, if anything, has replaced them; finally, there are new elements, and in that case the past is less useful, although there may still exist constant processes, or these new elements may be related to contexts that show constancy (Laslett, 1977; Laslett and Wall, 1972; Rapoport, 1990b). Housing as conceptualised above behaves in very similar ways (Rapoport, 1983) and the two domains mutually influence one another.

A good example is provided by Algeria (Mahdjoubi and Awotona, 1997) where both the Arab and the Berber communities are based on kinship systems ranging from the extended family, through clans to tribes. This is reflected in the organisation of rural space from the dwelling, compound and village to the larger settlement system. The dwellings, which may be large houses or compounds, in both communities are strongly influenced by the form of the household which is a patriarchal extended family, the basic socio-economic unit. In both languages the same word is used for compound and extended family, which comprises a number of conjugal families of married brothers and their offspring, the father and grandfather and married paternal uncles. Within the dwelling privacy and gender separation are very important and influence meeting places (Rapoport, 1977; 1986; 1990f). As already discussed, men typically utilise the public, outdoor domain and need to be visible, whereas women utilise the dwelling and should be invisible.

The next larger unit, the clan, is the largest socio-economic and political unit still based on kinship ties and found among the Bedouin, among others. Its lineage spans five or six generations and often shares an ancestral name, and includes several extended families. In this case the two communities differ: Arab villages consist of a single clan, and are separated from others; Berber villages consist of two or three clans which are, however, autonomous and lead a nearly separate existence. Until recently each had its own section of the village (ward or neighbourhood), cemetery, water sources and sometimes its own festivals, customs and even its own legend about its origins.

The tribe is an association of many clans claiming descent from a common ancestor from whom they derive their common name which replaces blood relationships in generating solidarity, cohesion and intense social relationships among members. The identity of the tribe is reinforced and maintained by shared institutions, such as water sources, mosques, assembly houses, cemeteries which are important in terms of ritual and symbolism as in the case of the Bedouin and other groups. At each social occasion women of the tribe socialise while men go to the same periodic markets where they meet and exchange views as was the case in China (Rapoport, 1977; 1983; Skinner, 1972).

Given my discussion earlier about the need for culture-specific design and supportiveness for and retention of, the culture core, and the mutual influence on each other of kinship and housing organisation, the discussion by Mahdjoubi and Awotona (1997) of accidental and deliberate inhibition of kinship patterns by planning and design policies during both colonial times and after independence are highly significant for planning policy and design generally, since the family and kinship are often among the most important components of the culture core (Rapoport, 1983; Stea, 1995) that are critically important mediating structures and form the social units that may need the support of appropriate physical units (Jaulin, 1971; Rapoport, 1978a; 1980; 1983).

Similar inhibitory effects occurred due to the inappropriate design of government housing in Zuni Pueblos with a consequent increased lack of congruence between Zuni social and spatial structures (Ferguson, 1996). Of course, some of the changes might have occurred in any case, due to modernisation, culture change and consequently new values and wants etc., but inappropriate planning and design decisions certainly contributed to the process and its speed. Thus, while the built environment reflects changes in Zuni society as described earlier, it also changes that society. For example, the provision of small houses inhibits the temporary gathering of larger groups that transcend the household. Another important element is the lack of kitchen/dining room combinations or, if they exist, their too small size, so that they cannot serve as a focus for social interaction among larger groups which may have a ritual component as in the case of the Apache described by Esber (1972); (Rapoport, 1978a; 1980; 1983; 1985).

In many of the examples discussed, and more generally as societies become more complex, the use of space becomes more specialised and hence the number of specialised settings, both inside and outside the dwelling increases (Cornell, 1997; Ferguson, 1996; Kent, 1991; Rapoport, 1969; 1990f). Since the rates of such changes, and therefore how far they have gone, varies among groups, this leads to another source of potential misfit between housing and culture.

This has been the case with housing for Australian Aborigines on which there has recently been a great deal of interesting research (Heppell, 1979; Memmott, 1991; Morel and Ross, 1993; Ross, 1987, among others). Although different variables play a role in the specifics of culturally appropriate dwelling and settlement design, one very important aspect is kinship, its broad definition based on a variety of connections (Stea, 1995), and the obligations it brings with it with a correspondingly wide sharing of resources. Unlike European Australians, who are an 'individualist' culture, Aborigines are 'collectivist'. Households expand to fill the space available, leading to many people sharing or trying to share dwellings with large kin-based households, even including visitors so that many people share bedrooms and other settings. This is more striking since the larger system of settings, particularly important in Aboriginal culture, has been ignored. Not only do small houses separated from other settings not work, but the household is in a constant flux, partly due to the use of mobility to handle conflicts as mentioned earlier (Rapoport, 1978d). Households and individuals move, either to other households or other camps, requiring a high degree of open-endedness. There are also same-sex households or camps, and settlement organisation is not only intimately related to the dwelling, but also reflects kinship. Thus wrong design at all scales has been highly inhibiting not to say destructive, leading to the current research effort.

An understanding of aboriginal patterns has also been used to understand the more general complex relationships between cultural norms and rules, social groupings and domestic space. This has been used to argue, for example, that in order to achieve sustainability in Australian housing one should avoid fundamental changes to social and spatial organisation, which should be the last option considered (Ross, 1991).

In line with my earlier argument about the generality of the model and approach, and the two-way interaction between households and housing, the above discussion can be applied to a very different group - Hasidic Jews in rural New York. Much of the problem is due to conflicts among governmental safety, zoning and other rules and community norms. The latter have resulted in the housing of 53 teenage boys in two ranch houses used as *Yeshiva* dormitories. Also, the very large families require significantly larger dwellings, and their absence leads to overcrowding and also to the use of three-family housing in areas zoned for two-family houses. Sabbath rules require greater density to make important institutions accessible to pedestrians, and the need for a variety of special culture-specific institutions means that they are located in houses, again violating zoning codes (Berger, 1977)[5]. The response has been to try and set up a culture-specific community, a village reflecting all these patterns, size and organisation of families, high levels of social interaction and other aspects of culture.

Such cultural conflicts are becoming more common as new immigrant groups move into very different societies, and many of those are related to various aspects of family and kinship. To conclude with just one more example, in the case of co-op housing for Vietnamese in Canada, transitional spaces between the unit of the household, the collectivity, the project and the neighbourhood were very different between the two cultures. Misunderstandings about the nature of boundaries, the cues marking them, the rules about appropriate play settings for children etc. all led to conflicts. Also, among Vietnamese in Canada, unlike in Vietnam, offspring do not take care of the elderly, who become isolated and this is exacerbated by their lack of English (Cooper and Rodam, 1995). The discussion earlier of the possibility of extended family living, household circles, granny flats, open-endedness etc. is clearly highly relevant in this case also.

A note on process

Although this chapter is mainly concerned with family/housing relationships at the level of product, it may be useful briefly to consider a few selected aspects of process.

It has been shown repeatedly that stable communities with similar cultural backgrounds, i.e. people with close relationships and tight social links, co-operate better and are thus more capable of working together (Salama, 1995). It seems intuitively clear that family and kin groups should, in general, be able to co-operate best. This should apply to initial construction as in spontaneous settlements, to ongoing maintenance and to changes, extensions and personalisations either in spontaneous or government housing. The extent of such transformations can be quite extraordinary, and many of the changes themselves, internally and externally, are related to family: relatives, more children, family size, number of married couples, number of sons/daughters, number of earners, gender relationship and privacy needs, and also the building skills of household members or relatives (Salama, 1995).

This is also the case in dealing with disasters, man-made or natural, where family and kinship networks and resources are important although not the only social coping mechanisms (Awotona, 1997). Family and kinship links are also important in the process of migration, adjustments to urban life, obtaining jobs and mutual help generally e.g. older relatives helping with household work and child-care, allowing mother to work when this is culturally acceptable or economically necessary. Families can also be helpful in accumulating and sharing necessary resources - money, materials, labour or skills - making the continuous housing modifications and transformations more likely and easier, particularly if housing is open-ended; they can also be helpful in self-housing. It should be noted that the increasing role of codes, regulations and rules make self-build, building by the family or kin group, and transformations more difficult, as do particular forms of land-subdivision, street and service layout etc. (Rapoport, 1980).

At the same time the percentage of self-built housing even in Australia (Holland, 1988) and Western Europe (Holman, 1997) remains high, and is even higher in developing countries and among specific groups. For example, among the Zuni architectural change has largely occurred in a piecemeal fashion with each nuclear family building, maintaining, demolishing and rebuilding and modifying their individual dwelling. This leads to many individual variations within a system of cultural norms, rules and schemata (Blanton, 1996; Ferguson, 1996, p.81; Rapoport, 1992a).

It should, however, be pointed out that there may also be negative consequences of family/housing relationships at the level of process. For example, the expectation of sharing among kin particularly when defined broadly can prevent capital accumulation and block housing improvements, leading to worse housing conditions and can also result in poorer maintenance, less transformation etc. This has been the case with one group in Colombia (Ashton, 1972) and is also widely reported in the case of Australian Aborigines and in sub-Saharan Africa. Such need to share may also influence activity systems in the dwelling, as when eating is done in secret to avoid the need to share. Obligations to share space may lead to crowding and other problems, as in the case of Alexandria, Egypt (El-Sherif, 1977) and among Australian Aborigines. Open-endedness in housing is again a prerequisite as households change in composition, structure and size (Benna, 1997; Rapoport, 1995, Ch.33, pp.529-562).

Conclusion

From the few examples I have used it seems that starting, say in 1900 and accelerating since the end of World War II there have been major changes to the family, including a clear shift to the nuclear family and to neo-locality. It also seems, however, that the nuclear family was always rather more prevalent than often thought (Laslett, 1977; Laslett and Wall, 1972; Stephens, 1963). Given that, and the apparently loose fit between family and housing, one might ask whether it is useful to worry about the relationship between family and housing.

However, housing not only reflects social and cultural change but also leads to it: housing which is inappropriate, and hence inhibiting or merely not supportive, may lead to undesirable changes in family structure, behaviour and other aspects of culture (Ferguson, 1996; Grenell, 1972; Grimaud, 1986; Jaulin, 1971; Rapoport, 1978a; 1983; 1990c; Wilmott, 1963; Young and Wilmott, 1962 etc.). It is also the case, as we have seen, that as change continues it may include 'reversals' or at least the persistence of earlier patterns (Despres and Murphy, 1997; Ferguson, 1996; Gaunt, 1997; Morgan and Hiroshima, 1983 etc.). In any case, one would not want unwittingly to destroy still viable family and kinship structures and their corresponding culture cores, by wrong planning policy and design. Two things follow with important implications for planning and design. The first is the need to consider the importance or potential importance of family and kinship and other aspects of the culture core for culture-specific design, and to provide support in cases where it is needed, i.e. in situations of high criticality (Badura, 1986; Rapoport, 1983). The second is to design open-ended site layouts and housing to allow for cultural variability, for unforeseen changes and also for changes 'back.'

Notes

1   One of my doctoral students, Mr. Yasser Moustafa, in studying Baladi housing in Cairo, recently proposed an interesting modification of my model which may have certain advantages. However, he is still in the process of developing it, and I have not yet been able to think through all its implications. Thus it seems too early to use here.
2   These residences may, of course, be in the same ward, neighbourhood or settlement, although they do not need to be.
3   This may also influence the larger cultural landscape as in the case of Anatolia, Turkey, where poplar forests were planted at the birth of a daughter to become her dowry (personal observations).
4   This work was reported in a news release by the Centre for Architecture and Urban Planning Research, University of Wisconsin, Milwaukee, in June 1997.
5   I ignore other conflicts unrelated to housing.

References

Ablon, J. (1971), 'The social organization of an urban Samoan community.' *SW Journal of Anthropology*, Vol. 27, No. 1 (Spring), pp.75-96.
Abu-Lughod, J. (1969), 'Migrant adjustment to city life: The Egyptian case', in Breese, G. (ed) *The city in newly developing countries*, Princetown University Press: Princetown, pp.376-388.
Ahrentzen, S. (1989), 'A place of peace, prospect and ... a PC: The home as office.' *Journal of Architectural and Planning Research*, Vol. 6, No. 4, (Winter), pp.271-288.
Ashton, G.T. (1972), 'The differential adaptation of two slum sub-cultures to a Columbian [sic] housing project.' *Urban Anthropology*, Vol. 1, No. 2 (Fall), pp.176-194.
Awotona, A. (ed) (1997), *Reconstruction after disaster: Issues and practices*, Ashgate: Aldershot, UK.
Awotona, A., and Briggs, M. (1997), 'The "enablement" approach and settlement upgrading in South Africa', in Awotona, A. and Teymur, N. (eds), *Tradition, location and community: Placemaking and development*, Avebury: Aldershot, UK, pp.59-77.
Badura, B. (1986), 'Social networks and the quality of life', in Frick, D. (ed) *The quality of urban life: Social, psychological and physical conditions*, de Gruyter: Berlin, pp.55-60.

Banning, E.B., and Byrd, E.F. (1987), 'Houses and changing residential unit: Domestic architecture at PPNB'Am Ghazal, Jordan.' *Proceedings, prehistoric Society*, Vol. 53, pp.309-325.

Barkow, J.H., Cosmides, L., et al. (eds) (1992), *The adapted mind: Evolutionary psychology and the generation of culture*, Oxford University Press: New York.

Baumgartner, M.P. (1988), *The moral order of the suburb*, Oxford University Press: New York.

Benna, U.G. (1997), 'Societal values in development process: Place-making in Sokoto, Nigeria', in Awotona, A. and Teymur, N. (eds), *Tradition, locatin and community: Place-making and development*, Avebury: Aldershot, UK, pp.173-187.

Berger, J. (1977), 'Growing pains for a rural Hasidic enclave', *New York Times*, 13 January, New York,

Blanton, R.E. (1996), *Houses and households: A comparative study*, Plenum: New York.

Bourdier, J.-P., and Minh-Ha, T.T. (1996), *Drawn from African dwellings*,   Indiana University Press: Bloomington.

Brazao-Teixeira, R. (1990), *Tradition and change in the domestic environment of unplanned urban settlements: A case study, Natal, Northeast Brazil*, MArch thesis, McGill University: Montreal, Canada.

Brown, P.L. (1996), 'A house that bends to a family's needs', *New York Times*, 19 September, New York,

Byrd, B.F. (1994), 'Public and private, domestic and corporate: The emergence of the Southwest Asian village.' *American Antiquity*, Vol. 59, No. 4, pp.639-666.

Carp, J. (1987), *A house: The flexibility of timeless architecture*, SAR-Network: Eindhoven, Netherlands.

Chira, S. (1994), 'Hispanic families avoid using day care, study says', *New York Times*, 6 April, New York,

Chua, B.H. (1988), 'Adjusting religious practices to different house forms in Singapore.' *Architecture and Behavior*, Vol. 4, No. 1, pp.3-25.

Cooper, M., and Rodam, M. (1995), 'Culture and spatial boundaries: Co-operative and non-profit housing in Canada.' *Architecture and Behavior*, Vol. 11, No. 2, pp.123-138.

Cornell, L.L. (1997), 'House architecture and family form: On the origin of vernacular traditions in early modern Japan.' *Traditional Dwellings and Settlements Review*, Vol. 8, No. 2 (Spring), pp.21-31.

Correa, C.M. (1978), *Third World housing: Space as a resource*, (Mimeo).

Despres, and Murphy. (1997), News Release by the Centre for Architecture and Urban Planning Research, University of Wisconsin, Milwaukee, June.

Doshi, S.L. (1969), 'Non-clustered tribal villages and community development.' *Human Organization*, Vol. 28, No. 4 (Winter), pp.297-302.

Duncan, J.S. (1981), 'From container of women to status symbol: The impact of social structure on the meaning of the house', in J.S., D. (ed) *Housing and identity: Cross-cultural perspective*, Croom-Helm: London, pp.36-59.

Duncan, J.S. (1985), 'The house as symbol of social structure: Notes on the language of objects among collectivistic groups', in Altman, I. and Werner, C.M. (eds), *Home environments*, Vol. 8, Plenum: New York, pp.133-151.

Ehrlich, A.S. (1971), 'History, ecology and demography in the British Caribbean: An analysis of East Indian ethnicity.' *SW Journal of Anthropology*, Vol. 27, No. 2, pp.166-180.

Elgohary, A.F., and Hanson, J. (1997), 'In search of a spatial culture', in Awotona, A. and Teymur, N. (eds), *Tradition, location and community: Place-making development*, Avebury: Aldershot, UK, pp.81-120.

El-Sherif, A. (1977), 'Location and development: People, place and power in Alexandria's inner city neighbourhoods', in Awotona, A. and Teymur, N. (eds), *Tradition, location and community: Place-making and development*, Avebury: Aldershot, UK, pp.121-139.

Esber, G.S. (1972), 'Indian housing for Indians.' *The Kiva*, Vol. 37, No. (Spring), pp.141-147.

Fedick, S.L. (1989), 'Dispersed organization: A consideration of prehistoric Maya domestic architecture, land use and settlement pattern', *Third International and Interdisciplinary Forum on Built Form and Culture Research*, Arizona State University, Tempe, 9-12 November, Paper presented at Conference. (Mimeo).

Ferguson, T.J. (1996), *Historic Zuni architecture and society: An archaeological application of space syntax*, part of the series 'Anthropological papers of the University of Arizona', Vol. 60, Arizona Press: Tucson.

Fox, R. (1980), *The read lamp of incest*, Dutton: New York.

Franck, K.A., and Ahrentzen, S. (eds) (1991), *New households, new housing*, Van Nostrand Reinhold: New York.

Frick, D. (ed) (1986), *The quality of urban life: Social, psychological and physical conditions*, de Gruyter: Berlin.

Gasparini, A. (1973), 'Influence of the dwelling on family life.' *Ekistics*, Vol. 36, No. 216 (November), pp.344-348.

Gaunt, L.N. (1997), 'The family circle: A challenge for planning and design.' *Journal of Architectural and Planning Research*, Vol. 8, No. 2 (Summer), pp.147-163.

Grenell, P. (1972), 'Planning for invisible people: Some consequences of bureaucratic values and practices', in Turner, J.F.C. and Fichter, R. (eds), *Freedom to build*, Macmillan: New York, pp.95-121.

Grimaud, V. (1986), 'Societé hierarchique et habitat en Inde.' *Architecture and Behavior*, Vol. 2, No. 3-4, pp.207-227.

Han, P.-W. (1991), *The spatial structures of traditional settlements: A study of the clan villages in Korean rural areas*, PhD (unpublished) thesis, Seoul National University: Seoul.

Hardie, G.J. (1980), *Tswana design of house and settlement - continuity and change in expressive space*, PhD (unpublished) thesis, Boston University: Boston, USA.

Heppell, M. (ed) (1979), *A black reality: Aboriginal camps and housing in remote Australia*, Australian Institute of Aboriginal Studies: Canberra.

Hole, W.V., and Taylor, J.R.B. (1978), *The housing needs of single young people and the use of older properties*. Current Paper, CP 43/78, May, Building Research Establishment: Garston, UK.

Holland, G. (1988), *Emoh Ruo: Owner building in Sydney*, Hale and Iremonger: Sydney, Australia.

Holman, C. (1997), 'Community self-build in Britain: The potential and the reality', in Awotona, A. and Teymur, N. (eds), *Tradition, location and community: Place-making and development*, Avebury: Aldershot, UK, pp.189-203.

Hull, R.W. (1976), *African cities and towns before the European conquest*, W.W. Norton: New York.

Jaulin, R. (1971), 'Ethnocide: The theory and practice of cultural murder.' *The Ecologist*, Vol. 1, pp.12-15.

Kent, S. (1984), *Analyzing activity areas: An ethnoarchaeological study of the use of space*, University of New Mexico Press: Albuquerque, USA.

Kent, S. (1991), 'Partitioning space: Cross-cultural factors influencing domestic spatial segmentation.' *Environment and Behavior*, Vol. 23, No. 4 (July), pp.438-473.

Kent, S. (1995), 'Unstable households in a stable Kalahari community in Botswana.' *American Anthropologist*, Vol. 97, No. 2, pp.297-312.

Knapp, R.G. (ed) (1992), *Chinese landscapes: The village as place*, University of Hawaii Press: Honolulu.

Laslett, P. (1977), *Family life and illict love in earlier generations: Essays in historical sociology*, Cambridge University Press: Cambridge, UK.

Laslett, P., and Wall, R. (eds) (1972), *Household and family in past time*, Cambridge University Press: Cambridge, UK.

Laude, O. (1992), 'Hekeng village, Fujian: Unique habitats', in Knapp, R.G. (ed) *Chinese landscapes: The village as place*, University of Hawaii Press: Hoholulu, pp.163-172.

Los Angeles Times. (1983), 'Proposition M: Minorities helped defeat measure', *Los Angeles Times*, 10 November, Los Angeles,

Madigan, R., and Munro, M. (1991), 'Gender, house and "home": Social meanings and domestic architecture in Britain.' *Journal of Architectural and Planning Research*, Vol. 8, No. 2 (Summer), pp.116-132.

Mahdjoubi, L., and Awotona, A. (1997), 'Planning and designing rural settlements: The Algerian experience', in Awotona, A. and Teymur, N. (eds), *Tradition, location and community: Place-making and development*, Avebury: Aldershot, UK, pp.141-159.

Martin, J.I. (1967), 'Extended kinship ties: An Adelaide study.' *Australia and New Zealand Journal of Sociology*, Vol. 3, No. 1, pp.44-63.

Memmott, P. (1991), *Humpy, House and Tin Shed: Aboriginal settlement history on the Darling River*, The Ian Buchan Fell Research Centre, University of Sydney: Sydney.

Morel, P., and Ross, H. (1993), *Housing design assessment for Bush communities*, Tangerntyere Council/NT Department of Lands, Housing and Local Government: Alice Springs, Australia.

Morgan, S.P., and Hiroshima, K. (1983), 'The persistence of extended family residence in Japan: Anachronism or alternative strategy.' *American Sociological Review*, Vol. 48, No. 2 (April), pp.269-281.

Netting, R.M., Wilk, R.R., et al. (eds) (1984), *Households: Comparative and historical studies of the domestic group*, University of California: Berkeley, USA.

New York Times. (1993), 'Parents fight to keep after-school program after a dispute', *New York Times*, 11 October, New York,

Osmont, A. (1986), 'Transformation des espaces habités à Dakar: Adaptations fonctionelles ou ré-interpretations culturelles?' *Architecture and Behavior*, Vol. 2, No. 3-4, pp.261-299.

Oyediran, O. (1994), 'Socio-cultural influences of the Hausas and Tivs of Northern Nigeria on their traditional architecture', in Neary, S.J. (ed) *Urban environment*, Spon: London, pp.45-59.

Pader, E.J. (1993), 'Spatiality and social change: Domestic space use in Mexico and the United States.' *American Ethnologist*, Vol. 20, No. 1, pp.114-137.

Payne, G. (1997), *Urban land tenure and property rights in developing countries*, IT Publications/ODA: London.

Pruchno, R.A., and et al. (1993), 'Multigenerational households of caregiving families: Negotiating shared space.' *Environment and Behavior*, Vol. 25, No. 3 (May), pp.349-366.

Rapoport, A. (1969), *House form and culture*, Prentice-Hall: Englewood Cliffs, NJ.

Rapoport, A. (1975), 'Toward a redefinition of density.' *Environment and Behavior*, Vol. 7, No. 2 (June), pp.133-158.

Rapoport, A. (1977), *Human aspects of urban form*, Pergamon Press: Oxford.

Rapoport, A. (1978a), 'Culture and environment.' *The Ecologist Quarterly*, Vol. 4 (Winter), pp.269-279.

Rapoport, A. (1978b), 'Culture and the subjective effects of stress.' *Urban Ecology*, Vol. 3, No. 3, pp.241-261.

Rapoport, A. (1978c), 'The environment as an enculturating medium', in Weidemann, S. and Anderson, J.R. (eds), *Priorities for environmental design research (EDRA 8)*, Vol. Part 1, EDRA: Washington, DC, pp.54-58.

Rapoport, A. (1978d), 'Nomadism as a man-environment system.' *Environment and Behavior*, Vol. 10, No. 2 (June), pp.215-246.

Rapoport, A. (1980), 'Site layout and housing.' *Architectural Association Quarterly*, Vol. 12, No. 1, pp.4-7.

Rapoport, A. (1980/81), 'Neighbourhood homogeneity or heterogeneity.' *Architecture and Behavior*, Vol. 1, No. 1, pp.67-77.

Rapoport, A. (1981), 'Identity and environment: A cross-cultural perspective', in Duncan, J.S. (ed) *Housing and identity: Cross-cultural perspectives*, Croom-Helm: London, pp.6-35.

Rapoport, A. (1983), 'Development, culture change and supportive "design".' *Habitat International*, Vol. 7, No. 5/6, pp.249-268.

Rapoport, A. (1984), 'Culture and the urban order', in Agnew, J. and et al. (eds), *The City in Cultural Context*, Allen and Unwin: Boston, pp.50-75.

Rapoport, A. (1985), 'Thinking about home environments: A conceptual framework', in Altman, I. and Werner, C.M. (eds), *Home environments*, Vol. 8, Plenum: New York, pp.255-286.

Rapoport, A. (1986), 'The use and design of open spaces in urban neighbourhoods', in Frick, D. (ed) *The quality of urban life: Social, psychological and physical conditions*, de Gruyter: Berlin, pp.159-175.

Rapoport, A. (1987), 'Learning about settlements and energy from historical precedents.' *Ekistics*, Vol. 54, No. 325-327 (July-December), pp.262-268.

Rapoport, A. (1988), 'Levels of meaning in the built environment', in Poyatos, F. (ed) *Cross-cultural perspectives in non-verbal communications*, C.J. Hogrefe: Toronto, pp.317-326.

Rapoport, A. (1989), 'On the attributes of tradition', in Bourdier, J.-P. and Al Sayyad, N. (eds), *Dwelling, settlements and tradition: Cross-cultural perspectives*, University Press of America: Lanham, MD, p.77105.

Rapoport, A. (1990a), 'Defining vernacular design', in Turan, M. (ed) *Vernacular architecture: Paradigms of environmental response*, Avebury: Aldershot, pp.67-101.

Rapoport, A. (1990b), *History and precedent in environmental design*, Plenum: New York.

Rapoport, A. (1990c), 'Housing and culture', in Taylor, L. (ed) *Housing: Symbol, structure, site*, Cooper-Hewitt Museum/Rizzoli: New York, pp.14-15.

Rapoport, A. (1990d), *The meaning of the built environment*, University of Arizona Press: Tucson.

Rapoport, A. (1990e), 'Science and the failure of architecture', in Altman, I. and Christensen, K. (eds), *Environment and behaviour studies: Emergence of intellectual traditions*, Vol. 11, Plenum: New York, pp.79-109.

Rapoport, A. (1990f), 'Systems of activities and systems of settings', in Kent, S. (ed) *Domestic architecture and the use of space*, Cambridge University Press: Cambridge, pp.9-20.

Rapoport, A. (1992a), 'On cultural landscapes.' *Traditional Dwellings and Settlements Review*, Vol. 3, No. 2 (Spring), pp.33-47.

Rapoport, A. (1992b), 'On regions and regionalism', in Markovich, N.C. and et al. (eds), *Pueblo style and regional architecture*, Van Nostrand-Reinhold: New York, pp.272-294. Paperback only.

Rapoport, A. (1993), *Cross-cultural studies and urban form*, part of the series 'The 1992 Lefrak Lectures', University of Maryland, Urban Studies and Planning Program, College Park, MD:

Rapoport, A. (1994), 'Spatial organisation and the built environment', in Ingold, T. (ed) *Eompanion encyclopeida of anthropology: Humanity, culture and social life*, Routledge: London, pp.460-502.

Rapoport, A. (1995), *Thirty-three papers in environment-behaviour research*, Urban International Press: Newcastle upon Tyne.

Rapoport, A. (in press-a), 'The courtyard house - a conceptual analysis', *The courtyard house and the urban fabric*, Aga Kahn Program, MIT, USA, 5-6 April 1997,

Rapoport, A. (in press-b), 'On the nature and role of urban neighbourhoods.' *Urban Design Studies*, Vol. 3,

Rapoport, A. (in press-c), 'On the relation between culture and environment', *Aris 3*, Department of Architecture, Carnegie Mellon University.

Rodman, M.C. (1985a), 'Contemporary custom: Redefining domestic space in Longana, Vanuatu.' *Ethnology*, Vol. 24, No. 4 (October), pp.269-279.

Rodman, M.C. (1985b), 'Moving houses: Residential mobility and the mobility of residences in Longana, Vanuatu.' *American Anthropologist*, Vol. 87, pp.56-72.

Rohter, L. (1997), 'Guatemala digs up army's secret cemeteries', *New York Times*, 7 June, New York,

Ross, H. (1987), *Just for living: Aboriginal perceptions of housing in northwest Australia*, Aboriginal Studies Press: Canberra.

Ross, H. (1991), 'Household composition and the use of space', in Cock, P. (ed) *Social structures for sustainability*, Australian National University, Centre for Resource and Environmental Studies: Canberra, pp.64-72.

Rosser, C., and Harris, C. (1965), *The family and social change: A study of family and kinship in a South Wales town*, Routledge and Kegan Paul: London.

Salama, R. (1995), *User transformation of government housing projects: Case study, Egypt*, MArch thesis, McGill University: Montreal. Unpublished.

Sancar, F.H., and Koop, T.T. (1995), 'Proposing a behavioural definition of the "vernacular" based on a comparative analysis of the behaviour settings in three settlements in Turkey and Greece.' *Journal of Architectural and Planning Research*, Vol. 12, No. 2 (Summer), pp.141-165.

Sastrosasmita, S., and Nurul Amin, A.T.M. (1990), 'Housing needs of informal sector workers: The case of Yogyakarta, Indonesia.' *Habitat International*, Vol. 14, No. 4, pp.75-88.

Schwerdtfeger, F.W. (1982), *Traditional housing in African cities: A comparative study of houses in Zaria, Ibadan and Marrackech*, Wiley: Chichester.

Sebba, R. (1991), 'The role of the home environment in cultural transmission.' *Architecture and Behavior*, Vol. 7, No. 3, pp.223-241.

Shami, S. (1989), 'Settlement and resettlement in Umm Qeis: Spatial organizationa and social dynamics in a Jordanian village', in Bourdier, J.-P. and Al Sayyad, N. (eds), *Dwellings, settlements and tradition*, University Press of America: Lanham, MD, pp.451-476.

Shokeid, M. (1971), 'Social networks and innovation in the division of labour between men and women in the family and in the coummunity: A case study of Moroccan immigrants.' *Canadian Review of Sociology and Anthropology*, Vol. 8, No. 1, pp.1-17.

Skinner, G.W. (1972), 'Marketing and social structure in rural China', in English, P.W. and Mayfield, R.C. (eds), *Man, space and environment: Concepts in contemporary human geography*, pp.561-601.

Stahl, P.H. (1991), 'Maison et group domestique étendu.' *APMOΣ*, Vol. III, pp.1667-1692. In French.

Stea, D. (1995), 'House and home: Identity, dichotomy or dialectic? With special reference to Mexico', in Benjamin, D. (ed) *The home: Words, interpretations, meanings and environments*, Avebury: Aldershot, pp.181-201.

Stephens, W.N. (1963), *The family in cross-cultural perspective*, Holt, Rinehart and Winston: New York.

Suttles, G.D. (1968), *The social order of the slum*, Chicago University Press: Chicago.

Tipple, A.G. (1977), 'Design a house game.' *Town Planning Review*, Vol. 48, No. 2, pp.141-148.

Tipple, A.G. (1987), 'Housing policy and culture in Kumasi, Ghana.' *Environment and Behavior*, Vol. 19, No. 3 (May), pp.331-352.

Troy, P. (1995), *The family and urban policy*, Australian National University , Urban Research Program: Canberra. Mimeo.

Vatuk, S. (1971), 'Trends in North Indian urban kinship: The matrilateral asymmetry hypothesis.' *SW Journal of Anthropology*, Vol. 27, No. 3 (Autumn), pp.287-307.

Vatuk, S. (1972), *Kinship and urbanization: White collar migrants in North India*, University of California Press: Berkeley.

Vayda, A.P. (1983), 'Progressive contextualization.' *Human Ecology*, Vol. 11, No. 3 (September), pp.265-282.

West, R.C. (1974), 'The flat roofed folk dwelling in rural Mexico', in Walker, H.J. and Haag, W.G. (eds), *Man and cultural heritage*, Vol. V, Louisiana State University, School of Geoscience: Baton Rouge, pp.111-132.

Wheeler, L. (1977), 'Behavioral and social aspects of the Santa Cruz riveside project.' *Man-Environment Systems*, Vol. 7, No. 4, pp.203-205.

Wilk, R.R. (ed) (1989), *The husehold economy: Reconsidering the domestic mode of construction*, Westview Press: Boulder, CO.

Wilk, R.W., and Ashmore, W. (eds) (1988), *Household and community in the mesoamerican past*, University of New Mexico Press: Albuquerque.

Wilmott, P. (1963), *The evolution of a community*, Routledge and Kegan Paul: London.

Yans-McLaughlin, V. (1977), 'The Italian family', *New York Times*, 6 July, New York,

Young, M., and Wilmott, P. (1962), *Family and kinship in East London*, Penguin: Harmondsworth, UK.

Young, M.W., P. (1973), *The symmetrical family*, Pantheon: New York.
Zgusta, R. (1991), *Dwelling space in eastern Asia*, Vol. 4, Publications of Osaka University Japan of Foreign Studies: Osaka, Japan.
Zich, A. (1997), 'Okinawa.' *National Geographic*, Vol. 191, No. 6 (June), pp.86-105.

Section II
Case studies from Africa

2 User modifications in public housing estates:

Some findings from the Nigerian scene

BEN C. ARIMAH

One of the measures adopted by authorities in developing countries to alleviate housing shortage is the construction of fully serviced housing units. For a variety of reasons, such houses may not be suitable for their intended beneficiaries. These units may then be abandoned or where occupied, are greatly modified to suit the needs of their occupants. User modification can be seen as a bottom-up approach which seeks to rectify some of the physical deficiencies associated with the direct construction of public housing estates. This chapter investigates the degree and nature of user modifications in a middle class housing estate: the Satellite town housing estate in Lagos, Nigeria. The empirical analysis reveals that 86 per cent of the units in the estate have undergone at least one form of modification or another. The major forms of modification include the construction of a surrounding fence, shops, additional rooms, carports, water closets and extension of kitchen facilities. The major reasons for these modifications are: safety considerations; the need to integrate income generating activities within the unit; increase in household size; and the need to improve the service component of the house. Finally, recommendations are proffered whereby modifications can be carried out without necessarily contravening planning and building regulations.

Introduction

A major challenge of urbanisation in developing countries pertains to meeting the housing needs of their cities' teeming population. High rates of urbanisation exert tremendous pressure on urban housing and land markets (Malpezzi and Sa-Aadu, 1996). This is partly reflected in the housing shortages that characterise developing countries. Such deficits as observed by Tipple (1994b) are manifested in overcrowded habitation, high levels of sharing and occupying dilapidated

39

structures, excessive rent burden and the breakdown of waste disposal arrangements among others.   In an attempt at reducing these shortages, governments in many Third World countries have responded with a plethora of programmes.   The most prominent of these are: direct construction of fully serviced housing units; sites and service schemes; provision of governments residential quarters at subsidised rents and slum and squatter upgrading schemes.

In Nigeria, such top-down approaches particularly the direct construction of housing units have been associated with a number of flaws, and as such, failed to achieve their intended objectives. For instance, as far back as the 1960s, the World Bank (1965, p.4) criticised Nigeria's public housing programme as: '... unsatisfactory because it produced too few houses and it also produced the wrong kind of houses.' The houses built were too expensive, limited in number *vis-à-vis* the urban population, of undue high quality, and a big drain on governments resources.   The high overhead costs often associated with constructing public housing estates meant that such housing projects required massive subsidies to be replicable and affordable for the low-income groups who indeed were intended to be the original beneficiaries (Buckley et al., 1993; Megbolugbe, 1983).   Where such subsidies were not forthcoming, such housing projects were simply retargetted to the upper and middle-income groups in order to be replicable.

Another oft-cited criticism of public housing programmes in Nigeria is that these units fail to take cognisance of the accessibility to jobs, as well as other public and private infrastructures and services. Criticisms have also been levelled against the inability of housing projects to include the cultural diversity characterising the country as well as the failure to integrate income generating components as part of the overall shelter design (Arimah, 1994; Awotona, 1993). Given situations where public housing meant for low-income groups filters down to upper and middle-income groups, where units are not accessible to work places and other activity nodes, where houses are not in conformity with the culture of the people, and where the household is unable to use the house as a work place, the house becomes unsuitable for the intended user. These houses may then be abandoned, or where occupied, are greatly modified to suit the housing needs of their occupants.

User modifications or alterations of public housing have in most cases been unacceptable to planning agencies in developing countries, and have in most cases been discouraged through planning regulations, fines and eventual demolition. Planners in Third World countries particularly have an aversion toward housing modification for income generation.   This perhaps can be attributed to a preoccupation on the part of planners with unifunctional land use theories and a moralistic bias against personal economic gains from public housing (Strassman, 1987).   Furthermore, planners contend that alterations may lead to over development of plots, thereby resulting in poor circulation, inadequate space between buildings and overcrowding among others (Tipple and Owusu, 1994). Households on the other hand, have a converse view of housing modification.

First, modifications apart from being viewed as incremental improvement to dwellings, are viable means of increasing housing supply and rectifying inappropriate design aspects of top-down housing approaches (Tipple and Owusu, 1994). Indeed, Tipple (1992, p.170) reminds us that user modification increases the housing stock without necessarily expanding the urban area and provides additional living space for both sitting and new tenants at affordable cost to users and virtually none to government. Second, occupants see the house as a place transcending home life. In this respect, the house is a production place, financial institution, marketplace and an entertainment centre (Laquian, 1983). In other words, apart from being a retreat, the house in developing countries is a work place which enhances the income earning capacity of the household. These views are rarely considered in the design of top-down housing projects. Consequently, modifications continue to proliferate and thus create conflicts between planning officials and occupants of public estates.

This chapter views user modification as a bottom-up approach to solving some of the deficiencies associated with the top-down direct production of housing units in developing countries. The purpose of this chapter, therefore, is to ascertain the degree and nature of user modification in a middle-class housing estate: the Satellite Town housing estate in Lagos, Nigeria. In so doing, we will provide answers to the following questions: What forms of housing modification have been undertaken? What are the mechanisms for carrying out such modifications? What are the factors responsible for housing modification? Finally, we will proffer recommendations whereby modifications can be undertaken without contravening planning and building regulations. With the limited number of systematic case studies of housing modification in African countries, there is the need to build up an inventory of case studies if precise knowledge is to be obtained. From such studies, generalisations can then be made with respect to housing modification in Africa.

The Satellite town housing estate

Satellite town which covers an area of about 486 hectares is located along the Badagry expressway and lies between Navy town and the International Trade Fair Complex in Ojo Local Government Area of Lagos State. The site which was acquired by the Federal Military Government in 1975 was a swampy area which had to be reclaimed. At the time of acquisition, villages identified included Ashogun Oshun, Ijegun and Oguntedo. The villagers were duly compensated and resettled. However, Ijegun still exists as a semi-squatter settlement. According to the Federal Ministry of Works and Housing (FMWH, 1992), Satellite town had a population of 22,489 in 1991.

The satellite housing estate in which residential development takes up 67 per cent of the land area was part of the Federal Government's housing programme under the Third National Development Plan period (1975-80), which envisaged the construction of 202,000 housing units nationwide, of which 46,000 were to be located in Lagos State. In 1976 the Federal Military Government in appreciating the enormity of housing problems being faced by residents in Lagos State decided to utilise the site for a housing estate. Consequently, the site was handed over to the Armed Forces Development Projects, which in turn allocated parcels of land to various government agencies and private organisations for the construction of houses for their middle cadre employees. Companies were also allocated land for commercial and industrial purposes, while a number of individuals were allocated land on Temporary Occupation Licence.

The Federal Housing Authority undertook the construction of units which were later sold on an owner-occupier basis to civil servants employed in the Federal Civil Service. This study is concerned with the owner occupier civil servants' area of Satellite town estate which had a population of 7,350 in 1991 (FMWH, 1992). This area comprises three housing types: two-bedroom semidetached units of which there are 154 units; 308 units of three-bedroom detached bungalows; and 588 units of four-bedroom bungalows. The price at which these houses were sold in the early 1980s ranged between ₦28,500 for a two-bedroom semi-detached bungalow to ₦81,300 for a detached four-bedroom bungalow[1] (FMWH, 1992). The civil servants' area is based on the *cul-de-sac* system and consists of 77 closes with 14 houses in a standard close.

With respect to infrastructure, the road network consists of main roads traversing the whole estate, with an average width of 7.5 metres. Collector roads with an average width of 6.7 metres convey traffic into the 77 streets. These roads were well constructed but are rapidly deteriorating due to poor maintenance and seasonal floods. The drainage system within the estate consists of both open channels and pipe networks made up of reinforced concrete and AC pipelines, respectively. The sewage system is integrated by the use of pipelines whereby, houses within each close are connected to a pipe running parallel to the close, which is connected to a larger collector pipe that joins the main pipe leading to the sewage treatment plant. Water supply to the estate is mainly from the Ishasi water works. This is irregular and does not meet the requirements of most households. Consequently, residents have to make alternative arrangements, which include the purchase of water from tanker drivers and the sinking of wells. Street lights are provided, but most have either been knocked down or had their appurtenances stolen. Health and educational facilities are also provided within the estate. As a dormitory settlement, Satellite town has the advantage of access to Lagos Island, Murtala Mohammed international and domestic airports, the Trade Fair Complex, the National Theatre and the ports at Tin-Can Island and Apapa.

Socio-economic profile of Satellite town housing estate

The socio-economic profile of Satellite town residents[2] is presented in Table 2.1. The table reveals that about 89 per cent of households within the civil servants' area are headed by males. This proportion increases successively from the two-bedroom units to the four-bedroom units. A similar pattern is replicated in the case

Table 2.1   Socio-economic characteristics of Satellite town residents

Socio-economic characteristics	Two-bedroom units	Three-bedroom units	Four-bedroom units	Entire estate
% of male-headed households	85.7	86.5	92.2	89.4
% of married households	75.0	80.8	90.8	85.4
% household heads aged 41-50	64.3	26.9	29.6	34.3
Mean household size	17.9	28.8	51.0	39.2
Average age of head of household	26.80	27.62	28.18	27.42
Persons per room	3.50	1.77	1.89	2.57
Years of completed schooling of household head	15.9	14.3	14.8	14.6
Per cent of household heads earning >=20,000	42.9	40.4	36.7	37.8

of married households. With respect to family life cycle, the table shows that a great proportion of household heads aged between 41 and 50 years live in two-bedroom units. The average age of the household paints a similar picture as the highest values occur in the case of four-bedroom units. This is an indication of the existence of a positive relationship between family life cycle and space requirements of households in our sample.

The table shows that larger households are more likely to occupy larger housing units. On the other hand, occupancy rates are highest in the two-bedroom units as the number of persons per room is 3.50. For the three- and four-bedroom units, occupancy rates are 1.77 and 1.89 respectively, with 2.57 persons per room being the mean for the entire estate. In terms of socio-economic status, the table reveals that 37.8 percent of the estates' heads of household earn more than ₦20,000 per annum and the average years of completed schooling is 14.6. The socio-economic status of Satellite town is quite high by Nigerian standards. An explanation for this lies in the fact that this is a middle class housing estate. This in essence implies higher levels of education and income compared with what obtains in the typical Nigerian urban setting.

Extent and nature of user modifications

The time horizon for the modifications being investigated is between the early 1980s and 1990. The extent and forms of user modification undertaken by residents of the civil servants' area of Satellite town housing estate are presented in Table 2.2. From the table it is quite clear that most houses have undergone one form of modification or another. The most pronounced form of user modification is the construction of a surrounding fence. In fact, all residents of the two-bedroom units have carried out this type of modification. In the case of occupants of three- and four-bedroom units, more than 85 per cent of them have constructed fences to surround their houses. The comparatively high proportion of fence construction among residents of two-bedroom units may be explained by the location of these houses. The two-bedroom units are the first two pairs of houses on either side of the close, and as such, highly susceptible to burglaries.

The high rate of fence construction *vis-à-vis* other forms of modification can be attributed to the fact that the original design of houses in the civil servants area did not include a surrounding fence or hedge. Initially, this may have fostered social cohesion and made for easy access between houses and different closes since pedestrians could walk through compounds. It however led to intrusion on privacy and most important, burglaries and break-ins.

A number of advantages accompany the construction of a surrounding fence. First, it enhances the safety of households, as it prevents easy break-ins at night and petty thefts during the day. Second, it serves to demarcate clearly the boundaries of each unit, thereby enabling occupants to secure their plot against trespassers. In Nigeria, it is not out of place for neighbours undertaking construction or development on their plots to cut into the adjoining or opposite plot if unfenced, to gain a few metres of land. This has been a common cause of conflict among neighbours. In order to prevent this, prior to the commencement of construction, prospective home owners may erect a surrounding fence to ward off possible trespassers. A final advantage of constructing a surrounding fence is that it increases privacy particularly from outsiders. As rightly observed by Tipple (1992), personal privacy is very much cherished among Moslems. The main problem with this form of modification is that depending on the height of the wall and type of materials used, it could reduce the amount of day lighting and

Table 2.2   User modifications undertaken in Satellite town

Modification (per cent)	Two-bedroom units	Three-bedroom units	Four-bedroom units	Entire estate
Construction of surrounding fence	100	88.5	85.7	88.8
Construction of shops	33.3	17.3	31.6	27.5
Additional rooms (attached)	21.4	11.5	13.3	14.0
Additional rooms (detached)	17.9	0.0	1.0	3.4
Construction of carports	7.1	30.8	50.0	37.6
Additional WCs	7.1	11.5	18.4	14.6
Extension of kitchen	0.0	11.5	11.2	9.6
Installation of sliding doors	0.0	0.0	1.0	0.56
Construction of ante sitting room	0.0	0.0	1.0	0.56
Construction of pillars in sitting room	0.0	0.0	1.0	0.56
Number of cases	28	52	98	178

ventilation, as well as result in a tightness within the now enclosed unit. The possibility of this occurring is real as the original designs of these units made little or no provision for the construction of a surrounding fence.

The construction of shops is another form of user modification. While some of these shops are permanent structures, most are makeshift structures constructed with wood and corrugated iron roofing sheets. These shops offer a wide range of services which include: retail sales, tailoring and shoe repair services, hairdressing saloons and the grinding of cooking ingredients among others. Table 2.2 shows that in the entire civil servants area, about one-quarter of the houses have been modified to include some form of Home-Based Enterprises (HBEs). This is even greater in the two- and four-bedroom units, as about one-third of these houses have been modified to integrate HBEs. The use of the house for income generating activities is not new in Nigeria. A casual observation of housing units within the traditional section of Nigerian cities reveals that HBEs occupy an important place within the house. This feature has perhaps been carried over to the country's public housing estates. For instance, Arimah (1994) has shown that in the Adewole and Kulende housing estates in Ilorin at least 92 per cent of the housing units have been modified to accommodate HBEs.

In stressing the importance of these enterprises, Tipple (1993, p.526) observes that: '... HBEs are an essential part of the economic and social fabric of most cities in developing countries.' This assertion appears most appropriate in the case of African countries as the house has traditionally been a place of employment. The harsh economic environment following the adoption of the Structural Adjustment Programme (SAP) has been associated with the retrenchment of formal sector employees and the ascendancy of the informal sector. This in turn has further accentuated the importance of the house as a productive economic unit, as a sizeable number of informal sector enterprises established in the SAP period use the house as their operating base (Abumere, 1997). While modification to accommodate various forms of HBEs allows households to supplement their income, without the necessary precautionary measures, the HBEs may themselves start a process of neighbourhood deterioration. This is because these HBEs may generate excessive noise and air pollution, excessive vehicular traffic, and alter the aesthetic quality of the neighbourhood. Furthermore, they may make additional demands on existing basic utilities. The successful integration of HBEs into the design and implementation of various top-down approaches to housing poses a major challenge to housing-related professionals in developing countries.

Another form of user modification pertains to the construction of additional rooms which may be attached to, or detached from the house. Previous studies (Arimah, 1994; Owusu and Tipple, 1995; Tipple, 1992; Tipple and Owusu, 1994) have shown that the construction of additional rooms and extension of existing ones are common forms of housing alteration in public estates. Table 2.2 indicates that a greater proportion of occupants of two-bedroom units have additional rooms attached to the house. The detached rooms are usually constructed as separate entities, and may be occupied by a household different from that in the main house. Once again, this type of modification is more pronounced in the two-bedroom units. This in part can be attributed to the high occupancy rate (3.5) of this class of houses. The implication of this is that for cultural reasons, two-bedroom units may not be suitable for the average Nigerian household. The non-construction of additional detached rooms in three-bedroom units may be explained by the arrangement of these units. In a standard close with 14 houses, the first four houses are two-bedroom units, while the next two and last two houses are three-bedroom units. The remaining six units are four-bedroom units. The way in which the first sets of three-bedroom units are orientated is such that every other house has its frontage leading into the close, while the frontage of the second set of three-bedroom houses leads into the adjoining compound, except where a fence separates them.   This type of arrangement does not leave enough space for additional detached construction.

Within the estate, the construction of additional rooms serves a number of uses. First, they are used to provide space for the family as the household size increases or life cycle changes in relation to existing space.   Among the middle class families who reside in the estate, a common practice is to append additional rooms onto the existing unit to serve as separate rooms for their adolescent sons.   This also doubles as guest rooms whenever the occasion arises.   On the other hand, Tipple (1992, p.186) observes that modification activity undertaken to increase living space such as the construction of additional rooms may indeed be at the expense of outdoor space.   Furthermore, population and densities are likely to be higher than were initially planned for.   These in turn have enormous implications for meeting additional requirements in terms of water, electricity, sewerage, refuse disposal and such like.

In the original housing design, no provisions were made for lock up garages or carports.   Being a middle-class housing estate where some families have more than one car, there was the need to modify the unit to include a more secure parking space.   Consequently, a major form of alteration undertaken by residents is the construction of carports.   In most cases this simply involves the use of corrugated iron or transparent plastic roofing sheets to cover enough space between the fence and a section of the house.   Table 2.2 shows that this form of modification is most prominent in the case of four-bedroom units as about one-half of the houses have had a carport appended to them.   While safeguarding the car, and protecting it from the vagaries of weather, this form of user modification may indeed reduce natural lighting and ventilation.   Finally, it is important to note that since all the units are bungalows, the addition of new structures such as shops, rooms and carports may not affect the structural stability of the main building, however, some of these new additions being of lower quality and usually ill-planned, collectively give the estate an air of planlessness.

The last major form of user modification entails enhancing the unit's service component.   In our case, this involves the construction of additional WCs and kitchen extensions.   Table 2.2 indicates that about 15 per cent of units in the entire civil servants' quarters have at least an additional WC constructed.   This proportion increases correspondingly from the two- to the four-bedroom units. With respect to kitchen extensions, these take place only in the three- and four-bedroom houses.   The construction of additional WCs has been occasioned by increase in household size as well as in the number of households residing within the unit.   The latter is more pronounced when additional rooms resulting from transformation activity are occupied by a household different from that in the main house. Kitchen extensions have primarily been necessitated by the small size of these kitchens in the original designs and by the fact that an extended kitchen may also serve as a dining room, a store and even a sleeping area for domestic servants.

Mechanism for undertaking housing modification

Given the high incidence of user modification in the civil servants' area of the estate, it will be instructive to examine the mechanism for carrying out these alterations. This would be examined with respect to approval, sources of finance and labour. In carrying out modifications, approval is rarely sought from the relevant authorities. In fact, only 36 per cent of residents who have modified their units sought official approval prior to transforming them. This is contrary to findings obtained for the *Suntreso* housing estate in Kumasi, Ghana, which indicated that more than 80 per cent of owners had obtained planning permission for their extensions (Tipple and Owusu, 1994). The remaining 65 per cent who did not seek official approval saw no justification for doing otherwise. This may be due to a number of reasons. First, since the modified house would eventually belong to them on completion of mortgage payments, they did not feel obliged to obtain approval before embarking on modifications. Second, following from the views of Tipple (1992) and Ameen and Raham (1996), the relevant authorities in developing countries for a number of reasons, appear to be tolerant or have a more relaxed attitude to user modifications of public estates. In essence, modifications take place, authorities close their eyes, and there are apparently no problems except the fact that the major part of these modifications are not appropriately applied for and approved. This indeed is a major contributory factor accounting for user modifications in public housing estates in Third World countries. This is also the reason for the proliferation of modifications that contravene building and planning regulations. Regulating user modification through development control in Satellite town has not been possible. In fact an unofficial view expressed by planners in the FMWH is that though illegal if approval is not sought, these modifications cannot be stopped because of the sterility of development control which arises from inadequate financing, poor commitment to work, politics, official corruption and the inadequacy of qualified staff.

In terms of the sources of finance used in carrying out these modifications, Table 2.3 shows that personal savings constitutes the single most important source as it is used in financing about three-quarters of the modified units. Other sources of secondary importance are: loans from relatives and friends; housing allowance from employers; retirement benefits; as well as banks and other related institutions in that order. Collectively, these sources provide about one-quarter of the finances expended on housing modifications. The picture painted here is similar to what occurs in Ghana as households finance housing transformation from personal or own funds (Owusu and Tipple, 1995; Tipple and Owusu, 1994). The strong dependence on personal savings or own funds is a reflection of the state of housing finance in most African countries, where the importance of formal sources of finance is limited. For instance, Okpala (1994) notes that formal sources account for between five and 20 per cent of financial resources for housing construction.

Table 2.3   Sources of finance for housing modification

Source of finance	% of respondents
Personal savings	74.7
Loans from friends and relatives	9.3
Co-operative allowance	5.3
Housing allowance from employer	4.6
Retirement benefits	4.1
Banks and related agencies	2.1

The proportion it accounts for in financing housing modification is likely to be much lower.

The various sources of labour employed by civil servants undertaking housing modifications are: small scale contractors, professional builders and family labour, in that order. The greater utilisation of small scale contractors is to be expected. This is because housing modification, given its incremental and small scale nature as well as the intermittent flow of funds, tends to attract this category of contractors (Tipple, 1994a). This has a lot of employment creating implications. Apart from creating jobs for small scale contractors and builders, user modifications have strong multiplier effects which they generate through the demand for the various local construction materials required in the alteration process.

Reasons for user modifications

In seeking to account for housing modifications, Tipple (1992) identifies and discusses six reasons for the occurrence of transformation activity in low cost public housing estates. These include: more generous space for the household; space for relatives; rental income; increased privacy from outsiders; privacy within the dwelling; and the need for increased services. In this section, we identify reasons why residents of the civil servants' area have modified their units and assess the extent to which these correspond with those identified by Tipple (1992).

The major reasons that prompt residents to modify their houses are listed in Table 2.4. These are presented in order of importance for the entire estate. The single most important reason explaining why user modifications occur pertains to safety and security considerations. The prominence accorded safety is in line with the finding that fence construction is the most pronounced form of user modification. Given that the units in Satellite town were initially constructed without a surrounding fence, it is not surprising that safety/security considerations constitute the major reason for carrying out housing modifications. Safety or security concerns do not feature in Tipple's (1992) 'theory' of housing transformations. This can be attributed to two factors. First, Tipple's (1992) case studies are all drawn from low-income public housing estates unlike ours which is a middle-income housing estate. This in itself makes Satellite town housing estate a sitting target for burglaries if steps are not taken by residents adequately to safeguard their houses. Second, Tipple's case studies included no housing estates from Lagos, Nigeria. If they had, perhaps safety/security considerations could have been identified as key reasons why houses are modified, given the fact that Lagos has one of the highest crime rates in the developing world.

Improving the service component of the house is another reason for user modifications. Given that the barest minimum in terms of basic housing infrastructures was provided in the original housing design, households with the

Table 2.4   Major reasons for undertaking housing modification

Reason (per cent)	Two-bedroom units	Three-bedroom units	Four-bedroom units	Entire estate
Safety /security considerations	49.1	72.8	63.6	64.0
Improving the service component of the house	9.1	6.3	18.2	14.6
Income generation	16.2	18.8	13.7	14.0
Increase in household size	25.6	2.1	4.5	6.7

necessary means have either upgraded or provided entirely new services. Instances were seen of households having constructed carports, additional WCs and extended their kitchens. This is in consistent with Tipple's (1992) demonstration that households see transformation activity as an opportunity to provide the services they lack.

A key reason for modifying units is to generate income. When houses are modified, income can be generated through a variety of activities. These range from retail trade, provision of different services and even the subletting of units which is seen as a 'passive' HBE. Such additional income as aptly pointed out by Ameen and Raham (1996) helps households to improve their economic solvency. In fact, Tipple (1994b, p.24) reports that HBEs account for about 40 per cent of income for households who have modified their units to accommodate them. In this respect, income generation therefore emerges as a universal reason why occupants of public estates modify their units. These findings concur with the notion that the house is a productive economic unit and that occupants will, if the situation demands, modify their houses in order to generate income.

Increased household size is the last major reason for housing modification. This is however only important in the case of two-bedroom units. This is not surprising given the high occupancy rate characterising this set of houses. In effect, this implies that while occupants of three- and four-bedroom units may to some extent be satisfied with their houses in terms of the number of rooms, this may not be the case of occupants of two-bedroom units. Given the prominence of the extended family system, Nigerians have large households, and as such, the two-bedroom units may not satisfy the space requirements of the average household. This is also the case in many African cities. In this respect, we are reminded by Tipple (1992, p.172) that households are obliged to provide free accommodation for job-seeking relatives who have just migrated to the city. Similarly, in times of hardship and distress, affected households may have no other alternative than to move in with relatives. It therefore follows that user modifications that involve the construction or extension of additional rooms provide some relief in such instances.

Concluding remarks

In this chapter, user modification of housing units in public estates has been viewed as a bottom-up approach which seeks to correct some of the deficiencies associated with the top-down, direct production of housing. This has been illustrated with the Satellite town housing estate in Lagos, Nigeria. Findings in the preceding sections have shown that user modifications are relatively widespread in the civil servants' section of the estate, and that these transformations are likely to continue in the future, since they serve many useful functions. Official development control has negligible impact on user modifications, and as such, some of these transformations contravene planning and building regulations. The question that arises at this juncture is: how can user modifications be undertaken without necessarily contravening planning and building regulations and minimise the problems associated with such modifications?

In order to avoid a situation in which user modifications result in the contravention of planning and building regulations, Nigerian architects and planners need to adopt more current and realistic approaches to the design of public estates. Conventional planning in Nigeria is one that designates different zones for residential, working and recreational purposes. The strict enforcement of zoning and land use ordinances apart from making it impossible to use favourably located sites for economic activity, also set higher standards than necessary, thereby, leading to illegal or unauthorised housing. The current trend is for mixed used settlements in order to exploit the economic potentials of such settlements. Consequently, physical planners will have to be flexible, and adapt their layout skills not necessarily to the traditional approach of segregating different activities, but one that for instance integrates employment activities within the unit. The issues to be addressed include: how can user modifications for various purposes such as income generation be integrated into housing projects without leading to the problems of conflicting land uses, environmental deterioration as well as other related problems? In this respect, the physical planner should regard HBEs as necessary and be seen to promote rather than discourage them. In the case of the architect, design skills should be such that allow for multiple use of space as well as modifications, should the need arise. In this regard, Tipple (1994b, p.537) stresses that housing designs '... which allow for adaptability, extensibility and flexibility should therefore be promoted.' All these are possible in Nigeria if architects, planners and other housing-related professionals learn to blend space for living with that for working. In this respect, the indigenous architectural designs have a lot to offer. For instance, indigenous housing designs make provision for the extended family system, place a high premium on privacy from both outside and within the house and have been able to incorporate mixed uses without the resultant problem of non-conforming uses. These are just some of the lessons to be learnt from indigenous architectural designs.

Finally, it is necessary for policy makers in Nigeria to move away from the narrow conception of housing which simply entails provision of core shelter. Where government still decides to embark on the direct construction of houses[3] rather than channelling its resources to creating an enabling environment to encourage the participation of the private and informal sectors in housing production, efforts should be made to create a liveable environment that is in consonance with the culture and socio-economic characteristics of the intended beneficiaries. This will to some extent stem the tide of user modifications and prevent the occurrence of some of the problems associated with these modifications in public housing estates.

Notes

1   In the early 1980s, the US dollar was exchanged for between $0.75 and $1.12 to the Nigerian naira (₦). As at June 1997, US $1 equals ₦86.
2   The data used in the empirical analysis were obtained from a questionnaire survey of the civil servants' section of the estate undertaken between June and July 1991. The survey was designed to obtain information on the extent, nature and reasons for user modifications of the housing types. The sampling frame utilised was the total number of housing units broken down by the three housing types. There is a total of 1,050 housing units of which 200 were sampled in proportion to the three housing types. The choice of the unit to be sampled was randomly systematic, as it involved a random choice of streets and a systematic choice of housing units. After eliminating improperly filled questionnaires and those with conflicting responses, 178 questionnaires were utilised in the final analysis.
3   Given the failure of successive Nigerian governments in implementing the programme of direct construction of housing units and the subsequent call for governments to move away from such top-down approaches to housing, it is rather surprising that in the 1994/95 fiscal year, the Federal Government embarked on a new National Housing Programme which entailed the direct construction of housing units. This again has run into a series of predictable problems.

Acknowledgement

This chapter was written while the author was visiting Shelter-Afrique in Nairobi, Kenya on a research fellowship. He is highly grateful to the authorities of Shelter for the necessary support and congenial working environment provided throughout the duration of the fellowship. The author is highly appreciative of the role played by Martin A. Ugboma in organising the survey on which the chapter is based. The usual caveats do apply.

References

Abumere, S.I., and Arimah, B.C., et al. (1997), *The role of the informal sector in Nigeria's development process*, Development Centre: Ibadan.
Ameen, M.S., and Raham, M.M. (1996), 'Transformation propensity in shelter generation: Study of government built low cost housing development scheme', in Ghosh, S. (ed) *Housing development and management*, Centre for Built Environment: Calcutta.
Arimah, B.C. (1994), 'Self-help housing modification for income generating activities: A study of two housing projects in Nigeria', *Second European Network for Housing*

Research Symposium on Housing the Urban Poor, International Conference Centre, Birmingham, UK, 11-14 April,

Awotona, A. (1993), 'The urban poor's perception of housing conditions', in Taylor, R.W. (ed) *Urban development in Nigeria*, Avebury: Aldershot.

Buckley, R.M., Faulk, D., et al. (1993), 'Private sector participation, structural adjustment and new national housing policy: Lessons from foreign experience.' *Economic and Financial Review*, Vol. 31, pp.53-67.

FMWH. (1992), *Master Plan for Satellite Town, Ojo, Lagos*, Federal Ministry of Works and Housing: Lagos.

Laquian, A.A. (1983), *Basic housing: Policies for urban sites, services and shelter in developing countries*, International Development Research Centre: Ottawa.

Malpezzi, S., and Sa-Aadu, J. (1996), 'What have African housing policies wrought?' *Real Estate Economics*, Vol. 24, pp.133-160.

Megbolugbe, I.F. (1983), 'The hopes and failures of public housing in Nigeria: A case study of Kulende and Adewole housing estates, Ilorin.' *Third World Planning Review*, Vol. 5, pp.350-369.

Okpala, D.C.I. (1994), 'Financing housing in developing countries: A review of the pitfalls and potentials in the development of formal housing finance systems.' *Urban Studies*, Vol. 31, pp.1571-1586.

Owusu, S.E., and Tipple, A.G. (1995), *The process of extension in Kumasi, Ghana*. Transformations Working Paper, 2, CARDO, University of Newcastle upon Tyne: Newcastle upon Tyne.

Strassman, W.P. (1987), 'Home-based enterprises in cities of developing countries.' *Economic Development and Cultural Change*, Vol. 36, No. 1, pp.121-144.

Tipple, A.G. (1992), 'Self-help transformations to low cost housing: Initial impressions of cause, context and value.' *Third World Planning Review*, Vol. 14, No. 2, pp.177-192.

Tipple, A.G. (1993), 'Shelter as workplace: A review of home-based enterprise in developing countries.' *International Labour Review*, Vol. 132, No. 4, pp.521-539.

Tipple, A.G. (1994a), *Employment implications of transformation activity: An introduction to the literature on housing and employment*. Working paper, No. 1, CARDO, University of Newcastle upon Tyne: Newcastle upon Tyne.

Tipple, A.G. (1994b), 'The need for new urban housing in sub-Saharan Africa: problem or opportunity.' *African Affairs*, Vol. 93, pp.587-608.

Tipple, A.G., and Owusu, S.E. (1994), *Transformations in Ghana as a housing supply mechanism: A preliminary study*. Transformations Working Paper, 2, CARDO, University of Newcastle upon Tyne: Newcastle upon Tyne.

World Bank. (1965), *Economic growth in Nigeria: Problems and prospects*, World Bank: Washington, DC.

3 Breaking through the barrier of standardisation:

The case of Tenth of Ramadan core housing scheme, Egypt

HALA KARDASH

Whenever the term 'informal housing' is mentioned, images of squatter settlements built throughout the developing countries by low-income groups to meet their housing needs immediately come to mind. Informal housing implies the existence of an informal decision making process behind it. A process by which low-income people, trusting their own instincts, manage to rely on their own scarce resources, plan their own settlements, and build their houses in complete absence of any governmental input.

On the other hand, low-income housing usually refers to rows of inexpensively built and frequently badly designed standardised housing units where low-income people are housed. The users' input in such housing is limited only to paying either rent or instalments and all other decisions are made by a higher authority.

This chapter presents a case study of a housing environment which lies in between the complete informal housing and the finished product provided by public housing. The case study discusses the transformation introduced by the users on a core housing scheme in the Tenth of Ramadan City, a newly built settlement near Cairo, Egypt.

In the Tenth of Ramadan core housing Scheme, the users managed to increase considerably their habitable space by building extensions to the initially provided core houses. This was achieved in the absence of any form of organisational, financial, or technical help from any formal authority. Ignoring the prototype plans, they defied the laws and regulations in order to create an environment more responsive to their needs, expectations and hopes. In other words they tried to introduce those unexpected qualities to the otherwise standardised rigid environment.

Relying on both quantitative and qualitative approaches, this chapter will analyse the components of the users' decision making process which resulted in the transformation of the project. It will also address the authorities' point of view concerning the transformation outcome. Finally, it will conclude by making some recommendations which aim to increase the responsiveness of similar housing schemes to users' priorities and requirements.

Introduction

In public housing projects, the quantitative aspects often receive more attention than those of quality. Quantity has its logic in serial repetition of systems and parts which are identical in all aspects. Consumer products are based on this logic. That which is produced by manufacturers of cars, TVs, clothes and the whole range of consumer durables is based on the mass production of element sub-systems co-ordinated to be assembled according to specific user requirements and level of performance. Into this equation the intrinsic value of materials and labour time elements which are consumed in the production process set the final index and quality value in monetary terms.

Public housing attempts too frequently to produce whole houses in which choice and variation are impossible. Even in the realm of self-help projects - where a part of the house (a core house) is provided, the degree of variation allowed in the extension of the property is limited to pre-determined plans and a set intrinsic value of materials to be used. Thus the outcome (quality) is prescribed from the outset of the project regardless of supposed users' input and minimising their freedom of choice. This applies as well to sites and services, schemes with pre-determined prototype plans, construction materials and development time.

For low-income groups it is essential to be able to decide on how much resources, at a certain time frame, one has to invest in his housing and what physical quality will result from such an investment in terms of space and construction. This is due to a greater need, more than any better off group, for a housing environment that is supportive of their life style. One does not force them to act according to values and norms borrowed from other groups.

On the other hand, standardisation is often considered as an essential perquisite by authorities. Even in self-help schemes standardisation is seen as one measure to reduce the chances of the scheme turning into a planned slum. In this context standardisation is sought after in the initial provision (e.g. plot size, services standards etc.) for the sake of organisational and administrative simplicity as well as reducing the implementation costs. Furthermore, some schemes force the users to adhere to prototype plans, methods and materials of construction in order to ensure a certain level of quality in what is built.

This chapter will address the issue of users' freedom of choice in low-income self-help housing through a case study of a core housing scheme which was implemented in one of Egypt's New Cities; 'the Tenth of Ramadan New City' in the early 1980s[1]. The 'Tenth of Ramadan Core Housing Scheme' (TORCHS) is considered by the official authorities as a failed experience that should never be repeated. As a result of the users' transformations introduced into this project the responsible authorities regard it as scheme that got out of control and turned into a planned slum. As will be demonstrated in this case study the users of TORCHS transformed the scheme into a housing environment that is more responsive to their individual requirements. The project and its planned development as envisaged by the designers and policy makers presented the users with standardised solutions which were unable to accommodate the varieties in their needs.

The aim of this study was to understand why did TORCHS users decide to ignore the proposed development plans, building and planning regulations. The study consisted of two levels of investigation. The first involved a general socio-economic survey of all households living in TORCHS. It also included a general physical development survey of the core housing units to record the general extent of the transformation of the scheme by its users. The survey took place in the winter of 1990. Out of the total 502 core houses in TORCHS about 140 were unoccupied at the time of the survey. It was only possible to include 251 units in the survey (about 73 per cent of the total number of occupied units). The second level involved a number of in-depth case studies (53 cases). The data collected in this level depended on series of interviews with the household members as well as observations and detailed drawing of the house plan. This level addressed the individual users' decision making process. It attempted to correlate the physical built results of the users' decisions with the various factors and constraints which had influenced their choice. The interviews took place in the summer of 1991.

The initial provision in Tenth of Ramadan core housing

In Neighbourhood 14 lies the core housing scheme. Neighbourhood 14 consists of 960 units of accommodation in four-storey walk-up blocks of flats and 502 core houses. The community facilities are situated in the middle of the core housing layout. An unplanned road from the south-east side of the neighbourhood is opened up for an informal mini-bus service to connect with centre of the neighbourhood. It became the main access road (Figure 3.1). There are four types of core houses in the scheme. Figure 3.2 illustrates those types and the proposed extension for each type. The plot areas range from 90 to 120 square metres and the built up area of the core from 18 to 24.6 square metres. The initial provision consists of a room, WC, an open kitchenette area and entrance situated along the front boundary of the plot. The construction of the core house consists of load-bearing break walls with strip foundation covering the rest of the plot.

The proposed extensions should have been from the load bearing brick walls and a concrete roof. As can be seen from Figure 3.2, the future development by the users as envisaged by the designers of this scheme should have resulted in only four types of plans. Each of them has just minor differences from the other three.

Figure 3.1   Neighbourhood 14

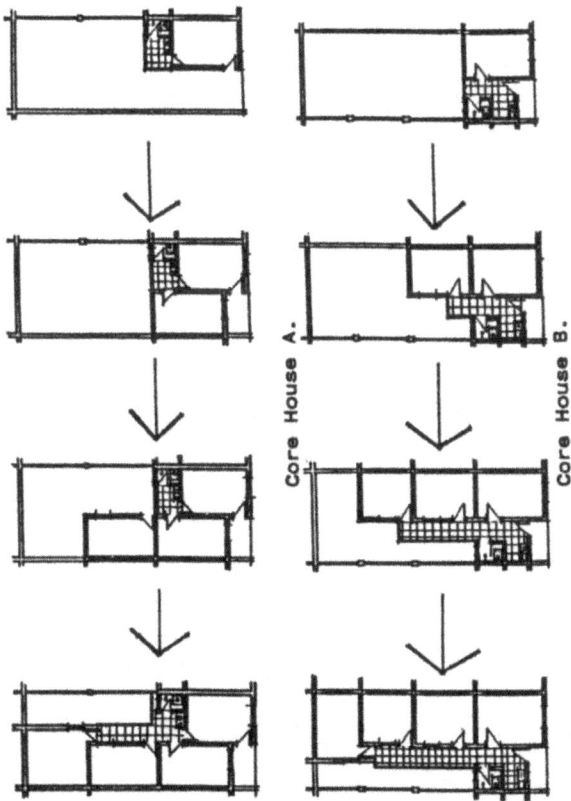

Figure 3.2 The four core house types and the proposed extensions

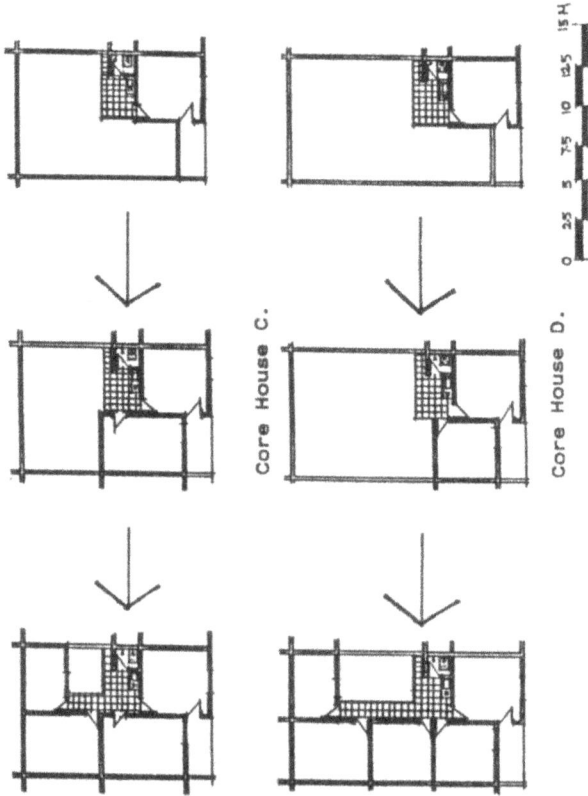

Figure 3.2   **The four core house types and the proposed extensions (continued)**

It is clear that if the users' additions to the scheme were to adhere to what was planned the result would have been sameness and uniformity. Both of which represent desirable qualities in a housing environment from the authorities' (the policy makers' and local authority) point of view. They reflect the predominance of order and control. Variety is only allowed if it is predetermined and only on a categorical and not individual basis (i.e. different plan types). As the following part of this study will show, the users had a different point of view concerning the issue of quality. Quality meant to the users a housing environment that met their requirements with all the variations and changes inherent in those requirements. Hence, quality became a function of variation and variation required an input that stems from free choice.

The transformation of Tenth of Ramadan core housing scheme

Out of 502 core houses 298 were extended. Just over two thirds of the unextended 204 units were unoccupied mainly because they were never allocated to the rightful beneficiaries. The initial prototype plans were continuously ignored by the users. Also in terms of the permissible number of floors which have been built the activity here exceeded the permissible limits. At the outset of the project all the core houses were meant to be developed on a ground floor storey only. After some negotiations between the authorities and the users the regulations were changed to allow the construction of an additional first floor. It was found that among the 298 extended core houses 260 houses had only a ground floor and just under half of these had already started a first floor extension; 33 houses had a ground and a completed first floor extension and five houses had ground, first and second floor extensions.

A mixture of building materials and construction methods was used in the core houses extensions - such as load-bearing mud bricks walls with tin or wood roofs, reinforced concrete skeleton with block or brick walls and load-bearing brick walls with reinforced concrete roofs. Salvaged building materials such as bricks, windows and doors were sometimes recycled in the construction of the extension.

The extensions varied greatly in their areas ranging form as large as 320 square metres to as small as 12 sq. metres. At the time of the survey it was found that 202 households have added 350 rooms to the habitable space of Tenth of Ramadan New City although 127 of them did not have security of tenure.

TORCHS users have also changed the scheme's planned central shopping pattern by opening shops within the residential blocks. Scattered around the settlement there were 22 informally operated shops. The shops usually occupied one of the front rooms in the ground floor of the house. They were, undoubtedly, rendering a much needed service for the community of TORCHS as well as the nearby neighbourhoods. Frequently the users have transformed parts of the public space surrounding the plots into private gardens. The gardens were usually very well looked after and maintained in contrast to the open public spaces which were always left unattended. As well as providing the settlement with green areas. The gardens are usually planted with vegetables to supplement the household's diet.

The local authority's view of TORCHS transformations

The local authority of The Tenth of Ramadan City - 'The Development Agency', did not approve of many of TORCHS users' building related activities. The local authority objections could be summarised as follows:

1. Over building on the plot area which resulted in lack of open space within the plot (light-wells and courtyards) necessary for ventilation and natural light purposes.
2. Exceeding the number of permissible floors.
3. The use of substandard building materials such as recycled bricks, adobe walls and tin roofs in the construction of the extensions.
4. Opening shops in the houses illegally.
5. Taking over public space and claiming it as private gardens.
6. Building small shacks on the roofs for pigeon and chicken rearing.

The local authority's role in TORCHS was limited to trying to control the quality of extensions. To accomplish this task, violators are sometimes forced to demolish what is built contrary to regulations, or else face financial fines. In some cases the violators are denied some of their rights such as the right to obtain additional connection to electrical services for the first floor.

Level one of the investigation

The influence of household characteristics on the decision process

How did the users' socio-economic parameters actually influence the decision to extend and determine the quality of the extension? It is only logical to assume that the need for more habitable space than the pre-built one room prompted the household to extend the core house in the first place. From the survey data it seemed that other factors in addition to the household size have influenced the number of added rooms. Those factors could have included among others the household income, household type or composition, security of tenure, availability of auxiliary finance and duration of stay.

Three different types of tenure were found among TORCHS' households. These were as follows: 80 owner occupiers, 38 tenants and 133 company residents[2]. Needless to say, the tenure type had a great impact on the quality and size of the built extensions.

In the cases where security of tenure was lacking, many users still extended their core houses but understandably with as little expense as possible. About 71 per cent of the company residents who did not have any form of security of tenure had built some kind of extension to their core units. However in such cases the amount of investment put in the extension was much lower than those who had ownership. About 90 per cent of the company residents, who had extended their core units built their extension out of cheap construction materials and often of a temporary nature. However among the owners 38 per cent had done just the same. The number of rooms added in the case of company residents rarely exceeded one or two rooms with an average of 1.00 whilst in the case of owner occupier the average reached 2.50 rooms and in some owner cases the number of rooms added has reached 11.

The average household monthly income in TORCHS was about E£158 (equivalent to approximately L30). About 63 per cent of the households had a monthly income somewhere between E£100 and E£299. Eighty per cent of the heads of household were factory workers while the rest were low ranking governmental employees. To a great extent, one can consider the majority TORCHS users to belong to the same socio-economic class. The extensions' cost ranged dramatically from E£25,000 for the most expensive to as low as E£.100 for the cheapest. The average extension cost about E£2200. Thus the average extension cost represents about 1.1 of the average household annual income.

This raises questions such as how the quantifiable economic and social factors would affect the users' decision in terms of what they decided to build (e.g. the number of added rooms and the construction materials). The following exercise was an attempt to shed some light on this issue. The impact of other unquantifiable factors will be discussed in the next level of investigation.

The quantifiable aspects in the decision making process

Multiple regression analysis[3] was selected as a statistical technique to test the relation between the number of added rooms and the size of the investment (the dependent variables) on one hand and the four socio-economic factors (the independent variables) on the other. The size of the investment expresses the number of added rooms and the construction type. It is a dummy variable which was achieved through multiplying the number of added rooms by a figure substituting the type of construction (an ordinal scale variable). For example the skeleton concrete structure with brick infill walls was given the highest score whilst an extension built out temporary materials such as recycled tin was given the lowest. Four main socio-economic variables were selected to describe household socio-economic characteristics:

1. The household total income.
2. The household size.
3. The age of the eldest child.
4. The duration of stay in the house.

These four factors were expected to be the ones that would have the strongest influence on the household's decision.

It was expected that the security of tenure would have a decisive impact on the user's decision making process in terms of the extension size and quality. Thus, the data of those who had secure tenure and those who did not were analysed separately. Only owners (80 households) and company residents (133 households) were included in this exercise. The tenant category was excluded because in many tenant cases doubts often existed regarding the actual tenure status of the householder[4].

In the case of company residents the variance in the number of added rooms was 52 per cent accounted for by the four independent variables . While in the case of owners the percentage dropped to only 19 per cent. As for the variance in the other dependent variable, the size of investment, the corresponding percentages were 35 per cent and 19 per cent respectively. The results of this analysis indicate that in the case of company residents the independent variables had a much stronger influence on the variance in the dependent variable than in the owners' case.

As can be seen from Table 3.1, in the case of company residents the household size had the most significant contribution to the change in both the number of added rooms and the size of the investment. The household income ranked second. While in the case of owners the most influential factor was the duration of stay followed by the household income.

The possible explanation of the stronger relation in the case of company residents than owners is that the latter are more free to choose when and how to built the extension. They do not necessarily act to satisfy their immediate needs for space but rather they might be aiming at other goals such as planning ahead for future needs. The company residents are extending the one-roomed core house because they, by necessity, require to fulfil basic accommodation needs. These include providing separate sleeping space for parents and children and for children of different sexes when they reach adolescence. So, one could predict more accurately the behaviour of this category than that of the owners, i.e. the former is forced to follow a certain path whilst the latter is not.

The following part of this chapter discusses the reasons behind the users' choices in relation to the building of the extensions through qualitative approach rather

Table 3.1   The regression analysis results

Tenure type	Size of investment				Number of added rooms			
	R²	F	T	SIG	R²	F	T	SIG*
Company residents	35%	11.5 0.0	3.49 4.77 -0.63 2.11	0.001 0.000 0.531 0.038	52%	23.6 0.0	1.58 8.29 -1.30 0.06	0.118 (1) 0.000 (2) 0.210 (3) 0.953 (4)
Owners	19%	4.2 0.004	1.66 1.50 0.89 -2.90	0.101 0.138 0.374 0.006	19%	4.1 0.005	1.93 1.20 1.31 -2.40	0.058 (1) 0.235 (2) 0.196 (3) 0.019 (4)

* The independent variables in order of entry are: (1) household income, (2) household size, (3) age of eldest child and (4) duration of stay at the house.

than the quantity oriented one which was presented in the previous part. Through the presentation of case histories the logic behind individual households' choices will be demonstrated.

Here it is important to note that for examining the users' decision making criteria, the results of the two levels of this study are indispensable to each other and they should only be considered together. To explain that further: the results of the first level would have revealed nothing but merely insufficiently substantiated guess work if the outcome of the second one had not conformed with them. At the same time the first level was essential to provide an overall picture and intuition on the direction that the second level investigation should take.

Level two of investigation

The unquantifiable aspects in the decision making process

From the previous brief attempt to investigate the relationship between the household quantifiable socio-economic characteristics and the extension decision it became obvious that the household quantifiables characteristics alone do not provide sufficient explanation for the users' decision especially in the case of owners where the process seemed very difficult to predict. This suggested that other factors might be influencing the process.

Meeting the basic needs for space

The following are two examples of owners who decided to invest as little as possible in the construction of the extension. In both cases they could have afforded to invest more but they decided not to for various reasons.

The first case is that of Samir; he thought that there are other more important priorities in life. The second case is that of Fatthy; he considered his extension to be all that he needed.

In spite of having sufficient resources to built a larger extension Samir was content with his two-roomed brick and concrete extension (Figure 3.3). As he explained:

> There are more priorities in life than living in a large house. I have six children who need to be educated. Three of them are receiving private lessons otherwise they will not be able to make it in school. Those lessons cost me a fortune each month. What good another two or three rooms will do them if they are unable to finish their education. I am not prepared to deny my children their right of education for the sake of some appearances.

In this case, using his income and his family size to explain his decision would have been totally misleading.

Fatthy managed to build himself the least expensive extension in TORCHS. He built two rooms out of adobe walls with a timber roof at the cost of E£100.00 (Figure 3.4). Fatthy has used soil dug out of his courtyard to make the adobe bricks. His household consists of himself, his wife and three young children, the eldest of them was about eight years old and the youngest was only two. Fatthy is a policeman. His monthly salary at the time of the interview was about E£90.00. He and his wife were supplementing their income by selling cigarettes out of one of the front rooms. In his opinion the adobe construction was good enough for him and his family. He was aware that the local authority considered his house to be of substandard quality because of the construction material he had used. He also was sure that some of the neighbours looked down at him because of that but

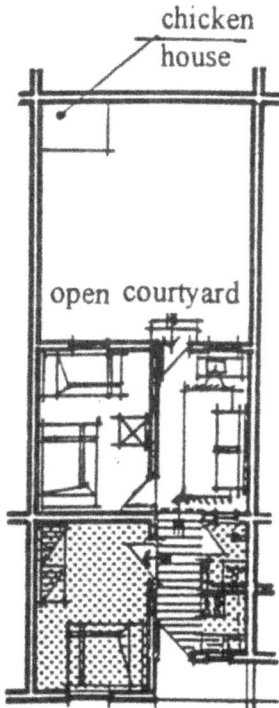

Figure 3.3   Samir's house

he did not care. He also added that he is used to living in adobe built houses in his village and he finds them much cooler in hot weather than concrete and brick houses. In this case too, trying to explain Fatthy's decision on the basis of the household income or need for space would have been misleading.

The house as a supportive environment

The next are examples of households who wanted the house to satisfy more than their basic needs of accommodation. Whether it was the need to house other members of the family in addition to the nuclear family members, to generate additional income out of the property or to act as a saving pot for the children's future, in each case the house plan had to accommodate those needs.

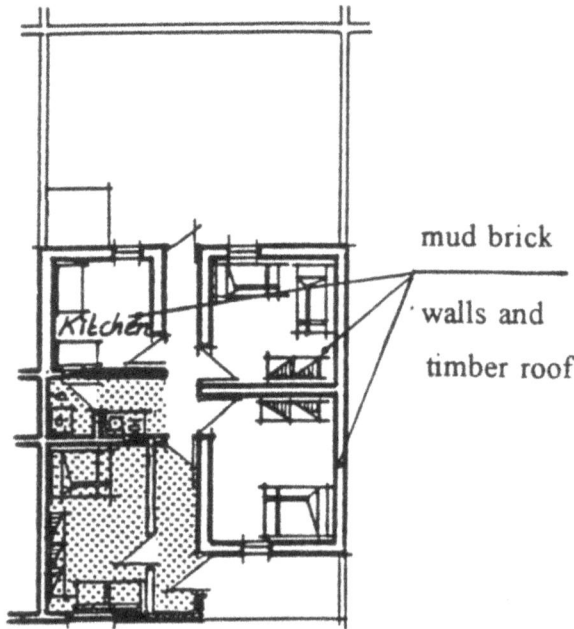

Figure 3.4   Fatthy's house

Supporting family life style There were many cases of extended family households in TORCHS. Examples included among others the following: a son or a daughter marrying and living with the parents' household; parents living with their son's household and a single sister (unmarried, divorced or widowed) living with her brother's household. The Ahmed household is an example of an extended family. The Ahmed's household consists of 11 persons. The household head is a labourer in a company factory in the Tenth of Ramadan. The family originated from Shoubra, Cairo. They left Cairo for the Tenth of Ramadan in 1984. The idea of the core house encouraged Ahmed to move to the Tenth of Ramadan City. He and his wife always wanted to have a house for an extended family. The core house seemed to offer them the opportunity to realise the dream. Ahmed was 51 years old in 1991. His household consisted of Ahmed, his wife, six children in addition to his daughter, her husband and their son. The total monthly income of the household was around E£470, of which the father contributed E£180, the son E£110 and his son in law E£180.

The extension built by Ahmed did not conform to the proposed plan provided by the local authority. In fact, it is different in almost every aspect of the plan, method of construction, number of floors, plot coverage etc. As Figure 3.5 shows, four habitable rooms were added to the initial core plus an additional WC and a very small kitchen. Also a staircase was built to give access to the second floor which was built but not finished at the time of the survey. This arrangement was made to accommodate his daughter who got married to a self-employed labourer. The daughter's husband was not convinced originally by the idea of living with his in-laws but when they tried to rent accommodation elsewhere in the Tenth of Ramadan, he found the rents too high for his income and they ended up staying with her father, who built the extension in this form in order to make a place for them. He specifically tried to build for them a residence separate from the rest of the family as far as possible. Ahmed was in a dispute with the local authority over the stair which he has built with opening for ventilation.

The first floor is divided into approximately two equal halves - one half will be for the daughter and her family and the other will probably be rented out for some time until it is needed by Ahmed's older son when he gets married. The structure is a concrete skeleton with brick walls. Being an end plot a garden was added along the side of the plot for growing vegetables and keeping chickens. The extension of the house was carried out in 1986 by a small contractor introduced to the family by a neighbour. The ground floor extension cost was about E£4,300 which they paid to the contractor in monthly instalments while the first floor cost (concrete skeleton and brick walls only) was about E£8,000. Ahmed with the help of his son and son-in-law did some of the interior finishing work such as wall painting and tiling. They intended to do the same for the first floor.

Investing for the future Although Gerges and his wife had only two teenage children (a boy of 14 and a girl of 12) they built a three-storey house of concrete skeleton frame and brick infill walls at the cost of E£25,000. In addition to the initially provided room, the house contains 16 habitable rooms (bedrooms and living rooms), four kitchens, five bathrooms and a large chicken house, see Figure 3.6. The ground floor is divided into two units. The unit in the front is let out to a widow and her daughter while the back unit is kept vacant for Gerges's daughter when she marries in the future. Similarly Gerges's son has a flat built for him in part of the first floor. The family lives in the rest of the first floor. The three rooms in the second floor are let out to lodgers. It is interesting that Gerges collected about E£170 each month as rents from his tenants and lodgers. This amounted to about 1.5 times his monthly salary as a rubbish collection truck driver for the Tenth of Ramadan City Authority.

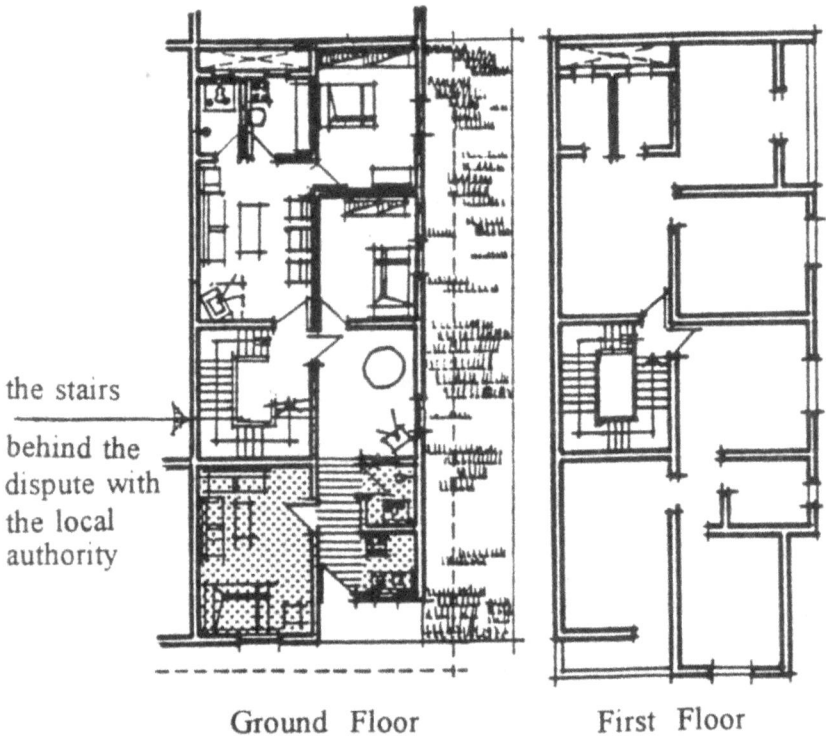

the stairs behind the dispute with the local authority

Ground Floor   First Floor

Figure 3.5   Ahmed's house

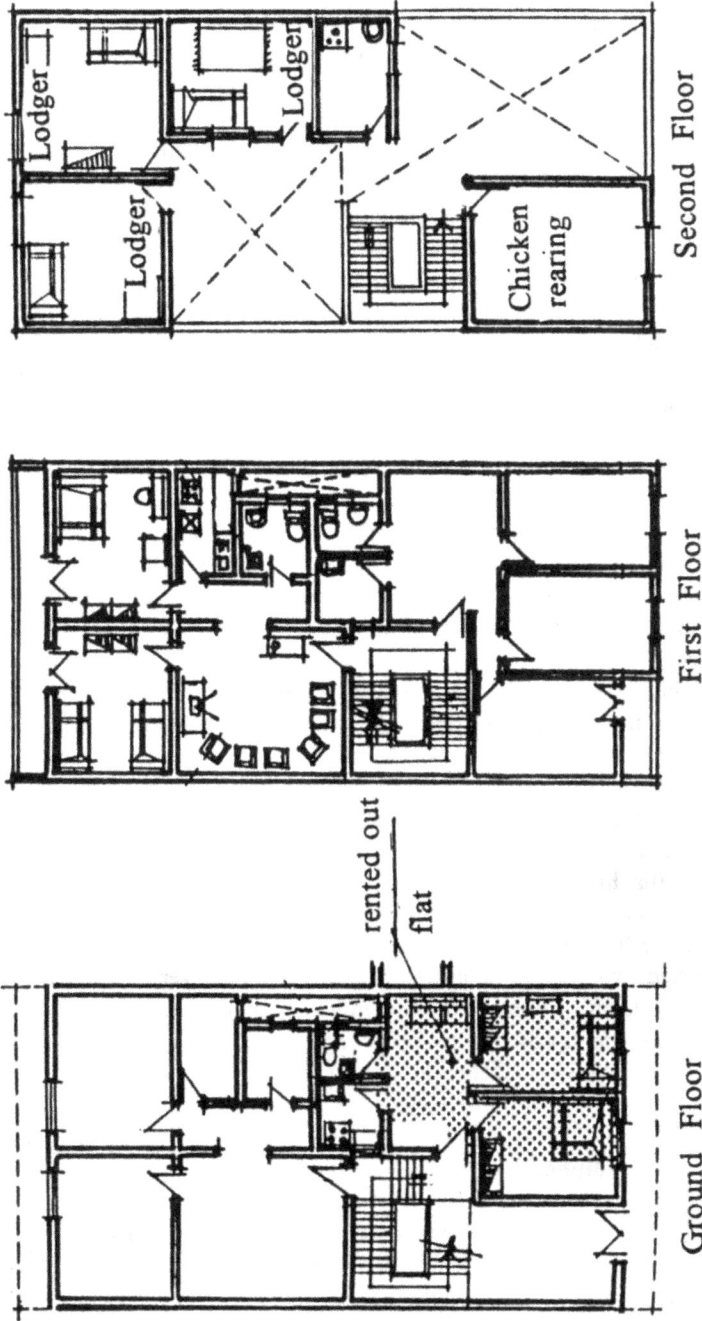

Figure 3.6   Gerges' house

To explain his decision to put such a big investment in the construction of the house Gerges said: 'I now have enough money to secure my children's future at least concerning their housing. Maybe tomorrow this money will not be enough to build the same construction. Also I might not be fit enough to supervise the work as I did. I bought every piece (construction) material myself and I sometimes did the bricklaying. As I get older I am not sure I can do that again.' Then he goes on to say : 'I had to sell a piece of agriculture land my father left me in Suhag to finance the construction. If I were to leave my children a piece of agriculture to inherit what could they do with it? They are not going to farm it, they would sell it and might not be wise enough to use the money in sensible things. At least I know I will have left them something they could use'. Needless to say, Gerges' investment in the house was already paying him back in addition to the expected future benefits for his children.

Generating income In TORCHS the house is often used to generate some additional income for the household. The income generating activities found in TORCHS included letting out of rooms (as in the previous case of Gerges, running shops, growing vegetables, keeping chickens and livestock. Most of these activities require a space set aside from the dwelling. In many cases the profits of such activities contributed to the extension's costs as the following case will demonstrate.

As mentioned before, there were a total of 22 informal shops in the TORCHS at the time when the survey was done. The following case explains the user's own logic behind his decision to have a shop in one of the rooms of his house. Attia's house consists of two roofed rooms in addition to the room of the initial core house. Three other rooms have been brick walled but not yet roofed. One of the total of the three roofed rooms is utilised as a shop (Figure 3.7). Attia's family consists of Attia, his wife and four children in addition to his mother who is living with them permanently. The whole family including Attia's mother live in only two rooms. When asked about the contribution of the shop to the household income he said: 'without the shop we could hardly live, never mind completing the rest of the extension. All my four children go to school and three of them receive private lessons which cost me E£60.00 each month. This is half of my salary. How could I feed and dress them with just 60 pounds?'

Conclusions and implications

What TORCHS users had built constituted a wide variety of standards and design solutions. This reflected a rich mixture of people with different priorities and different social, economic and cultural requirements. Some of the extensions which had been built required very large investments considering the average household income in TORCHS which reflected the ability of low-income earners to manage their own resources and direct them successfully into investments in their own housing. Lack of security of tenure was the reason why many households chose to spend as little as possible on the extensions. The project lacked a local management system which is indispensable in projects where housing is not provided in the form of a finished product. Due to the absence of such a system the project was treated from the local authority's side as any other low-income public housing scheme. The authority's responsibility was only to try to control the standards of the extensions. A good opportunity to set an example of users-local authority partnership in self-help housing projects was lost in this scheme. However, the project demonstrated the ability of low-income households to rely on their own financial and organisational skills to extend the core houses.

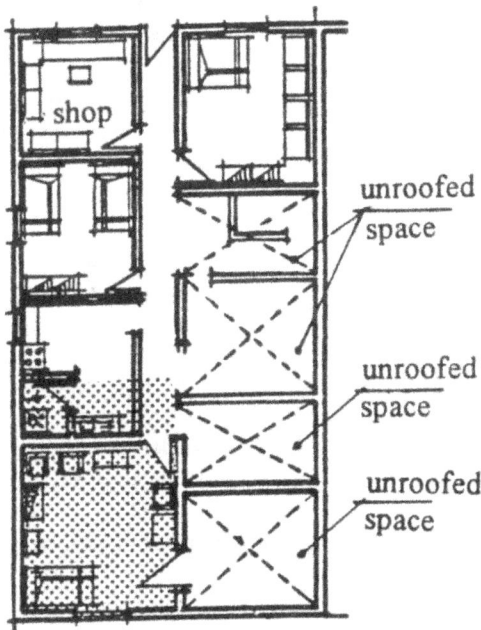

Figure 3.7   Attia's house

TORCHS, after being transformed by its users was successful in answering their communal, economic, social and cultural requirements. This is because it allowed them the freedom to choose when and how to extend the core houses while ignoring any pre-determined plans. Various needs, in addition to the household's basic need for accommodation space, influenced the decision making process regarding the construction of the extensions. These needs could be referred to as the life-style supporting needs. In the case of TORCHS the house played a role in supplementing the household income, meeting the social responsibilities to house extended family members and offering the opportunity to invest for the future.

The two main negative aspects of transformed TORCHS built environment, as conceived by the authorities, are the low standards of construction in some cases and violation of building regulations. The first, is in many cases the result of a mistake made by the policy makers when they decided to sell some core-houses to factory owners to be used as company-residences for their workers. This led to lack of security of tenure. The lack of security of tenure, in turn, forced the residents to minimise the amount of investment they put in the extension. Thus cheap and recycled building materials were often used in those cases. The violations of the building and planning regulations is a symptom of existing mismatches between the actual requirements of the users and those envisaged by the policy makers, planners, and authority parties. Although this problem is by no means one of TORCHS' residents exclusively but is widespread in the Egyptian environment as a whole, it had an alarming effect in TORCHS case. This is partially due to the fact that it is situated in a new city where every development should contribute to an image of a strictly formal and planned environment.

Extensible core housing is a housing solution which has great potential for Egyptian low-income households in general and in particular in the context of the New Cities. Sizeable improvements in the quality of the built environment could be achieved if the following aspects were taken into account:

1. Supportive political and social climate which encourages the mobilisation of financial resources.
2. Well designed projects in terms of their ability to be less deterministic and more accommodating to users' inputs and interventions from the early stages of projects.
3. The political will from the authority's side to reach compromise agreement on issues of standards.
4. Good management which envisages its role as providing assistance and help rather than merely policing and control.

Lastly, the idea of the 'Gradual Consolidation of Layout' must be brought up. In planned self-help schemes gradual consolidation of the layout can take place, as it does in unplanned settlements thus avoiding development according to pre-determined norms. It is a process which maximises the flexibility and adaptability of planned settlements such that users are not faced with many limitations to their freedom of choice. Simulation exercises and hypothetical scenarios are examples of the tools which researchers interested in this process have experimented with. (For further information see Bhatt and Navarette, 1991; Hamdi, 1991). To conclude, a recommendation is made here for further research in this concept and its viability for application in the context of Egypt's New Cities.

Notes

1 Since the mid-1970s it became one of Egypt's strategic national policy aims to construct new settlements in the desert outside the Nile valley. Tenth of Ramadan was one of the first among those new settlements to be implemented. At that time foreign aid agencies were pushing the idea of aided self-help housing to be tried in Egypt. The typical low-income housing built in the New Cities is usually in the form of two to three-roomed apartments in four- to five-storey walk-up blocks. As in the core housing Scheme of the Tenth of Ramadan the beneficiaries of such housing are required to pay a down payment of 10-20 per cent of the unit price. The rest is paid in monthly instalments over a period of 20 to 30 years.

2 More than half of the project core house units were sold to business owners in the Tenth of Ramadan City as an incentive for investment. The employees (mostly factory workers) are then housed by their companies as a form of housing tied to employment. This practice undoubtedly was counter productive in the case of the core housing scheme. With the lack of ownership the residents built the extensions with minimal costs as much as possible. The concept of investment in the house became inapplicable. This clearly defies one of the main objectives of aided-self help housing.

3 Multiple Regression is a method of analysing the collective and separate contribution of two or more independent variables, to the variation of a dependent variable.

4 In some cases the tenant could actually have bought the house from its original owner. As a result of not paying off the loan on the house, the transfer of ownership becomes illegal according to the project regulations. To avoid legal complications the house title remains in the possession of the original owner. The house sale is documented by the issuing of a 'Primarily Sale Contract'. Meanwhile, a rent contract is issued for the new owner to ensure his right to live in the house.

Bibliography

Bhatt, V., and Navarette, J. (1991), 'The self selection process: A simulation exercise.' *Open House International*, Vol. 16, No. 4,

Hamdi, N. (1991), *Housing without houses*, Van Nostrand Reinhold: New York.

Mathéy, K. (ed) (1992), *Beyond self-help housing*, Mansell: London.

Peattie, L. (1982), 'Some second thoughts on sites and services.' *Habitat International*, Vol. 6, No. 1/2,

Peattie, L. (1983), 'Realistic planning and qualitative research.' *Habitat International*, Vol. 7, No. 5/6, pp.227-234.

4 Post-occupancy evaluation of five-storey walk-up dwellings:

The case of four mass housing estates in Algiers

MAGDA BEHLOUL

Because of the acute shortage of housing in Algeria, resulting from a high birth rate and the migration of the rural population to the cities, large mass housing programmes have been launched since the late 1970s, providing the urban population with dwellings and housing facilities just outside the existing urban perimeters. The urgency of unmet housing needs has meant that certain qualitative aspects of dwelling design, such as its adaptability to users' needs and its social adequacy, have generally been overlooked or somewhat ill considered.

This chapter investigates residents' reactions to the design of their housing environment in four selected estates in Algiers. The research methodology is based on a combination of questionnaires, interviews, photography and records of physical traces. A sample of 128 housewives has been interviewed and different indicators have been used in order to assess their evaluation of the various physical and non-physical features of their housing environment. Adaptive changes made to the original design of the dwellings have been recorded, as well as the space use patterns of the main living areas. The relationship between residents' satisfaction with their dwelling and their perception of the various features of their housing environment has also been investigated.

The research findings have resulted in a number of recommendations which are applicable to the programming, the design and the management of future mass housing estates in Algeria.

Introduction

Algeria is the second largest country of Africa, with a surface area of 2,382,000 sq. km. The Sahara desert, in the south, occupies five-sixths of the whole surface area. The French occupied Algeria for more than a century (1830-1962) and were concentrated in the Northern regions. They focused on agricultural exploitation of the best lands along the Mediterranean coast. A significant proportion of the population (40 per cent) is therefore located in the coastal strip, which represents only 1.7 per cent of the whole surface of the country (ONS, 1988, p.9). Between 1954 and 1962, urban growth was directly linked to the circumstances of the war of liberation, which resulted in the gathering of the rural population and its migration to the cities. The urban population increased from 25 per cent in 1954 to 31.4 per cent in 1966 (ONS, 1988, p.21). After independence in 1962, the Northern part of the country was the only part that had the necessary infrastructure for any immediate development. Consequently, the first economic development plans undertaken by the Algerian Government were all located there, aggravating the already existing unbalanced growth and exacerbating the exodus of the rural population. After a few years of independence, the Algerian Government launched a large programme of industrialisation. The first National Development Plans, (1967-69) and (1970-73) concentrated on establishing heavy industries, such as the hydrocarbon and steel industries. The Government priority was to industrial investments at the expense of those of a more social character, such as housing.

It was not until the end of the third National Development Plan (1974-77) that housing problems emerged as being one of the urgent priorities in the development policy of the country. The combination of high natural population increase and the intense migration of the rural population to the urban centres created acute shortages of housing. Faced with such a situation, the Algerian Government has embarked on a massive prefabricated building programme. Taking the experience of Europe in the past three decades as a model, industrialisation of the building process was thought to be the ultimate solution for responding quickly to the increasing needs in housing. During the period 1974-77, different national companies were allowed to import industrialised building systems to Algeria without any particular conditions being imposed. Consequently, some 26 different heavy prefabricated systems were imported from 200 different companies (Yahiaoui, 1983, p.170). Realising that housing industrialisation was being carried out without any organisational framework and that the development of urban areas was progressing without much control, the Government felt it necessary to set up the first political structure responsible for housing policy and the development of urban planning. This structure was created in 1977 as the Ministry of Urban Planning, Construction and Housing (MUCH). The new Ministry was faced with two alternatives: either continue to use heavy prefabricated building systems and set up large industrial units for their manufacture in Algeria, or set up smaller industrial units, possibly on building sites, that were more appropriate to local conditions and more suited to the ability of the local workers (Yahiaoui, 1983, p.170). There were several problems associated with the introduction of the heavy prefabricated systems and so they did not have the expected results (Boubekeur, 1986). Thus the second alternative was chosen resulting in the development of small building companies using more flexible and more manageable industrialised building techniques such as the framework construction system, the panel system or a combination of different systems called hybrid systems.

Whereas housing programmes used to be merely isolated operations not conforming to any urban planning scheme, they have rightly come to be seen as major urban determinants since the implementation of the New Urban Housing Zone (ZHUN) policy. The first Ministerial circular set the main strategy for developing and implementing the ZHUN programme, which became the major frame within which large scale urban housing projects were to be implemented in the suburbs of several Algerian towns. An evaluation of the housing situation in 1979 estimated the short and the long term needs and set two goals for housing production. The first goal was the production of 100,000 urban dwellings per year, to be reached between 1980 and 1985, and the longer term goal was to reach a production of 200,000 urban dwellings per year by 1990 (INERBA (Institut National d'Etudes et de Recherches du Batiment), 1980). An analysis of the housing production between 1980 and 1984 shows that, four years after the decision to build 100,000 dwellings per year, actual production had hardly reached 88,000 dwellings per year in the best circumstances (Boubekeur, 1986, p36). Whereas some 700,000 dwellings were intended to be built between 1980 and 1984 (Guerroudj, 1990), only 458,000 dwellings were in fact finished (El-Moudjahid, 1988). The fixed targets for housing production have never been reached. This is not only because of the poor productivity of the building sector and serious delays, the causes of which have been largely analysed by empirical studies (Benamrane, 1980; Benmatti, 1982; Boubekeur, 1986) but also because of the worsening economic conditions in the country. The sudden fluctuations of the oil market have had serious implications for the National Economy. As a consequence, the five year development plan (1980-84) emphasised the necessity for more involvement of the private sector in the construction of housing, so as to lift the burden off the state as far as house building was concerned. The housing shortage has since been worsening, making housing mobility impossible for the vast majority of the households.

The planning of the ZHUNs has been strongly influenced by the ideology of French concepts for new towns. The structure of the ZHUN estates is usually based on three levels: the district, the neighbourhood and the residential grouping. Each level is defined according to a specific number of housing units within which different types of facilities are made available. Each ZHUN operation is on the scale of thousands of dwellings grouped into mainly five-storey walk-up blocks of flats. The programme is obviously affecting a significant proportion of the Algerian urban population. Furthermore, the ZHUN programme has had a considerable impact on the shape of the urban space and the quality of the built environment. The approach to the planning of the ZHUNs has usually been superficial, resulting in poor integration of the new housing estates with the existing urban environment. Consequently, a landscape of scattered prefabricated blocks of flats, lacking any urban character, has invaded the urban space of several Algerian cities.

Because of the urgency of the housing problem, planning and architectural studies of mass housing estates have frequently been allocated only a limited amount of time, resulting in important aspects of the design being neglected or overlooked. The same programme of housing was aimed at all possible types of households and was widely built within different climatic regions of the country. The specific needs of Algerian households have not been considered in the design of the mass housing dwelling because it was assumed by the decision makers that Algerian households were evolving towards 'a modern way of life' and possibly hoped that the inhabitants' behaviour would change within the new housing environments and thus adapt to the new type of dwellings. The average size of the mass housing dwelling unit has been fixed as three-roomed flats (two bedrooms and a living room) for an 'average household' of seven people (ONS, 1988, p82). A number of important questions are raised in this chapter with regard to the extent to which the average size and the different features of the mass housing dwellings in Algeria are adequate and responsive to their residents' needs. The results presented here were obtained as part of a PhD research programme completed by the author in 1991 (Behloul, 1991).

Research methodology

A total of eight ZHUNs have been launched in Algiers between the 1970s and the beginning of the 1980s. Each programme consisted of thousands of dwellings with an overall total of 46,620 dwellings. Four representative estates have been selected from those eight for examination in the present study. The selection has been made according to the location and the size of the ZHUNs and the year in which they were launched. Two estates have been selected from the largest ZHUNs that were commenced in the 1970s: the *Bab Ezzouar* ZHUN with 10,800 housing units, and the *Ain Nadja* ZHUNs with 11,000 housing units. The two others have been selected from the smaller ZHUNs that were launched in the 1980s: the *Garidi* ZHUN with 4,820 units, and the *Ain Allah* ZHUN with 3,300 housing units. All four ZHUNs are located in the suburbs of Algiers within a maximum distance of 15km from the city centre. They are located near a new network of motorways linking the east part of Algiers suburb to its west part.

Sampling

The survey was carried out within the earliest built parts of each of the selected ZHUNs. A sample of 30 to 33 occupied dwellings was selected, resulting in an overall sample of 128 housewives being interviewed. Cluster sampling was used. In each estate, a systematic selection of blocks of flats was made and within each selected block of flats a number of households were interviewed at random. Although cluster sampling can reduce the randomness of the sample, one of its advantages was that if a selected household was absent, or not available for the interview at the time of the survey, the researcher could simply try to obtain an interview from another cluster household. The size of the sample was fixed with reference to the researcher's capacity to carry out the survey herself. Since the research aims were relevant to the qualitative understanding of people's feeling about their residential environments, it was considered appropriate to have a sample of at least 30 households per estate. In each of the four studied estates, a sample of 30 to 33 housewives was interviewed.

Data collection

Structured face-to-face interviews were carried out by the author. The interviews were usually conducted within the confines of the respondents' dwellings. The average time for each interview was 30 minutes and was followed by an informal discussion and a record of the furnishing layout of the various rooms in the dwelling unit, when this was permitted. Systematic observation and record of activities taking place and changes made to the housing environment were carried out in both the inside of the dwelling and the outside environment. Observing physical traces meant systematically looking at the physical surroundings to find a reflection of previous activity and/or physical adaptive changes and recording them. The value of such unobtrusive measures lies in their non-reactivity, allowing for behavioural assessment free from threats to validity found in the use of questionnaire and interviews. Used in conjunction with the questionnaire, these unobtrusive measures can provide valid and informative data necessary for an objective evaluation.

Data analysis

Different indicators were used in order to assess residents' evaluation of the various physical and non-physical features of their housing environment. Among the aspects examined were the housewives' perception of the design qualities of their dwelling units and the spaces within the units; their alteration to the original layout; their space use pattern; and their overall level of satisfaction with their dwelling. Respondents' housing aspirations and possible preferences for more traditional arrangements were also assessed. In addition to the physical attributes of the dwelling units, the respondents' perception of their estate was assessed through their perception of the appearance of their estate, the use of the external spaces, the level of maintenance and up-keep, as well as social relations between neighbours. After reviewing distribution data covering the survey responses, hypothesised relationships between variables were examined. Dwelling satisfaction was used as a criterion variable in a conceptual and operational model, where variables measuring physical, social and contextual attributes of the residential environment as well as individual characteristics were used as predictors of satisfaction. The analysis then involved examining relationships between the variables and conducting statistical tests as to their significance.

Respondents' characteristics

The sample obtained using cluster sampling consisted of a wide cross-section of the population. This can be explained by the fact that mass housing programs were not aimed at a specific socio-economic group but were to house families from different social backgrounds. A typical block of flats could include a variety of household types ranging from middle-income nuclear households, where both parents were working and educated, to low-income extended large households re-housed from poor over-crowded housing areas in Algiers. When considering household types and size, more than two thirds of the studied households (77 per cent) were families of the nuclear type and 23 per cent of them were extended households. Most of the extended households consisted of one of the grandparents living with their married son or daughter, or married children living with their parents on account of the housing crisis and the impossibility of getting their own flats. The size of the households studied varied from two to 15 people. Almost half the sample (45 per cent) consisted of households of five to nine people and almost a third of the whole sample consisted of households whose size exceeded 10 people. More than half the 128 households studied (56 per cent) contained more than three children. The majority of the households had children of different ages, varying from young children to adults.

In any household type, women are usually responsible for all family management that occurs in the home such as cleaning, cooking, laundry and caring for children. They are often spatially confined to their dwellings by social customs. Although they are increasingly joining the work force, employed women form a decided minority and withdrawal from the work-force is common during childbearing years. Consequently, women are likely to spend a considerable amount of time inside their flats and are the ones who are the most aware of the quality and adequacy of the dwelling design in meeting the needs of their household. Therefore, the women were the ones who were interviewed. About half of the 128 housewives interviewed in the four estates (53 per cent) were young women whose age varied from 23 to 35 years old. Almost one third of the sample consisted of housewives between the age of 35 to 45 years old and only a small proportion (15 per cent) were over the age of 45. More than two thirds of the 128 respondents (70 per cent) were non-working housewives. Only a small proportion had worked previously and slightly less than a quarter of those interviewed (22 per cent) were still working at the time the survey was carried out. When comparing the proportion of interviewed working housewives within the four estates, it appeared that a higher proportion was interviewed in the Garidi estate. The majority of the working respondents were either teachers in primary or secondary schools or were university lecturers.

The environment outside the dwellings

Residents' overall opinion about their estate

The first question respondents in the four estates were asked was what they generally thought about their estate. The question was deliberately left open in order to identify the criteria by which housewives judged their housing environment and the aspects which appeared to matter most to them. The responses revealed important differences amongst the four estates. Different criteria were clearly used by the various respondents in their overall evaluation of their estate. However, residents seemed to be more likely to identify and point out negative aspects rather than positive ones. The negative aspects mentioned dealt with both physical and non-physical features. Poor constructional quality and poor site layout were raised along with poor management and maintenance of the estate. The relationship between neighbours living in the same block and general upkeep of the adjacent external spaces seemed also to be important aspects from the point of view of the residents as they were the criteria most frequently mentioned in comparison with other parts of the estate were perceived as being better. When respondents were then specifically asked to assess various aspects of their estates, it was confirmed that the relationship between neighbours living in the same block, the maintenance and upkeep of the external spaces and the shared stairways, the landscape quality of the external spaces, as well as the construction quality of the dwellings, were important sources of concern for the majority of the respondents.

Relationship with neighbours

Responses revealed that in most cases residents living in the same block of flats and sharing the same staircase tended to avoid having any relationship with each other. It appears that when families of different social and economic status dwell in the same block, there is less likelihood of relationships developing. A greater homogeneity between neighbours seems more likely to occur when residents have chosen to live in a particular development. This is not the case for the majority of the households living in large scale housing estates, where residents have little or no choice of flats and where the flats are rented at the same subsidised prices for the different social categories. Moreover, there is seldom an effort in the housing allocation policy to ensure a certain degree of homogeneity between neighbours living in the same block of flats. A 'good' relationship between neighbours was described by the respondents as the ability of neighbours in certain blocks of flats to organise themselves in order to share the cost and responsibility for the maintenance and up-keep of their communal staircase and the external spaces adjacent to their blocks of flats. Such cases coincided with blocks with a greater social homogeneity and a high proportion of owner occupiers.

The communal staircase and security

In almost all multi-storey residential units, access to individual flats is gained by means of a common stairway. In both the *Bab Ezzouar* and the *Ain Allah* estates a stairway serves eight to ten dwellings, giving access to two dwellings per floor. In the case of the *Ain Nadja* and the *Garidi* estates, the stairs serve 10 to 20 dwellings giving access to two to four dwellings per floor. In general, the flats' entrance door is directly accessible from the stairway landing. The main entrance to the block is generally open and therefore the stairs are accessible to anyone. Moreover, no-one within the blocks of flats appears to have responsibility for the shared stairway, as there are no resident caretakers. Consequently, the level of up-keep and maintenance was generally poor. Furthermore, entrances to flats were reinforced with an additional iron door in order to reduce their vulnerability to burglaries. Such security measures were also taken for windows and balconies to which iron grills were added.

External spaces and appearance of the estates

The quality, the scale and the maintenance of the spaces between the blocks of flats tended to lower or improve respondents' overall perception of the estate. In the *Bab Ezzouar* estate, the large spaces between buildings remained undefined and unused, the scale of the spaces is such that the same housing density could have been achieved with two to three-storey blocks. The repetition of the same blocks, and the lack of space definition, were reported by the respondents as causing problems of orientation as all parts of the estate look the same. The lack of landscaping caused huge amounts of mud in winter and a very dusty environment in the summer. On the other hand the quality of the external spaces in the *Garidi* estate was praised by the respondents (Plate 4.1). In the *Ain Allah* estate, the small distance between some of the blocks (Plate 4.2) caused privacy problems for the dwelling units.

Site observations showed that some of the residents have taken the initiative to fence and landscape the spaces immediately adjacent to their blocks (Plate 4.3). Their claims for these spaces were evident in the four estates, despite the regulations which supposedly prevented them from taking the spaces over and personalising them. Such initiatives presented several advantages: not only did they reduce the scale of the public spaces and consequently reduce the maintenance cost, they also created important buffers between the ground floor flats and the public spaces. Moreover, they improved the overall appearance of the estates and the cumulative effect of residents' different initiatives in some areas of the estates had resulted in a naturally occurring complexity and variety in the external environment. It was also found that these initiatives did not necessarily come only from the residents living in the ground floor flats. It seems that residents are likely to invest energy and money in taking care of their entrances and the external spaces immediately adjacent to their blocks. However, the problem of how to divide the external spaces adjacent to the blocks and allocate them to residents without raising conflicts, and how to ensure that these spaces are not used for other purposes than gardens and/or yards, remains an important area of the design of multi-family housing which needs future investigation and experimentation.

Plate 4.1   The *Garidi* estate

Plate 4.2   The *Ain Allah* estate

Plate 4.3   The *Bab Ezzouar* estate: landscaped spaces adjacent to the blocks
of flats

This section has presented the respondents' evaluation of the environment outside their dwellings. The next section will concentrate on a detailed analysis of residents' perception, use and alteration of their dwelling units, as well as their overall level of satisfaction.

The dwelling units

All the flats in the selected estates (with the exception of some of the flats in the *Ain Nadja* estate), have a modern European distribution of functions. The flats are organised along a corridor that serves, on each side, the living room, bedrooms, bathroom and kitchen. The kitchen is usually provided with a tiny loggia to 'compensate' for the lack of a traditional courtyard and sometimes the living room or one of the bedrooms is provided with a balcony.

The main issues that were investigated and are discussed in this chapter are:

1. To what extent the size and the internal organisation of mass housing dwelling in Algeria are responsive to their residents' needs;
2. What type of adaptive changes (if any) the residents in the mass housing estates make to their dwelling in order to make it more responsive to their needs;
3. To what extent traditional space use patterns and traditional activities are still carried out within the 'modern' urban dwelling and to what degree traditional housing arrangements are regarded by the respondents as preferable to their present dwelling's organisation;
4. What are residents' preferences for the location of private external spaces and what are their perceptions and uses of the existing private external spaces;
5. How satisfied residents' living in the five-storey walk-up dwellings are and what physical and non-physical features of their housing environment are likely to promote a higher degree of dweller satisfaction.

Respondents' overall perception of their dwelling unit

The perception of the residents to the adequacy of their dwelling as a whole was assessed through their responses to some initial open-ended questions, that were quite general in nature, followed by some very specific ones. The first questions dealt with what the residents liked and disliked about their flat and what they thought about its organisation. At this stage the questions did not prompt the respondents to give approbation or to comment on their dislike of any particular characteristics. The topics raised, therefore, were those which occurred to the respondents and were thus, it seems reasonable to assume, uppermost in their minds. The most frequently shared source of dislike in the four estates was the constructional quality of the dwellings. However, the specific constructional items that raised complaints among the respondents varied from one estate to another. In the *Bab Ezzouar* estate it was the inappropriate choice of plastic as a material, for doors and floor tiling, which led to a quick deterioration of these. In both the *Garidi* and the *Ain Nadja* estates, it was the frequent occurrence of cracks in the walls and the poor quality of floor and wall finishes resulting in costly maintenance and repair work. In the *Ain Allah* estate, although the internal finishes of the dwellings were achieved to a high standard, it was the apparent fragility of the prefabricated facade and the concern about the life-span of the buildings which were complained about.

The majority of the respondents perceived the general organisation of their flats as reasonably satisfactory, with the exception of the *Ain Nadja* estate where an attempt was made in the design to recreate the traditional central space within the dwellings (Figures 4.1a, b, c & d). The central space is either a circulation space in some of the flats, or the living room itself. Such arrangements have been strongly criticised by the respondents and were subject to various alterations (Figure 4.2). A number of features of the dwellings in the *Ain Nadja* and the *Bab Ezzouar* estates were disliked by the majority of the respondents. The case of these two estates allowed the identification of a number of design details that should be **avoided** in future dwelling design. These are as follows:

- a long, dark and narrow corridor;
- lack of a proper entrance hall resulting in the entrance door leading directly onto a narrow corridor;
- an entrance door too close to the living room door;
- a WC door facing the living room;
- bedroom windows with a fixed part causing difficulties for airing the bedding;
- large spacing between louvres of window shutters allowing flats to be overlooked at night from facing blocks;
- access to bedrooms from living room or guest room;
- lack of natural light and ventilation in the bathroom and the WC.

This last aspect has been heavily criticised by the respondents in almost all the estates, suggesting that both the bathroom and the WC should have windows opening to the outside. However, the physical features of the dwellings in both the *Garidi* and the *Ain Allah* estates were mostly liked by their residents: two design details strongly appreciated by the residents in these two estates and which should be considered in the design of future dwellings are:

- the availability of built-in storage spaces within the corridor and/or the kitchen;

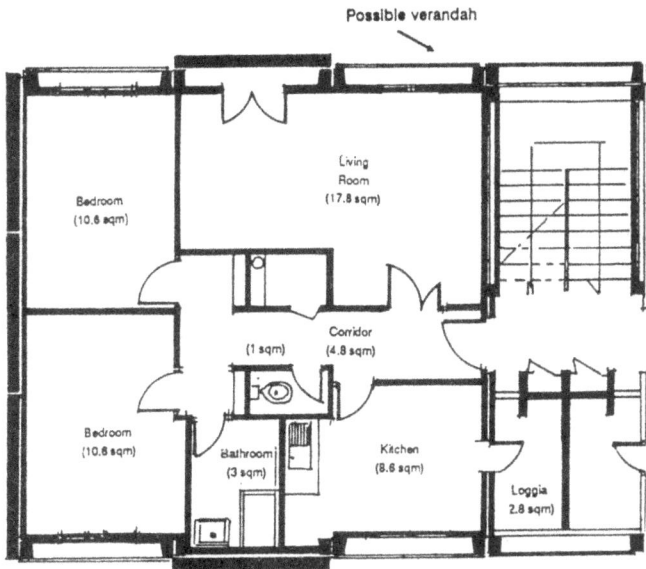

Figure 4.1a   Dwelling layout in the *Bab Ezzouar* estate. A two bedroom flat. Floor area 65 sqm

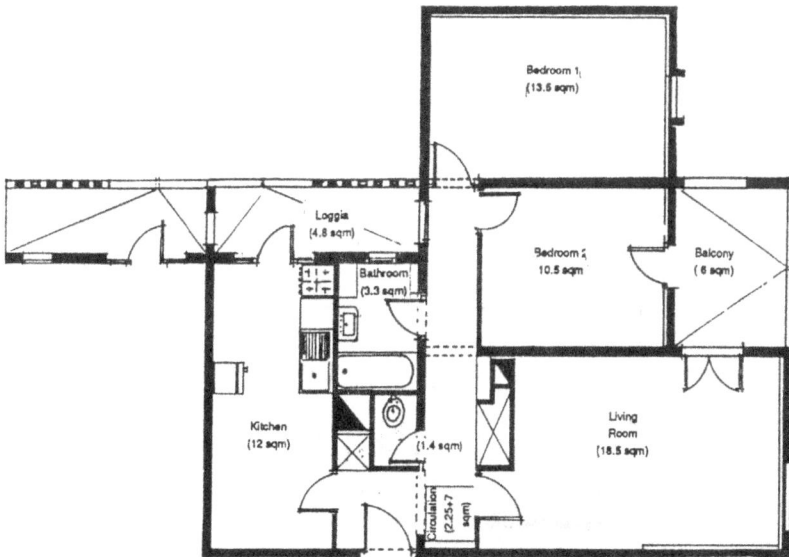

Figure 4.1b   Dwelling layout in the *Garidi* estate. A two bedroom flat. Floor area 83.5 sqm

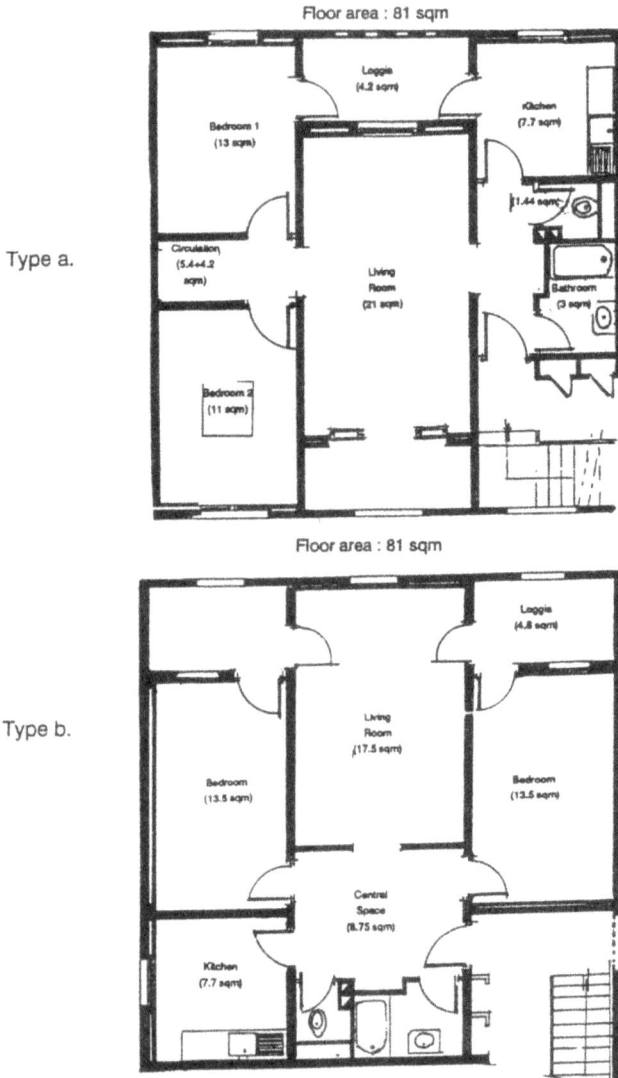

Figure 4.1c   Dwelling layout in the *Ain Nadja* estate. Two bedroom flats

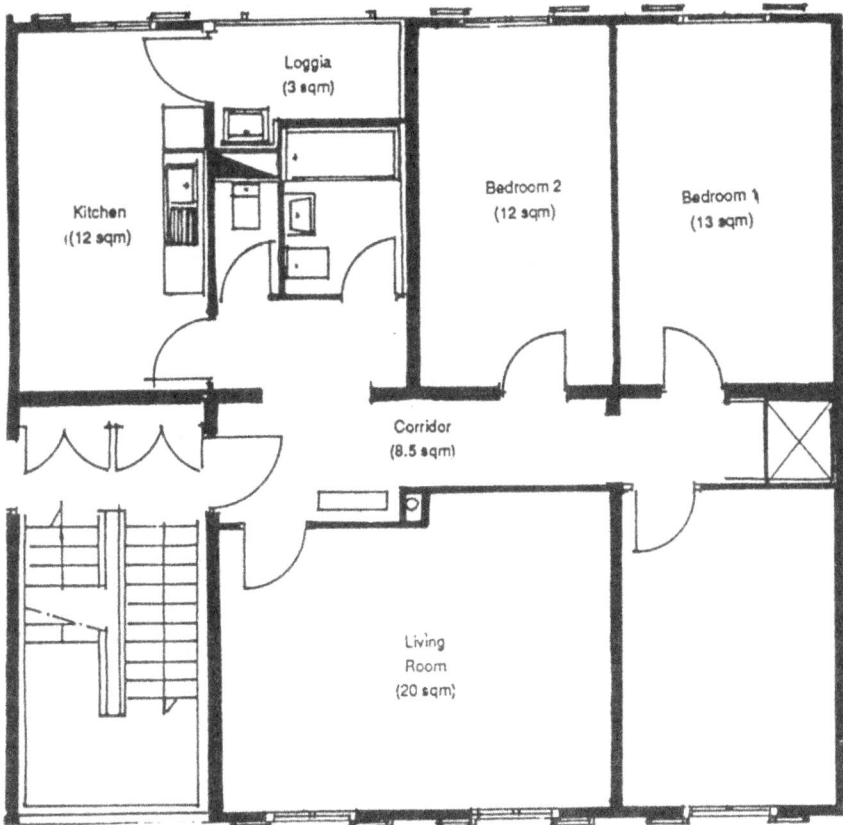

Figure 4.1d **Dwelling layout in the *Ain Allah* estate. A three bedroom flat. Floor area 93.5 sqm**

- a clear separation between the circulation leading to the kitchen, the bathroom and the WC and the circulation leading to the bedrooms and the living room. The arrangement of the kitchen, the bathroom and the WC in the *Ain Allah* estate seems to be the most satisfactory when compared with the arrangements found in the three other estates.

The examination of respondents' comments with regard to the internal organisation of their dwellings shows that housewives were able to evaluate and criticise their dwelling design accurately. Their evaluations ranged from general matters such as flat size and general organisation, to detailed matters such as the quality of the finishes. It is appropriate to point out that responses to the open-ended questions gave what was believed to be a wide ranging view of the different problems within the dwellings, as aspects which might not have been mentioned by one respondent were mentioned by another.

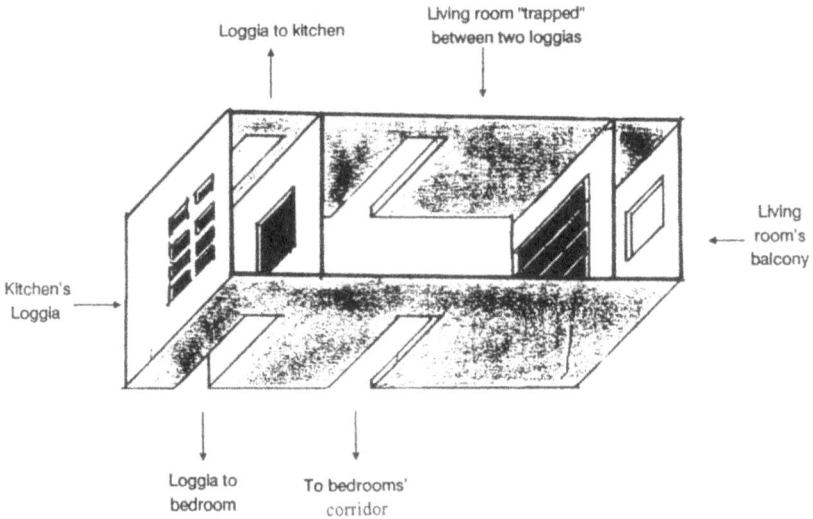

Figure 4.2   The central space in the *Ain Nadja* estate and alterations

Adaptive dwelling alterations

When considering the physical alterations that residents made or wanted to make to their dwellings, it appears that the most frequently reported type of alteration concerned the private external spaces such as the loggias and the balconies. These were closed off in an attempt to gain desperately needed additional habitable floor area. Moreover, the kitchen's loggia was subject to conversion in the Garidi and the Ain Nadja estates (Figures 4.2 & 4.3). This was done in an attempt to gain an

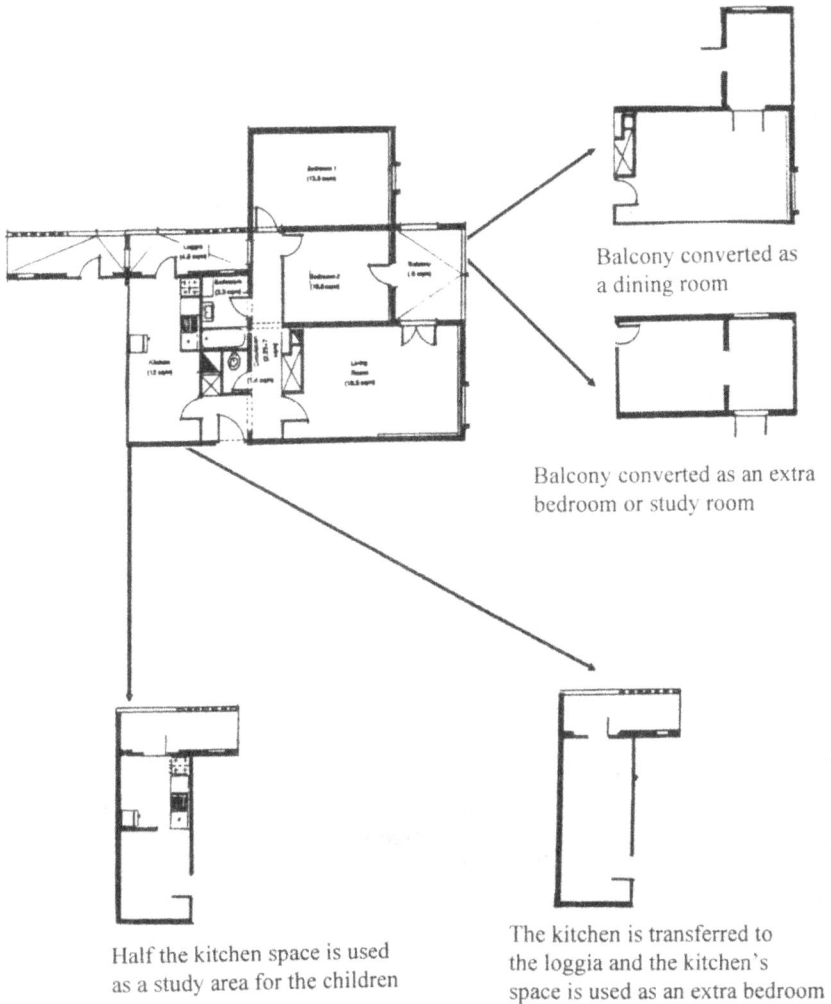

Balcony converted as a dining room

Balcony converted as an extra bedroom or study room

Half the kitchen space is used as a study area for the children

The kitchen is transferred to the loggia and the kitchen's space is used as an extra bedroom

Figure 4.3   **Dwelling alterations in the *Garidi* estate**

extra bedroom, by transferring the kitchen to the loggia and using the kitchen space as a bedroom. This suggests that the average size of the dwellings is an important problem. The only alterations that were carried out as a result of poor layout were found in the *Ain Nadja* estate. Some residents created a corridor and divided the central living room into two rooms: a small living room and a guest room. Less radical alterations were also carried out by the residents and concerned the finishes of the dwellings, such the change of floor tiling in the *Bab Ezzouar* estate and the addition of bathroom wall tiling in the *Garidi* and the *Ain Nadja* estates.

Preference for a traditional courtyard house layout

When respondents were asked whether they would have preferred a traditional courtyard organisation, 73 per cent were so minded. Reasons for their preference revealed that housewives lacked contact with external spaces and had difficulty in carrying out certain activities. Non-working housewives complained that they felt that they were somewhat suffocated inside their dwellings, missing the direct contact with the natural elements: air, sunlight and plants. The practice of sexual segregation for a woman confined to a cramped European housing type results in restricted light and air as well as a reduced level of social relations. The courtyard in the traditional house provided women with a constant contact with the outside world as well as the required level of privacy. Furthermore, the accessible roof in the courtyard houses also allowed visual contact with the city and social interaction with the women living in the adjacent courtyard house. Whereas the roof was used for drying the washing, the courtyard served routinely for a variety of activities such as laundry, children's play, wool weaving and preparing couscous (a traditional North African dish). Therefore the functional suitability of the courtyard houses was acknowledged by the respondents. This was the result of the various functional problems they had encountered in their current dwelling rather than a previous housing experience in a traditional courtyard house.

While most respondents preferred a traditional courtyard house to their current dwelling because it was perceived as solving a number of functional problems, their actual housing aspirations were either a larger apartment or a 'modern' villa. There is an obvious conflict here. While courtyard houses may be convenient in themselves, they are clearly associated with backwardness, poor social categories and somewhat undesirable circumstances such as location in old centres and overcrowded conditions. The aspiration to improve social standing seems more important than a functionally suitable traditional house. A study carried out by Waltz (1985) about women's housing needs in Tunisia, found that the common desire of 30 families with modest income was for a house with functionally specific rooms and no courtyard.

Several conversations with the housewives about the type and location of the private external spaces within the 'modern' dwellings, as well as their potential use, revealed a strong preference for an accessible roof on their block. In addition a private loggia attached to the kitchen appeared to be a necessity within the dwelling unit. An accessible terrace roof was required for fresh air and to allow traditional courtyard house activities to be carried out. These activities included drying the washing, drying the couscous, washing and drying carpets, mattresses and wool.

The following section presents the results arising from more specific questions regarding the various spaces within the flats. In order to understand more thoroughly residents' general responses, and to suggest possible design solutions for future mass housing dwellings, a detailed analysis of residents' use of the various spaces within their dwelling units, and their perception of their design, shape and spaciousness, has been carried out.

Space perception and space use patterns

The living room An examination of respondents' perception of their living room size showed that even a floor area of 21 square metres was still perceived by the majority of the respondents as small (Figure 4.4). The perception of the living room size was not only influenced by its actual size but also by its shape and the amount of furnishing intended to be placed within it. Many complaints were made by some residents about the fact that they had to get rid of a number of furniture items when they moved in. A strong tendency for having a 'modern' large living room suite, a wall unit and a dining area within the available living room space was evident (Plate 4.4). Those who did not have such a suite expressed the aspiration of acquiring it when their financial situation improved or when the size of the household reduced. Rectangular shapes where the difference between the width and the length was quite large tended to be strongly disliked and irregular shapes, due to built-in wall units, tended to cause difficulties in the placing of the furniture. The living room tended to contain the best furniture items and tended to be under-used in order to keep it clean and tidy for the possible visit of guests.

The living room versus the guests' room When space was available within the dwelling unit, a clear separation was made by the residents between the living room and the guests' room. One of the bedrooms became the living room where members of the household could relax and watch television, whereas the original living room space became the guests' reception room. The living room then contained flexible traditional furnishing consisting of bunks with cushions for sitting on during the day and sleeping on during the night (Figure 4.5). The modern and best furniture items were 'displayed' in the guests' room, which remained closed most of the time.

Plate 4.4   Modern furnishing in the living room

The examination of the way the living rooms and the bedrooms were furnished confirmed the hypothesis that there is a conflict between the tendency of residents to conform with modern ideas, by using stereotyped modern furniture arrangements, and the persistence of traditional space use patterns which were found in, for example, the children's bedroom. The guest room became a modern facade claiming a certain social status, whereas the living room was the comfortable traditional space with flexible multi-purpose furnishing. However, such separation was not possible for the majority of the residents who had very large households and complained about the lack of space within their dwelling unit. In these cases the living room was used as a bedroom at night by laying a number of mattresses on the floor. The availability of a balcony adjacent to the living room was perceived as important for sitting outside and having fresh air. However, the observed uses of such spaces revealed that this was not the case. The need for space resulted in most of the balconies being closed off and used as an extension of the living room.

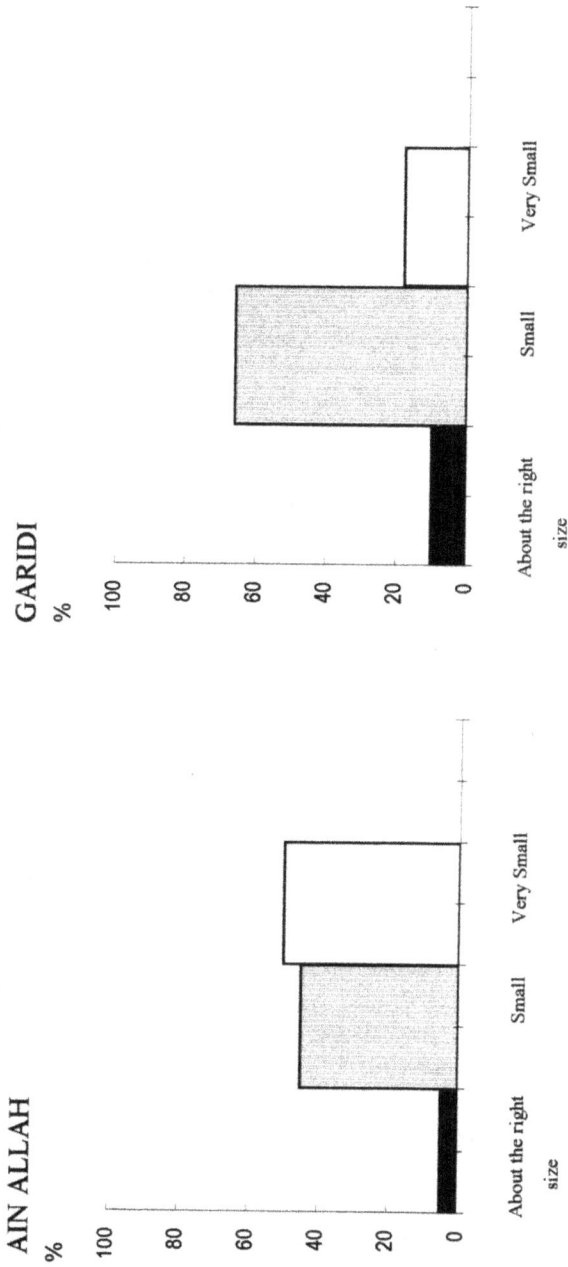

Figure 4.4   Respondents' perception of their living room size

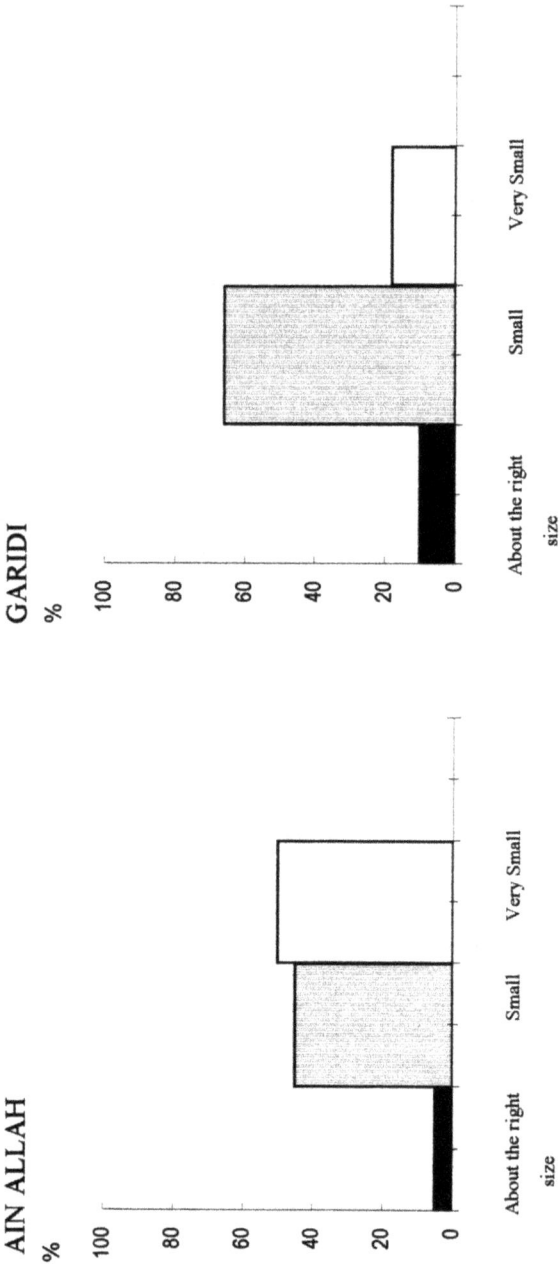

Figure 4.4 **Respondents' perception of their living room size (continued)**

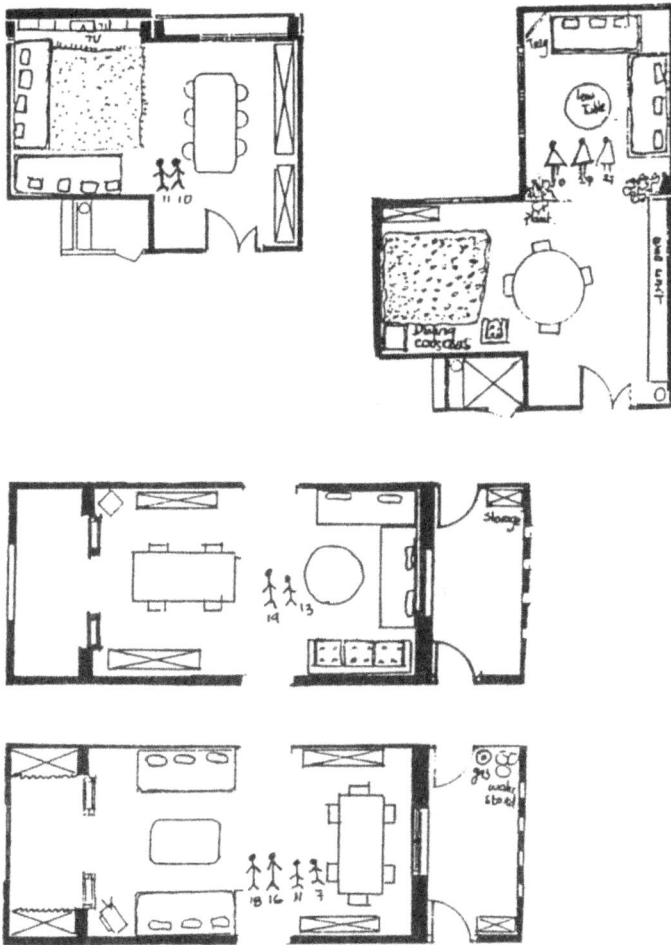

Figure 4.5   Traditional living room furnishing

The kitchen   All respondents in the *Bab Ezzouar*, the *Ain Nadja* and the *Garidi* estates perceived the size of their kitchen as either small or too small. However, the majority of the respondents in the *Ain Allah* estate described their kitchen as being the right size (Figure 4.6). This coincided with a floor area of 12 square metres. Because of the large household sizes in general, women tend to spend a considerable amount of time in the kitchen, preparing meals and drinks. This is usually a very time consuming activity as ready made meals and processed food do not exist in the local market. Furthermore, the majority of the respondents reported that all meals were generally taken in the kitchen. In the case of very large households, meals were taken in shifts - adults /children and/or men/women. When available, the dining table placed in the living room area was used only for guests or on special occasions. When respondents were asked about the shape of the kitchen and the facilities provided in it, it was clear that a shape that is closer to a square rather than to a rectangle was generally preferred. The available working surface was perceived as inadequate and insufficient in most cases. As mentioned previously, kitchens in all the estates are provided with a loggia directly accessible from the kitchen.

The kitchen's loggia   The kitchen's loggia appeared to be the most important private external space within the dwelling unit itself, primarily because of the number of activities taking place there. In addition to the tasks which are complementary to those occurring in the kitchen, the loggia was used for storage and drying the laundry. Other activities which could be described as 'traditional' and which used to be easily carried out in the traditional house courtyard and/or its accessible terrace roof, were sometimes found taking place in the loggia, although there were some difficulties.

  The size, orientation and design of the loggias was subject to criticism particularly in the *Ain Nadja* estate. Whereas a certain degree of privacy is required for the housewife in the loggia, the architectural response to such a need has been extreme in the case of the *Ain Nadja* estate (Plate 4.5). The need for good exposure of the laundry to the sunlight seems to be stronger than the need to have a high degree of privacy within the loggia. The availability of a wash basin as well as a storage space within the loggia seemed to be much appreciated by the residents. When considering the size of the loggias, it appears that a floor area of three square metres was perceived as too small whereas a floor area of 5.5 square metres was not subject to criticism. As regards the shape and location of the loggias, it seems that a long rectangular shape that allows a greater exposure of the washing to the sun's rays would be preferable. Direct access to the loggia from the bathroom would be extremely helpful, not only for a direct transfer of the washing to the drying lines but also for good ventilation of the bathroom. This would

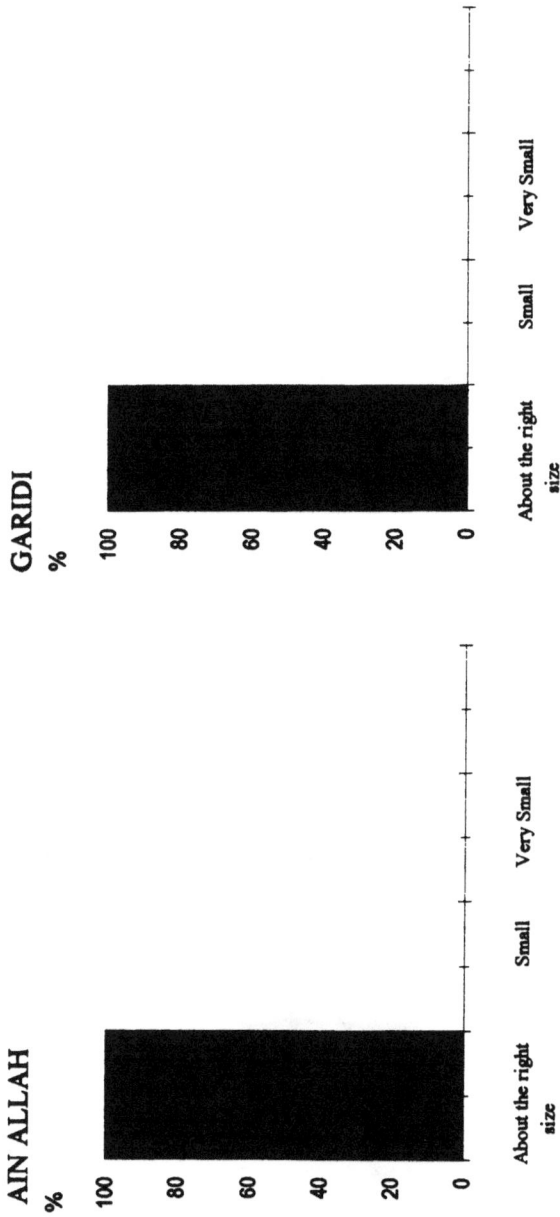

Figure 4.6 **Respondents' perception of their kitchen size**

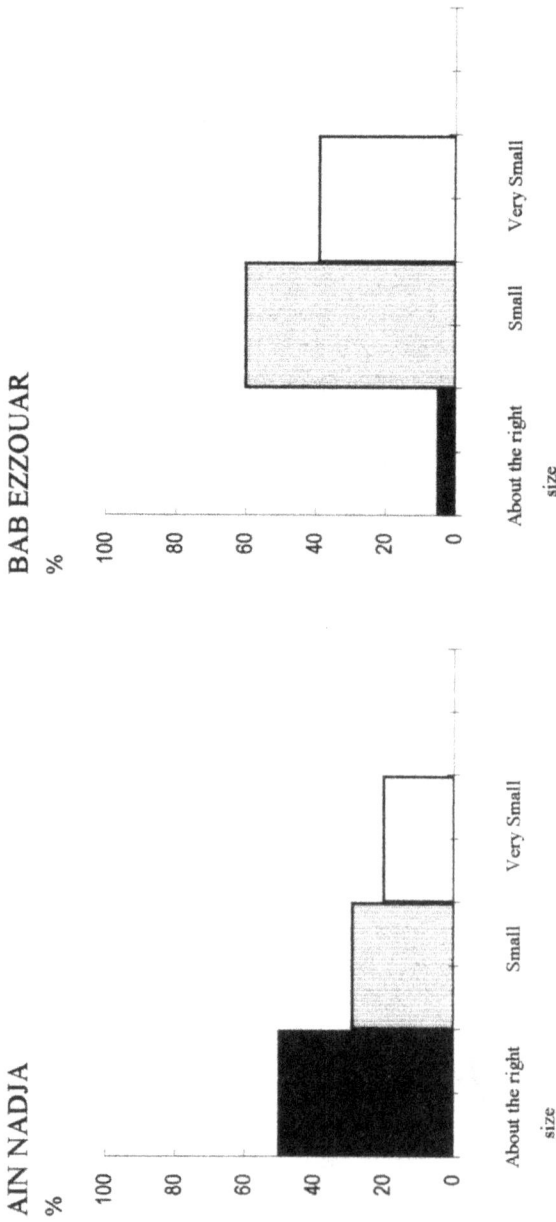

Figure 4.6   Respondents' perception of their kitchen size (continued)

Plate 4.5   Inadequate loggia design in the *Ain Nadja* estate

ensure a higher degree of comfort for the housewife when doing the laundry in the bathroom.

The bedrooms Apart from the *Ain Allah* estate, the vast majority of the dwellings in the three other estates consisted of two bedrooms and a living room. Both the number and the size of the bedrooms were heavily criticised by the respondents in the four estates. The examination of residents' perception of the size of their bedrooms shows that a floor area of 12 to 13 square metres for each bedroom is likely to be satisfactory. The number of bedrooms was found insufficient for a significant proportion of the households studied as 62 per cent of the respondents expressed the need for an additional one or two bedrooms. The need to separate mature boys and girls and to provide privacy for the couple would dictate three bedrooms as a desirable minimum, since households rarely move from one dwelling to another as their circumstances change. Moreover, when a household is at the stage where the children are grown up, the children will frequently be still living at home. The following circumstances could take place:

- Reduction in household size due to children marrying and moving away or
- An increase in the number of extended family households - the parents may house a married son because of the housing crisis which makes it difficult for young couples to find a flat.

With the worsening housing shortage, the second scenario is definitely on the increase. The comments with regard to the size and shape of the bedrooms revealed that almost all households faced difficulties with furnishing the bedrooms because of their small size and/or the large number of people sharing them. Most parents' bedrooms contained stereotyped furniture items that left very limited circulation space. The children's bedroom however could in several cases not contain a bed for every child so a number of mattresses were found piled up in a corner during the day and laid on the floor during the night. When comparing respondents' perception of the size of the bedrooms and their objective size, it appears that a floor area of 12 to 13 square metres is likely to be satisfactory.

Respondents' evaluation of various features of their dwelling units and their housing environment made it possible to identify various aspects that can be improved in the design and management of future housing estates. However, in order to find out which aspects should be given priority for improvement, the relationship between residents' satisfaction and their perception of both physical and non-physical attributes of their housing environment has been analysed.

Dwelling satisfaction

Residential satisfaction may be considered as the response of residents to their residential environment - the positive or negative feeling that the occupants have for where they live. As such, it is a representation of the affective response of people to the social-physical environment which they inhabit. All respondents in the four selected estates were asked how satisfied they were with their present accommodation. Because any response to a question about satisfaction is bound to depend on the context in which the question is asked, including the question which immediately precedes it in the interview, the same question was asked twice, on different occasions in the interview, so that a more accurate record of the respondents' expressed satisfaction could be made. The first record of the respondents' satisfaction was made in the early stages of the questionnaire, after respondents had answered general questions. The second record was made towards the end of the questionnaire after the respondents had assessed various detailed aspects of both their housing environment and their dwellings. The two records of satisfaction were then considered in relation to housewives' perception of the various attributes of their housing environment, with the aim being to identify the contribution of both physical and non-physical attributes to residents' satisfaction.

Despite the identification of a number of deficiencies in the design of both the external environment and the dwellings themselves, the overall recorded satisfaction from the two questions in the four selected estates was rather positive - almost two-thirds of the sample (62 per cent of the 128 respondents) were either fairly satisfied or very satisfied with their dwellings. This somewhat unexpected result may partially be explained by the fact that other non-physical factors may have a stronger influence on the residents' satisfaction than the physical characteristics of the dwellings. Among these non-physical factors may be the residents' awareness of the local housing crisis and their low expectations resulting from their experience of what might be available in the local housing market. Marcuse (1971) suggested that 'A person may express satisfaction with an incongruent situation out of a sense of fatalism and powerlessness to alter the situation'. He explains that fatalistic resignation results in lower aspirations, higher tolerance and hence higher satisfaction. Rapoport (1985, p278) argues that people tend to express satisfaction with their home environment, and 'misfits' may be 'solved' via other mechanisms and strategies such as modifying the home environment, changing life style and behaviour, or by changing expectations.

Satisfaction was found to vary a great deal from estate to estate. Records of residents' satisfaction show that the *Bab Ezzouar* and the *Ain Nadja* estates had a significant proportion of dissatisfied respondents, as more than half the 33 respondents in each estate had mixed feelings or were either fairly dissatisfied or very dissatisfied. The *Ain Allah* and the *Garidi* estates had a much higher proportion of satisfied residents with more than two thirds of the respondents being either very satisfied or fairly satisfied.

Previous studies on satisfaction (such as Francescato et al., 1979) suggest that residential satisfaction is related to three sets of factors:

1. objective characteristics of the housing environment
2. objective characteristics of the residents (such as age, gender, previous housing experience)
3. the subjective beliefs of the residents, their perceptions and aspirations.

The precise nature of the linkage between these three components is, however difficult to define (Weidemann and Anderson, 1985). Different users assign different priorities to various properties. It is not clear to what degree the variations in subjective response are a function of personality or of cultural or social variables among users. There is still no general agreement on what features of the built form produce which degree of satisfaction or dissatisfaction among which sub-cultural group. The relationship between 45 variables measuring physical and non-physical features of the housing environment and the two records of residents' dwelling satisfaction was statistically examined. The conclusions drawn in this study only deal with those factors that have been found **significantly** related to **both** records of residents' satisfaction.

Results from the present study show that both physical and non-physical attributes of the housing environment contributed to respondents' satisfaction with their dwellings. The most strongly associated factor of dwelling satisfaction was not associated directly to one of the features of the dwellings themselves but concerned the respondents' perception of their estate. Those who had negative opinions recorded the lowest levels of satisfaction. Responses to open ended questions revealed that such overall opinions were not only shaped by physical features of the environment, such as the general appearance of the estate and the design quality of the external spaces separating the different buildings, but also by non-physical features of the environment such as the general maintenance/upkeep of the estate and the type of relationship that exists between neighbours living in the same block. This last factor has itself been found significantly related to both records of satisfaction, particularly with regard to the degree of agreement between neighbours to share the price of cleaning and maintenance projects within their block of flats. Such agreements, which resulted in a higher level of upkeep of the communal spaces, appeared to be possible only where a certain degree of social homogeneity was found among residents living in the same block of flats.

Among the physical variables found strongly associated with both records of satisfaction and at a very high level of significance ($p < 0.01$) was the perceived size of the kitchen. A floor area of 12 square metres was perceived as being the right size and this seems to contribute in promoting a high degree of satisfaction among housewives. The adequacy of the internal organisation of the dwellings was also found to be related to residents' satisfaction. Dwelling layouts in both the *Ain Allah* and the *Garidi* estates appeared to be more satisfactory than in the two other estates. The necessity felt by some respondents to make some alterations to the internal organisation of their dwellings reduced their satisfaction significantly. Contrary to what would have been expected neither the overall size of the dwelling nor the degree of crowding within the dwelling unit were found to be significantly related to the respondents' satisfaction.

Whereas physical factors related to satisfaction can be altered in future housing projects, some of the non-physical factors related to dwelling satisfaction in the present study are not within the scope of architecture itself. These factors are directly related to the residents themselves such as their childhood housing experience, their length of residence in their present dwelling and their moving intentions. Other non-physical features of the housing environment, which might be alterable, are related to respondents' satisfaction and confirm the findings from previous studies. Such factors include the type of relationship that exists between neighbours, the degree of up-keep of the estate and the perceived degree of security. Furthermore, the symbolic value of the mass housing dwelling, which results from its association with 'modernity' and social promotion, seems to have a stronger impact on residents' satisfaction than the functional deficiencies in the dwellings' design. For example, residents' satisfaction with their present dwelling was found to be significantly associated with their previous as well as their childhood experience. Respondents from a rural background appeared to be more satisfied than those from an urban one.

However small the impact of the built environment may be in promoting residential satisfaction, it is an area in which the architect has some control. On the other hand, concentrating on improving dwelling quality alone may have little impact on overall residential satisfaction. It is likely that the kinds of findings shown in this study are not confined to the four selected estates. Further research on these lines could contribute significantly to the practical usefulness of residential satisfaction research, particularly in terms of cultural differences.

Conclusion and recommendations

One of the major findings of the present research was that the mass housing dwellings are not necessarily unsatisfactory, as the overall recorded satisfaction in the four estates was rather positive with almost two thirds of the 128 respondents being either fairly or very satisfied. This was despite a number of deficiencies that have been identified in the design of both the external environment and the dwellings themselves

The shortage of space within the dwelling units resulted in various types of physical alterations being made to the dwellings by the residents. The constructional quality was subject to severe criticism in almost all the estates and was a major source of dislike. In addition to the size and constructional quality of the dwellings, the spaces left between the blocks of flats appeared to be one of the detrimental aspects common to all the estates. The lack of any space hierarchy and landscape, as well as the lack of maintenance of those spaces, resulted in a poor quality of external environment which tended to affect residents' perception of their estate and lower their satisfaction with their dwellings. Whereas some efforts had been made in parts of the *Garidi* and the *Ain Nadja* estates to landscape the external spaces, and were very much appreciated by the residents, such efforts remained in general very rare. However, residents' claim for the spaces adjacent to their blocks and their initiative to landscape those spaces appear to be an alternative which should be encouraged.

The research findings suggest a number of recommendations which are directly applicable to the programming and the design of future mass housing estates in Algeria. It must be emphasised that a degree of uncertainty remains when dealing with recommendations. This means that the recommendations should be implemented initially within an experimental context and be evaluated at that stage before they are applied on a larger scale.

The public external spaces adjacent to the blocks of flats

The first items that should be subject to change in the four estates evaluated, as well as in other existing mass housing estates in Algeria, are the public external spaces adjacent to the blocks of flats. One of the findings of the present research is that residents living on different floors of the five-storey walk-up dwellings may be prompted to invest in fencing and personalising the public external spaces adjacent to their blocks. It is highly recommended that these spaces should be legally allocated to the residents. Not only is the alteration of these spaces likely to increase residents' satisfaction with their dwellings by changing their opinion about their housing environment, it will also provide the residents with a number of benefits. These benefits are as follows:

- Compensation for the small size of the dwellings by allowing a certain number of activities to be carried out in the external spaces.
- Ensuring that housewives have access to fresh air and sunlight.
- An increase in the privacy and security of the ground floor flats, which in turn should increases their popularity.
- Achieving a better definition and hierarchy in the external spaces.
- Reducing the spaces that need to be maintained by the local council. The local authorities cannot generally afford to water and nurture large public green spaces and so their maximum privatisation would result in a more pleasant overall environment with more greenery and more shade.
- Enhancing the visual quality of the environment. The use of the spaces adjacent to the blocks as private gardens would increase the amount of greenery, creating a gentle micro climate during the summer period. Furthermore, the greenery would also provide the ground floor dwellings with visual buffers and more pleasant views.
- Facilitating the upkeep of both the dwellings and the shared stairways by reducing the amount of dust in the external environment.

Such benefits depend on the willingness of the residents to maintain and landscape the external spaces, which in its turn depends partially on their size and the accessibility. How to divide the external spaces adjacent to the dwellings and how to allocate them to the residents without raising conflicts between neighbours, as well as how to ensure that the spaces are not used for purposes other than gardens or yards, remains an important area of the design of multi-family housing. This area of work would benefit from future investigation and experimentation. A number of suggestions can be made, however. It seems reasonable to believe that residents would use the spaces only if they had some degree of control over them. Such control would obviously not be possible if the residents did not have an easy visual and physical access to them. For these reasons it is suggested that the spaces adjacent to the blocks should be allocated in the main, to the residents living on the ground and first floors of the blocks. Each of these flats would be able to have a well defined fenced area. The ground floor flats should preferably be allocated the spaces immediately adjacent to them and might well have independent entrances from such spaces. An arrangement of this sort would not only provide the ground floor flats with a much greater degree of privacy and independence from the main entrance of the building, but would also eliminate the notion of unused spaces around the perimeter of the buildings. Moreover, if the ground floor flats were allocated to households with a large number of children, the number of children using the main entrance of the building and the stairways would be considerably reduced. This would have a significant impact on the level of maintenance and upkeep of these spaces. Some of the spaces adjacent to the blocks might be allocated to the residents living in the first floor flats. This means that some of the windows on the ground floor flats might open directly on the gardens belonging to the first floor flats. While this did not seem to cause problems for the cases observed during site visits, it is possible that such an arrangement could cause inconvenience for the residents living on the ground floor. However, it would still be a significant improvement for the ground floor flats to have their windows opening on their neighbour's garden rather than on noisy public spaces. Design solutions might possibly be found where some of the inconveniences caused by such arrangements could be eliminated. A number of other suggestions can be made with regard to the possible uses of the external spaces. Such suggestions include the availability of a water supply with a proper drainage system, the provision of a paved or hard surface for washing carpets and similar tasks, and a pergola or a lattice system to prevent the gardens from being overlooked. However, further research is needed in order to determine in more precise terms the floor areas of the external spaces that are to be allocated as well as the type of services that should be provided. In addition to design considerations, the legal and financial frameworks within which such space allocations are to be made also need investigation.

While the flats on the ground and the first floors would be allocated the spaces adjacent to the buildings, the flats located on the second, third and fourth floors might be given more control of private external spaces located on the flat roof of the building.

The blocks' roof

The results of the survey clearly reveal that a significant proportion of the residents were in favour of an accessible roof in order to carry out a number of activities such as washing and drying large items for which there is generally not enough space in the loggias. The allocated spaces on the top of the building should be designed, as far as possible, to allow the same activities that are carried out in the gardens to take place. The roof could be divided into private fenced spaces and each space might have its own water supply and drainage. Access to the roof should be limited to the residents living in the upper floor flats. The size of the private external spaces would obviously depend on the size of the roof and the number of households sharing it: the smaller the number of people sharing the roof, the less noise and fewer disagreements. Reducing the number of households sharing the same terrace roof means that there is more chance of the various neighbours coming to an agreement in setting their own 'rules' for preventing possible problems.

The recommendations just stated are more likely to be successful if a certain degree of social homogeneity within the blocks of flats is achieved. The adoption of a particular housing allocation policy appears to be a factor in the running of future similar housing estates which is very likely to promote a higher degree of residential satisfaction.

The Housing Allocation policy

A sensible allocation policy regarding those living in the same block of flats would seem to be one which respects the following guidelines:

- Ensures that households with reasonably similar backgrounds dwell within the same blocks of flats. A degree of social homogeneity of neighbours living in the same block of flats was found to be significantly related to a higher level of maintenance and upkeep of the shared stairways which, in turn, was significantly related to residents' satisfaction with their dwelling;
- Ensures that large households are allocated the ground and the first floor dwellings;
- Avoids the concentration of a large number of children within the blocks of flats. A low child density within the different blocks would reduce the noise generated by the children and would facilitate the maintenance and up-keep of the communal spaces;
- Ensures that the largest households are allocated the largest flats within the estate. The field study showed that this was not the case in several instances.

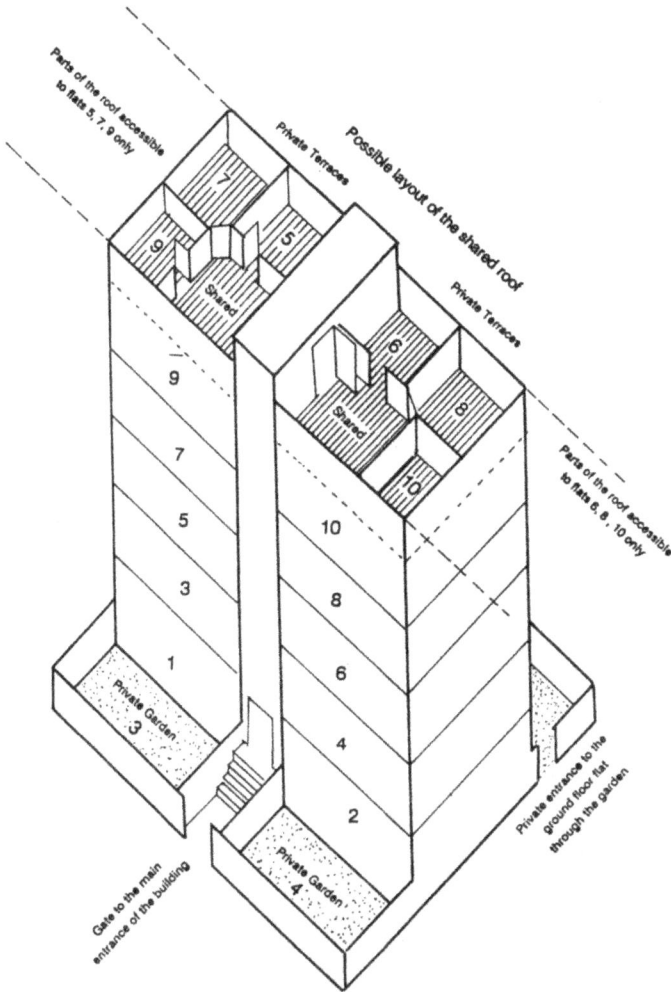

Figure 4.7 The mass housing block: possible allocation of roof and external spaces

Maintenance and upkeep

A key element in the design of multi-family housing estates is their capacity to be easily managed and easily maintained. Various types of repair work were found to be carried out within the flats in the four estates by a significant proportion of the respondents (81 per cent). Such repairs included plumbing, changing wall tiling or floor tiling, as well as filling in cracks in the walls. The availability of a maintenance office located within the estates is highly recommended, as it should not only ensure the quick repair of faults but would also prevent a rapid degradation of the fabric of the mass housing dwellings. In addition to the repair work, the maintenance office would also have a number of cleaners with clearly laid out responsibilities for cleaning the staircases of the different blocks. As well as frequent cleaning of the communal spaces, a number of other factors have been found related to the cleanliness of those spaces. These factors are:

- The number of households using the stairways;
- The child density within the block of flats;
- The degree of agreement between the neighbours living in the same block.

As stated in the previous section, these factors could well be brought about through a more rational housing allocation policy. Other factors where design improvements might be made are:

- In the physical features of the communal stairways, in terms of their day-lighting quality and the type and quality of the finishing materials, such as floor and stair tiling and wall painting;
- A restriction on access to the communal stairways in order to give the residents more control of, and a responsible feeling towards, the communal spaces.

The private external spaces adjacent to the block of flats should provide a transitional space between the public spaces and the semi-public stairways. This would to some extent prevent strangers' access to stairways. The flats' entrances should **not** be located on the part of the landing immediately adjacent to the stairs (this raised some complaints among the respondents) but should be placed within a semi-private space extending from the landing. Such arrangements would provide the flats with a transitional space leading to the staircase and would ensure more privacy within the dwellings.

Whereas the recommendations previously stated are directly applicable to either existing or future mass housing projects and deal mainly with the housing environment **outside** the dwellings, the following recommendations are applicable to the design of the dwellings themselves.

The dwelling

A number of features in the design of the mass housing dwellings were criticised by the respondents in the four studied estates. The examination of the *Bab Ezzouar* and the *Ain Nadja* estates allowed the researcher to identify a number of aspects that tended to be strongly disliked by the majority of the respondents. On the other hand, the examination of dwelling design in the *Garidi* and the *Ain Allah* estates made the identification of positive features possible. Among the features of the dwellings found to be significantly related to residents' satisfaction was the size of the kitchen..

The kitchen

The kitchen is one of the spaces in the dwelling that should undoubtedly be given priority in the design process. The results of the present study show that a floor area of 12 square metres is very likely to be satisfactory and promote a higher level of dwelling satisfaction. The location of the kitchen and the loggia doors, as well as the location of the window, should allow enough free wall surface for hanging storage units and for placing the refrigerator. More wall surface could be made available if the sink and the working surface were placed under the window. If the shape of the kitchen is rectangular, the working surface should preferably be placed along the width rather than along the length of the kitchen. Sufficient wall tiling should be provided next to the working surface and should not be limited to two rows only. The cooker should **not** be placed near the kitchen or the loggia doors. All the kitchens should have direct access to the loggia, for the reasons outlined in the next section.

The kitchen's loggia

There seemed to be contradictory needs in relation to the degree of openness of the loggia. Whereas a certain degree of privacy was required for the housewife standing in loggia, the need for good exposure of the laundry to the sun's rays seemed to be more important, as a significant number of complaints were raised regarding this matter. Privacy in the loggia should not be achieved at the expense of a good ventilation and good exposure to the sun's rays. It appears to be preferable for the loggias to have two parts: one which would be open and used for drying the washing and a second which would be screened and could be used for washing and/or cooking. Another alternative would be a flexible design allowing the housewives to open or screen the loggia, depending on the activity taking place. The loggias should be provided with a number of facilities such as a sink and adequate water drainage as well as a built in storage space. A North orientation for the loggia should be avoided and its floor area should be a minimum of five square metres.

The bathroom and WC

Because the vast majority of the respondents use the bathroom for washing the laundry either in a washing machine or in the bath itself, it appears that a satisfactory arrangement would be to have a direct access from the bathroom to the loggia in order to aid the transfer of the washing to the laundry lines. The opening of the bathroom to the loggia would also ensure better ventilation and a comfortable level of daylight within the bathroom. However, such an arrangement should not affect the privacy within the bathroom. The WC should also have natural light and ventilation with an opening directly onto the facade or on the loggia.

The living room

The size of the living room should be determined according to the type and size of the furniture items generally available on the local market and which tend to be used by the residents. Twenty square metres should be satisfactory providing that the shape of the space is closer to a square. The positions of the doors and the window should allow maximum free wall surface. The size of the living room should be increased by not providing a balcony but adding its floor area to the living room total floor area.

The dwelling size

The results of this study also show that flat size is one of the major problems residents face with their dwelling and is the major reason for closing off the private external spaces provided with the dwellings. The small number of available bedrooms is further aggravated by the worsening acute shortage of housing. This results in a return to the extended family within the two bedroom dwelling, which may then be subject to either minor or major alterations ranging from the closing off the balconies to the conversion of the kitchen into a bedroom and the conversion of the loggia into a kitchen. Such alterations have also been observed in similar housing projects in other countries such as Egypt (Steinberg, 1984) and

Baghdad (Al Noori, 1987). The distress brought about by overcrowded housing conditions may provoke uncontrolled extensions and construction activities by the inhabitants. Such activities have been observed in similar mass housing estates in Egypt (Steinberg, 1984; Tipple et al., 1985), where the shortage of housing is even worse than in Algeria. Although the general tendency in the present housing construction policy is to reduce the size of the dwellings in order to produce a greater number of dwelling units, the results of the present work suggest that, in order to avoid problems in the future and in order to avoid a rapid degradation of the newly built housing stock, a larger proportion of three-roomed flats should be provided within the mass housing estates and these should be allocated to large households. Because of the limited degree of housing mobility available, adaptations and extensions should be conceived as part of the long term future of mass housing dwellings in order to allow for the changing needs of the residents. Extensions could be planned through either the closing off of available private external spaces, or through actual extensions of the building structure. Recent changes in Algerian housing policy encourage the involvement of the private sector in solving the housing problems of middle class households. This means that low-income households should have priority in the allocation policy of the subsidised mass housing dwellings. A better knowledge of the future residents of the mass housing dwellings, and their involvement in a number of decisions concerning the design and the management of their housing environments, is highly recommended.

It is likely that the findings of this study are not confined to the four selected estates. More studies are needed at a national level in order to improve the design of the mass housing dwellings in different parts of the country. Small scale experimental projects should be built where the present recommendations could be brought about in a variety of ways. These experimental projects should themselves be subject to further evaluative studies. Post-occupancy evaluation should be carried out as routine, on a cyclical basis, with effective feedback mechanisms. Such mechanisms should permit the regular updating of design recommendations and the formation of databases necessary for the improved design of housing.

Bibliography

Al Noori, W. (1987), *Environmental design evaluation of multifamily housing in Baghdad: Users' satisfaction with the external areas*, PhD thesis, Department of Landscape Architecture, University of Sheffiels: Sheffield.

Behloul, M. (1991), *Post occupancy evaluation of five-storey walk-up dwellings: The case of four mass housing estates in Algiers*, PhD thesis, Department of Architectural Studies, University of Sheffield: Sheffield.

Benamrane, D. (1980), *Crise de l'habitat: Perspectives des développement socialiste en Algérie*, Crea-Sned: Algiers. In French.

Benmatti, N. (1982), *L'Habitat du tiersm-monde: Cas de l'Algérie*, Sned: Algiers. In French.

Boubekeur, S. (1986), *L'Habitat en Algérie, Stratégies d'acteurs et logiques industrielles*, Office des Publications Universitaires (Opu): Algiers. In French.

El-Moudjahid. (1988), *Supplément Social*, 18 April, Algiers, p.7. In French.

Francescato, G., Weidemann, S., et al. (1979), *Residents' satisfaction in hud-assisted housing: Design and management factors*, US Department of Housing and Urban Development: Washington, DC.

Guerroudj, T. (1990), 'L'Habitat en Algérie', International Seminar on *Stratégie D'habitat et Cohérence Urbaine*, Algiers, 1-12, Unpublished paper presented at conference. In French.

INERBA (Institut National d'Etudes et de Recherches du Batiment). (1980), *Procédés de construction: Etudes générales de développement du secteur du batiment*, Ministère de l'Urbanisme, de la Construction et de l'Habitat: Algiers. In French.

Marcuse, P. (1971), 'Social indicators and housing policy.' *Urban Affairs*, Vol. 7, No. December, pp.193-217.

MUCH (Ministry of Urban Planning Construction and Housing). (1979), *Prescriptions fonctionnelles et techniques, normes, recommandations et instructions relatives au logement social urban*, Algiers.

ONS. (1988), *Statistiques, armature urbaine, 1987*, part of the series 'Les collections des statistiques', Vol. 4, Office National des Statistiques: Algiers.

Rapoport, A. (1985), 'Thinking about home environments: A conceptual framework', in Altman, I. and Werner, C.M. (eds), *Home environments*, Vol. 8, Plenum: New York, pp.255-286.

Santelli, S. (1987), 'Self-built urban housing, Rabat and Tunis.' *Minar Architecture In Development*, Vol. 17, pp.41-48.

Steinberg, F. (1984), '*Ain El Sira* in Cairo - The architecture of poverty.' *Open House International*, Vol. 9, No. 2, pp.35-42.

Tipple, A.G., Wilkinson, N., et al. (1985), 'The transformation of Workers' City, Helwan multi-storey extensions observed.' *Open House International*, Vol. 10, No. 3, pp.25-38.

Waltz, S. (1985), 'Women's housing needs in the Arab context of Tunisia.' *Ekistics*, Vol. 310, No. Jan/Feb, pp.23-33.

Weidemann, S., and Anderson, J.R. (1985), 'A conceptual framework for residential satisfaction', in Altman, J. and Werner, C.M. (eds), *Home environments*, Vol. 8, rienum Press: New York.

Yahiaoui, M.S. (1983), 'Complexité technologique et perspectives de l'industrialisation de la construction en Algérie', *Le développement économique, theories et politiques en Afrique*, Office des Publications Universitaires (OPU): Algiers. In French.

5 The attitude of Libyan families to their traditional and contemporary houses

ABUBAKER M. SHAWESH and ADENRELE AWOTONA

Introduction

The geographical location, socio-cultural values and climate played a major role in shaping the urban pattern as well as the house form in the old town of Ghadames. The Ghadamesian house clearly reflects the user's response to the harsh environmental conditions, the need to sustain the social organisation and to respect social and cultural traditions. This chapter examines user perception of both the traditional and 'modern' (Western) houses by determining the degree of satisfaction with them. The study is based on a survey carried out in the Ghadames oasis in November 1995. Ghadames is located in the Libyan Sahara Desert and forms a part of the sub-region of Gharyan, one of the five sub-regions of the Tripoli region. It lies 630 km south-west of Tripoli, close to the junction with the borders of Algeria and Tunisia and is situated at an altitude of 350 metres above sea level (Figure 5.1). It is one of the most important trade routes, connecting central Africa with the Mediterranean sea coast. All these factors make Ghadames the most important of the Libyan cities. In fact, Ghadames has been inscribed on the world Heritage list of historic monuments by UNESCO since 1987.

The social structure among the Ghadames population is based on a tight hierarchy. The tribal division is clearly part of the political and social structure of the oasis community (Eldblon, 1968). Confederations are subdivided into tribes, tribes into clans, and often clans into subclans. However, the family is the simplest and most important form of social structure in the old town of Ghadames. It is still highly patriarchal; its cohesion is protected and maintained by the system of matrimonial alliances and also by different social measures designed to keep the families as strong as possible. The influence of the family upon the house can be clearly seen in the house design particularly in the organisation of space.

117

Social life in the old town of Ghadames oasis was most conservative. Females were usually separated from the public life. For this reason the traditional Ghadamesian house was the outcome of the socio-cultural factors as well as climatic requirements and experiences, all contributing to its design. The main considerations were the necessity for privacy, security and proximity to water. However, more important is the social way in which divisions were reflected in physical terms by the division of the house into two distinct sections: a strictly private space to ensure that family life was completely protected from the outside world, where no glimpse could be caught from the street, even when the house entrance remained open, and a semi-private space where male guests could be entertained.

The city now also has a new Government built settlement. There are 616 housing units in this project which was designed and built by a foreign company. They were built in the 1980s as the ideal solution to the housing demand in the city.

This chapter consists of four sections. The first looks at the character of the traditional house. The second discusses the growth of Ghadames city as a result of the large revenue from petroleum during the oil boom period. The third documents the characteristics of the contemporary house. The fourth reports the main findings from the survey of user satisfaction with their traditional and contemporary houses.

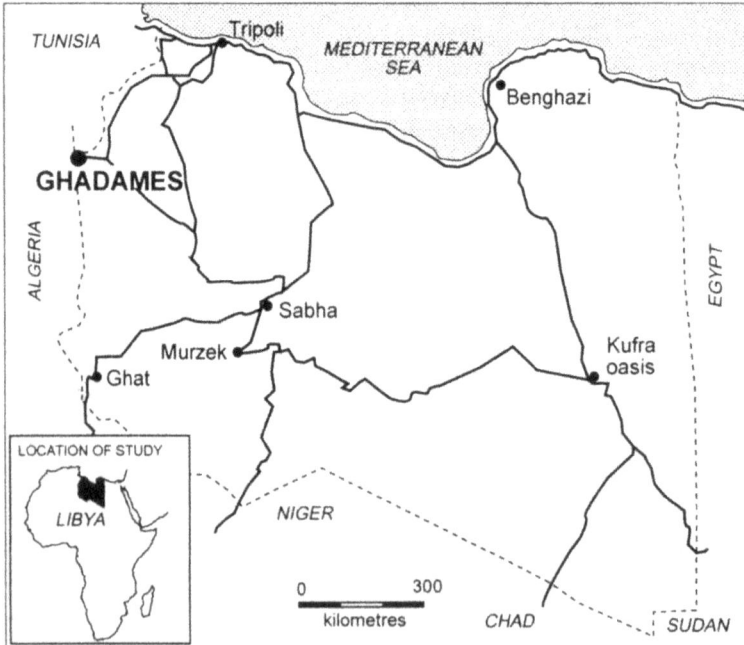

Figure 5.1   Geographical location of Ghadames

The character of the traditional home

The traditional settlement was organised and governed according to socio-cultural and climatic needs, and this clearly shows that an overall social unity was established in this settlement. Despite the fact that the settlement dates back more than 2,000 years, the townscape features proved that the spatial pattern of the traditional residential area related directly to the traditional social organisation. According to Piccioli (1935, p.209),

> In few places on earth, I believe, is one dominated, as at Ghadames, by that singular charm which is exercised by traces of a vanished way of life, of a world that has lasted from immemorial times. Everything here is as it has been for centuries.

Consequently the separation of spaces into a hierarchy, from totally private to completely public, can be seen clearly.

The old settlement of Ghadames is located in the south-west of the oasis and forms one large agglomeration of houses (Figures 5.2 and 5.3). It consists of about 2,120 dwelling units, markets, mosques and other public spaces.

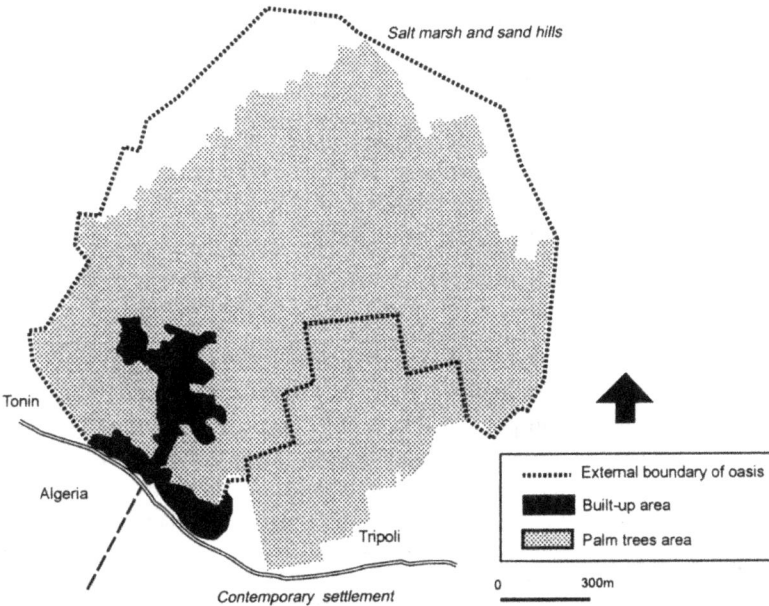

Figure 5.2   Location of the traditional Ghadames settlement
Source: After Eldblon (1968)

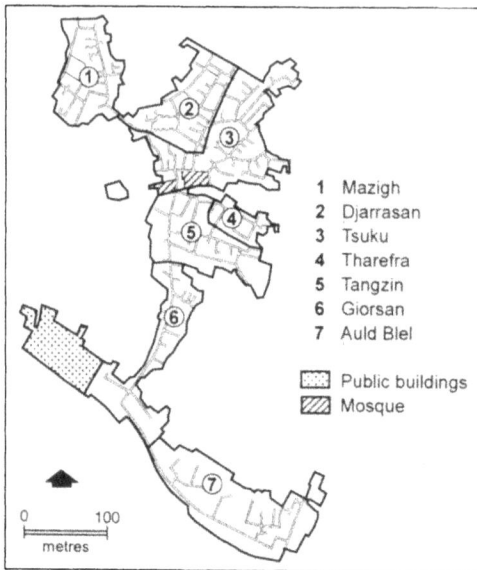

**Figure 5.3   The seven neighbourhoods of the traditional Ghadames
settlement**
Source: After Eldblon (1968)

Ghadamesian house design represents a clear expression of the socio-cultural
values held by Libyan society and provides a clear illustration of the way in which
the original architects responded to the climate and users' living requirements in
the settlement, neighbourhood and house in particular.

House form and size

When one looks at the traditional Ghadames house for the first time, one is
surprised because the eye sees something that it has never seen before. One also
gets a strange feeling about the place, because the homes are well designed and
beautifully constructed. The Ghadamesian people put all their abilities into
building their homes. They make their homes very comfortable in terms of climate
and social needs. The architectural form in the old town of Ghadames suits local
requirements, climatic conditions and ethnic needs. It is a compact architecture to
protect its users from the hostile environment. All buildings are constructed
entirely from local building materials. The house form allows only a few visible
facades, rising in an almost fortified manner to a height of about 10 metres. The
houses in this complex are of the same basic design, only slightly different in size

and decoration, for example, in the number of bedrooms, or in the area of the living room in the middle of the house. Despite the differences in some of these elements, the uniformity of the houses is apparent. The similarity in scale, colours and main forms are the reasons for this.

Interestingly, houses in old Ghadames town are characterised by the lack of open courtyards, which is a distinct feature of most houses in other parts of the country. It seems that the people of Ghadames may have paid more attention to the house form and its articulation as an important mechanism responding to climate and social conditions.

There is a shortage of agricultural land and therefore the plot area of these houses may range from 25 to 50 square metres with the house area ranging between 70 to 80 square metres. There are some standard areas for the inside elements of Ghadames houses: the area of the bedrooms is between five and 12 square metres, the area of the living room is between 10 and 16 square metres, the area of the bathroom is between four and six square metres, and the area of the store rooms 20 square metres. The actual age of the building form is very difficult to assess, due to it having evolved over a long period of time. Ghadames does not seem to have been influenced by colonial architecture style, whether Phoenician, Garamants, Greek, Roman or Italian. It is unique amongst Islamic style and design. It is also argued below that the plan and architecture of the town is part of the original ancient Arab traditional architecture (Figures 5.4, 5.5, 5.6 & 5.7 show Ghadamesian house plans).

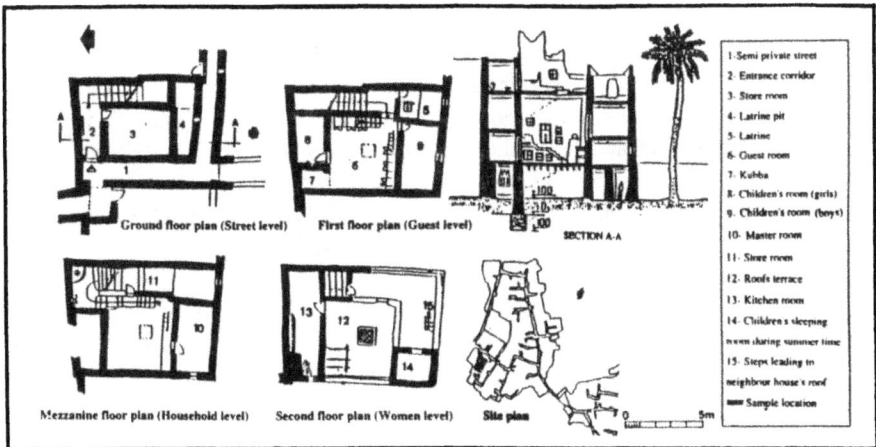

Figure 5.4   Layout of a traditional Ghadames house

House design and space use

According to the house plan shown in Figure 5.4, it can clearly be seen that the Ghadamesian house is an institution, not just a structure, founded for a complex set of purposes. Building a house is a cultural phenomenon, its form and organisation are greatly influenced by the socio-cultural environment and way of life. This has been reflected in the physical form of the Ghadamesian traditional house. There are three distinct floors in the house, each floor adapted to a different use. The main entrance is on the ground floor where there is a single entrance door, made of palm tree trunk. This entrance usually opens directly on to the covered semi-private street about 1.40m wide. It is fitted with a heavy iron lock which can be operated by means of a key from outside. To secure this door from inside there is also a sliding wooden bolt. The common features of this door emphasise the sharp line between external public areas and private internal ones. Leading from the main door is the entrance hall, *sqifa*. In the entrance hall there is often a bench for sitting where the house owner may rest as he comes from his work, or the visitor who comes to call at the house. This is a private and secure place where a person is given the feeling of relaxation and safety.

Two interesting features can be observed in the *sqifa*, one is that it is considered very important to hang gazelle or antelope horns above the door frame to prevent an evil spirit from entering the house, the other being a niche for an oil lamp near the main door. When the oil lamp is placed in the middle of the niche, it indicates that the family is willing to receive visitors. If placed to the right, the visitor will know that this a time of family happiness, such as a wedding or a new baby's arrival is being celebrated, and the visitor will therefore know whether he can meet the household members. If the lamp is placed on the left it is a sign that there is sadness in the house, perhaps a death, and if the light is turned off this is a sign that the household wishes to be left alone. On the ground floor there is access to a store room used for agricultural tools; it measures 4.75m by 3.50m and is quite dark. It is usually located near the main entrance corridor. The whitewashed staircase is designed to enable visitors to ascend or descend without being seen by people on the different floor levels. It is built like a piece of sculpture, and leads to the upper floors. As a general rule, each corner and each available space of the house has a function. Drinking jars are placed in a round niche in the wall of the last landing of the grand staircase. These jars form a very beautiful decoration, which are usually brought by the bride at wedding time. Additionally there is a room with a pit for the latrine above.

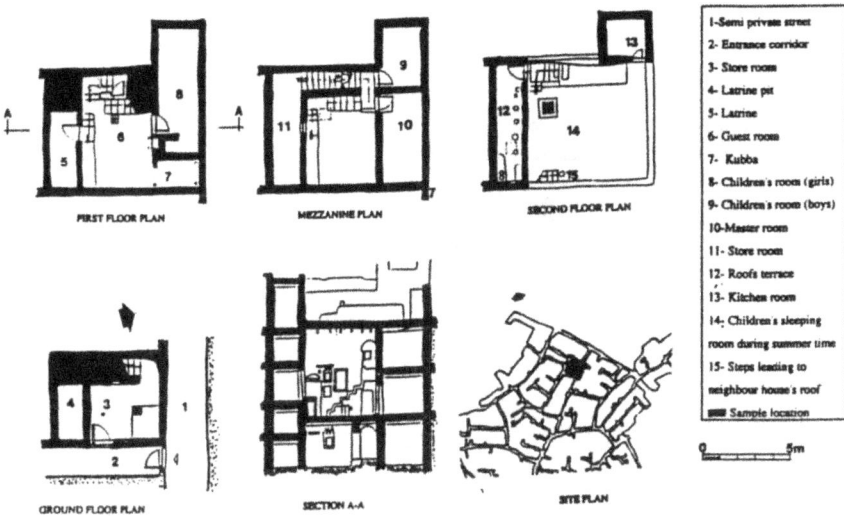

1- Semi private street
2- Entrance corridor
3- Store room
4- Latrine pit
5- Latrine
6- Guest room
7- Kubba
8- Children's room (girls)
9- Children's room (boys)
10- Master room
11- Store room
12- Roofs terrace
13- Kitchen room
14- Children's sleeping room during summer time
15- Steps leading to neighbour house's roof
▬ Sample location

0 _____ 5m

Figure 5.5   Layout of a traditional Ghadames house in the Djarrasan neighbourhood

One of the design features of the Ghadamesian traditional house reflects the modesty between males and females. This need for modesty is achieved by the vertical arrangement of the house; the males have free movement in streets and squares at the ground floor level and females having free movement above street level, and in a big living room with a double floor to ceiling height known as the 'middle home' (*wast El-Housash*). This central space is used as the living area of the house, and is the most important room of the house. It also functions as a guest room in which the owner receives his guests, and it is here that the decoration is concentrated. Generally this room is arranged in a way that allows male visitors and guests easy access without disturbing the privacy of female members of the household.

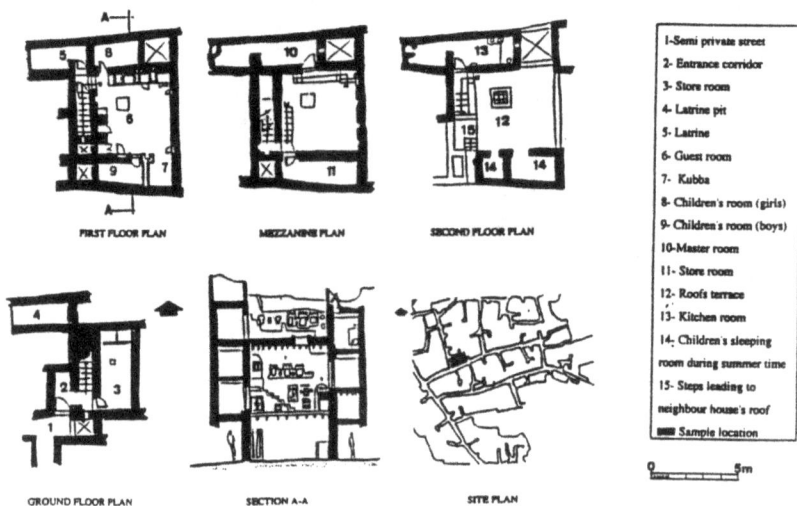

1-Semi private street	
2- Entrance corridor	
3- Store room	
4- Latrine pit	
5- Latrine	
6- Guest room	
7- Kubba	
8- Children's room (girls)	
9- Children's room (boys)	
10-Master room	
11- Store room	
12- Roofs terrace	
13- Kitchen room	
14- Children's sleeping room during summer time	
15- Steps leading to neighbour house's roof	
▬▬ Sample location	

FIRST FLOOR PLAN   MEZZANINE PLAN   SECOND FLOOR PLAN

GROUND FLOOR PLAN   SECTION A-A   SITE PLAN

Figure 5.6   Layout of a traditional Ghadames house in the Tangzin neighbourhood

The most interesting room is at the same level as the middle home, and is called *elkubba*. It is a small space and is reserved for two special occasions, the first being when a women marries and the second when her husband dies. The space is used for one night only, for the first night of the marriage (when it is richly and traditionally furnished and decorated) and when the husband dies, when the widow spends the night there. Her son, if living in the same house, could bring his newly married wife to spend the first night in this place. Additional rooms have access directly from the living room, either at floor level or at mezzanine level; in the latter case, with a flight of steps inside the room. The mezzanine level mainly consists of the master bedroom and two stores for clothes and grain. This floor is used by all members of the household during day time, and used by husband and wife at night in complete privacy. All these rooms are ventilated and lit through the main living room sky light, and some windows opening into the well. They are furnished simply and adequately with carpets and mats, although the living room, where male guests are entertained, receives more attention than the other rooms.

Figure 5.7   Layout of a traditional Ghadames house in the Tharefra neighbourhood

The Ghadamesian house layout ensures visual privacy from outside or adjacent areas, yet allows members of the household to be in contact with nature via the roofs. Thus, the roof level was considered to be one of the most important parts of the house (Figure 5.8). It played a significant social role, containing a cluster of kitchen cubes, courtyards and terraces reserved for the women to conduct most of their activities, including cooking, washing and traditional crafts such as making mats and carpets. It also serves as their meeting place, allowing them to visit their neighbours in any part of the town. This is possible because all the town houses are connected to each other by terraces covering the lower streets. This allows the women considerable freedom of movement and communication which parallels the men's movement and communication in the lower streets, and gives opportunities to meet each other in complete privacy and security without contravening the traditional segregation of the sexes. The roofs are surrounded by a high parapet wall, about two metres in height, to ensure privacy. Moreover, household members use the roof extensively during the summer nights for gathering and sleeping, enjoying cool night breezes.

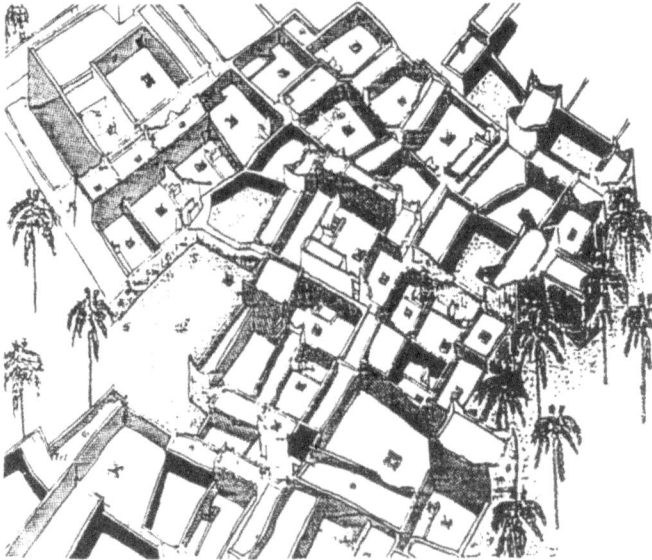

Figure 5.8   Plan of traditional rooftop area in Ghadames

When a death occurs in the family, the women in the house climb to the upper passage: and their lamenting can be heard by their neighbours, who share in their grief and sadness. On happy occasions such as marriages, the women also gather together to sing and dance and celebrate, and they convey the bride across the roofs to her new home. The beautiful view from the top of the houses adds to the pleasure of happy celebrations and gives solace at times of sadness. The men, at these times of mourning or happiness, gather together in the street squares, and on the ground floor.

Ghadamesian house decoration

The Ghadamesian house also has unique characteristics where decoration is concerned, for it is one of the most outstanding, and regarded as one of the best, desert habitations developed by local builders with a richness of decoration (Hassan, 1982). Ghadamesian people are extremely concerned with their home's decoration; they use many expressive materials, ranging from locally made paint, to mirrors, brass, tapestries, pictures of saints, objects of local handicraft, and souvenirs inherited from the caravan trade. All these elements are arranged on the walls, mainly by the Ghadamesian women, but are concentrated within the living room. Interior doorways are framed and decorated by the women of the household who choose and decorate the living room walls with stucco moulding.

The most adapted form of decoration in the Ghadamesian house is the wall paint which the women are proficient at making. The interior walls are all plastered with gypsum and whitewashed and decorated with motifs painted in a bright red. Red is the preferred colour, used inside the rooms, and, together with mirrors and various utensils hanging on the walls, combines to make a delightful interior. The external walls have a general appearance characterised by the brownish and pale yellow colours of the sundried clay bricks. Conical patterning on the top of the walls and the stepped finials at the corners are whitewashed, providing a characteristic feature to the external appearance of the house. Besides the spectacular visual effect, these measures also improve the capacity of the walls to resist weathering and general deterioration. Moreover, a particular conical pattern on the top of the external walls was an ancient form of protection against evil spirits in the days before Islam became the religion of the people. This design can also be seen on the city walls showing that the people wished to protect their city. This pattern was also brought into the interior walls when the dwellers were decorating their home with red to protect their family members.

Building materials and methods

All buildings are constructed entirely from local materials, mainly limestone or sun-dried clay brick for walls. Gypsum or lime and clay are used for mortar, and bisected and smoothed trunks of palm trees for ceilings and roofs. The buildings are integrated into one complex structure in which it is hardly possible to distinguish the individual houses. The Ghadamesian house structural system has resulted from the types and strength of building materials that were found available in the oasis or near Ghadames, such as lime and gypsum which are produced in the village of Tonin, three kilometres west of Ghadames.

In the horizontal floors, divisions are constructed by bisected and smoothed trunks of palm trees; the wood should be kept to dry for one year before use and treated twice with a wood preservative made from a solution of dates, salt and lime. About 30 different kinds of palm trees provide materials of varying properties: gypsum and lime for plaster were produced in the vicinity of Ghadames, but only a few people now practise the old craft of providing these materials. For example craftsmen preferred to use *Tamudi* palm trees in floors because they provided more flexibility and resistance to deflection. Ribs of palm leaves are left in water for three months before plaiting to provide support for the upper floor slab. The slab consists of light stones and mud with a floor screed of gypsum (Figure 5.9).

The latrine is situated on the first floor next to the main staircase. It empties down into a pit located in a separate room in the ground floor. The latrine pit is constructed of stone and measures about two metres square. When used regularly by one family it is necessary to empty it only once a year. After each visit, ashes from the pit are thrown into the latrine pit to prevent any smell coming from the latrine. The fermented contents of the pit become dry and friable, providing a useful fertiliser for the fields.

The building materials which were available for building the old town houses are:

1. Mud
2. Hard lime stone
3. Pumice stone
4. Palm trees - trunk, leaf stalks and leaves
5. Gypsum
6. Chopped straw

With these six very simple building materials, Ghadamesians used to build their houses in the middle of the Sahara Desert. Many factors determine the selection of specific types of materials: the economic structure of the society, experience with certain types of materials and methods of construction, the level of technology, the urge to adapt certain dwelling forms and climatic conditions.

All load bearing walls are constructed of sun-dried clay brick on a foundation constructed of hard limestone in a mud mortar. The foundation trench does not exceed one metre in depth. The thickness of the walls diminishes from the bottom of the house to the top, corresponding to the size of the bricks. The walls measure 60 by 40 by 15 centimetres at ground floor level, 50 by 40 by 15 centimetres at first floor level and 40 by 40 by 15 centimetres at second floor level. The bricks

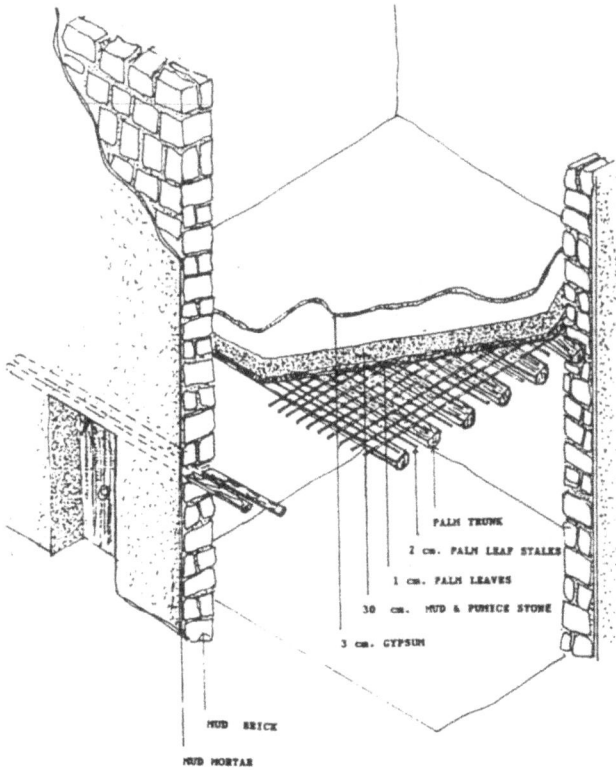

PALM TRUNK

2 cm. PALM LEAF STALKS

1 cm. PALM LEAVES

30 cm. MUD & PUMICE STONE

3 cm. GYPSUM

MUD BRICK

MUD MORTAR

Figure 5.9   Building materials used in traditional Ghadames houses

are made from mud mixed with straw. The raw materials should be left in moist conditions for at least one year before being used to produce bricks.

The main materials used in the floors and roofs are palm trunks used as beams, either as whole pieces or cut into lengths. They are spaced 50 to 70 centimetres apart. On top of these beams the palm leaf stalks are placed horizontally. On top of these more palm leaves are laid in the opposite direction. Mud mixed with small pumice stones is then laid on top of the structure. The last stage is a layer of gypsum as a floor or roof finish.

The stairs are usually constructed with light pumice stone and gypsum mortar. First, an arched structure is constructed carrying the steps of the stairs then, these steps are finished in gypsum. The lintels above the doors and windows are constructed by two methods: the palm trunk lintel, which works like a beam to distribute the load in two directions, and is used always in the main entrance, other doors and windows. The second method can be found in traditional houses which have been built by the self-help process, which usually takes a period of about one year to complete. Materials needed usually are 20,000 mud bricks, 800 metres of palm trunk, 1,500 palm branches, 20,000 kg. gypsum and 2,000 kg. lime. As in many desert habitats, openings are very limited and the small Ghadames house contains about 10 doors and 3 to 5 windows (Shawesh, 1992).

Finally the Ghadames traditional dwelling, successfully preserves its ancient history in its artefacts, decorations and architecture. The traditional Ghadames house could be described as a museum representing the family and its preceding generations. Socio-cultural forces and environmental forces are the boundaries which affected both the settlement and its architectural contents. The house reflects an ingenious method of shelter design using limited resources and space to meet physical, functional and socio-cultural needs as well as to modify the harsh conditions for the benefit of the human inhabitant.

Development of Ghadames city

The economic growth that resulted from oil production affected the socio-physical characteristics of Ghadames city like the other cities in Libya. The city witnessed a massive modern building boom in both public and private sectors, especially in terms of housing, which transformed Ghadames from a small town to a large city (Figure 5.10). The main purpose of these new dwellings was to meet the pressing need for housing. However, the issue of the socio-cultural values that influenced the Ghadames traditional settlement had been completely ignored in their design. This fact was emphasised by Ben Swessi (1993, p.16) 'the new housing project was crude and is lacking in sensitivity to local traditions, values and climate'. It was designed by foreign architects in complete conflict with traditional housing design, construction methods and building arrangements. Furthermore, it is located outside of the Ghadames oasis, in a harsh unprotected area where there is no water or greenery.

Characteristics of the contemporary house

The contemporary settlement of Ghadames was affected by the concept of the master plan, which was based on Western models of development. It was characterised by isolated structures, high standards of construction and building materials, large spaces and modern infrastructure as well as dwellings randomly grouped (Figure 5.11). From the new master plan proposal, it can be seen that there was a greater amount of attention given to public open spaces, roads,

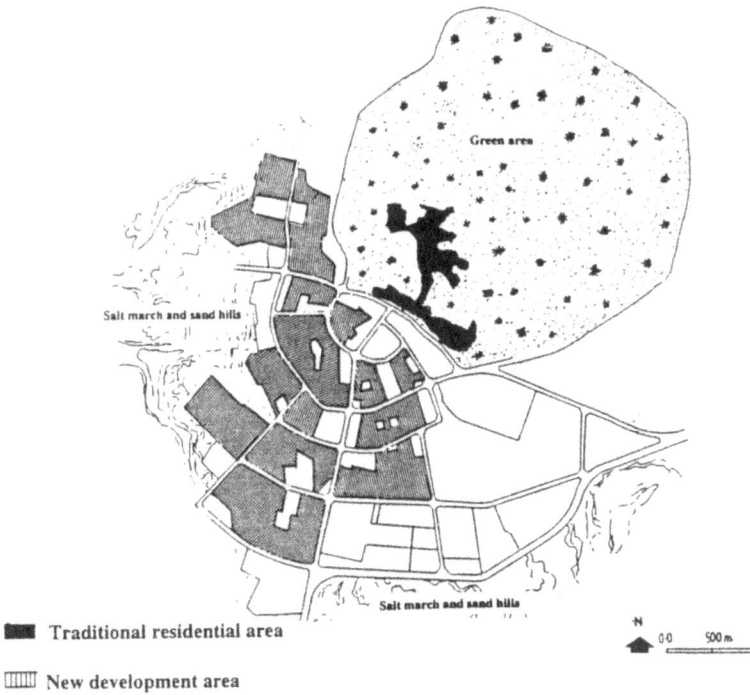

Traditional residential area

New development area

Figure 5.10   Ghadames new development
Source: Fieldwork (1995)

commercial activities and car parking spaces than to the residential areas. Despite the fact that the dispersed layout provided more space, better access and facilities than the compact traditional layout of the old town, it is clear that it did not respond effectively to the social and climatic conditions of Ghadames. The new plan for housing did not take into consideration the importance of kinship, religion and family structure, which had been the basis for the traditional way of life and so has created problems and friction between neighbours, leading to social disharmony.

The structural system of the new dwelling can be simply described as a skeleton structure, where reinforced concrete is used for columns, beams, floors and roofs, and hollow cement blocks are used for walls. The dwelling unit is based on separate architectural masses, new building codes and new building materials. Sometimes there is a mixture of residential and commercial activities in the same building. If we look at the dwellings' plan and sections in the new town from the

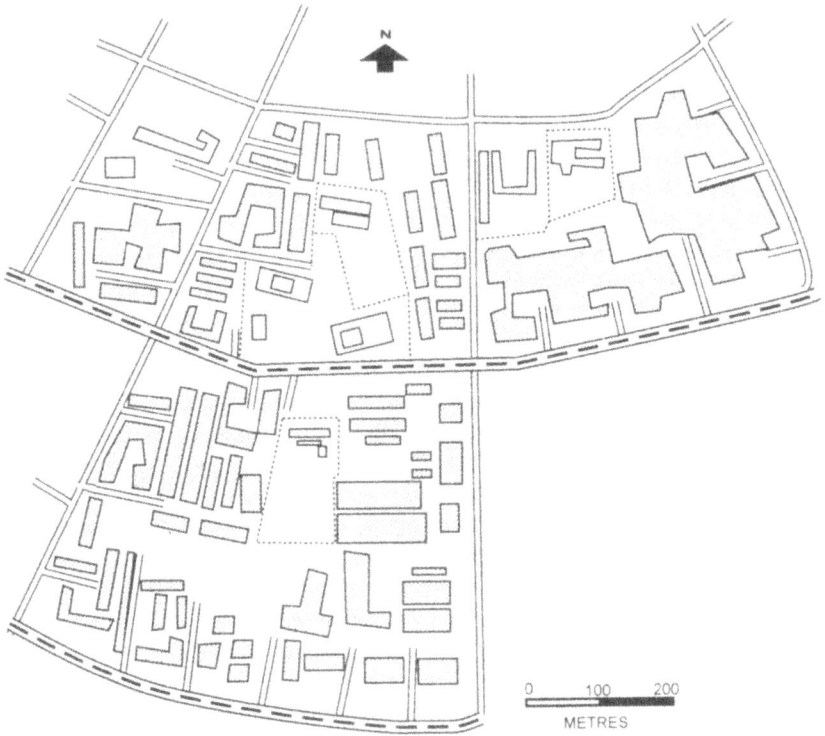

Figure 5.11 Ghadames contemporary settlement master plan
Source: Fieldwork (1995)

inside, it consists of different levels, depending on the type of dwelling.   The
contemporary dwellings are characterised by a lack of similarity in terms of form,
size and distribution of elements.   All the dwellings' openings are large and face
directly onto the outside public space.   In addition, there are large unprotected
openings overlooking the neighbouring houses, the wide asphalt unshaded streets
and passages.   The size and position of these openings have a great impact on the
private indoor space.

   Figures 5.12, 5.13, 5.14 and 5.15 represent the typical space arrangements in
contemporary dwellings.   The ground floor in the plan shown in Figure 5.12 has
only a single main entrance, a living room, a guest room, a bathroom used by the
visitors and family members located in front of the guest room.   The kitchen,
where the women normally spend much of their time, is located on the ground
floor near the guests' area.   In addition, the kitchen window opens directly to the
outside, or to the neighbouring dwelling creating privacy problems.   There is also a
room used by family members or female visitors and a staircase up to the next
floor.   The first floor is designed as a family sleeping area only and includes one

room used as store or kitchen, as well as a balcony. The balcony is a foreign element inherited from the Italians. Its purpose is to give additional space to the dwelling but the socio-cultural and climatic problems make the use of the balcony extremely difficult.

The built environment in general, and housing in particular, reflect changes in society. In Ghadames contemporary town this is clearly evident in the development of the housing design, from traditional houses to various housing types. The contemporary dwelling was influenced by the Western plan which affected the internal arrangement of space and made access to such houses, particularly when the family has a visitor, very difficult. This happened because the contemporary dwelling was designed by architects who did not have adequate information about the socio-cultural factors and ways of life of the people for whom they were designing.

In an area like Ghadames where the socio-cultural values and hostile climatic conditions are dominant, outdoor and open spaces need to be treated just as carefully as indoor spaces. In other words, both of them need to respect people's socio-cultural conventions and the need to be protected from the hostile climate. However, in Ghadames contemporary town the dwellings are free standing, the asphalt streets and passages are wide and lack any place for users to meet or sit and also lack any shade to protect people from the heat. Another important point is that the new settlement lacks harmony and unity due to the different and alien building forms.

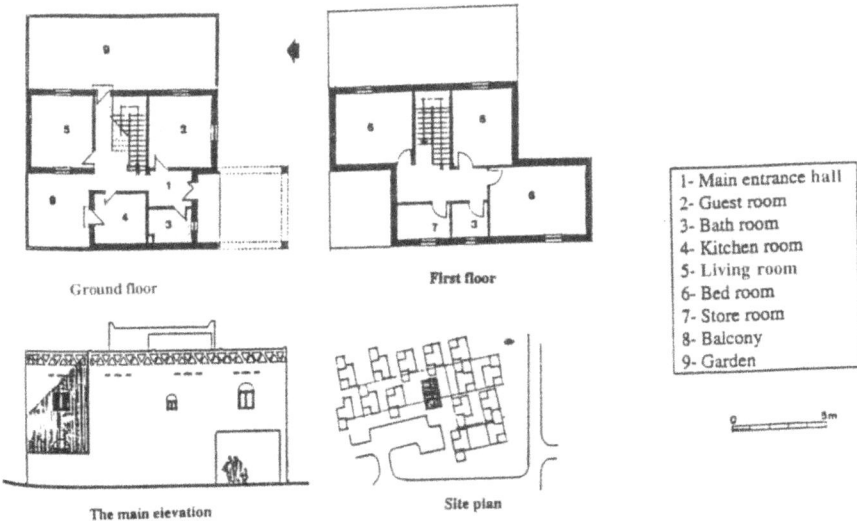

1- Main entrance hall
2- Guest room
3- Bath room
4- Kitchen room
5- Living room
6- Bed room
7- Store room
8- Balcony
9- Garden

Ground floor

First floor

The main elevation

Site plan

Figure 5.12   Plan of a three bedroom contemporary Ghadamesian house
Source: Fieldwork (1995)

The fact that the inhabitants of the new town always return to their old houses during religious, wedding and fraternal occasions, as well as during the hottest periods, demonstrates the functional achievements of the traditional architecture. It ought to be seriously considered that the local traditional house form should provide a model for new building in the desert.

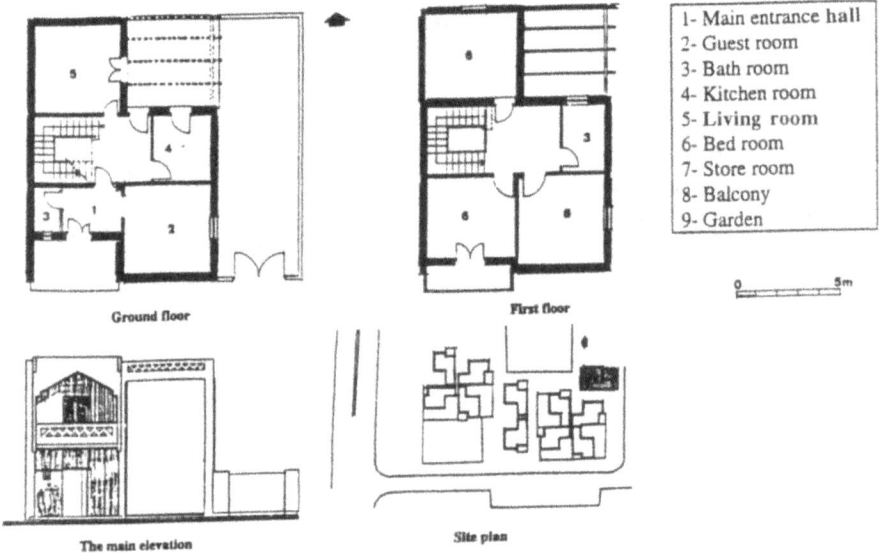

1- Main entrance hall
2- Guest room
3- Bath room
4- Kitchen room
5- Living room
6- Bed room
7- Store room
8- Balcony
9- Garden

Figure 5.13   An alternative plan of a three bedroom contemporary Ghadamesian house
Source: Fieldwork (1995)

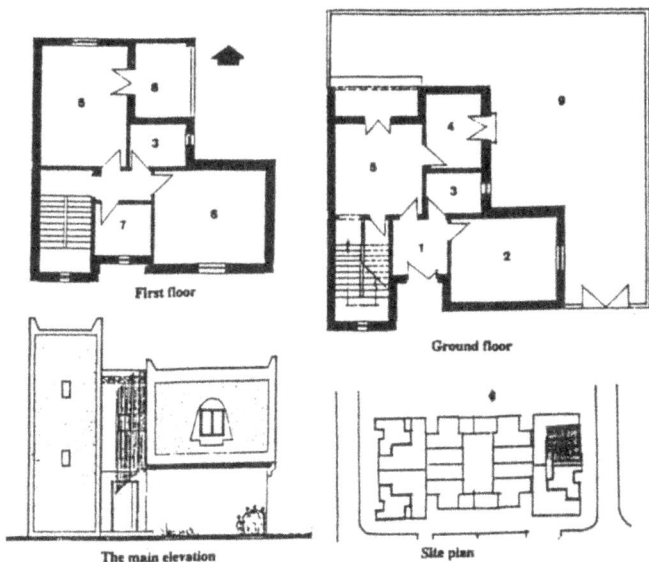

Figure 5.14 Plan of a two bedroom contemporary Ghadamesian house
Source: Fieldwork (1995)

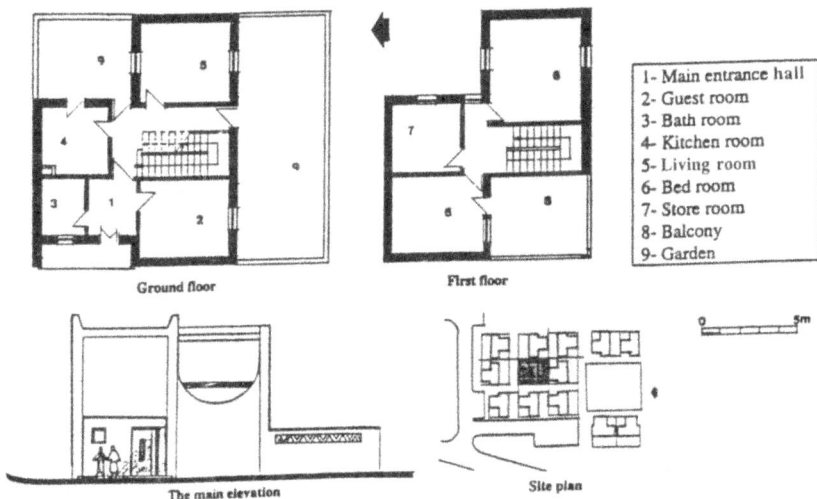

1- Main entrance hall
2- Guest room
3- Bath room
4- Kitchen room
5- Living room
6- Bed room
7- Store room
8- Balcony
9- Garden

**Figure 5.15   An alternative plan of a two bedroom contemporary
                     Ghadamesian house**
Source: Fieldwork (1995)

Users' satisfaction with their traditional and contemporary house

Fieldwork was undertaken in Ghadames in November 1995 in order to measure users' satisfaction with their traditional and contemporary houses in terms of meeting their social life needs. According to theoretical and the empirical studies, five social factors were chosen: choice, privacy, security, religion and prestige in order to examine respondents' satisfaction with their houses. A sample of 120 households was selected at random from a traditional settlement that has been occupied for more than six generations, and from the contemporary settlement. Twenty-four variables were examined in this study in order to assess users' satisfaction with their traditional and contemporary housing environment in terms of response to their socio-cultural needs.

Computation of the index of satisfaction

The first step in the computation of the index of satisfaction (IS) is to express decimally the percentage frequencies for each variable in all the three response categories: Satisfaction, Neutral and Dissatisfaction. For example, if one takes the interviewees' response to the question about satisfaction with the settlement in terms of social life (variable 24) as an example, Satisfactory (83%) = 0.83; Neutral (5%) = 0.05; Dissatisfaction (2%) = 0.02.

The second step is to assign the following weights to each of the response categories: +1 for Satisfaction; 0 for Neutral; and -1 for Dissatisfaction. The decimal value in each response category is then multiplied by the appropriate weight. The maximum index that a variable can have is +1.00 when all respondents are satisfied; the minimum is -1.00 when all respondents express dissatisfaction; and 0.000 when all respondents are neutral.

Main findings

Co-operation in the choice of the dwelling

Respondents were asked to state their feelings about the opportunities they were given to co-operate in the design decision of their two residential areas both traditional and contemporary, and if were they satisfied or dissatisfied with them. Eight variables were selected to examine respondents' perception; they were asked about the neighbourhood level in terms of location, type of neighbours, and relation with neighbours, and, at dwelling level, about location, type, size, layout and building materials. The analyses indicate that years ago members of housing committees gave their people the opportunity to co-operate in residential area design processes, and in the past people have done better than the Housing Authority today. The high degree of satisfaction with those traditional houses is not surprising; from this study it was found that the majority of respondents were more satisfied with their traditional houses in terms of the choice given to them to co-operate in the selected variables than contemporary ones (Chart 5.1). Although there are some complaints relating to the physical characteristics of the traditional houses, such as its size, building materials' durability, and inadequacy of the sewage system, these traditional dwellings were considered by the majority of the residents to be satisfactory. Their criticism of their contemporary dwellings is the result of not being allowed to share in the design process. Ghadamesian households were moved from traditional houses to the contemporary ones because they needed more space, due to increased households' sizes and there being no development in the traditional housing sector which was left without maintenance or a proper sewage system. These reasons forced occupants to leave their houses in the traditional settlement and to move to the new one. The people who had moved tried to introduce some of the design features which they had liked in their traditional dwellings. For example, balconies were closed so that the space could be used for another purpose, and rooms and entrances were altered so as to make the dwellings conform to their choice. This confirms the findings of Rossi (1985), Ermuth (1973) and Ward (1985): dwellers who have the opportunity to co-operate in the design processes of their houses are happier and more satisfied than those who have no such opportunity.

In view of the large number of people whose lives are affected by their housing it is desirable to make an effort to consult as many as possible when considering house design. Meetings should be arranged with individual groups wherever possible and ideas exchanged about housing design. If this is not possible, a survey of opinions could be made and published. The purpose of such consultation would be to co-ordinate the work between architects and users, which helps to rationalise the construction and consequently avoids demolishing or modifying parts of the dwelling as a result of mistakes.

Security/safety considerations

'A good environmental image gives its possessor an important sense of emotional security' (Lynch, 1960, p.4). The desire for protection against street crime and the ensuring of the safety of their possessions from crime was found in almost all of the respondents in Ghadames. The traditional houses are designed according to their users' needs for security/safety, and are safer than the contemporary dwelling. The majority of Ghadamesian people were very satisfied with their traditional houses where they lived in the past and did not take any additional security measures there. People in traditional houses live together according to their blood relationship, which increases the level of security and provides suitable places for

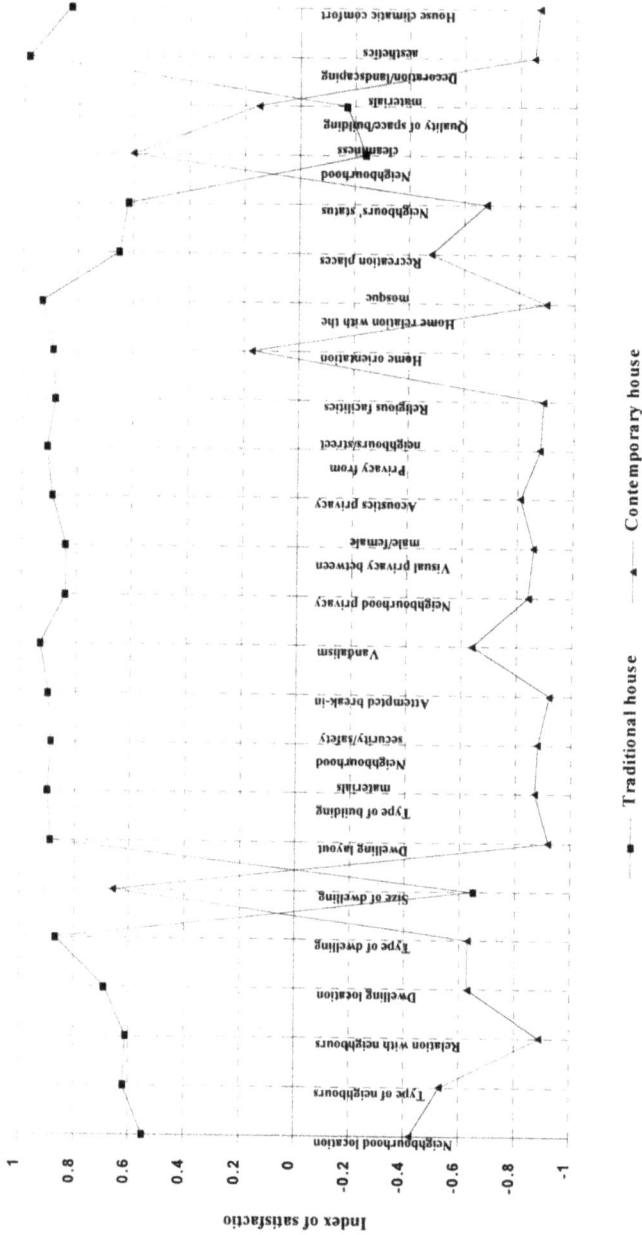

Chart 5.1 Comparative users' level of satisfaction with 24 environmental variables within their traditional and contemporary houses

schools, children's play areas. It decreases the vandalism caused by children and reduces traffic accidents. Moreover, the presence of greenery, vegetation and trees around the houses, increased the people's sense of security. However, most were dissatisfied with their contemporary dwellings and took important security measures such as inserting an additional metal door and/ or metal grille on their windows. The lack of homogeneity between neighbours, and the absence of children's play areas were the most important factors affecting security and vandalism levels in the contemporary settlement.

It was discovered from the empirical evidence collected, how the right decision was made about the most preferred dwelling design in terms of security/safety. Taking into consideration the housing experiences of dwellers in both traditional and contemporary houses, people preferred the traditional neighbourhood and house rather than the contemporary, particularly in terms of security and the prevention of crime and, at neighbourhood level, traffic accidents and, at dwelling level, attempted break in and vandalism (Chart 5.1). The main reasons why the contemporary dwelling was unacceptable to the users were that the people expressed anger, feelings of vulnerability, grief for lost and damaged things, many children were suffering and some had died from car accidents. This causes a psychological impact on the person's relationships with others and affects the general level of satisfaction with the residential area design.

Preservation of household privacy

Informal discussion which took place during interviews, revealed that the influence of the physical characteristics of a neighbourhood and dwelling on the residents' perception of the level of privacy inside and outside the dwellings, was important. The arrangement of the exterior space where social activities could take place, as well as internal space, such as location of the guest room, main entrance, women's section and kitchen, and placement of openings in relation to the street, passers-by or neighbours, have to be considered with care. It is important to say that the preservation of privacy of the household members (women and men) constitutes an essential prerequisite of Islam, particularly in Arab society. Analysis of data suggests that Ghadamesian people preferred the traditional house design because it is a direct interpretation of their privacy patterns by taking into account their need for privacy in the areas immediately outside the dwelling (at neighbourhood level), visual and acoustic privacy inside the dwelling and privacy from neighbours and street (Figure 5.16). For example, its interior space arrangement and placement of the openings were the result of the privacy convention. However, this requirement was completely missing in contemporary dwelling regulations. From observation of the traditional residential area design and interviews with its residents, the major types of privacy which Ghadamesian household are concerned about are:

1. Places for meetings at neighbourhood level, for carrying out the daily activities such as playing cards, drinking cups of tea under the shade of trees, and squares, where social activities such as weddings or funerals could take place and sitting without disturbing others.
2. Household visual privacy between male guests and household quarters, particularly the female section, was found to be the most important factor determining dwelling design in Libya. This was found to be affected by the interior space arrangement such as the placement of the main entrance, guest room, bathroom, female section and location of kitchen.
3. Acoustic privacy and avoidance of sound transmission between male visitors and household quarters was found, by an overwhelming majority of respondents, to also be an important aspect of privacy.
4. The need to prevent passers-by and neighbours looking into the house and the need to keep out noise. Findings showed that in the traditional houses of Ghadames, house openings were usually made to avoid looking into the neighbour's dwelling and internal space, and the height of these openings, especially windows, was above the level of a man passing-by and these were not positioned where they could be overlooked by people in the street or by neighbours.

The concern of religious needs

Ibrahim (1979, pp.66) said of religious needs in Islamic communities:

> The mosque should be considered the major dominant element in the designing of residential areas or towns. As a symbol of religion and the place where prayers are offered and as a centre of daily life of Islamic communities, it should be given the utmost consideration and highest priority in the various planning projects.

The Islamic religion has influence on the built environment, especially in Saharan communities, such as Ghadames. This study examined the level of satisfaction in both house types (traditional and contemporary), and it appears that the traditional houses are totally responsive to their users' religious needs, but the respondents in the contemporary dwellings complained that there was a lack of any relationship between dwelling design and religious values. The majority of Ghadamesian people prefer the traditional dwelling because it successfully responds to their religious needs, particularly in terms of neighbourhood religious facilities, dwelling relation with the mosque and orientation, unlike the contemporary one (Figure 5.16). The following were the factors which concerned people about the necessity for adapting their dwelling to meet religious needs.

1. Mosque system; every neighbourhood should have its own small mosque, or mosques, depending on the population. A central mosque is larger and more imposing, and is often provided and maintained by endowment to serve a wider area. This is sometimes called the *Jummah*, or Friday mosque, as people from the whole settlement gather to make their Friday prayers.
2. The dwelling relationship with the mosque is the most important variable. This process could be seen in the Ghadames traditional houses where religious trends translated into a practical design; houses were concentrated around the mosque and in close relationship with the mosque, but the contemporary dwelling has no such relationship.
3. The dwelling orientation: People are not concerned too much about their dwellings' orientation because no specific rule or recommendation exists for this. However, users in our study were concerned about the orientation of bathroom 'siphonic water closets'. The user of the bathroom prefers not to turn his back or face away from the direction of the holy Makkah, which means that water closets must be correctly positioned in accordance with their users' religious needs.

Users' desire for prestige

The need for prestige or self-esteem involves the desire for self-respect, a sense of personal worth, and the esteem of others (Maslow, 1970). Prestige is an important value and planners and architects must take it into account when designing any residential area. The analysis of data shows that people get respect from other groups, particularly those from outside of the settlement, according to the degree of their neighbourhood's recreation places, cleanliness and neighbours' status as well as the dwellings' aesthetic quality and climatic comfort. Respondents in the sample preferred the traditional house design because it met their prestige needs better than the contemporary design in terms of satisfaction with these aspects (Figure 5.16). A study done by Shawesh (1992; 1995) revealed that people living in Ghadames' traditional houses survived the summer months without mechanical ventilation, and the winter without heating, by gently migrating around the house. However, they recorded dissatisfaction with respect to the quality of the home in terms of the building materials and space. Experience of traditional house design definitely influenced people's perception about their present dwelling design. The users desired the contemporary built environment whilst having the traditional house design. Despite this, they had some complaints about the traditional house which they felt needed some improvement in terms of an increased amount of interior space, better building materials and a more efficient sewage system. It is obvious from the findings of the study that the following variables were found to be relatively strong and to have a significant relationship with prestige.

1. The upkeep of the neighbourhood has been recognised as a very important factor influencing satisfaction with neighbourhood environment. A similar conclusion was reached by Lansing *et al* (1970, p.130): 'Upkeep of housing estates has been recognised as a very important factor influencing satisfaction with the housing environment'.

2. The spaciousness and size of the guest rooms as well as the size of the kitchen, the size of space for female household members and visitors, and the size of the storage area and other rooms were related to the users' desire for prestige and satisfaction with their dwelling. The results confirm the findings of Tognoli's (1985) study, which noted that room size is one of the features of the dwelling likely to be associated with the users' level of satisfaction.

3. From the findings of this study, it appears that the aesthetic aspects of the dwelling are strongly influenced by the amount of decoration (which represents the household's status and prestige), the choice of building materials, texture and the amount of greenery outside and inside the dwelling. These are the most important factors linked with the residents' levels of satisfaction with the aesthetic qualities of traditional and contemporary dwellings.

4. Users' opinions showed the importance of flexibility and the ability to design houses to conform to climatic needs. This means dwellings should be able to provide protection against the harsh climate.

Conclusion

The findings of this investigation lead to the conclusion that the success of the traditional forms of settlement, neighbourhood and dwelling is the result of successfully consulting with the users during the design and construction processes, and dealing with their socio-cultural values. The contemporary design failed to adapt to the social life needs of the Libyan household. Turning back the clock is not possible because modernity has affected some aspects of the residents' lifestyle, and changes in furniture and new household domestic technology have caused specialised room usage and created the need for more regularly shaped and bigger rooms. Moreover, the use of new systems of transportation, such as cars, need new road systems, particularly in terms of width, and the new sewage system also needs different space dimensions caused by the use of new fittings and equipment. However, lessons can by learned from the traditional housing design system and from the residents' experience with it. For example, through spatial analysis, it was shown that respondents accepted the traditional design system but they recommended some change in the dwelling's physical components, such as the sewage system inside and outside. On the other hand, they desire more spacious housing, particularly in regard to the amount of interior dwelling space.

They would also like to improve the traffic system according to their present lifestyle needs.

Note

The original version of this paper was first presented at the 12th Conference on 'The Small City and Regional Community', held at the Centre for Urban and Economic Research, University of Louisville, Kentucky, USA, 22-23 October 1996.

Bibliography

Ahmed, S. (1985), *City of Ghadames*, PhD thesis, University of Krakow: Krakow, Poland.

Awotona, A. (1988), 'The perception of housing conditions in Nigeria by the urban poor.' *Habitat International*, Vol. 12, No. 1, pp.75-96.

Been Swessi, A. (1993), 'The development of the City of Ghadames: Between the lost identity and the search for meaningful and productive rural architecture', *Hassan Fathy Conference*, Cairo, Egypt, 1993, Paper presented.

Eldblon, L. (1968), *Structure fonciere, organisation et structure social: Une etude comparative sur la vie socioeconomique dans les trois oasis Libyennes Deghat, Mourzouk, et Parti Culierment Ghadames*, Meddelard fran Lund Universities Geografiska Institution: Lund. In French.

Ermuth, F. (1973), *Urban environmental preferences*, University of York: York.

Hassan, M.A. (1982), *Understanding the traditional built environment: Crisis change and the issue of human needs in the context of habitations in settlements in Libya*, PhD thesis, University of Pennsylvania

Ibrahim, H. (1979), 'Planning standards for mosques.' *Albenaa Magazine*, Vol. 1, pp.66-69.

Lansing, J., Marans, R.W., et al. (1970), *Planned residential environments*. Ann Arbor Institute of Social Research, University of Michigan:

Lynch, K. (1960), *The image of the city*, MIT Press: Cambridge, MA.

Maslow, A.H. (1970), *Motivation and personality*, Harper & Row: New York.

Piccioli, A. (1935), *The Magic Gate of the Sahara*, Methuen: London. Translated from the Italian by Angus Davidson.

Rossi, P.H. (1985), *Why family move*, Sage: London.

Shawesh, A.M. (1992), *The impact of climate on housing in the Libyan desert: A case study of Ghadames City*, MIHSc thesis, School of Architecture, University of Newcastle upon Tyne: Newcastle upon Tyne.

Shawesh, A.M. (1995), 'Traditional settlement in the oasis of Ghadames in the Libyan Arab Jamahiriya.' *Libyan Studies*, Vol. 26, pp.35-47.

Tognoli, G. (1985), 'Residential environment', in Stokols, D. and Altman, J. (eds), *Handbook of environment psychology*, Vol. 1, Chapter 7.

Ward, C. (1985), *When we build again*, Pluto: London.

6 Housing and difference in Cape Town, South Africa:

Case studies and policy concerns

ANDREW SPIEGEL, VANESSA WATSON and PETER WILKINSON

South Africa's current housing policy, strongly influenced by 'supply side' considerations, appears to be based on certain unexamined, and possibly over-simplistic, assumptions about the needs and priorities of potential beneficiaries. As a result it remains immured in a mode of 'homogenising' or 'normalising' discourse about the nature of housing need, and is generally insensitive to the diversity of situation and experience among the people to whom it is directed. The chapter uses case study material to illustrate some of the lack of fit that results.

Offering a summary history of South African urban housing policy as backdrop, the chapter illustrates a persistent lack of fit between urban housing policy and on-the-ground housing need amongst African residents of greater Cape Town. By tracing the experiences of a number of individuals from households with extremely disparate sizes and compositions, as well as diverse trajectories of domestic change and consolidation, the chapter offers an indication of the diversity of a specific population. The individuals, some of whom have come to Cape Town from a remote rural region and some of whom have spent much of their lives in various parts of this metropolitan area, have all confronted the common problem of obtaining suitable housing, but in very different ways depending on their particular economic and social circumstances, their experience of urban life, and their 'world-view'. They have also all found themselves, in very different ways, necessarily responding to the particular sets of opportunities and constraints imposed by current and past housing and urban development policies.

After identifying some of the obstacles to effective housing delivery in present policy, we conclude that, to be more effective, South African housing policy needs to be formulated in ways that are accommodative of the diverse situations of the people to whom it is directed, and sensitive towards their experiences and understanding of urban living.

Introduction

A recent survey of Cape Town's African population[1] revealed that 71 per cent of all senior males and 62 per cent of all senior females in the households surveyed were originally from rural areas (Mazur and Qangule, 1995, tables 4.1 & 4.3). The survey also confirmed that migration within this population continues to follow the kind of oscillating pattern associated with the imposition of apartheid legislation and policies that precluded long-term urban settlement by African people, particularly in Cape Town.   In a context of high unemployment rates and job insecurity, the pattern appears to have become embedded in the risk management strategies adopted, to greater and lesser effect, by many African households.

   One result is that many such households are 'stretched', in the sense of including, as members, individuals who live in different parts of the country for greater or lesser periods, and who contribute to, or draw from, a common resource pool. Households thus constitute networks of domestic relationships stretching across the subcontinent and focused on an idea shared by their members that they are, and ought to be, entailed in intensive reciprocity with one another.   The aim of the reciprocity is twofold: to maintain the members of the household; and to develop a secure long-term resource base for them, in other words, to 'consolidate' the household.   Domestic consolidation in this sense has a different meaning from what current housing policy documents refer to as 'consolidation', a term coined by John Turner (1968; 1972) to describe a process whereby newly urbanised households incrementally improve their housing conditions, usually through the investment of their own labour ('sweat equity') and other resources.

   The processes of domestic consolidation that have emerged from an in-depth study conducted by the authors during 1992-93, amongst African people in Cape Town[2], reveal the commitment of some to a pattern of the kind outlined above in which households are stretched to accommodate diverse interests and opportunities for creating long-term security for their domestic units.   One result is that residential groups are very fluid in composition and size (Spiegel et al., 1996b) and that domestic fluidity and change have become common as people attempt in diverse ways to construct units that will offer them some long-term security. Moreover, domestic fluidity and change is experienced not only by those households stretched between urban and rural areas, but also, frequently, by households within the city.

   Various factors either constrain or enable people's efforts to achieve their intentions of establishing secure domestic units, and not all households experience the same pattern.   One result is that the ability of at least some households to utilise the kinds of urban housing that is promised by present housing policies is severely undermined, precisely because the policy, based on an urban transition model of migration (Zelinsky, 1971), assumes that urban households are small, settled and stable in composition, and that their members' ties with rural areas steadily diminish in intensity as they embed themselves in urban communities and secure, reliable, income-generating work.

The purpose of this chapter is to examine how current housing policy in South Africa addresses (or fails to address) the particular domestic circumstances and consolidation strategies of some African households in the metropolitan area of Cape Town. The varied nature of a few households' experiences and expectations of urban life, are summarised using case material drawn from the authors' 1992-93 study. The chapter is as much concerned with what might be described as people's domestic 'life projects' (how they actively seek to use the resources and opportunities represented by the city to construct or maintain their households) as with the constraints that circumstances impose on their ability to realise such projects.

First, however, we sketch some historical background to the development of the housing conditions currently confronting Cape Town's African residents. We indicate how these conditions were shaped under apartheid by deliberate strategies to 'contain' African urbanisation, particularly in the Western Cape Province, and, subsequently, by efforts to initiate an alternative 'self-help' and market-driven approach to housing provision. We then review four cases that illustrate how differently households have responded to these developments. We focus on their capacities to pursue specific, individual strategies of domestic consolidation. We understand that such selective accounts cannot be considered as representative of the African population as a whole. Yet we believe that they are indicative of the diversity of urbanisation experiences and domestic consolidation processes within that population. Recognition of diversity leads us to pose questions about the relationship between the assumptions on which current housing policy seems to be based and the actual housing requirements of the heterogeneous population at which that policy is targeted. We conclude by suggesting that the relationship is profoundly problematic and that policy-makers need urgently to reconsider the axiomatic bases of their current approach to housing provision to meet the real needs of people.

Housing conditions in Cape Town: historical background

South African housing policy was subject to wide-ranging debate and review in the period immediately before, and after, the election of the country's first democratic government in mid-1994. Yet the current housing programme remains strongly influenced by earlier positions on housing policy and constrained by the pattern of low-income urban settlement inherited from the apartheid era. Both aspects need to be understood within the context of previous governments' efforts to contain and direct African people's urbanisation patterns.

Already in 1923 the Natives (Urban Areas) Act established the principle that the franchise could be denied to African residents of 'white' urban areas only if their right to permanent residence there (defined as the right to acquire freehold tenure) was withheld (Wilkinson, 1984). In the era of 'grand apartheid', initiated from 1948, the problems of removing existing freehold rights of Africans in 'white' urban areas, and of controlling the influx of Africans from the 'homelands'[3], were addressed *inter alia* through mass construction of public rental housing in 'properly planned townships', where occupancy could be closely monitored and regulated. During the 1960s, the logic of 'separate development' increasingly emphasised accommodation of the growing African labour force within 'homeland' areas, from where, it was expected, they would commute to jobs in 'white' towns and cities. Provision was made for the temporary accommodation of migrant workers in single-sex hostels. From the late 1960s, therefore, housing resources were increasingly directed to 'homeland' locations, and in 1968 a state directive ordered the cessation of all provision of African family housing in townships in the 'white' urban areas.

In Cape Town and the surrounding region, the harshness of these provisions was compounded by the implementation in 1955 of the 'Coloured Labour Preference Policy', which declared the Western Cape region the natural home of the coloured people, and an area in which they were to enjoy a degree of protection in the labour market. The policy was aimed, originally, at the eventual removal of all Africans from the region, and to this end influx controls (the pass laws) were tightened and were applied particularly vigorously against African women in an attempt to prevent the permanent settlement of African families in the region (West, 1982). Inevitably, these measures gave rise to severe housing shortages, high levels of overcrowding, and widespread illegal informal settlement (Fast, 1995).

Increasing political resistance to apartheid rule through the early 1970s, culminating in the 'Soweto revolt' of 1976, threw the basic tenets of apartheid and 'separate development' dramatically into question. Lack of clarity about the direction of necessary 'reform' in the urban policy arena, coupled with the onset of severe economic recession, enabled non-governmental agencies (particularly the big business-supported Urban Foundation) to establish a new approach to housing provision. From the end of the 1970s, therefore, state intervention in the housing process was effectively limited to the provision of serviced sites and 'core' housing, a change in keeping with emerging international emphasis on self-help approaches (World Bank, 1974).

The shift towards a new approach to housing provision cannot be divorced from broader political and social developments. Continuation of widespread and intense urban unrest throughout the country during the 1980s, forced reformist policy makers to recognise that African urbanisation was inevitable and would have to be managed on a different basis from that prevailing during the 'grand apartheid' era.

A key problem faced was how to provide housing for a generally very poor and rapidly growing African urban population under conditions which would support emergence of a primarily market-driven process. Moreover, establishment of a property-owning African middle class would, it was hoped, provide a buffer against popular demands for more fundamental transformation.

In Cape Town, the 1970s marked the start of a period of frequent battles by 'squatters' to establish various informal settlements, some of which survive to the present. By the late 1970s and into the 1980s, divisions and conflicts also began to emerge within the African population, essentially over the control of access to informally settled land. They resulted in large scale destruction of several informal settlements and the creation of a sizeable refugee population within the metropolitan area (Fast, 1995). The consequences of these conflicts have shaped present patterns of settlement in certain parts of Cape Town.

In 1983, in an attempt to take control of the increasingly unstable situation in the city, the state opened up an extensive parcel of land for African settlement on the south eastern periphery of the metropolitan area. Known as *Khayelitsha*, it was intended to accommodate some 450,000 people, partly on serviced sites and partly in small formal 'core' houses, in both cases for eventual freehold ownership. Concerted, and often unsuccessful, efforts were made to consolidate many of the scattered informal settlements around Cape Town into this area, but its distance some 35km from the central areas of Cape Town, its lack of work and service facilities, and its bleak and sandy, wind-swept nature, has meant that for many people it was a residential area of last resort.

Nationally too, housing policy remained an issue of concern throughout the 1980s and into the 1990s. The most important features of the most recent policy framework (Department of Housing, 1994) derive directly from earlier policy debates and initiatives. A central plank of the new framework is the concept of state-assisted self help housing and a commitment to an incremental approach to housing. This is realised through the provision of a one-off capital subsidy on a sliding scale of up to R17,500 (£2,378)[4], to provide serviced sites or, at best, small core houses for occupation under freehold tenure. Thereafter the onus is on beneficiaries to improve on or 'consolidate' their accommodation by drawing on their own resources. In addition, the policy enables provision of formal rental accommodation by housing co-operatives and non-profit social housing agencies although, under current circumstances, it is likely to play only a limited role. In principle, the new policy framework brought South Africa into line with a position promoted for some years by agencies such as the World Bank, and with policies adopted by many developing countries. In practice, however, the overall effect has been to continue to reproduce the social and spatial inequities characterising urban development in the apartheid era (Spiegel et al., 1996a).

In the Cape Town context the new policy has, so far, done little more than extend or supplement schemes already underway. Development of serviced sites and core houses has continued in *Khayelitsha* and in pockets of land around the older formal African townships. Most older informal settlements remain, and have expanded. Some have had basic services provided; some have not. Most hostel accommodation is now occupied by families living under highly overcrowded conditions (Jones, 1993; Ramphele, 1993), while plans for upgrading have yet to reach implementation stage. In the older formal townships, services have been deteriorating and levels of overcrowding increasing.

The central housing concern of poorer African households in the city has therefore continued to be to gain access to land and shelter under highly constrained conditions. The cases we review next indicate some of the ways particular individuals and households, each with different sets of needs and priorities, have, with greater or lesser degrees of success, managed to secure urban shelter for themselves and how that process relates to their attempts at domestic consolidation.

The dynamics of domestic consolidation: some indicative cases

The four cases below serve, firstly, to indicate the diversity of experience and expectations people's domestic trajectories embody and, secondly, to identify various factors that constrain their consolidation efforts. We have selected cases that range along a continuum of consolidation trajectories from what, at one end, appears to be an example of successful rural consolidation enabled by access to urban-based resources, through examples of patently unsuccessful or not yet achieved consolidation in either the rural or the urban context, to an example of provisional but currently successful urban consolidation. In each instance, we endeavour to present some necessary contextualisation of the household's circumstances at the time of the interview and, through reported speech, a sense of our respondents' own perceptions of their individual situations[5].

Case 1: Successful rural consolidation using urban resources

BD (file G1) was in his mid fifties when he was interviewed for our project. The interview was conducted in the migrant workers' hostel room that he shared with two of his brothers and their respective wives plus a 'homeboy' (friend from the same rural area) and his girlfriend. Both BD's wife and the homeboy's wife remained in the Transkei region[6] of the Eastern Cape Province where they cared for their rural homesteads and children. BD's brothers' children were also 'back home' although their wives were temporarily visiting Cape Town at the time of the interview.

For BD, his brothers and homeboy, Cape Town was a place where they had come to earn money for building their rural homesteads:

What do you think I am doing here in Cape Town? I have cows there (in the Transkei). Fifteen of them. We also have sheep and goats and my wife has fowls. I save money for them (my house and family). I also save for my old age, and in order to buy cattle. I use my savings if I want to buy cattle, or a plough.

These men maintained a view of Cape Town as a place just to earn money even though some had been in the metropolitan area for over 30 years. BD, for example, had been in Cape Town for 33 years, having come at a time when apartheid policy was still such that he could have qualified to remain permanently in the city and rented one of the few small council-owned African township houses in Cape Town, had he brought his wife and children to live with him. Yet he had always lived in one or another hostel, in most instances finding hostel accommodation either through his employer or through relatives and homeboy connections. He clearly preferred the hostels to the townships:

I like to live here because it keeps me away from the ills of the townships. We have come here to work, and not to complain. The place is not ideal, but I know deep down that I do not belong here. I belong in the Transkei where my real home is. This place is just temporary.

BD's only concern for upgrading the hostels was that the rooms be made larger so that he could more easily accommodate short-term visits by relatives from the Transkei. Although he did not object to their visiting occasionally, he was adamant that his wife and children should never come to live in the city. He thus saw no reason to want to own a house in Cape Town, nor indeed to rent one. The hostel room was adequate for the kind of short-term co-residential arrangements, commensality and income pooling that he and his brothers engaged in, so that they could save as much as possible of their earnings for investment in their rural homesteads. If it were a little larger, however, it would permit easier accommodation of visitors and thereby improve their chances for consolidating extended networks of reciprocity.

BD, his brothers and co-resident homeboy, all had relatively secure albeit poor incomes from work in Cape Town. There were others whom our study came across who shared these men's world view that placed their rural homes at the centre of their social universes and saw Cape Town as just a place to earn a living. Among them, however, were a number who lacked a regular or secure source of income and who had therefore failed to realise their dream of Cape Town as a place to earn an income for utilisation in building and consolidating a rural home.

Case 2: Unsuccessful consolidation: rural or urban

When interviewed in 1992, PZ and his wife OZ (file B4) were in their mid-thirties. Both were unemployed. They were then living with two of their four children in a plastic sheet shelter in a shack settlement on invaded land neighbouring an old formal African township. Most residents there were refugees from violence that had for a number of years marked shanty settlements and had resulted in whole settlements being razed to the ground. This had been the experience of PZ and OZ whose already minimal resources had been lost in one such fire and who had then moved to the area where we now found them.

PZ had been in the Greater Cape Town area for nine or ten years. When he first arrived he had found work, and a place to stay in a hostel in Paarl, a small town on the periphery of the metropolitan area, through friends from their Transkei district. For a few years he began to develop a life trajectory of the kind BD (above) had realised. He lived and worked in Paarl, and visited his wife once annually, remitting some earnings for her to support herself and their young children and to begin to develop a rural homestead and resource base by purchasing some sheep that they left in an old village man's care. Occasionally she visited him for short periods in Paarl, but for the most part she remained in the Transkei: 'I hated to come to town. I felt more comfortable there at home.'

The pattern was broken, however, when PZ was retrenched by the brick factory for which he worked, and was unable to find further employment. In addition, the old man who had cared for their sheep died, and his son claimed all the sheep had been lost. On the advice of OZ's father's brother, PZ moved closer to the city where he was assured a site in a shack settlement, and hoped to find a job. When this occurred, OZ had been visiting, and they thus moved and lived there together for some months until OZ left again to return to her childcare duties with their four children whom she had left with her sister in the Transkei.

But from then on PZ found only occasional work. It was insufficient to support regular remittances, or to allow regular travel for either of them between Cape Town and their Transkei home. When two of their children fell ill, OZ managed, with financial help from her father's brother, to bring them to Cape Town for treatment. But then they were trapped: without the resources to purchase further tickets, the two children remained with PZ and OZ in their Cape Town shack, while their other two children remained in the Transkei with OZ's sister, and their Transkei house was left unoccupied. This was despite OZ's insistence that she would have preferred that none of her children live in the city: 'I must live here with my husband, but not with my children. Then if it (the violence) is bad again, we can easily move on because we won't have children with us.' Later, discussing their likely immediate future, she added:

> I intend now to stay here in Cape Town because I have no means to live there in the Transkei. I cannot plan to move away (from this shack area) when there is

no way for me to move out. You can plan to move out of an area (only) when you have an option or means to achieve that. You cannot just move if you do not have money. For this moment I am here because I am suffering. But my heart is there in the Transkei. I think I shall stay here a bit longer because we are looking for money.

A number of our interviewees had found themselves in predicaments similar to those of PZ and OZ in that their incomes were so low and erratic that they undermined any attempt to realise a project of domestic consolidation, in whatever form. For people such as these, provision of urban housing for small stable households with a regular income source, is bound to miss the mark. Firstly, such people's incomes are highly erratic and extremely low. They can therefore not afford such housing. Moreover, their risk-spreading activities disincline them from investing heavily in any one place or resource. Secondly, their experience of repeated violence in town undermines any inclination they might have towards permanent urban settlement, particularly if that involves their children. Indeed, as Case 3 below shows, commitment to urban living reflects, for some, a kind of fatalistic pragmatism rather than a belief that urban life is appropriate and right.

Yet our study also provided examples of people who were indeed committed to urban domestic life projects, despite their being relatively recent migrants into the city. We need therefore always to differentiate between those whose circumstances allow them to succeed in achieving their goals, and those whose circumstances will not.

Case 3: Attempted urban consolidation

The largest co-residential group recorded in our study was that headed by MN (file B2) a man in his mid fifties. It comprised 11 persons, including MN and his wife and four of their six children plus a grandchild as well as MN's brother, his wife and two of their children. MN's remaining two children were at their small Transkei home. At the time of interview MN's co-resident group occupied a shack in the same shanty area as PZ and OZ. They too had been forced recently to relocate there as a result of township violence that had destroyed all their possessions in another shanty area that was razed.

Unlike PZ, however, both MN and his brother were employed, MN in a relatively secure job albeit with a low wage. Unlike PZ and OZ (Case 2), they saw their future in Cape Town rather than in the Transkei. Although they owned a small house in the Transkei with a field that MN's wife returned to every summer to tend, they were quick to indicate that:

We have family there at home, but we are planning to bring them here. I want to stay here for the rest of my life because my relatives and friends are here. The hospital is here. I want even to die here and I will, no matter we do not have houses. Tell me, who in his right mind would want to live in the Transkei? Life there is very difficult, everything is here, the schools, the doctors and everything.

The problem people in such a predicament faced regarding urban housing was multifold. They desperately wanted a formal brick house to replace their shack. Indeed, that was their hope when, with the lifting of influx control legislation in the mid 1980s, they had come to settle in Cape Town, but all they had found was a severe housing shortage. That was why they had settled in the earlier shanty area that had been razed - the leader there had promised residents an upgrade and had taken a regular 'rent' from them, ostensibly for this purpose. Had they obtained such a house it would, in any case, have been too small for the extended family that constituted their residential group, a problem that many of those who did live in such houses complained about. While MN and his dependants were clearly intent on an incremental strategy to improve their housing conditions (as is the current policy norm for all households) they were constrained by the lack of available housing stock, their own poor incomes and the fact that what might become available could not provide for the large urban household they had assembled as a means to cope with the exigencies they had found themselves having to face.

Others who had indeed managed to make the upgrade to a formal township house and begun the upgrade process also complained of lack of space. For the most part this was because·they had large households they needed to accommodate and did not constitute small nuclear families, as the next case illustrates.

Case 4: Currently successful urban consolidation

When interviewed for our study 37 year old GR and his 34 year old wife PR (file A2) were the owner-occupiers of a small formal house in the *Makhaya* area of *Khayelitsha*. They had purchased in 1989 on the basis of GR's reliable income from a formal sector job as a driver and PR's employment as a char.

GR had been born in the Transkei but had come to Cape Town as a child. PR was born in Cape Town. Both spent their formative years in various townships and shanty settlements and, for significant periods during their teenage years, at school in the Transkei. They were formally married in 1982 after GR's father died and when their first two children were already three and one year old respectively. But they had lived together much longer, first in GR's parents' township house, then in various backyard shacks, sometimes rented, sometimes with other relatives. They eventually returned to GR's widowed mother's house which they hoped to take over from her, an arrangement, they said, bureaucracy prevented them from finalising.

Given pressures of space in GR's old family home, and the fact that he was precluded from formally taking it over, they decided to purchase elsewhere:

> We stayed there, but we could see that we had no future there because we had children, and we felt our kids should grow up in our own house. So we decided to buy this house. We found that we could pay for (afford) it. There were other houses that we could find and which were better than this one, but because of our standard and the money we earn we could see that we cannot afford those better houses.

Even though they hoped, eventually, to be able to move upmarket they began improvements within months: first by laying carpets and installing an electricity supply, then by replastering and tiling some walls, and more recently by installing a ceiling and adding a veranda. They intended adding further rooms since:

> ... this house is small and since we have this large family (eight residents at time of interview) we are 'packed'; we want to extend it, as you see we do not have a dining room we have only a lounge. I want to build a new bedroom and extend the kids' bedroom. I will change our bedroom and make it into a dining room.

Although GR and PR were tied into networks that stretched to the Transkei, they felt no need to maintain a homestead there or to send their children there as they had been sent during their high school years. PR expressed fear of trying to do so, both for the demands it would make on their income, and for the implications she understood it would have on her children's upbringing:

> I could not send my child to the Transkei, even though my husband's home is there. We would be obliged to send extra money in addition to what we occasionally send to my husband's father's wife. All in all, I like my children to stay in the place I'm in and eat what I'm eating, and (for me) to oversee their needs in order for them to grow up well. This is because children who grow up in different places acquire different moral lessons.

An issue of concern to many of our respondents, including some referred to above, was that a decent house ought to be large enough to accommodate sleep-in visitors from afar. It was an issue of particular concern to those with some resources, such as BD (Case 1) and who felt it was crucially necessary to create and maintain social networks of mutual support. Being able to offer accommodation was one clear way of engaging in the reciprocities that encouraged such network maintenance. By contrast, those such as GR who had recently found themselves new formal housing accommodation, seemed to need to create distance between themselves and their networks, partly because of the strain it would place on resources which were now committed to consolidation in Cape Town.

Housing supply and housing need: the problem of 'policy fit'

Our description of four households above clearly cannot be used simply to generalise about Cape Town's entire African population: we have no indication of just how 'representative' these four cases are. However, they serve to illustrate the diversity of consolidation experiences. This allows us to raise some questions about the degree to which current housing policy 'fits' with the range of housing needs to be found amongst poorer households in a city such as Cape Town.

The primary focus of current housing policy on home-ownership, and the incremental approach to housing provision, does not suit the needs of rural consolidators such as BD (Case 1). BD's primary concern is to minimise his expenditure on housing in the urban area. He has therefore little choice but to occupy the only cheap rental accommodation available (a hostel bed) although many others like him choose the option of informal rental, usually in a backyard shack behind a formal township house. While both of these options are cheap, neither provides an adequate standard of shelter or sufficient space to allow the development of networks of reciprocity by accommodating family or other members. For people such as BD, ownership of property in the city (and the recurrent rate and service charges which this implies) and investment in extending the minimal 'core' house which the housing subsidy allows, would simply detract from the realisation of his domestic life project in the Transkei. The failure on the part of current policy to consider significant support for cheap urban rental accommodation seriously constrains the housing options open to some urban residents.

The policy focus on home-ownership and incrementalism, together with the assumption that credit to expand the basic 'core' unit will be supplied by the private banking sector, also restricts the ability of other kinds of households to gain access to housing. Home-ownership assumes that households can contribute to service and infrastructure costs on a regular basis: a recent policy document (Republic of South Africa, 1995) suggests that households earning under R800 (£108.69) a month should be provided with sites with basic services (communal water standpipes, on-site sanitation, graded roads with gravel, open stormwater drains and streetlights) and be charged for these at a rate of R35-R50 (£4.75-£6.80) per month. However, households such as that of PZ (Case 2), who are unable to afford even the train fare to reunite the family, and who feed themselves by begging from neighbours, would be entirely unable to meet such financial demands. Even households such as that of MN (Case 3), with two income earners (but nine dependants) would find this level of payment difficult, while GR's smaller household (Case 4) with two formal-sector income earners, can afford no more than an unsuitably small unit in one of the poorest locations. Mazur and Qangule's (1995, p.44) finding that, in 1995, 41 per cent of African households in Cape Town earned less than R800 (£108.69) a month, and that more than a third were often unable to purchase their full food requirement, suggests that many households find themselves in circumstances similar to those described in our cases.

Moreover, credit assistance from financial institutions is out of the question for all but those in GR's position (Case 4). Even for these relatively better off households, bank rates are higher than for middle class South Africans, small loans are very difficult to secure, and many are faced with the fact that poorer townships have been 'redlined' by banks attempting to minimise their risks. It is no surprise, therefore, that survey results (Mazur and Qangule, 1995, table 6.2) reveal that only six per cent of African households would consider approaching a formal financial institution for assistance.

Where households have no choice but to draw on their own resources to achieve adequate shelter, maintenance of reciprocal networks becomes all important. However, the process is seriously constrained by the small size of both older formal township houses and newer units, which means that network members can be accommodated only with great difficulty. MN's household, with its 11 residents, (Case 2) would certainly not have fitted into one of the completed houses currently on offer; GR's family (Case 4) had been forced by space considerations to move to a *Khayelitsha* house which nonetheless provided inadequate space for the eight permanently resident family members. Significantly, the highest levels of housing dissatisfaction in Mazur and Qangule's (1995, p.34) survey were recorded in the new formal township areas of *Khayelitsha* and this correlated closely with levels of overcrowding. The implicit assumption in both past and current housing policy, that families consist of stable and nuclear households, requires re-examination.

Issues of housing tenure, cost and size aside, an overall constraint to meeting housing needs has been created by the very slow rate of delivery of serviced land and housing. Households such as that of MN (Case 3) want to gain access to better levels of service and shelter, but their relatively low-income forces them to wait in a lengthy queue for state-subsidised houses. Reasons for the slow delivery of housing, in Cape Town and throughout the rest of the country, are complex, and factors such as lack of bureaucratic capacity and the slow nature of public participation processes must be numbered amongst them. A particularly important stumbling block, however, has been the central assumption of present policy that delivery can largely be left in the hands of private sector property developers and construction companies. While the approach has recently been modified in that local authorities should now take increased responsibility for housing provision, it is still a requirement that partnerships be formed with the private sector. Yet the high-risk and low-profit nature of low-income housing construction (Tomlinson, 1995) reduces the likelihood of large-scale delivery through the private sector.

Conclusion

We have argued that the current South African national housing policy framework is likely to produce only a very limited set of housing options for the majority of African households. Given the diversity of these households in terms of their size, their composition and their domestic change and consolidation trajectories (at least as we have observed them in Cape Town) we have further suggested that the policy is unlikely to provide adequately for the housing needs of the poorest sector of the population.

It is not our intention here to propose an alternative policy framework which might achieve a better 'fit' between policy outcomes and the heterogeneous - perhaps increasingly segmented - contextual realities of urban life for African residents of South Africa's cities and towns. Our purpose has necessarily been more limited and we have sought only to uncover what seem to us to be immanent problems in the current policy framework.

At best, we hope to alert policy makers to what may be the unexamined assumptions that shape their policies and to the unintended consequences that may result from the policy's implementation. We have indicated that the possibilities and constraints people face in trying to manage their lives are extremely diverse. Given that South Africa's political transformation is rapidly changing the circumstances in which people must make personal and domestic decisions, the nature of that diversity is also changing, as are the ways people perceive the value of urban living. We would argue, therefore, that work based on empirically grounded critique is now, more than ever, both important and necessary as the new, democratic South Africa attempts to deal with the extraordinarily complex set of urban problems it has inherited from its apartheid predecessor.

Notes

1   Cape Town is South Africa's third largest city. Of its total 3 million people, 800,000 are Africans. African refers to a category, legislated under apartheid to comprise descendants of indigenous Bantu-speakers, and most severely discriminated against (West, 1988). While the legislation has now been repealed, the category remains significant because of the legacy of its effects.
2   The study was based on in-depth interviews conducted, during 1992-93, in 37 domestic units in seven different types of African residential area in greater Cape Town (see Spiegel et al., 1996a; 1996b; 1996 (in press)). It was

conducted under the auspices of the Urban Problems Research Unit (UPRU), University of Cape Town. We acknowledge financial assistance from the Centre for Science Development, but bear full responsibility for views expressed here. We also gratefully acknowledge the assistance of interviewers Anthony Mehlwana and Ayanda Canca.

3   'Homelands' were labour-reserves set aside for exclusive African occupation where, under the apartheid principle of 'separate development', Africans should govern themselves according to their own 'traditions'. They constituted less than 13 per cent of South Africa's land area.

4   £1.00 = SARand7.36 (12 June, 1997).

5   Our interviews were coded A to G according to which of the seven different types of housing area in the African areas of Cape Town they were conducted in. They were then numbered chronologically. We cite interview codes in the text to identify where the case material is located in the project files.

6   The Transkei region is a former 'homeland', its nearest point being about 1,000km east of Cape Town.

References

Department of Housing. (1994), *White Paper: A new housing policy and strategy for South Africa.* Government Gazette, 254(16178), Pretoria.

Fast, H. (1995), *An overview of African settlement in the Cape Metropolitan Area to 1990.* Working Paper, 53, Urban Problems Research Unit, University of Cape Town: Cape Town.

Jones, S. (1993), *Assaulting childhood: Children's experiences of migrancy and hostel life in South Africa.* Witwatersrand University Press: Johannesburg.

Mazur, R., and Qangule, V. (1995), *African migration and appropriate housing responses in metropolitan Cape Town.* Report, Western Cape Community-based Housing Trust: Cape Town.

Ramphele, M. (1993), *A bed called home: Life in the migrant labour hostels of Cape Town,* David Philip: Cape Town.

Republic of South Africa. (1995), *Urban development strategy of the government of national unity.* Notice, 16679, Ministry in the Office of the President, Republic of South Africa: Pretoria.

Spiegel, A., Watson, V., et al. (1996a), 'Devaluing diversity? National housing policy and African household dynamics in Cape Town.' *Urban Forum*, Vol. 7, No. 1, pp.1-30.

Spiegel, A., Watson, V., et al. (1996b), 'Domestic diversity and fluidity among some African households in Greater Cape Town.' *Social Dynamics*, Vol. 21, No. 2, pp.7-30.

Spiegel, A., Watson, V., et al. (1996 (in press)), 'Women, difference and urbanisation patterns in Cape Town, South Africa.' *African Urban Quarterly*, Vol. 11, No. 1,

Tomlinson, M. (1995), *From principle to practice: Implementors' views on the new housing subsidy scheme.* Research Report, 44, Social Policy Series, Centre for Policy Studies: Johannesburg.

Turner, J. (1968), 'Housing priorities, settlement patterns and urban development in modernising countries.' *Journal of the American Institute of Planners*, Vol. 24, No. 6, pp.354-353.

Turner, J.F.C., and Fichter, R. (eds) (1972), *Freedom to build: Dweller control of the housing process*, Macmillan: New York.

West, M. (1982), 'From pass courts to deportations: Changing patterns of influx control in Cape Town.' *African Affairs*, Vol. 82, No. 352, pp.463-477.

West, M. (1988), 'Confusing categories: Population groups, national states and citizenship', in Boonzaier, E. and Sharp, J. (eds), *South African keywords: The uses and abuses of political concepts*, David Philip: Cape Town, pp.100-110.

Wilkinson, P. (1984), 'The sale of the century? A critical review of recent developments in African housing policy in South Africa', *Carnegie Conference in Poverty and Development*, University of Cape Town, Paper No. 160.

World Bank. (1974), *Site and services project: A World Bank report*, IBRD: Washington, DC.

Zelinsky, W. (1971), 'The hypothesis of the mobility transition.' *Geographical Review*, Vol. 61, pp.219-249.

7 Do grassroots publicity and media success guarantee successful housing?

A case study of 'bottom-up' approaches to housing and urban regeneration in District Six, Cape Town, South Africa

OLA UDUKU

In this chapter the author will discuss the case of the former residents of District Six, a former multi-cultural, mixed social class neighbourhood in Cape Town, South Africa. Housing in District Six has been a mixture of owner-occupied and 'tenanted' multiple occupancy dwellings inhabited by all racial groups in the city. The Group Areas Act was used as the main legislative instrument by which to achieve the forced dispersal of the neighbourhood from 1966 until the repeal of the Act in 1990.

All buildings except religious sites in District Six were demolished, and the area, renamed *Zonnenbloem*, was declared a 'White' residential neighbourhood in the late 1960s. More recently a proportion of the area has become the site for the *Cape Techknikon* (polytechnic). The forcibly removed former residents of District Six set up a formidable campaign throughout the apartheid era which has continued into the present 'New South Africa' to call for their right to former property and land owned in the neighbourhood.

This chapter analyses how the District Six residents have been able to sustain and generate world media attention to their plight. It examines specifically the role of memory and material memorabilia in providing a focus for the community to further articulate their demands for adequate restitution for their displacement from District Six. It fundamentally questions whether the 'direct action, bottom-up' approach of the former District Six residents, successfully employed in publicising internationally the plight of neighbourhood, will be as useful or successful in ensuring the delivery on new physical domains in similar situations elsewhere.

Introduction

'District Six' is well known both within South Africa and further afield as the celebrated multiracial neighbourhood which was destroyed as a result of the planning policies in place during the 'apartheid era' in the country. Prominent writers such as Alex La Guma and political families such as the Goules were known to have come from the neighbourhood[1].

Whilst today most of what remains of District Six is below the foundations of the *Cape Technikon*, the District Six museum, within an old Methodist Church, stands as a testimony to the area's past. The District Six Land Trust and various constituted former residents' associations also are physical and statutory symbols of the continued importance of 'District Six' as an issue at local and national level.

In the first section of this chapter the context in which District Six existed is described to provide the background to the second section which analyses the success of the District Six protest campaign at publicity media levels and also at practical level in ensuring the provision of housing for the displaced residents. The final section considers the issues that the District Six case study highlights which are of universal relevance to other 'unempowered' communities who suffer political, socio-economic or other disadvantage.

Throughout the chapter the author critically considers the status and situation of District Six and its residents in relation to the typical position in which most urban dwellers in developing countries find themselves. Its premise is that, although it is rightly acknowledged that District Six was a unique housing situation, there are crucial lessons that the community based approaches adopted to demand the reinstatement and repopulation of the neighbourhood can teach other communities in urban areas. It argues that even in totalitarian political states there are often avenues for community action through non conventional ideas and methods such as those used by the District Six residents which can have very effective results.

An equally candid analysis is given of the specificity of the urban housing and community organisational structure in District Six to contrast with the received imagery of the neighbourhood. This chapter thus puts forward a counter-argument that high profile community action can only have limited success in delivering its goals if it is unable to deliver practical physical goals. Housing need and provision requires more tangible practical solutions than conceptual media coverage.

This brief introduction, the contextual analysis and the conclusions to the work are intended to bring to this volume a discussion or debate on the necessity and appropriateness of community exploration of unconventional methods of raising awareness by self-promotion through advertising and media activities, as the piece's study of District Six has shown.

The context to District Six

In this section the analysis that follows begins with a description of Cape Town, the city in which District Six is located, as the urban setting for this study. This is followed by an in-depth discussion of the historical and contemporary development of District Six. The section concludes by describing the scenario in which District Six was left before the forced removals took place in 1966.

Cape Town

Cape Town metropolis is reputed to have the largest urban conurbation in Southern Africa. It comprises a multi-cultural population, comprising all Southern African racial groups[2]. In the pre 'self-determination' Nationalist party era, Cape Town was officially legislated as a 'coloured preference' area. This meant that there was a government-enforced employment system ensuring jobs were given to 'coloured' South Africans in the Western Cape in preference to 'Blacks', unless there was no 'Coloured' labour available to fill in jobs[3].

This employment restriction on Black labour in the Cape Region was also enforced through Government imposed controls on Black migration to cities and townships in the Province throughout the period[4]. This led to a fall in the provision of state- and self- built housing for Blacks in the Province. Contrastingly the period saw the manifold increase in the construction of 'shanty' housing in and around urban areas in the Western Cape, especially in Cape Town.

Before 1948, prior to the Nationalist era, Cape Town had been a multi-cultural seaport. Known as the 'Tavern of the Seas', it was a thriving seaport embracing sailors, immigrants and cultures from throughout the world. Although within the structures of a greater Republic, Cape Town up until 1948 remained a relatively autonomous city, despite its connection with the South African hinterland. Thus the city's central- and port- areas had neighbourhoods which became the home to different ethnic groups. These included the *Bo Kaap* or '*Malay Quarter*', *Oranjezchist* or 'Gardens', the Jewish Quarter, and District Six, a mixed neighbourhood (Figure 7.1).

This forms the context to the next part of this section which describes the situation existing in District Six. The area designated as District Six was obliterated from the street maps in Cape Town after the forced removals in 1966. The former community which resided there however kept the memory of District Six alive through various activities which are discussed in this work.

District Six

This analysis considers specifically the housing development in District Six, from its pre-Nationalist Party years through to today. However to set the context to this

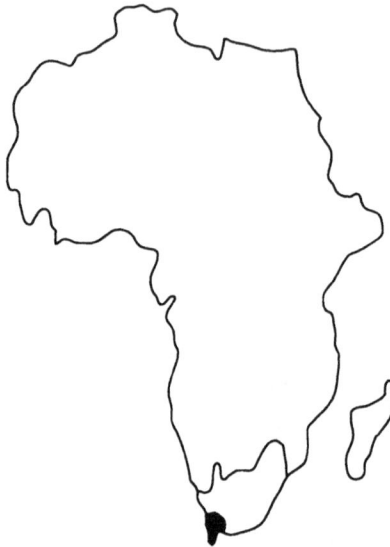

Figure 7.1   Cape Town, South Africa

analysis we first provide a short description of District Six. The neighbourhood has its origins in the early development of greater Cape Town in the last century, when it was a connecting area between the city and the garden and farm areas south of the Port[5].

Archival records suggest that the area originally was built for the middle class residents of the City[6]. The development of the Southern suburbs led to the flight of the affluent residents further away from the city, and to the development of a multi- class and multi-cultural community in District Six in its place. Past street municipality records show the variety of backgrounds and ethnicities that street inhabitants came from[7].

The socio-economic circumstances of District Six have been equally varied. Although it was a predominantly working class neighbourhood, there were also a number of middle class residents in listed professions[8]. Thus it remained a community within a formal context throughout its existence, it had a higher socio-economic status than shanty towns and most townships which had sprung up in the racially divided South Africa. Its culturally heterogeneous population also ensured that there was a mixed religious and cultural focus to the neighbourhood's existence.

Its multi-cultural status began to change relatively early this century initially with the removal of a sizeable black community to the first Black Township, *Ndabeni* following a plague epidemic in 1903. District Six however reached its heyday after this event in the 1940s and 1950s. By then District Six had become the cultural and intellectual focus for many liberal Capetonians and South Africans. It was also a well known haunt for sailors, writers, such as Alex La Guma, politicians such as the Goules, and aspiring professionals lived in the community amongst other residents who owned or rented their homes.

The change of government in 1948 and the subsequent implementation of its 'apartheid' policy, led to the official legislation to implement the forced removals of residents of District Six. The neighbourhood was proclaimed a 'white' area and its non-white residents were deemed illegal residents who were expected to move to new housing built in outlying townships of Cape Town. The official reason given for the demolition of the neighbourhood, (as opposed to its simply changing its racial categorisation) was the need to eradicate the slum environment and attendant vices which the neighbourhood encouraged. A series of other issues however equally worked to ensure the forced removals and the eventual attempted official obliteration of the neighbourhood took place. These issues were both physical and socio-cultural and are discussed in the following paragraphs.

Geography The geographical and physical location of District Six, close to Cape Town, meant its identity would come into conflict with the more 'formal' and 'ordered' parts of the city. Thus the official terminology 'black spot' used to describe other such multiracial areas in what would otherwise have ostensibly been 'white' has metaphorical and physical resonance[9] (Figure 7.2).

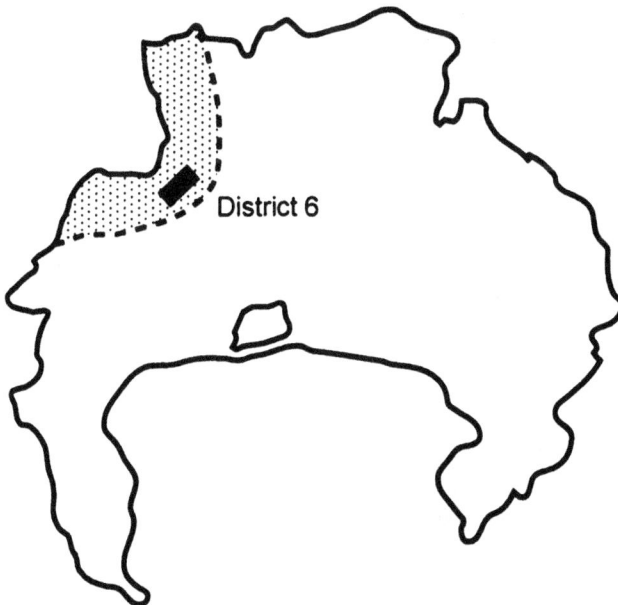

Figure 7.2   Location of District Six

Racial fears and socio-politics   District Six and other multi-racial neighbourhoods in the Nationalist-ruled South Africa were cultural aberrations which could not be tolerated. The central thesis of apartheid was the separation of the races, the close proximity of racial groups except for necessary work purposes was not encouraged. Miscegenation, resulting from 'illicit' unions was unacceptable as it flew in the face of established social mores and, in the long run threatened the supremacy of the white race. Embodied in District Six therefore was the existence of a multicultural and multiracial society which the government of the day chose through its apartheid policies to obliterate.

   The patently challenging views and lifestyles of the more radical residents of District Six were also at odds with the conservative political outlook of the ruling party. The dangerous precedent of having such a substantial number of residents in opposition to key issues in the new 'apartheid' policy must have had some bearing on the decision to 'remove' or relocate residents from District Six. It has also been pointed out that District Six was considered too close to the main transport networks - road, rail, and access to the sea- and air-port. Thus for strategic reasons also the neighbourhood had to go.

Real estate economics and planning   The real estate value of District Six due to its proximity and relationship to prime Cape Town land cannot be underestimated. From an economic perspective the area therefore had profit potential under the somewhat uncertain construction which epitomised the area just before it was demolished. The more desirable parts of District Six, located near Table Mountain have, since the area's demolition, been sold and built on by private speculators (Figure 7.3).

   Similarly the strategic location of District Six as part of the greater Cape Town metropolis led in the 1960s and 1970s to large tracts of its land being given over to road networks. More recently the *Cape Tecknikon* was built on a substantial portion of the remaining parts of District Six. Generally much of District Six's physical boundaries have been transformed or obliterated through the effects of developer speculation on prime land in a free market economy.

The eviction

In 1966 the Cape Provincial Council proclaimed the housing in District Six unfit for human occupation and the area a 'white group area'. Forced evictions and relocations of 'coloured' and black residents to segregated 'townships' in Mitchell's Plain, *Athlone, Manenberg* and *Guguletu* rapidly followed this.

   Most of the residential accommodation and built infrastructure in District Six was demolished, and the Cape Government pronounced new development initiatives for the area, now renamed *Zonnenbloem*[10].

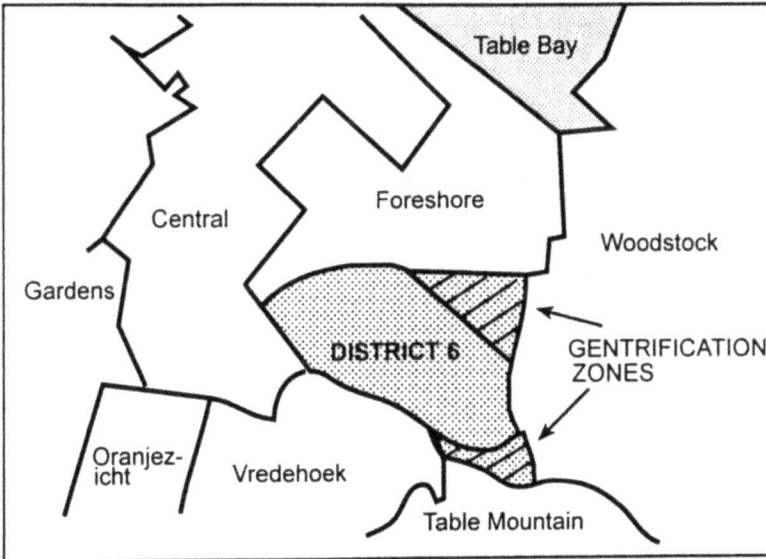

Figure 7.3   Closest Cape Town wards to District Six

These plans came to nought, except for the construction of a polytechnic, the *Cape Tecknikon*, on part of the site in the 1980s. The government was unable to generate the financial backing which it expected to get for the site's redevelopment. Similarly the plan to erase the name 'District Six' was successful only in policy and official documentation. The local memory of District Six and the community it embodied was not obliterated. *Zonnenbloem*, the newly christened territory remained only an 'official name' and a written reminder of the government's wishes and plans for the area.

In the next section we consider the campaign that the District Six community set up to fight for the recognition of the injustice done through the forced removal of the entire community. The battle also was waged to gain government recognition and restitution to the owners of properties demolished during the forced removals.

This section has summarised the background to the events and also the activities that preceded the formation of the community initiatives discussed in the following section which led to the continued campaigning and publicity given to the forced removals and loss of community housing and livelihoods in District Six. It is unlikely that the community would have formed such strong allegiances and commitments to the cause if the history of the neighbourhood and the form of removals had not been as ingrained in the local memory. This background is crucial to understanding the events which have followed the forced clearances more than thirty years ago.

The struggle for District Six

The campaign

The campaign for District 6 has been fought on many fronts, the most successful and sustained being the media's involvement and influence in portraying the District Six saga on the international stage. Because District Six, in its hey day had a number of prominent South African residents of all races, living within its boundaries, it could draw on a rich and varied past cultural history. In this section the various forms of community involvement in the advertisement of, and wooing of, the media to the plight of District Six.

The key campaigns which have been staged to highlight District Six have been the following:

The cultural component

Literature - including books, poetry and plays There is a substantial amount of literature which has been written on District Six. A lot has been written by former residents in the form of memoirs, stories and sometimes poetry. The visual imagery of the place was captured by the local photographer, Jansjie Wissema, whose photographs have gained international acclaim[11].

Music District Six the musical, and the work of various formerly District Six resident artistes. As with the literature component, there have been a series of songs and a musical written about District Six. Many of the community's best known musicians also were able to leave South Africa and act as ambassadors for the community in far flung parts of the world. The musical 'District Six', also toured internationally which further promoted the District Six cause.

The District Six museum Situated in the former Methodist Church in the heart of what was District Six, the museum began as a temporary exhibition of various elements of the material culture of District Six. It was so successful that it over-ran its expected duration and became a permanent exhibition of the material culture of the District Six community.

Since its establishment the museum has had artefacts such as street signs, photographs and taped interviews donated to it by members of the former community and others who had an interest in the neighbourhood (Plate 7.1). The museum is also intensively used by the various focus groups and former community members for cultural activities such as concerts and book launches. It has essentially become the most potent symbol of the former community's existence and continuing presence in contemporary Cape Town.

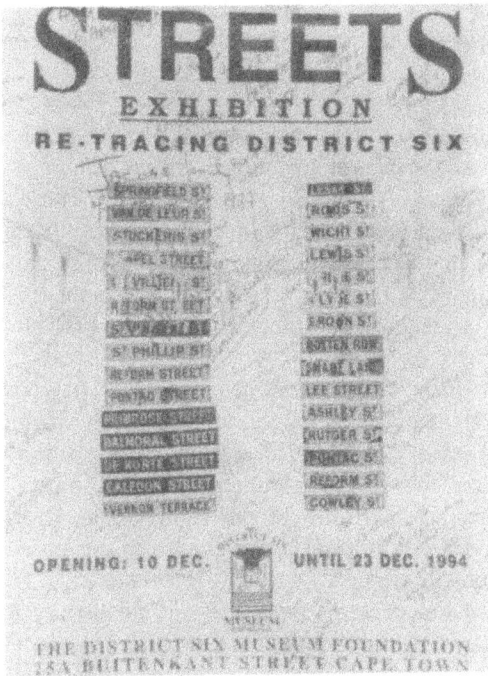

Plate 7.1   District Six Museum poster

The other activities which the community has been involved in have been more conventional, they included:

The action and protest groups This title includes all the protest groups which were constituted since the removals.   Many of these groups have achieved some successes in bringing various issues relating to development on what remains of the District Six territory to the public attention.   It is probable that it was through the underlying influence of these groups that there has been limited development aside from government projects on the site of the former District Six.

Through the sustained high profile protests from the 1960s to the present day there has been very limited private interest in developing new properties or housing estates in the officially designated *Zonnenbloem* area.   Also a few years after the final clearances of the area the then nationalist government redesignated an area adjoining District Six as a 'coloured' area.   This would seem to be a concession granted to the protest groups who had been vociferous in their opposition to the move.

In contemporary times the action groups have continued to challenge the now democratically elected government's attempts at the urban regeneration of the area.

The group also takes a critical view of the formal planning and community groups who have been legally entrusted with District Six's regeneration.

The committees This group includes a number of formally constituted committees which have more direct links with the current government bodies that are involved in the re-planning and regeneration of District Six and other areas. These groups have the remit to act 'on behalf' of local communities at governmental level in order to ensure that the plans for regeneration meet with local consultation and approval, and also that whatever settlements, through land compensation or redistribution, the community or individuals within it are entitled to, are given accordingly.

The activities and groups which this section has described have worked successfully to incorporate different strands of the former District Six communities in the protest movements involved in keeping the memory of the community alive. Whilst the constituted associations and committees had the most formal organisations involved in campaigning for the various rights of the District Six residents, the more community-focused cultural activities such as the museum and the musical had more far-reaching influence.

The museum represents the best example of the success of community focused activity as a vehicle for publicity and spontaneous local support. Its success as a museum owes as much to local association and identity with the 'project' as it does to the international interest in its contents. As a symbol the museum has been able to project local feelings about the events in District Six and also indirectly act as a protest symbol about the continuing problems that the District Six's redevelopment is beset with. The museum has acted as a receptacle or container of community material culture and memory which have resulted in it being more successful than any of the other interventions in projecting the history and plight of District Six onto the national and international stage.

Thus as a community based initiative the museum project has shown that this non-conventional initiative has proved successful as a community approach to publicising the housing and infrastructure requirements of the former residents and their relationship to the new regeneration plans for the re-established District Six area.

The achievements of the community based interventions

Although none of the community protests which took place before the forced removals were able to halt the process, various concessions have been made to the area. A few years after the declaration of District Six as a 'white' area, an area of District Six, close to the then neighbourhood of Woodstock was redefined as being 'coloured'. This meant that a few District Six residents who lived or had moved to this area were guaranteed legal status as residents.

In more recent times the high profile community activities such as the museum and committees have succeeded in keeping District Six constantly in the media attention. The District Six museum attracts visitors from all over the world and it has 'links' with museums in Europe. There has also been a series of publications on District Six which have similarly kept the public gaze on the neighbourhood. The residents' committees and action groups have also raised the debate about the area's regeneration and have begun to ensure that forms of financial restitution or resettlement are available to surviving and remaining District Six residents.

The setbacks to the community based approaches have also been notable. As at 1996 District Six residents had no more than promises that some would be resettled in new housing in the neighbourhood. There remains the unresolved debate as to how District Six should be redeveloped and regenerated. Other contributors to the debate and the regeneration process argue that the area would have to be open to other residents if it were to become a truly multicultural community. There is also an ongoing discussion with the educational planners as to the future of the Tecknikon which exists on District Six land and an earlier plan which had proposed that the area should be transformed into an 'educational quarter'.

Despite the setbacks, District Six is likely to have a regeneration plan which will incorporate some if not all of its former residents in its housing plans. The high profile which the redevelopment of the neighbourhood has received is due considerably to the community based interventions which this section has discussed. Other neighbourhoods which suffered the same fate such as *Sofiatown* in Johannesburg and *Cato Manor* in Durban have had less success in achieving what the District Six community movements have.

In the final section the work discusses why the District Six community approach to highlighting housing need and regeneration has been relatively successful, and what lessons can be learned by other developing countries from the community based interventions discussed as case studies in this section.

Do grassroots publicity and media success guarantee successful housing ? An analysis

The current scenario

The new political and social scenario which began with the negotiations and discussions in the late 1980s has led to the re-emergence of District Six, both as an issue and as a memory. As with two similar areas in Cape Town, the *Bo Kaap*, and *Mowbray*, there have been moves to redevelop what property remains standing in

District Six, amounting to 'gentrification'. The main players in this redevelopment game are the more affluent or outright property speculators.

As a counter to this free market redevelopment also in existence are the various District Six pressure groups. The group discussed in detail in the previous section has established the District Six museum, with archival, oral and material records of District Six up until its demolition.

This group and others have been successful in ensuring that all discussions about the area's future development are discussed openly with past residents who can and do claim ownership of much of the bulldozed land.

It is uncertain at present what this course of events will do to shape the redevelopment of the re-christened District Six. However it is clear that there remains a conflict between the developer-driven aspirations for its redevelopment and the past residents' views on its reclamation. Furthermore the publicity which the area generates, largely through sustained community actions such as the Museum project, has resulted in its future development remaining a high profile affair.

The analysis

For District Six, the community's role in generating the publicity, and the media attention which followed this has been crucial in raising the debate about the area's future. However whilst the grassroots involvement in raising the profile of the debate has been successful, future housing delivery in the area is still fraught with difficulties. The families who will eventually be rehoused or will be entitled to housing in the regenerated District Six are unlikely to be representative of all families who had lived in the area in the past.

Many families who had originally lived in District Six up to its forced demolition were tenants or subtenants and thus have been unable to claim property or land restitution from the government. Furthermore the dispersal of District Six happened more than twenty years ago, this has meant that many families no longer have the links or are interested in resettling in the area, whilst there are other families without a direct claim to restitution who would like to have access to housing in the area.

There is also a culture structure which remains prevalent in the continuing debates and publicity about District Six. The successes it has had in organising community actions to highlight the injustices of the past legislation have been made possible by the unique cultural and social history of the community resident in District Six. Whilst by the time the removals took place in the late 1960s the area could not have been described as an affluent middle class neighbourhood, the kinds of resident who lived within its boundaries made up an alternative community. Many of the families who lived in the community were thus well educated and had professional members who can still be identified in the diaspora of residents from the area.

This is likely to have had a great effect on the local interest in redeveloping or 'gentrifying' the area, which has taken place elsewhere in Cape Town. The local knowledge of the families who had lived in District Six such as the Goules meant that many investors and property speculators were unlikely to have felt tempted to purchase or develop property which might at a future date be challenged by surviving family members, which is the situation which now pertains to the remaining vacant land in the area.

This has meant that the publicity generated has had a greater than local audience. For example the writings of Alex La Guma and the jazz artistry of 'Dullah Ibrahim are internationally acclaimed. Also the organisational skills and perseverance of effort has been better handled than it might have been in communities with fewer skills or resources available. Similarly, although most of the poor in South Africa would be considered equally poor elsewhere in the developing world, the inhuman situation that the 'apartheid' policies enforced in South Africa put its ethnic minority urban dwellers in, through group areas legislation, led to the District Six campaign and publicity generating higher profile publicity and interest on the international stage.

Also District Six, although racially mixed in the eyes of the then National Party government, had already become a lighter mix than it had been prior to the earlier forced removals of most blacks to the first township of *Ndabeni* earlier on in the century. Areas such as Elsie's River, known for its shanty town population of poor blacks from all over Southern Africa, were in essence more racially mixed, poorer and had worse facilities. District Six therefore could not be considered to be the worst or poorest mixed race neighbourhood in the Cape Town metropolis, and so had considerable clout in developing and sustaining its protest groups.

Within the District Six context the grassroots publicity and media success that its community interventions have produced have had a very beneficial effect in guaranteeing a wide debate about the urban regeneration of the area and also a limited amount of housing provision for former residents of the area. Its validity as a replicable case study for other communities is less certain.

District Six, South Africa and the local community who lived in the neighbourhood have all been seen to have been unusual if not unique. In most urban communities suffering relocation their physical locale, socio-cultural importance, and urban-political relationship are of little or no publicity value. Thus at that level the District Six case study does represent a unique record.

However the success of the District Six Museum and the other local history projects which its foundation has spawned does provide a case study in cultural development and recording for other communities. Whilst most of District Six's physical fabric has been demolished and its community remains in diaspora

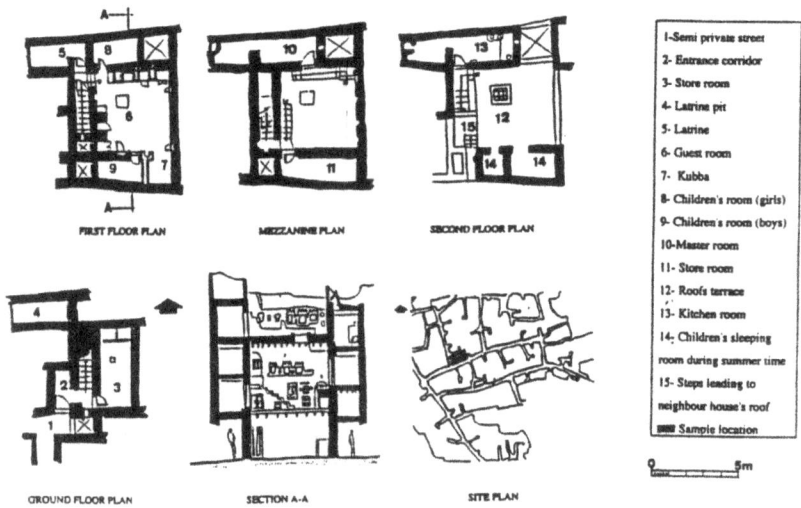

	1-Semi private street
	2- Entrance corridor
	3- Store room
	4- Latrine pit
	5- Latrine
	6- Guest room
	7- Kubba
	8- Children's room (girls)
	9- Children's room (boys)
	10-Master room
	11- Store room
	12- Roofs terrace
	13- Kitchen room
	14- Children's sleeping room during summer time
	15- Steps leading to neighbour house's roof
	Sample location

FIRST FLOOR PLAN   MEZZANINE PLAN   SECOND FLOOR PLAN

GROUND FLOOR PLAN   SECTION A-A   SITE PLAN

Figure 5.6   Layout of a traditional Ghadames house in the Tangzin neighbourhood

The most interesting room is at the same level as the middle home, and is called *elkubba*. It is a small space and is reserved for two special occasions, the first being when a women marries and the second when her husband dies. The space is used for one night only, for the first night of the marriage (when it is richly and traditionally furnished and decorated) and when the husband dies, when the widow spends the night there. Her son, if living in the same house, could bring his newly married wife to spend the first night in this place. Additional rooms have access directly from the living room, either at floor level or at mezzanine level; in the latter case, with a flight of steps inside the room. The mezzanine level mainly which, in the District Six case, was almost entirely at a conceptual 'past memory' level. For most communities in developing countries the locations of the shanties, townships, slum dwellings or informal settlements remain real and physical, thus the task that District Six was able to overcome was more difficult. As a case in point the success of District Six should serve as encouragement to all communities which today struggle for the right to exist and retain their urban spatial identity.

Notes

1 Alex La Guma's most well known writings were published as short stories entitled *A Walk in the Night* (La Guma, 1967). Whilst for the role of the Goul family in politics see Davenport (1992, pp.286-287).
2 The racial group categories used throughout this paper are as classified by the past administration: White, Coloured, Black and Indian, including also the 'Malay' sub-category.
3 Throughout this chapter the words 'Black', 'Coloured' (mixed race) and 'White' are used in the South African racial terminology.
4 'Influx controls' had been in force before the Nationalist Party came into power in 1948, but became more strictly enforced in the early 1950s and stayed in existence until the late 1980s in the Western Cape Province.
5 There are various sources that have written about the history of Cape Town (see Bickford Smith (1995); Fowler (1990)).
6 Personal viewing of District Six Museum documentation, Cape Town, September 1995.
7 District Six in the 1940s comprised residents who were Black, White, Coloured, Muslim, Jewish, Christian, minor professionals, traders and civil servants, to name a few.
8 As shown in archival street records displayed at the District Six Museum.
9 *Sofiatown*, *Cato Manor* in Johannesburg and Durban, were other 'black spots' in the Apartheid Town structure.
10 For more on 'forced removals' see Davenport (1992, pp.343-346 & 380) and Platzky & Walker (1985, p.36).
11 See Smail & Wissema (1986).

Bibliography

BA (Econ. History) thesis (1989), *Building developments in District Six, BPSA's proposal.* Unpublished.
Baines, T. (1852), *History of the commerce and town of Liverpool*, Longman: London.

Barnett, N. (1993), *Race, ousing and Cape Town c. 1920-1940, with special reference to District Six*, MA (History) thesis, University of Cape Town: Cape Town. Unpublished.

Berelowitz, I. (1989), 'The Jews of District Six', *Weekend Argos*, 21 January, Cape Town,

Bickford-Smith, V. (1995), *Ethnic pride and racial prejudice in victorian Cape Town*, Cambridge University Press: Cambridge.

Bradlow, F., and Cairns, M. (1978), *The early Cape Muslims: A study of their mosques, geneology and origin*, Balkema: Cape Town.

Cape Times. (1981), *Cape Times*, May, Cape Town, General article on new housing built in District Six.

Cape Times. (1990), '"Headstart" Proposal', *Cape Times*, 5 April, Cape Town,

Cape Times Property Section. (1996), 'Zonnenbloem', *Cape Times*, 11 August, Cape Town,

Cape Times/Argos. 'Fracas over land claims', *Cape Times/Argos*, 7 August, Cape Town,

Cape Town Community Land Forum. (1996), *District Six development project planning process and financial approach*, South African Government:

Centre for Intergroup Studies. (1983), *Group areas*. Occasional Paper, 7, 1983, Centre for Intergroup Studies, University of Cape Town: Cape Town.

Citizen, T. (1990), 'District Six declaration as a free area', *The Citizen*, 29 March, Cape Town,

Davenport, T.R.H. (1992), *South Africa - A modern history*, 4th Ed., Macmillan: London.

District Six Steering Committee. (1993), *District Six: redevelopment process and planning relations document*, South African Government:

Fowler, H., and Fowler, F. (1990), *The concise Oxford dictionary of current English usage*, 8th Ed., Clarendon Press: Oxford.

Hall, M. (1992), *People in a changing urban landscape: Excavating Cape Town*, University of Cape Town: Cape Town. Inaugural lecture, 25 March.

Hart, M.D. *Master plans: The South African Government's razing of Sophiatown, Cato Manor and District Six*, PhD thesis, Department of Geography, University of Syracuse, USA Unpublished.

Heliburth, B. (1983), 'Scruples not at home in restored District Six', *Star*, 14 February, Cape Town,

Home, R. (1997), *Of planning and planting: The making of British colonial cities*, Spon: London.

Jeppie, S., and Soudien, C. (eds) (1990), *The struggle for District Six*, Buchu Books: Cape Town.

Marks, R., and Bezzoli, M. (1996), 'The urbanism of District Six', *Africa's Urban Past*, School of Oriental and African Studies, London. Paper presented at conference.

Mayson, J.S. (1963), *The Malays of Cape Town*, African Connoisseurs Press: Cape Town.

Nasson, B. (1986), 'Oral history and the reconstruction of District Six', *Western Cape Roots and Realities*, University of Cape Town. Paper presented at conference.

Pama, C. (1977), *Bowler's Cape Town: Life at the Cape in early victorian times 1834-1868*, Tafelberg: Cape Town.

Rand Daily Mail. (1983), *Rand Daily Mail*, 3 May, Cape Town, Article alleging homes bought by Whites at subsidised government rates (approx. R35,000) were resold privately at R75,000, making a R40,000 profit.

Saunders, C., Phillips, H., et al. (eds) (1988), *Studies in the history of Cape Town*, Centre for African Studies: Cape Town.

Schoeman, C. (1994), *The Spirit of Kanala*, Human and Rousseau: Cape Town.

Smail, A., and Wissema, J. (1986), *District Six*, Fontein: Cape Town.

Smith, D. (1982), 'Urban and social change under apartheid: Some recent developments', in Smith, D. (ed) *Living under apartheid*, Allen and Unwin: London, pp.32-37.

South African Government. (1994), *Restitution of land rights Act No. 22*. Government Gazette, Section 34, 25 November, South African Government:

Uduku, O. (1996), 'Beneficial sustainable urban redevelopment? A Cape Town Liverpool comparison', *IAPS*, Sweden, August, Unpublished.

Western, J. (1982), 'The geography of urban and social control: Group areas and the 1976, 1980 civil unrest in Cape Town', in Smith, D. (ed) *Living under apartheid*, Allen and Unwin: London, pp.217-226.

Section III
Case studies from Asia

8 Housing adaptable to changing conditions:

A physical analysis of the older neighbourhoods of *Yokne'am Illit*, Israel

IRIS ARAVOT

Yokne'am Illit is a town of 25,000 inhabitants near Haifa. *Shehunat HaTemanim* - the Yemenite neighbourhood and *Shehunat HaKurdim* - the Kurdish neighbourhood, the two older areas of *Yokne'am Illit*, were built in the fifties to house new immigrants. Currently these two districts are enjoying an upsurge of spontaneous revitalisation on private initiative.

These neighbourhoods can, therefore, be considered as good examples of successful housing patterns, adjustable to changing conditions. This chapter offers a detailed analysis of their physical attributes, and some conclusions about possible adaptation of these attributes to new housing solutions.

The analysis concentrates on the three following groups of aspects:

1. Figure/ground relationships.
2. Characteristics of houses.
3. Characteristics of the unbuilt areas.

Some principles for future housing schemes in *Yokne'am Illit* are also recommended.

Introduction

Yokne'am Illit (Upper *Yokne'am*) is a new town of 25,000 inhabitants, situated in a hilly area some ten kilometres south of Haifa. *Shehunat HaTemanim* - the Yemenite neighbourhood and *Shehunat HaKurdim* - the Kurdish neighbourhood, the two older areas of *Yokne'am Illit*, were built in the fifties as humble housing solutions for new immigrants.

181

Shehunat HaTemanim and *Shehunat HaKurdim* are located on two adjacent hill tops and are bounded by the steeper slopes of the hills. They are composed of 250 housing units extending over an area of 200,000 square metres.

There are many interrelated reasons for revitalisation in this area including:

1. The rapid expansion of *Yokne'am Illit* during the last decade, due to government initiative.
2. Development of two big industrial areas in the vicinity.
3. The plan for Route 6 - the cross-Israel-toll-road to pass nearby.
4. Increasing demand for quality housing in the Haifa area.
5. Rising costs of Haifa inner-city apartments.

These and other related issues encourage the private market tendency to explore housing potential in the outlying region of Haifa and in *Yokne'am Illit* area in particular.

Here we may ask: what are the qualities of the specific urban surroundings which ultimately benefit from this general trend towards revitalisation? What makes one existing neighbourhood more attractive than another in the same regional context? Within these local parameters two factors apparently play significant roles, namely, housing patterns and socio-economic image.

Shehunat HaTemanim and *Shehunat HaKurdim*, originally inhabited by new immigrants of African and Asian origin, have never embodied any cultural or socio-economic prestige. On the contrary, for some decades they contrasted sharply with the relatively affluent *Moshava Yokne'am* - the rural village founded at the beginning of the century by European immigrants. So we must consider planning attributes as major components of the success of these two neighbourhoods' revitalisation.

However, it is apparent that their adaptability to new conditions has played a major role in this recent process, rather than the housing patterns themselves. For example: the plans of the original apartments were unimportant, because they were completely integrated in the schemes of the new dwellings. In this respect, the distances between neighbouring houses - and thus perimeters of possible extensions - had much more impact.

The following is a detailed analysis of the physical attributes of the two neighbourhoods and some conclusions about possible adaptation of some attributes to new housing solutions.

Analysis

The analysis concentrates on three issues: a) 'the positive' - i.e. the built objects (housing units); b) 'the negative' - i.e. the unbuilt areas, either privately owned or shared by several households and functionally defined or undefined; c) the relationships between 'positive' and 'negative', i.e. a) and b).

The third issue will be discussed before the first and the second. In contradiction to the classifying categories which were a-priori defined, sub-categories for analysis were suggested by the reality of the revitalised neighbourhoods themselves:

1. Aspects of 'figure/ground' relationships:
   a) Adjacent houses, b) Dimensions, c) Density and d) Height of buildings.
2. Characteristics of houses:
   a) The built volume, b) Siting of houses, c) Typical building elements, d) Perceived density and e) Outlook from the neighbourhood.
3. Characteristics of unbuilt areas:
   a) General impression, b) Public open space, green strips, c) Streets and paths and d) Private open spaces.

The analysis is based on the conditions of the early nineties. The original plans for the neighbourhoods are referred to as and when relevant.

Aspects of 'figure/ground' relationships

Figures 8.1 and 8.2 present the relationships between open spaces and built-up areas by means of figure/ground analysis (i.e. regardless of the function of the open space as street, public garden, private yard etc.).

The extensiveness of the 'ground' (in black) is easily noticeable. This relationship has several quantitative and qualitative attributes.

Adjacent houses

There are broad spaces between adjacent houses. even when they are close to each other on one side, other directions enjoy unobstructed views (Plate 8.1). In quantified terms:

'close' = 7 metres distance between houses (on one side)
'remote' = 25-40 metres between houses in two or more directions.

Dimensions

The original residential units were small. Even the present day bulk of the extended houses does not dominate the streets, and the views from the streets are unimpeded by long or high facades. Fences are low and do not produce 'wall'

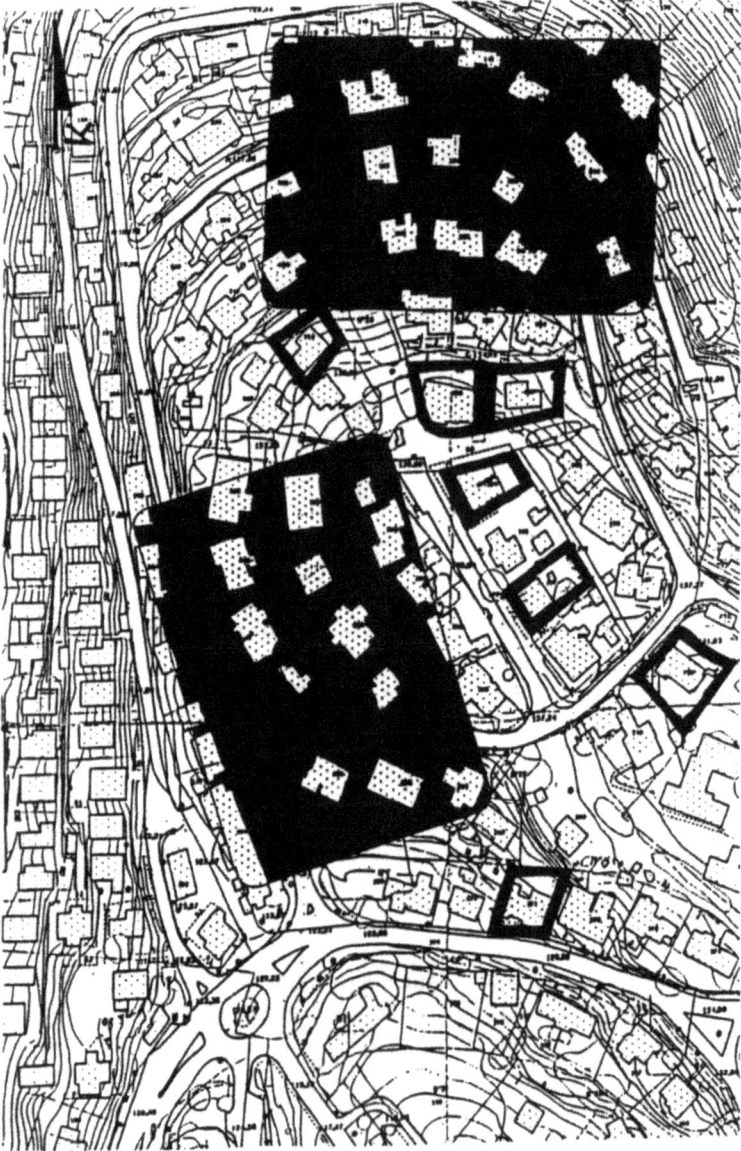

Figure 8.1   **Figure/ground relationships in *Shehunat HaTemanim***

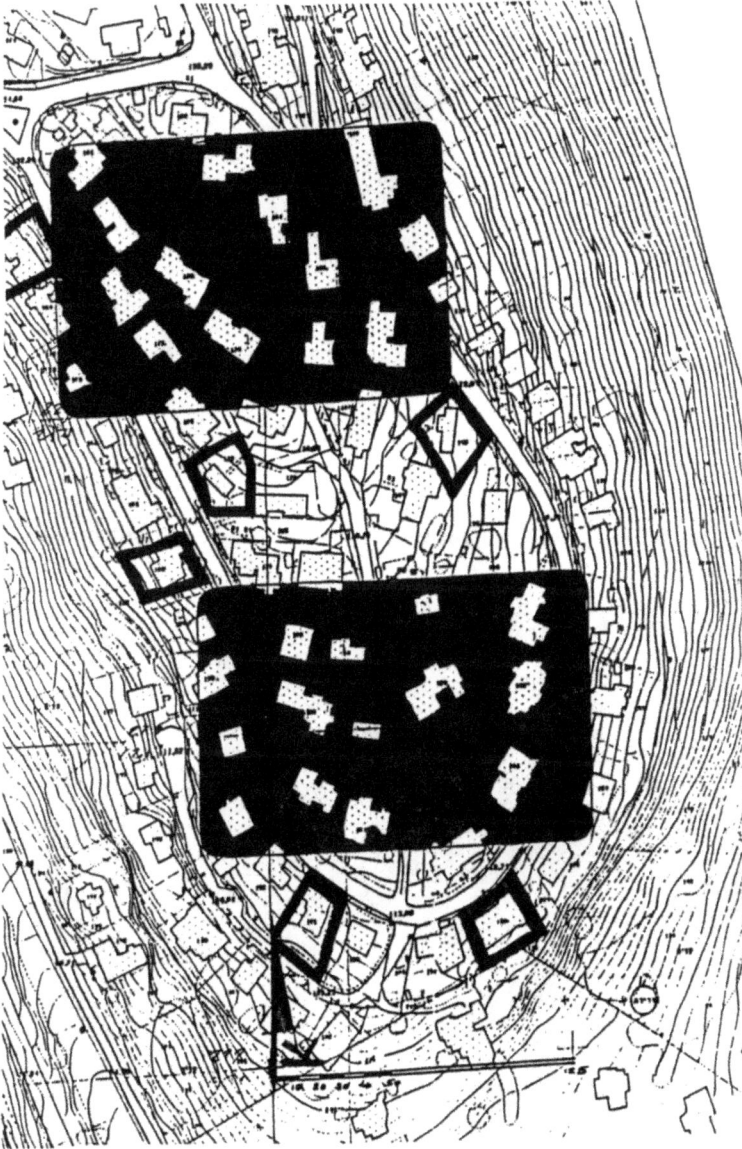

Figure 8.2   Figure/ground relationships in *Shehunat HaKurdim*

Plate 8.1a **Overall image of low density due to vegetation and unobstructed views**

Plate 8.1b **Overall image of low density due to vegetation and unobstructed views**

images. In quantified terms:

Maximum extent of facade of a residential building: 40 metres
Overall extent of facades of residential buildings: 12 x 20 metres

Density

The original building density was very low in comparison with contemporary urban density in Israel, particularly in terms of percentage of floor space. However, the original density is now undergoing profound modification according to recent local urban planning. In quantified terms:

Original density: 1 dwelling unit (house) per plot of 770-900 square metres, i.e. 1-1.3 dwelling unit per 1,000 square metres.
Current density, according to recent plans: 50-60 per cent F.A.R., i.e. up to 6 dwelling units per 1,000 square metres.

Height of buildings

The original houses were low (one to two storeys) and appeared even lower because of their small overall volume. Many of them were situated below street level so that only their red roofs were visible. Houses built above street level, located *vis á vis* those below street level, were set back far enough from the street to create an open perspective and not overshadow those passing by (Figure 8.3). Thus the sections of most of the streets were originally and still are asymmetrical.

Original building height: up to two stories high with sloping roof
Current modifications: two to three stories with basement and sloping roof.

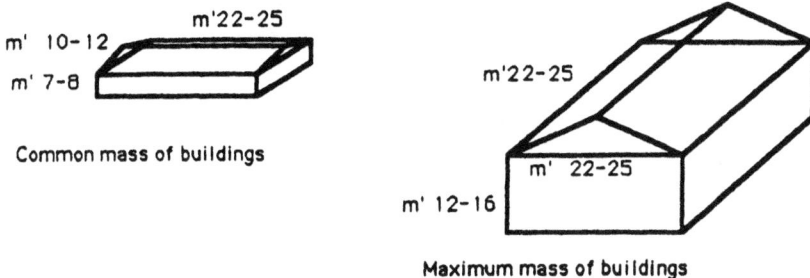

m' 10-12 m'22-25
m' 7-8

Common mass of buildings

m'22-25
m' 22-25
m' 12-16

Maximum mass of buildings

Figure 8.3   **Sections of most of the streets were originally and still are symmetrical**

Characteristics of houses

There were four original types of housing units - detached, semi-detached, row houses (terraces) and two-storey apartment blocks of four apartments with communal staircases (Plate 8.2). Of these, only a few have retained their original characteristics. Most of the existing houses at the time of this study are extensions of the original modest units.

The older extensions are also relatively modest. They are small and are easily recognisable as distinct additions to the original house (Plate 8.3). Recent extensions, on the other hand, are very large (up to 200 square metres) and virtually engulf the original houses (Plate 8.4). The following are quantitative and qualitative expressions of some of the buildings' characteristics.

Plate 8.2a   Few houses maintained their original form

Plate 8.2b   Few houses maintained their original form

Plate 8.3a   Older extensions are relatively modest

Plate 8.3b   Older extensions are relatively modest

Plate 8.4a   Recent extensions virtually engulf the original houses

Plate 8.4b   Recent extensions virtually engulf the original houses

The built volume

The overall built volumes, including those of extended units, are relatively small in the Israeli context.   This may be due to the predominant housing types, i.e. detached, semi-detached, terraces and two-storey apartment blocks (Figure 8.4).

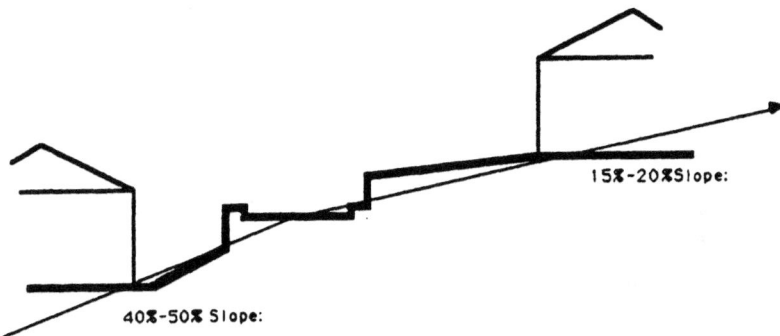

Figure 8.4   The overall built volumes are relatively small

Siting of houses

The buildings are only marginally aligned with the streets. Each building is sited according to the terrain. Since the streets also follow topography there are only a few complementary examples of classically urban street sections. Usually there is no general feeling of constriction or closure.

As regards arrangement of houses in relation to the street - one facade is parallel or nearly parallel to the street (Figure 8.5) though houses are rarely parallel to each other, but are laid out to follow the topography (Figure 8.6).

Typical building elements

The building elements are modest and functional, very commonplace and of the popular kind. They may best be classified as 'modernist Israeli vernacular'. They may also be regarded as 'the ugly and the ordinary' - to quote Robert Venturi's seminal distinction in his book *Learning from Las Vegas* (1972).

Typical building elements are:

- flat facades;
- basic, usually rectangular, plasticity (the house as a cube, the roof as a triangular prism, verandas as cubes);
- simple, unsophisticated coating materials (plaster, aluminium, PVC);
- pale colours (off white, light grey, light brown; no bold colours);
- almost complete absence of symbolic elements;
- stone fences, and
- exterior concrete paving (in private yards).

The place seems completely uninfluenced by the varying architectural styles of the last 15 years, and the houses do not seem to bear the touch of professional architects.

Perceived density

The perceived density is low. There is no sense of urban density. On the contrary, one feels the place is spacious, extensive, open. Perceived density is always a function of actual measured density, but it may be moderated by various factors. (See Cooper-Marcus and Sarkissian, 1986). Here these moderating factors are:

- vegetation screening, part (usually a major part) of the building (Plate 8.5),
- varied use of front and side setbacks of the plots,
- open view to distance,
- repetition without uniformity in building elements, and
- restricted street perspectives and few parked cars on the street.

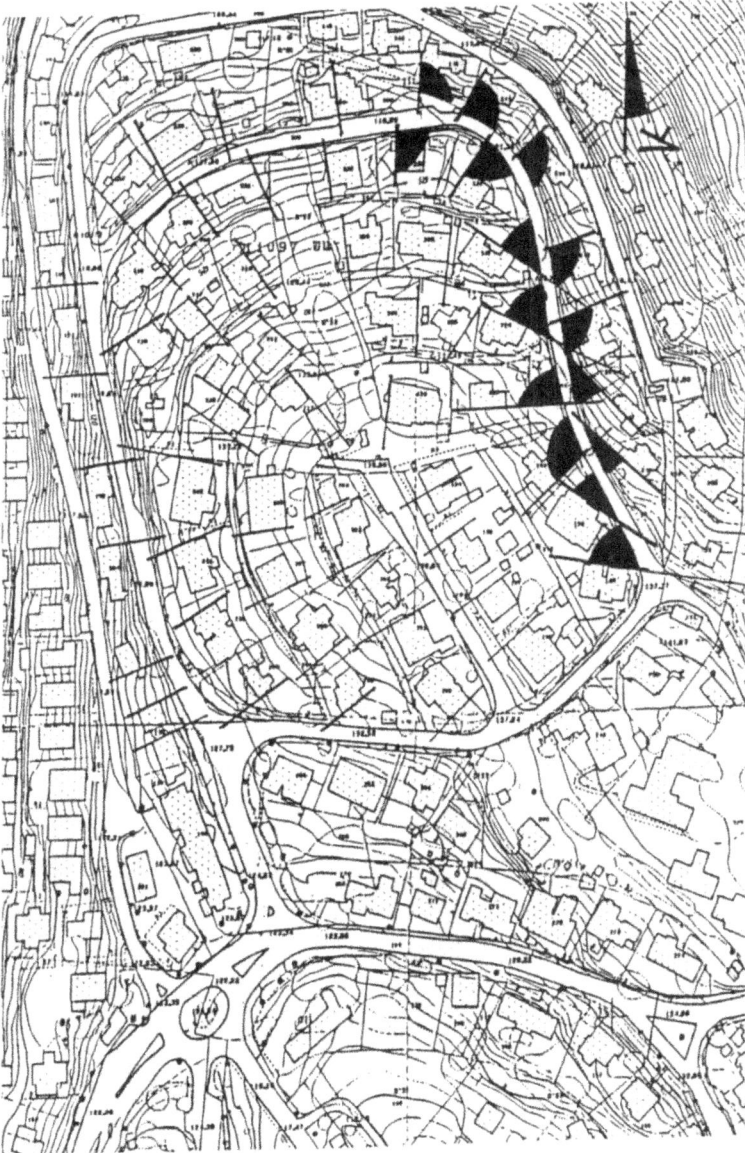

Figure 8.5   Arrangement of houses - one facade is parallel or nearly
              parallel to the street

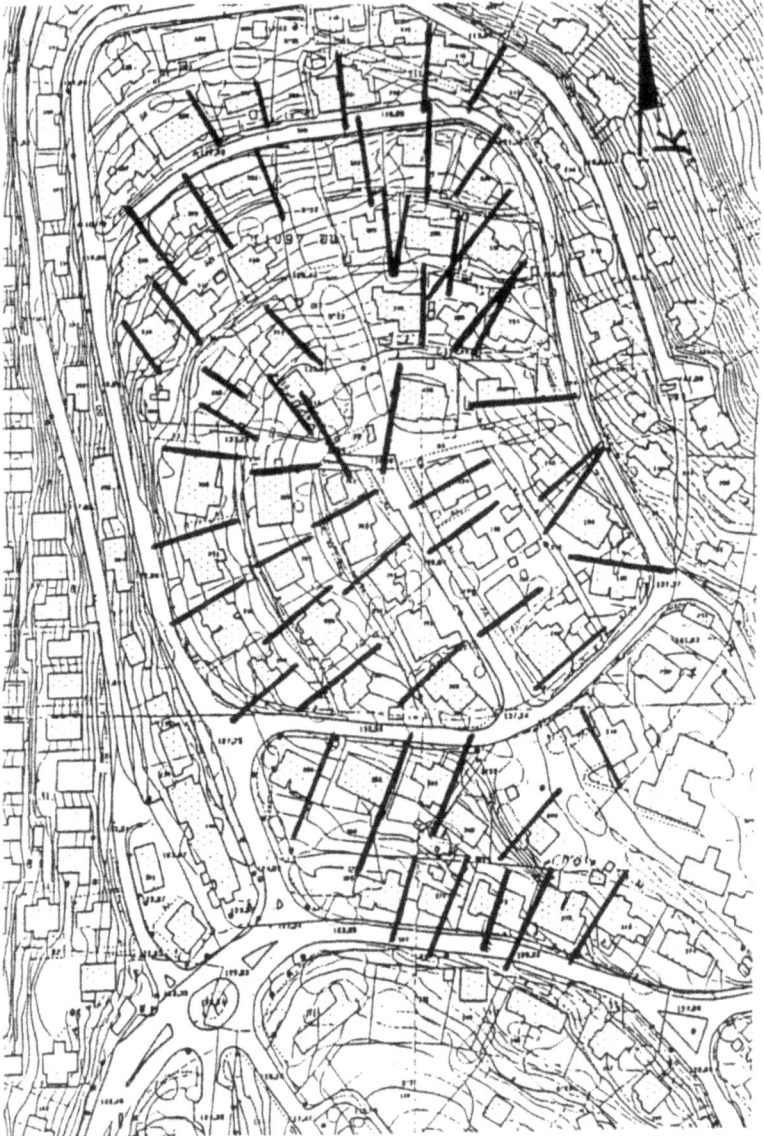

Figure 8.6   Houses are rarely parallel to each other, but are laid out to follow the topography

Plate 8.5a   Vegetation screening

Plate 8.5b   Vegetation screening

Outlook from the neighbourhood

Concerning the perceived low density, many views of landscapes beyond the neighbourhood should be mentioned since these reinforce the feeling of 'here' versus 'there' (see Cullen, 1971). Perceived space is usually much more extensive than functional space: one can see into the distance, to places which are inaccessible on foot. The places comprising the 'there' are natural, such as Mount Carmel or the agricultural zones of the *Kibbutzim* of Jezreel Valley (Plate 8.6).

Characteristics of the unbuilt areas

General impression

There is a strong feeling of abundance of open spaces, although some of it is illusionary. The eye does not rest on built sequences. Many views are dominated by vegetation e.g. towards the neighbourhood from regional roads numbers 66 and 70, from the neighbourhood to the landscape and internal aspects inside the district. Figure 8.7 presents clusters of vegetation randomly located both in private and public spaces. It comprises grown trees and small shrubs. The abundance of trees on the skyline also contributes to the green impression from a distance. Since houses are screened by trees, the illusion of extensive natural and rural areas is created within the neighbourhood.

Public open space: green strips

Both neighbourhoods are crossed by strips of public green space, 20-25 metres wide. Unbuilt plots with pine trees are also visible. (The plots were originally assigned for gardens but were not cultivated.) The sloped terrain permits simultaneous views of much greenery.

Street and paths

Streets are narrow. Sometimes the distance between opposite fences does not exceed six to seven metres. Recent improvements, such as paving and lamps, emphasise the small scale. In the author's view, the narrow streets are an important asset rather than a drawback. Most parking lots are located inside the private yards. Back paths and tracks perpendicular to the topography enhance the sense of ease and tranquillity.

Plate 8.6a   One can see into the distance, to places which are natural or
              agricultural zones

Plate 8.6b   One can see into the distance, to places which are natural or
              agricultural zones

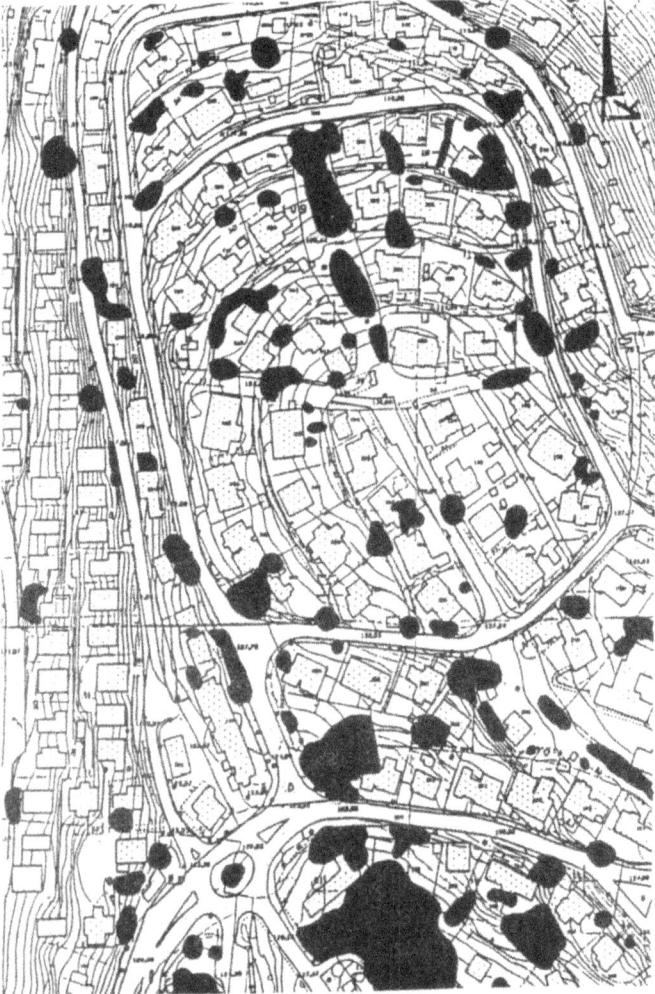

Figure 8.7   Clusters of vegetation randomly located

Private open spaces

Many private open spaces (setbacks, yards, gardens) are set out with paved terraces, fruit orchards and flower gardens. Some of them are not cultivated but all have mature trees, creating a sense of nature rather than neglect.

Summary

Three characteristics form the unique image of the old neighbourhoods of *Yokne'am Illit*:

1. Original housing of very low F.A.R.
2. Gentle following of the topography by arrangement of housing and streets.
3. Mature vegetation.

Each characteristic is achieved through a series of attributes, as explained above. Some of these are quantifiable, others are not: some are dependent on planning, others depend rather on abstaining from planning; some are the result of the passing of time, others - less.

We may ask: what could be concluded from this study in relation to future developments which might seek to emulate the older areas of *Yokne'am Illit*? Although low density housing is categorically unsuitable for urban areas of Israel in the late nineties, principles which enhance the illusion of low density may be applicable to new housing schemes. These, according to the *Yokne'am Illit* analysis include:

- leaving one open view (remote vicinity);
- intensive use of setbacks;
- planning according to climatic factors;
- modest dimensions and careful consideration of size and proportions of building elements;
- preference of muted colours, textures and forms;
- street sections creating a sense of 'here' and 'there';
- selecting vegetation: location, preferable types for private and public spaces, consideration of rate of growth;
- building height restriction beneath trees' level;
- planning for change, for full realisation of housing potential only in the future;
- parking inside private plots, not on the street, and
- an abundance of paths and walkways for pedestrians.

These are recommendations which should be considered in conjunction with the needs, aims and restrictions of future residential projects which aspire to the charm of *Shehunat HaTemanim* and *Shehunat HaKurdim*.

Acknowledgement

This research was supported by the fund for the promotion of research at the Technion.

References

Cooper-Marcus, C., and Sarkissian, W. (1986), *Housing as if people mattered*, University of California Press: Berkeley.
Cullen, G. (1971), *The concise townscape*, Architectural Press: London.
Venturi, R., and et al. (1972), *Learning from Las Vegas*, MIT Press: Cambridge, MA.

9 Housing processes in war-torn areas:

Family case studies from Lebanon[1]

SOUHEIL EL-MASRI

Introduction

The chapter focuses on the housing processes of three families from one of the war-damaged villages in Lebanon, namely *al-Burjain* (the two towers[2]). It uses family case study method to examine, in-depth, their survival and shelter provision strategies. The **stories** of the three families give detailed insights emphasising issues of shelter, reconstruction and their inter-relationships with socio-economic conditions. All these are put in a human context by using some phraseologies and expressions of the families themselves. Additionally, the living picture given by the three families, convincingly questions the effectiveness of top-down approaches to housing provision after disasters. Despite the limitations of case study method, the discussion is extended to generate patterns and relations of theoretical importance, related to shelter provision in disaster prone areas.

This chapter starts by discussing top-down and grass-root approaches to reconstruction, stressing the need for partnerships between victims and interveners. It also provides a brief background of the village, followed by a discussion of the family case study method within the context of the fieldwork. Then the **stories** of the three families are reported by focusing on their socio-economic backgrounds, displacement patterns, housing processes before and after displacements, and priorities in and opportunities for reconstruction. The chapter ends by highlighting important issues for interventions in disaster prone areas.

Top-down versus bottom-up

In recent decades, awareness has grown that intervention in disaster-prone areas should shift from top-down approaches to community-based projects. It is a shift from professional and official judgements of what should be done, to building local capacity, to promoting participatory actions, to using local resources, and to supporting existing socio-economic and building processes.   This holistic approach, which integrates reconstruction and development, aims to speed up the victims' recovery process, to maximise the use of available resources, and to respond to people's needs and aspirations.

A crucial requirement of grass-roots approaches is the clear understanding of local conditions and victims' needs, based on close consultation with the affected community.   In fact, one of the recurring mistakes of top-down reconstruction programmes is the simplification of housing to a **quantified** object by ignoring the dynamic of human settlement with its various dimensions.   Counting the number of houses damaged and people affected is of limited benefit because it does not elucidate priorities, opportunities, problems and alternative courses of action. Taylor (1981, p.139) argues that:

Quantification is useful and may be necessary at a later stage when the needs have been hypothesised, but over-enthusiasm for the questionnaire as a tool often obscures rather than enlightens a situation.

Bottom-up approaches to reconstruction after disaster, solicit facilitating the process rather than imposing and directing.   They necessitate building appropriate bridges between the community and interveners in order to gain insights into local circumstances and processes.   Therefore, fieldwork should shed light on the victims' socio-economic conditions, the ways they have organised their world, their thoughts about their built environment, their experiences in housing provision, and their perceptions regarding future reconstruction of their houses. As Peattie (1983, p.231) explains:

To understand the processes of housing and the invisible structures which shape those processes we need stories which correctly represent the World out there into which housing programmes intervene.   We need, in other words, correct stories about process, about connections, and about the working rules of the housing system or real estate market.

The case study

From 1975 to 1991, Lebanon (Figure 9.1) was eclipsed in the shadow of unprecedented civil strife resulting in massive population displacements, extensive destruction of property and severe disruption to the normal ways of life.   The appellation of the country as 'Switzerland of the East' was quickly replaced by

'Death of a Nation' (Mackey, 1989) and 'Tribes without Flags' (Glass, 1990). Khalaf (1989, pp.20-21) captures accurately the tragedy by saying:

> Violence and terror have touched virtually everyone. They are everywhere and nowhere. They are everywhere because they can no longer be confined to one specific area or to a few combatants. They are nowhere because they cannot be identified or linked to one concrete cause. Recurring cycles of violence erupt, fade, and resurface again for no recognisable or coherent reason.

The crisis had aggravated already existing socio-economic and housing problems, and increased demand for shelter in 'safer' areas. With the lack of emergency housing programmes, the majority of displaced people relied on their own initiatives to shelter their families in war-torn Lebanon.

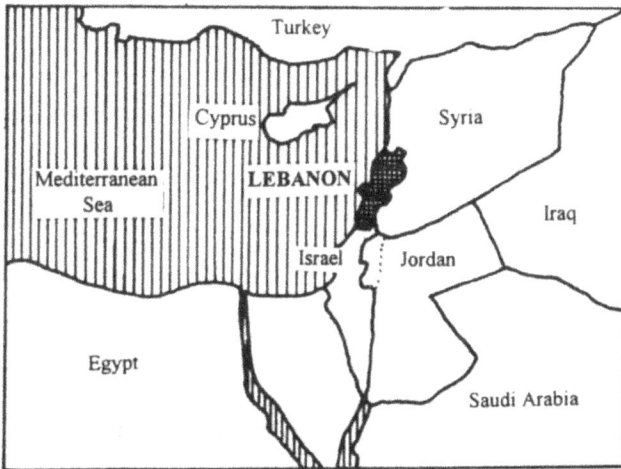

Figure 9.1   Location of Lebanon

Al-Burjain village is a vivid example of the war calamity in Lebanon. From 1982 to 1985, Muslim and Christian groups who inhabited the village, suffered from the upheaval in the Mountain Area. Both groups were forced, for a variety of reasons, to escape to safer parts of the country and their pattern of displacements developed according to the military actions in the different areas. After 1985, the Muslim families were able to return to the village to find most of the village was razed to the ground. By the time of the fieldwork, July-August 1991, three groups of families could be identified in terms of the housing situation (Figure 9.2a and 9.2b).

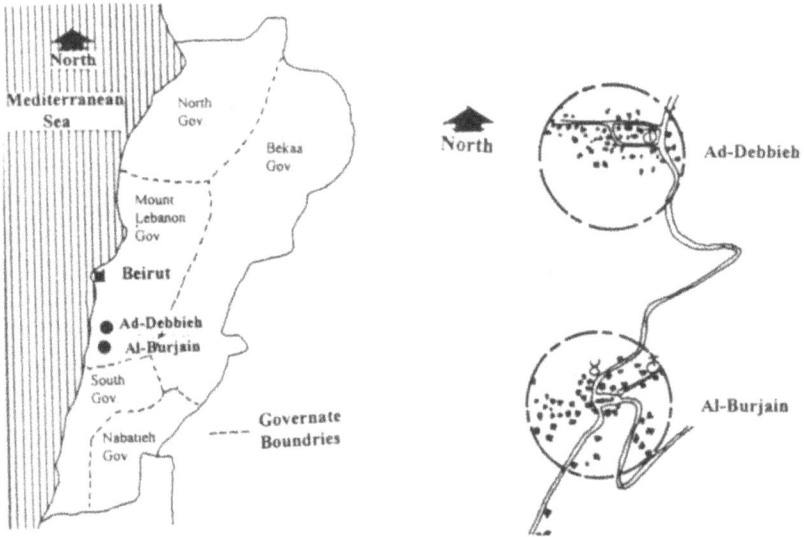

Figure 9.2a **Locations of original village (*al-Burjain*) and place of refuge (*ad-Debbieh*)**

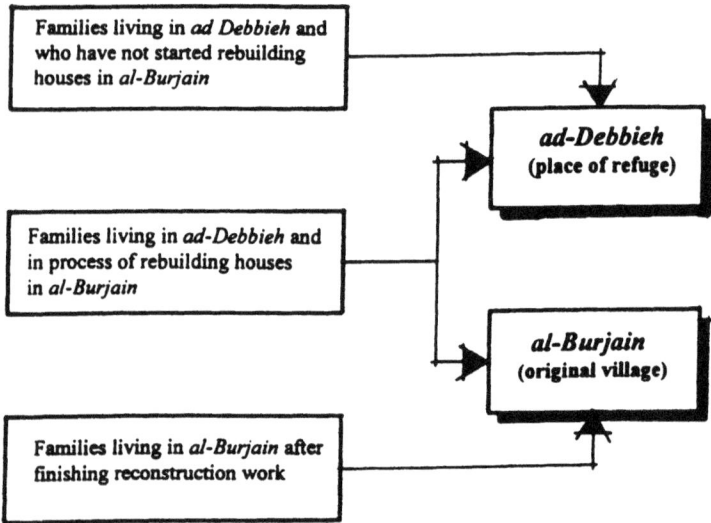

Figure 9.2b **Groups of families from *al-Burjain* defined by housing situation**

- Families who were living in *ad-Debbieh*[3], the place of refuge, and were in the process of rebuilding their houses in *al-Burjain*.
- Families who were living in *al-Burjain* after finishing most of the reconstruction work on their original houses.

Family case study method

The case study method was used in the second stage of the fieldwork: the first method was discussions with key figures and the third one was semi-structured interviews. These methods were used in a complementary way; one stage prepared the ground for the next one. This mixture capitalises on the strengths of each method and provides opportunities for cross checking of data (El-Masri, 1997, pp.57-72). The methodology of the fieldwork, including the family case study, emphasised, as Patton (1990, p.37) puts it, the 'phenomenological inquiry, using qualitative and naturalistic approaches to inductively and holistically understand human experience in context specific settings'. This approach is referred to as 'Grounded Theory'; it is a theory that originates from data rather than being abstract and tentative. It is developed by (1) entering the fieldwork place without a hypothesis; (2) describing what happens; and (3) formulating explanation (Bailey, 1987, p.54). Walker (1985, p.19) describes this theory as 'grounded in the experiences ... of those likely to be affected by a policy decision'. Plummer also stresses this point:

> One of the principles of my work is to allow people to speak for themselves, to whatever extent this is possible, and in turn to communicate to them, in our conversations as well as in my writing, that it is their words I seek, and not material for the generation of something that ultimately transcends their words and hence their lives.
>
> (Cottle, 1978, p.xii cited in Plummer, 1983, p.84)

The family case study was used in an exploratory manner to gain insights into local conditions and processes. As Hakim indicates (1987, pp.61-75), it serves as an 'equivalent to the spotlight or microscope' involving detailed examination of a few families from which a great deal could be learned. This detailed examination is not only descriptive, but includes comments and discussion of alternatives. In addition, important issues are highlighted to provide solid grounds for future reconstruction. The method is flexible and provides rich and in-depth information. However, this flexibility requires effective note-taking, recording, observing and conversational ability from the investigator. Despite the depth and the flexibility of the case study method, softness and generalisation are often perceived as the major drawbacks. However, Yin (1989, p.26) argues that: 'the softer a research technique, the harder it is to do', because it requires creativity and improvisation. Moreover, Yin (1989, pp.21 & 38) stresses that the objective of a case study is not to generalise the findings from a sample to a population by using frequencies and enumeration (statistical generalisation), but to develop patterns and linkages of theoretical importance (analytical generalisation). Generalisation could be achieved when the theory is tested through examining the findings in similar cases. Once such tests have been made, the results might be accepted for a larger number of similar situations (Yin, 1989, p.44). Peattie (1983, p.232) also explains that 'We generalise from the particular in much the same way that the historian takes the story of a very particular individual as a way of understanding the politics or social history of his time'.

Case study no. 1: A displaced family living in *ad-Debbieh* who have not started rebuilding in the original village of *al-Burjain*

Socio-economic background

This family is a nuclear type of six persons with two working members: the father and the oldest daughter. The oldest son is married and lives in a separate dwelling above his parent's house (Figure 9.3). The interview was conducted with the mother, the oldest daughter and the second oldest son, in the presence of the President of the Village Committee. The family was very reluctant to give an exact figure of its income, which was generated from different sources. Cash income included the father's and daughter's wages and income 'in kind' was gained from agricultural activities (olives, figs, grapes, vegetables). Obstacles were also faced in obtaining a detailed pattern of expenditure. However, the mother listed the priorities in spending the family's income as follows: '... food, medical care, education, clothing, and the necessities of life. We are just managing with the expensive prices and sustaining the basics which enable us to survive'. One point that should be mentioned is that the family owns various plots of land in different parts of the village, which were inherited either by the mother or the father on different occasions. This separation of plots make them less manageable and productive for agricultural activities.

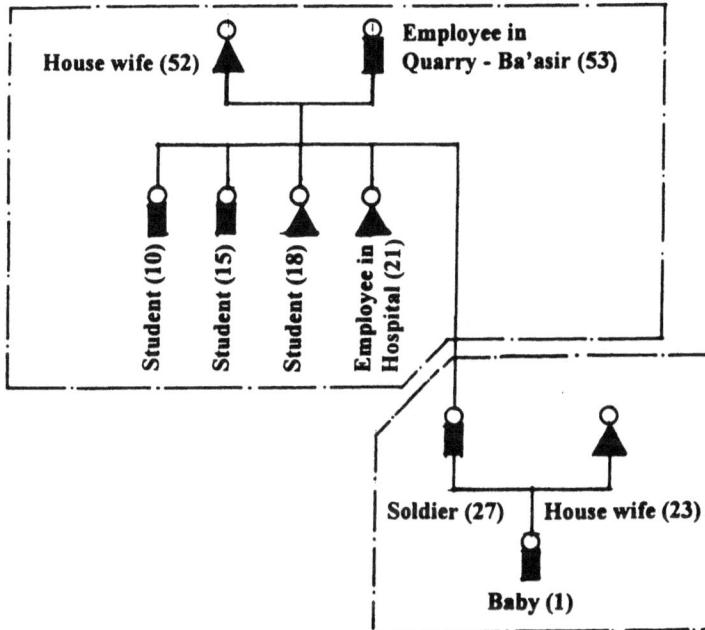

Figure 9.3   Family No.1: Household composition

Displacement pattern

The daughter, with interference from her brother who tried to correct her or add more details, described the pattern of their displacement:

First, we fled, leaving behind our clothes and furniture, to our father's work place where we all lived in one room. After one week, due to the unbearable living conditions, we moved to *Barja* to stay for a few weeks with some relatives. Then we left for *Daraya* where we shared the house with our father's cousin. From *Daraya*, we left for *Sh-him* to be nearer to our house and land in the original village. In *Sh-him*, we stayed in a room in one of the public schools which was occupied by other displaced people from *al-Burjain*. Problems in sharing facilities, difficult living conditions and continuous shelling on the area, forced us to move to a more secure area; this time to *Ketermaya*. There, we rented a house of two rooms with utilities (kitchen and toilet). After 25 April 1985, we were able to go back to our village to find our house had been razed to the ground. So, we moved to *ad-Debbieh* to stay in this house, where we have lived ever since. (See Figure 9.4).

Original home

The members of the family had lived in *al-Burjain* in the same house all their life. The house was extended incrementally with the growth of the family. The parents married 27 years ago and all the children were born and raised in the same house. The mother told the story:

> The house was built on a plot of land inherited by my husband. Firstly, with the help of my father-in-law he built two rooms. One was used for living and the other was divided into a kitchen and a bathroom. Additionally, a garden for growing vegetable and fruit, and a terrace for a variety of activities (washing, cooking, receiving guests, etc.) were also provided. Another floor was added with the growing size of the family. This floor was built using the family's saving. My husband helped during the building process by carrying materials, supervising construction activities, and contributing unskilled labour. We had many problems especially with carrying building materials, because the plot is far from the main road.

In terms of infrastructure, the mother continued: '... the house was equipped with electricity; sanitation was a type of pit latrine and refuse was dealt with on site by burning it or by throwing it in the bushes, but water was, and still is, the major problem especially during the summer'.

The original house was built from 'modern materials' (reinforced concrete for the roof and columns, and concrete blocks for the walls). The family did not use the traditional building materials (limestone for the walls and pitch red tiles for the roof) because of the cost involved and the lack of availability of materials and skills. This point was supported by a builder from the village who joined the discussion circle on the terrace. He elaborated by saying: 'Traditional materials are better in terms of appearance, character and for the climatic conditions. But this technique is expensive and faces many problems: transportation of materials, lack of skills and availability of materials. It is a luxury which becomes affordable only to rich people'. The family seemed positive about what had been said. At this point the President added:

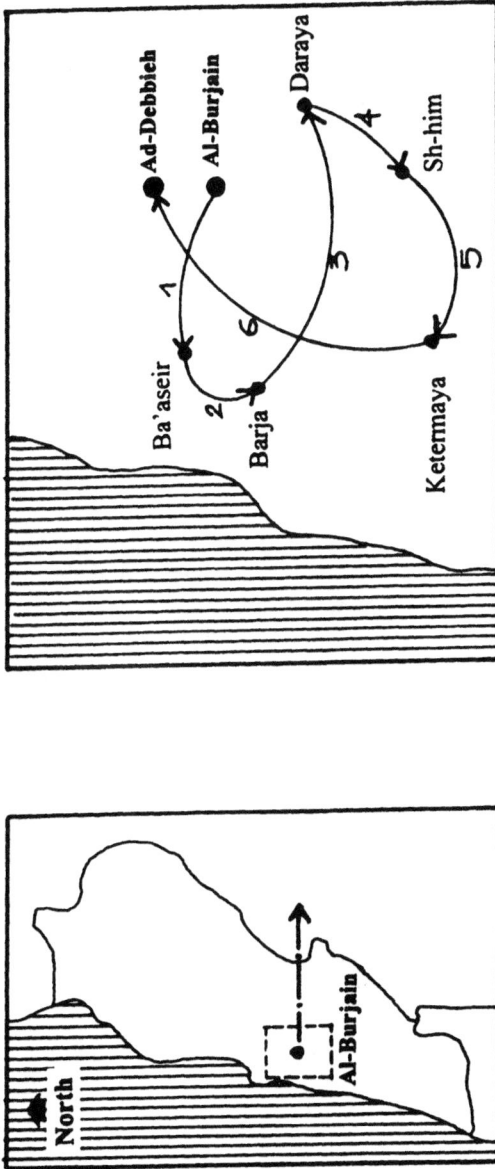

Figure 9.4   **Family No.1: Displacement pattern**

In the past, building a house was a social occasion and all the people of the village contributed; everybody had to do something. Even old people used to come and sit, to supervise the process. At the end, a meal was provided for the helpers by the family, to celebrate the construction of their home. These customs have disappeared with the change in rural life and the influence of urban life.

The married son, who joined the circle of discussion on the terrace, had another view concerning the use of traditional materials. He argued: 'Traditional buildings are good as monuments. The house form is not important; the house form and materials should be compatible with the modern life. You cannot ask me to live in the same way as my grandparents lived; nowadays there are televisions, washing machines, refrigerators and other modern equipment.'

Present dwelling

The present dwelling consists of two rooms, a kitchen, a toilet, a terrace, and a terraced-garden for agriculture (Figure 9.5). A well for collecting rain water is also available near the house. Infrastructure facilities are similar to those previously mentioned and the availability of water is still the crucial problem. Despite having a roof to protect them, the family felt insecure and uncomfortable. 'This house is not ours; we have no incentives to improve or repair it (the house suffers from water penetration, cracks and missing window panels). We hardly satisfy our needs for living which are very expensive nowadays. If we have money, we will invest it to rebuild our own house.' Comparing life in *al-Burjain* and *ad-Debbieh*, the family strongly expressed that the original village and home '... mean everything in life representing roots, security, comfort and shelter. They are the place of our ancestors and the memories of our infancy. We invested all our saving in the house and we were going to improve it when we have enough money. We are very attached to our village because it is our preferred place.' In this sense the symbolic meanings of the village/home exceeded its physical meanings. Therefore, the family described its original house as '... perfect and without faults in terms of construction, style and design.' However, experience has shown that an incremental house built by a builder from the village is expected to have some problems in terms of partitions, spaces and facilities.

Reconstruction

Previous points brought up the issue of reconstruction for discussion. There was a common agreement that all people should be able to return to the village except the ones responsible for the crisis. 'All our life, we lived together Muslim and

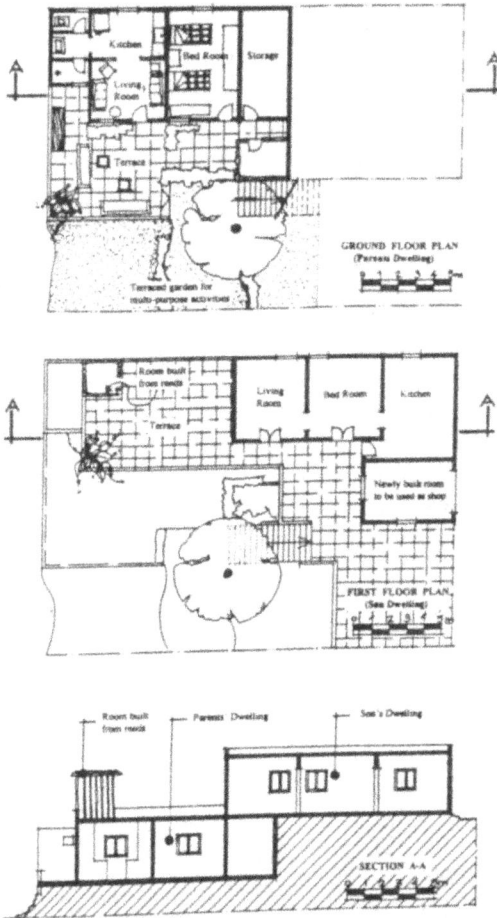

Figure 9.5   Family No.1: Dwelling occupied by the family in *ad-Debbieh*

Christian and we are willing to do so again.' When asked about the character of the reconstructed village/home, there seemed to be a clear contradiction. The mother wanted them as they were, while the builder and the President favoured traditional forms and materials, but with reservations. The married son talked about the opportunity for providing '... a typical village with tourists facilities', and expressed that planning and design should be compatible with modern life. However, all of them recognised that reconstruction should be more than physical, as the socio-economic crisis is more important and serious. '15 per cent to 20 per cent of the young people have emigrated either to the city or outside the country.

Most of the agricultural production for marketing has stopped (grapes, olives, figs, wheat, etc.) and this production is now only for family consumption.'

The discussion continued by shifting to the role of the government in the reconstruction process. At the beginning, the participants wanted the government to provide everything. However, the author explained the difficulties of such an approach, saying that the government could not build every damaged village and city. As a result, two priorities began to emerge from the discussion. First came issues of communal concern because '… it will benefit everybody and improve life in the village.' These are: (1) re-planning the village to solve the problems of roads and access to plots, (2) providing adequate infrastructure especially water supply, (3) and supporting the agriculture sector (co-operatives, irrigation projects, loans, market protection). Second emerged concerns at the household level; they asked for financial and technical assistance to help them rebuilding their houses. The family acknowledged a great role for the Village Committee to organise reconstruction activities with the government. The author felt that the oldest son tried to exaggerate the Committee's role because the President was present. However, the discussion ended with the oldest son asking the author a question which nobody could answer: 'How long will *al-Burjain* stay destroyed?'

Case Study No. 2: A displaced family living in *ad-Debbeih* who have started rebuilding in the original village

Socio-economic background

Mr Y., born in *al-Burjain* 60 years ago, is the head of a five person family (Figure 9.6). The discussion was carried out with him at the original house in al-Burjain while he was doing some construction work. At the beginning of the war (1975), he lost his original job in a textile factory due its the location near the 'Green Line' which divided Beirut into two parts. Since that time, he has worked on the land. Support from the oldest son and land revenue are used to cover living expenses.

Displacement pattern

The father told the story of displacements:

> We escaped from *al-Burjain* to the South of Lebanon where we were offered a house with one room, a toilet and a kitchen. After one year, we decided to move to *Sh-him* as it is nearer to the village and land. In *Sh-him*, the family was offered a house with two rooms, a kitchen and a toilet. On the 28 April 1985, we went back to *al-Burjain* to find our house had been razed to the ground. We

lost the saving of a life time and now we need to restart again. We moved to *ad-Debbeih* to shelter ourselves in a house with two rooms, kitchen, toilet and a terrace. (Figure 9.7)

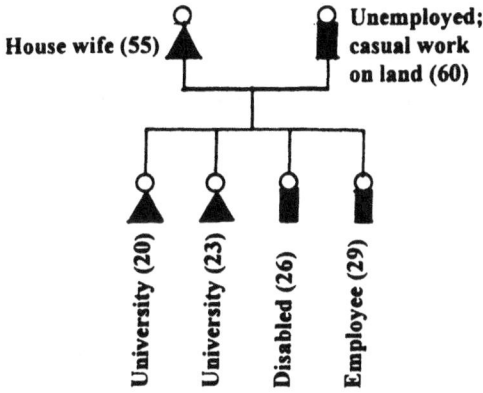

House wife (55)

Unemployed; casual work on land (60)

University (20)

University (23)

Disabled (26)

Employee (29)

Figure 9.6   **Family No.2: Household composition**

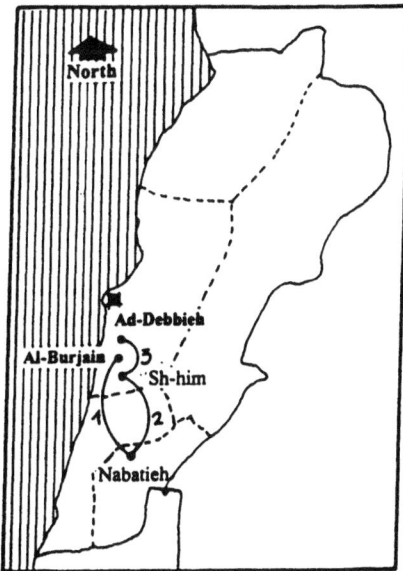

North

Ad-Debbieh

Al-Burjain

Sh-him

Nabatieh

Figure 9.7   **Family No.2: Displacement pattern**

House rebuilding

Mr Y. rebuilt his house on the same site as the old one. He started rebuilding one year and two months ago. 'We (he and his brother) sold a plot of land (34,000 sq. metres) to support rebuilding activities. We wait hoping that the officials will do something but nobody cares and prices are increasing.' In rebuilding the house, he reused some of the salvaged steel from the destroyed roof and columns. Mr Y. also used tree trunks for scaffolding the roof. On a large scale, using trees for construction activities can cause negative environmental consequences. The reconstructed house consists of two floors; a ground floor with a living room, a bedroom, a kitchen and a bathroom, and a basement to be used for storage and as a family room in winter (Figure 9.8). The building is still unfinished; 'We limited rebuilding to the available resources. In the future, I am going to add another floor on the roof. (vertical extension). A builder from the village has done the essential work (foundations and columns) and the father is building partitions, carrying materials and supervising construction. Infrastructure is similar to the previous case and water and roads were identified as major problems. An essential point was that the grapevines, fruit trees (lemons, oranges and pomegranates) and vegetables were already cultivated in front of the house, which was still unoccupied. The father explained that by the time the family occupies the house, the trees will be grown up providing shade and fruit.

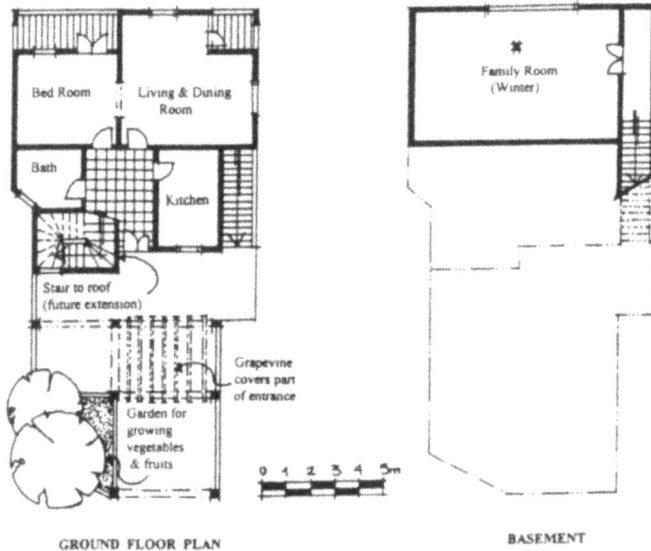

GROUND FLOOR PLAN   BASEMENT

Figure 9.8   Family No.2: Reconstructed house in *al-Burjain*

Reconstruction

Mr Y. recognised that, before the war, life in the village was not perfect, but it was secure and relaxed. He also elaborated on the issue of future symbiosis between the two groups: Christian and Muslim lived together but the war separated them.

> Good and bad people are found in both communities and we are willing to live as before with the good people. Of course, I will not accept the one who destroyed my house returning to the village. My home was my security for old age. I invested all my saving to build something for my children. It was the home of memories and the village was the place of ancestors and grandparents. No better place than *al-Burjain*; it is the whole world for me. What is better than to have your house and land in your village? We heard many promises for rebuilding the village, but nothing was achieved and prices were escalating with inflation. Many people came here, like you, asking questions and taking photos but no results.

Mr Y. was rebuilding his house to the best of his ability and knowledge. On the issue of government involvement, he believed that the government should address the communal facilities: roads and access to houses, infrastructure and specially the water supply, and social facilities (mosque, school, medical care centre, post office, etc.). On the household level, the involvement could be in providing loans to enable families to go back and rebuild their houses.

> I am building my house from my pocket, if they are going to give money they should compensate me for what I have already spent. Assistance and support should be equally distributed and should not benefit only the powerful people. The government should show us support and goodwill and the people will be willing to do their best. In *al-Burjain* a good number of educated young people is available (architects, engineers, doctors, teachers, etc.) who are familiar with the problems of the village. They should be involved in the reconstruction process; it is an opportunity to provide them with jobs.

Mr Y. also preferred the reconstructed village to have a traditional character and houses separated from each other. However, he recognised that social reconstruction between the people of *al-Burjain* is the first pillar for a comprehensive reconstruction. 'Things could be more organised; infrastructure and access to houses could be solved by re-planning. Instead, some families are rebuilding their houses relying on their knowledge and money but without any guidelines.' Mistakes are repeated and reconstruction is targeted in an individual limited manner. Who is going to remove rubble scattered in the village? Who is going to deal with public facilities and infrastructure?

Case Study No. 3 : The family living in the original dwelling and in the process of rebuilding

Socio-economic background

The family consists of seven persons (Figure 9.9). The father, Vice-president of the Village Committee, works in the Institute of Agricultural Research (*al-Bekaa*). The family's income is supported by some agriculture and farming activities. As expected, an exact figure of the family income was hard to determine. However, priorities in expenditure were '... food, medical care, education, clothing, house repair and improvement, and emergency events.'

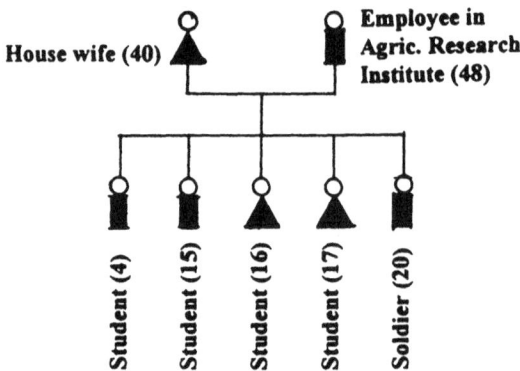

Figure 9.9   Family No.3: Household composition

Displacement pattern

The family moved three times (Figure 9.10). Firstly, it fled from *al-Burjain* village to *Sh-him* to rent a house with three rooms, a kitchen and a toilet, for one year and eight months. Due to the escalation of military activities in the area (the Mountain War), they left for *al-Bekaa* area, a more secure area, where they rented a house with two rooms, a kitchen and a toilet. On the 28 April 1985, the family returned to the village; '... as the house is located on the outskirts of *al-Burjain*, it escaped complete destruction, but it was inflicted with severe damage.'

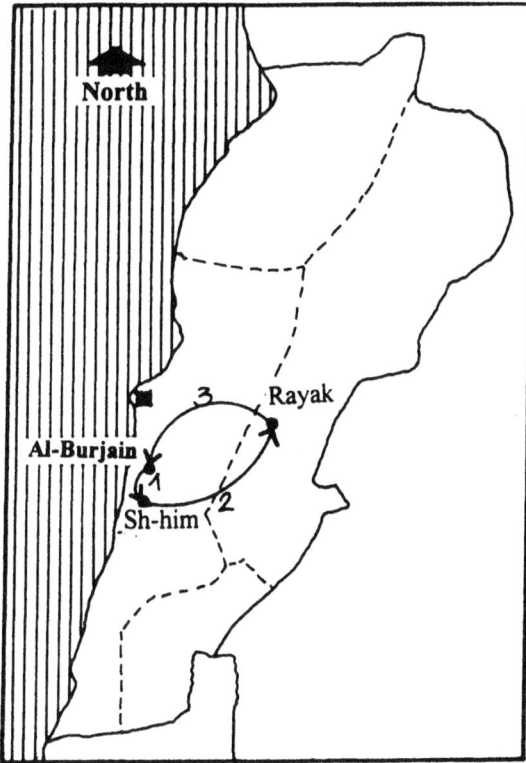

Figure 9.10   Family No.3: Displacement pattern

Original house

The original house consists of five rooms and utilities (a kitchen and a bathroom). In front of the house, there is a large terrace; underneath it a part is used as a well for collecting rainfall from the roof. Also, there is a garden (*Jidar*) for growing vegetables, as well as a sitting area (*ifriz*) shaded by a Carob tree (Figure 9.11). The land surrounding the house is used for farming (chicken, ducks) and for growing olive and fruit trees. Regarding the infrastructure, a pit latrine is used for sanitation, electricity is available although power cuts are frequent and water is a problem despite the well.

The father described the building process as follows: 'The land was bought a long time ago. In 1979, the foundations and columns were erected by a builder from the village. In 1980, I sold a plot of land in the village to finance the construction of the roof and partitions. The other finishing work was done in stages according

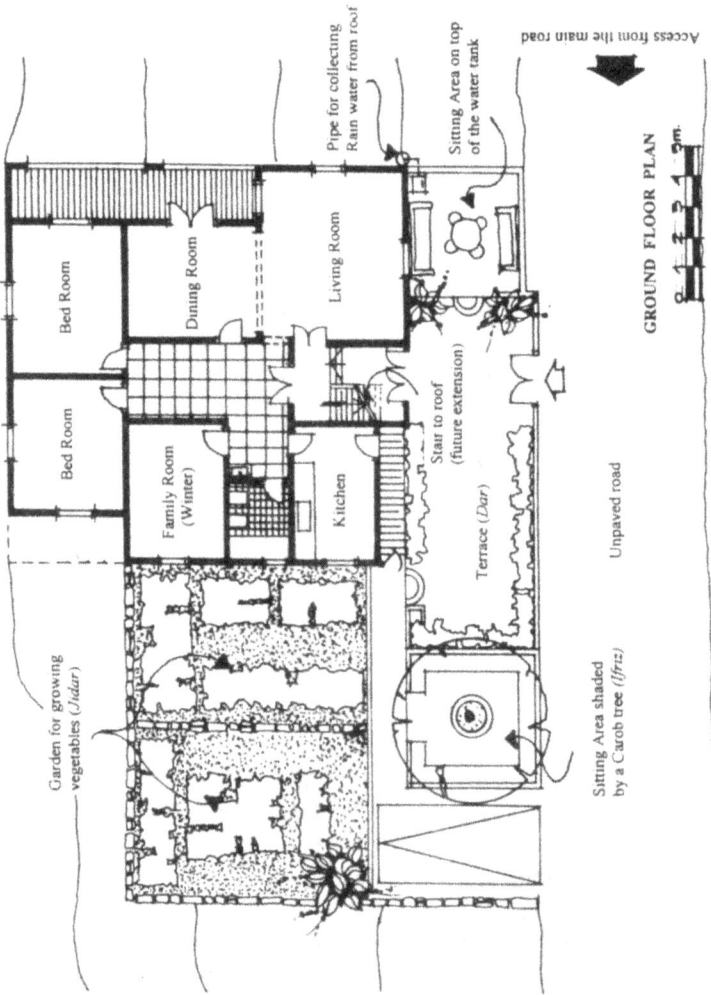

Figure 9.11 Family No.3: Original dwelling in *al-Burjain*

to the availability of money.' The father helped in the construction by supervision and in unskilled labour whenever he had free time from his work. The house is one floor of about 245 square metres. It was built from modern materials bought from the surrounding areas. The father acknowledged the appropriateness of traditional materials in terms of climate and providing the real character of a Lebanese village, '... but they are very costly and skills to build with them are scarce. Our priority is to have a house which we can afford and manage.' The design was done on site through discussions between the builder and the father; and the criteria were: (1) big and naturally lit rooms; (2) access to the roof and future vertical extension; (3) separate entrances to the living room and kitchen; (4) terrace in front of the house including the *Ifriz* (sitting area); and (5) a well for collecting rainfall from the roof. Despite these considerations, some problems were identified: 'One bathroom is not enough for such a large family, and the rooms are not effective in relation to privacy, circulation and space usage.'

Reconstruction

The village and home mean a great deal to the family; they represent security, settlement, memories and roots. The father emphasised having a house in the village as a continuity for the family and providing an identity for the children. Village and home give a sense of belonging to a certain environment and to a certain social group. Therefore, it is rare to find houses in the village rented to outsiders. The father summarised this attachment to land by saying: 'I do not like to stay more than 24 hours outside the village.' Living in their houses gives the family a sense of security, therefore, the mother described her family as lucky because the house escaped complete destruction. She also elaborated on economic hardships for future house improvements.

Before displacement, we had a plan for improvements (tiling, painting, stone facing for the facades) and for adding another floor for the children. We had the important thing (the structure) and we were going to improve it when money became available. Instead, we spent our saving on renting houses during displacements and on repairing the damage (in the roof, tiling, paint, and glass for windows and doors).

The father recognised that reconstruction should respond to the ambitions of the younger generations in providing job opportunities (agriculture projects) and social facilities. He called for establishing

... a Reconstruction Council for the Mountain Area to provide development programmes at regional and provincial levels. Priorities in reconstruction should concentrate on infrastructure, especially road improvements, and public facilities (mosque, school, post office, medical care centre, and social club). Also, the government should support and help people to rebuild their dwellings (loans, technical assistance). The reconstructed village should reflect the character and identity of the region. We like our village to have a Lebanese character (limestone and red tiled pitch roofs) and separated houses.

As a Vice President on the Village Committee, the father recognised that the people have to contribute (management, labour and supervision) during reconstruction, but

... we need affirmation from the government. The Committee has already done some projects in terms of repairing some electricity networks, providing a well and distributing cement offered by a leader from the area. Now all reconstruction activities are carried out by some families on an individual level. They are repeating the same mistakes as before by building close to each other and common facilities have not been addressed.

Conclusion

The case studies contradict many conventional assumptions which still are, unfortunately, guiding many intervention programmes in disaster prone areas. These assumptions are related to victims' ability, building process, rural life and reconstruction programmes. The cases clearly demonstrate:

- the effectiveness of the people's social mechanisms, as opposed to victims' helplessness. In coping with the homelessness issue people relied on different networks: savings, existing housing stock, and relatives and friends.
- the high degree of changes in the socio-economic conditions, as opposed to traditional rural ways of life. Nuclear family, salaried jobs and high levels of education are common characteristics within *al-Burjain* community.
- the people's control over the building process, before and after the war, as opposed to public centralised housing projects. Houses are built in an incremental manner and people make the major decision regarding materials, design, stages and finance and the like.
- the complex social, cultural, economic and physical aspects of reconstruction, as opposed to only building houses in the top-down approaches. As explained by the people themselves, reconstruction should be a developmental process of multifarious dimensions: social, economic and physical.

These issues confirm that the complexity of reconstruction after disaster requires a holistic and evolutionary approach to deal with the varied aspects (physical and non-physical) of the damaged settlements. The complexity can be tackled when the route of reconstruction filters through these different aspects and their reciprocal relations. This will be achieved by examining the pre and pro-disaster situations of the settlement in order to identify needs, priorities, opportunities, difficulties and constraints. This approach will make it possible: (1) to maximise the use of available resources (human and material); (2) to capitalise on the victims' resources for meeting their own needs; (3) to rectify existing problems for improving conditions; (4) to provide opportunities for enhancing the well-being of the affected community (5) and to identify appropriate levels of individual, communal and governmental intervention; (6) and to reduce conflict and envy among families in order to enhance social coherence. It is a developmental process in which adequate inputs into the built environments could help in economic generation, in promoting socio-cultural identity, in providing opportunities for co-operation and integration within the affected community. It also helps to establish a link between the past, the present and the future which enhances a sense of belonging to the rebuilt settlement.

Notes

1 Family case studies: This chapter is based on the author's PhD research entitled: 'Reconstruction After Disaster; A study of war-damaged villages in Lebanon: the case of *al-Burjain*'. The research was conducted under the supervision of Dr Peter Kellett at University of Newcastle - Centre for Architectural Research and Development Overseas (CARDO). For the proof reading of this chapter, the author would like to thank Mr Clive Standring from the English Language Centre - University of Bahrain.

2 Villages names: except for *al-Burjain* (the two towers), meanings of the names of other villages mentioned were not available.

3 *Ad-Debbieh*: During the upheaval in the Mountain Area, many villages were damaged on different scales. *Ad-Debbieh* was one of the lucky cases which escaped complete destruction. Therefore, safe houses were the refuge for people from *al-Burjain*.

References

Bailey, K. (1987), *Methods of social research*, Macmillan: London.

222 Housing provision and bottom-up approaches

El-Masri, S. (1997), 'Learning from the people: A fieldwork approach to war-damaged villages in Lebanon', in Awotona, A. (ed) *Reconstruction after disaster: Issues and practices*, Ashgate: Aldershot, pp.57-72.

Glass, C. (1990), *Tribes without flags: A journey curtailed*, Secker & Warbury: London.

Hakim, C. (1987), *Research design: Strategies and choices in the design of social research*, Unwin Hyman: London.

Khalaf, S. (1989), *Besieged and silenced: The muted anguish of the Lebanese people (Prospects for Lebanon)*, Centre of Lebanese Studies: Oxford.

Mackey, S. (1989), *Lebanon: Death of a nation*, Longdon and Weed: New York.

Patton, M. (1990), *Qualitative evaluation and research methods*, Sage: London.

Peattie, L. (1983), 'Realistic planning and qualitative research.' *Habitat International*, Vol. 7, No. 5/6, pp.227-234.

Plummer, K. (1983), *Documents of life: An introduction to the problems and literature of a humanistic method*, Allen & Unwin: London.

Taylor, A. (1981), 'Assessment of victims needs', in Davis, I. (ed) *Disasters and the small dwelling*, Pegamon: Oxford, pp.134-137.

Walker, R. (ed) (1985), *Applied qualitative research*, Gower: Aldershot.

Yin, R. (1989), *Case study research: Design and methods*, Sage: London.

10 Chinese vernacular dwellings:

A popular approach to housing supply

YING LIU and ADENRELE AWOTONA

Introduction

China, with its long history and a vast territory, is a multi-national country. It has 56 ethnic groups and has an abundant cultural heritage. As an important part in the cultural heritage of Chinese architecture, the traditional vernacular dwellings in various areas are rich and colourful. They have been closely related to the social, cultural and political aspects of the Chinese people. Today, the local dwellings are scattered among various areas and nationalities. Passing through the whirligig of time and experiencing dramatic historical changes, countless wars and natural calamities, the traditional dwellings and their functions still remain and are used by the broad mass of the people.

This chapter examines the variety of traditional vernacular dwellings in China. In this context, vernacular dwellings can be classified into three main categories: courtyard dwelling, stilt dwelling and cave dwelling. The study investigates the physical forces, such as climatic and natural environments, and other basic determinants which have directed the evolution and development of these three main styles of traditional vernacular dwellings. Special emphasis is placed upon the influences of physical factors and socio-cultural traditions on the development of the traditional courtyard house form. The socio-cultural implication in traditional Chinese courtyard houses is also addressed. In order to explain the popularisation and continuance of the traditional courtyard houses in China, various forms of the courtyard houses in different areas (South and North China) and in different historical periods are explored for analysis and comparison. The layout, the spatial organisation and the functions of those typical courtyard houses with their socio-cultural meanings are analysed in detail.

223

The various traditional vernacular dwellings in China

China is a large country with a long history and rich cultural traditions. It has a territory of 9.6 million square kilometres and a population of 1.19 billion. As a reflection of its own indigenous environment, independent society, specific socio-cultural tradition and social changes, a unique style of classical architecture and many diverse forms of traditional vernacular dwellings have been handed down. Reliant on independent economic development, outside influences on indigenous Chinese culture were limited because of natural barriers in the form of oceans in the east and south, vast deserts to the north, and steep mountains to the west. Inside China, natural environments differ from region to region. They encompass plains, plateaux, basins, grasslands, mountains, deserts, ridges and valleys. Settled by 56 ethnic groups such as *Han, Man* (Manchu), *Mongol, Hui, Zang* (Tibetan), *Zhuang, Uygur etc.*, the economic life and customs vary greatly among the different nationalities, placing tremendously divergent demands on architectural design. On the other hand, the continuous increase of population throughout the nation's long history also imposed heavy and diverse demands on Chinese architecture.

The classification of Chinese vernacular dwellings

In the study of the Chinese local dwellings, different ways and views exist in classifying traditional dwellings, as listed in Table 10.1 below.

Table 10.1   The existing classification of Chinese local dwellings

No.	Classification	Basis for Classification
1	Plan Classification	Plan form
2	Contour Classification	The contour of local dwellings
3	Structure Classification	Building structure
4	Climate-geographic Classification	Climate zones and geographic divisions

The first is called the 'plan classification' which classifies local dwellings according to their plan form. The second is called the 'contour classification' which uses the contour of local dwellings as the standard of classification. The third is called the 'structure classification' the basis of which is the building structure. The fourth is called the 'climate-geographic classification' of which the standard is the climate zones and geographic divisions. Shan Deqi in his 'Classification of traditional dwellings in China' (Shan, 1992) commented that although each classification method has its own characteristics of simplicity, they share a common problem of being treated separately and locally, and hence lack inner links among them. In the authors' view, these classification methods probably ignore the facts that 'a house is not only a tool with practical utility, but also a clear response to a society's economic, social, aesthetic and psychological needs as a complex object' (Gullestad, 1993). This complexity in the nature of the dwellings is addressed well by Oliver: 'Every culture has some form of house ... They are shaped as much by belief systems and concepts of status, territory and security, as by economy, material resources, technology, and climatic conditions' (Oliver, 1987, flyleaf).

Shan Deqi proposes a new way for the classification of traditional local dwellings. This classification is based on human and natural conditions. Human conditions include production, life, customs, beliefs, aesthetic standards etc., while natural conditions include climate, geography, land forms, materials and other factors. Among all of the factors, the natural conditions are the main factors which determine the distinctive national features of traditional local dwellings and their differences in various areas. According to this classification he suggests that the different styles of the Chinese vernacular houses could be divided into three groups: (1) **courtyard dwellings**; (2) **stilt dwellings**; and (3) **cave dwellings**. The advantages of this classification may be stated as follows:

- It is based on the life of inhabitants: meeting and expressing the requirements of residents are the most important things for a dwelling.
- It makes the study of the dwellings easier by tracking down the origin of existing vernacular dwellings and exploring the evolution and the transformation of the local dwellings in the process of their development.
- It could reflect the natural and ecological environment of vernacular dwellings, and could also image some of the social characters of local areas and nationalities.
- It could vividly show the spatial characters of the vernacular dwellings.

The geographical divisions in China

The analysis of this chapter is based on the search for geographical divisions according to the following sources: (1) a geographical book published by government (Qin, 1993), and, (2) the individual view by Chen Chengxiang (Chen, 1981). Considering the major differences in climate and topography, China can be divided into four major zones. The main characteristics of China's geography and the geographical divisions would be stated as follows.

The surface of China's mainland slopes down from west to east in a three-step staircase. The top of the staircase is the Qinghai-Tibet plateau, with an average elevation of more than 4,000 metres above sea level, and hence known as 'the roof of the world'. Even its lowest area lies at least 3,000 metres above the sea level.

The major mountain ranges are the Kunlun, Gangdise and Himalaya in the Qinghai-Tibet plateau. The second step consists of the Inner Mongolia, Loess and Yunnan-Guizhou plateau, and the Tarim, Junggar and Sichuan basins, at an altitude of 1,000-2,000 metres. The third step, about 500-1,000 metres in elevation, begins at the line from the Greater Hinggan, Taihang and Xuefeng mountain ranges eastward to the sea coast. Here, spreading from north to south are the Northeast Plain, the North China Plain, and the Middle-Lower Yangtze Plain (see Figure 10.1).

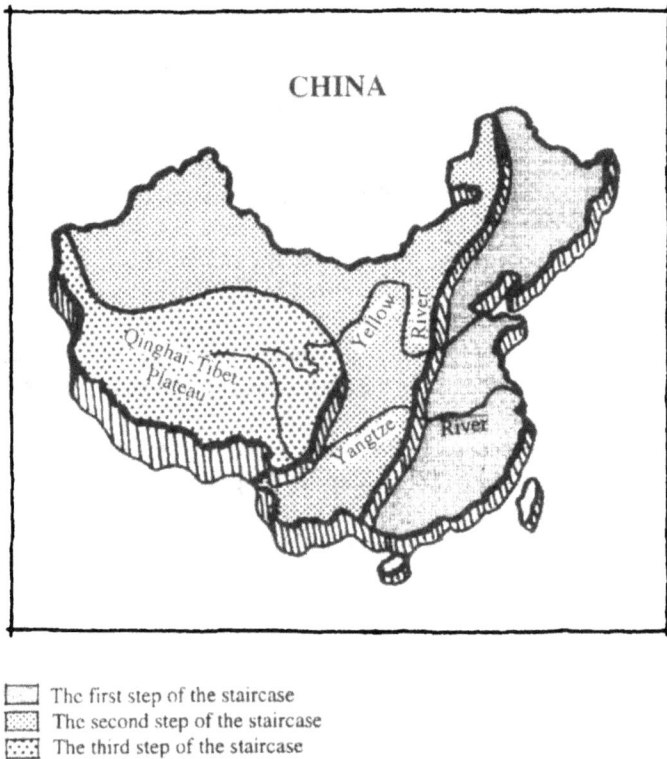

The first step of the staircase
The second step of the staircase
The third step of the staircase

Figure 10.1   China's topographical staircase

The major mountain ranges in China can be divided into the following three categories, according to the directions in which they run: (1) west to east mountain ranges, including the Tianshan-Yinshan mountain system and the Kunlun-Qiling mountain system; (2) north-west to south-east mountain ranges, including the Altay, Qilian and Gangdise, Himalayas mountains; and (3) north-east to south-west mountain ranges, including Changbai, Greater Hinggan, Taihang, and Xiefemg ranges (see Figure 10.2).

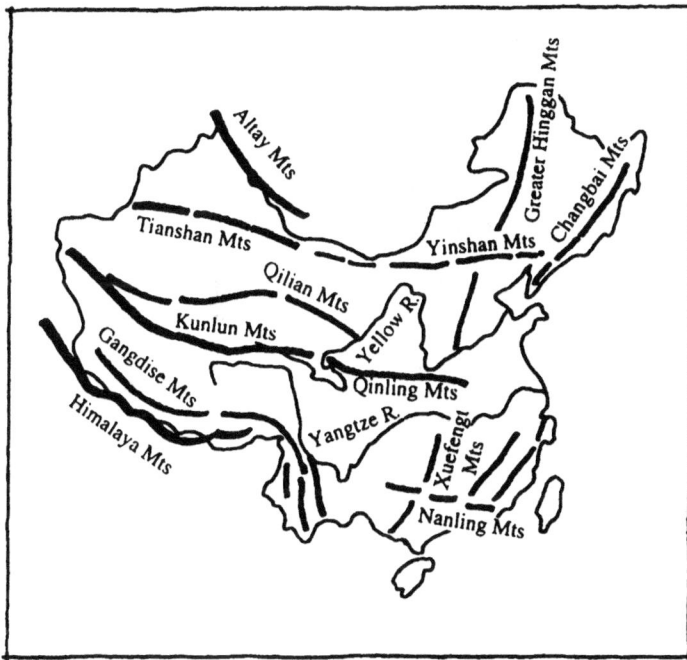

Figure 10.2   China's major mountains
Source: Qin (1993, p.5)

Most of China's rivers flow from west to east into the Pacific Ocean, except a few in south-west China that flow to the south. The Yangtze River, 6,300 kilometres long, is the longest river in China. It is the major inland-river and regarded as the transport artery in China. The Yellow River, stretching over 5,464 kilometres, is the second longest. The region along the both sides of the Yellow River is the birthplace of ancient Chinese civilisation and has a wealth of historic sites and relics, many of them buried underground.

Two of the four zones in the geographical divisions are a semi-arid zone and an arid zone, and they are divided by the topography and the mountain ranges. The semi-arid zone is the Qinghai-Tibet plateau on the top of the staircase and the arid zone, is Tarim-Jungger Basin and Inner Mongolia plateau on the second step of the staircase in the north of China. They shear the Qilian mountain range and eastern part of Kunlun mountain range, and the line joining mountain ranges is located to the north of the Qinghai-Tibet plateau. The border of arid zone to the north-east is formed by Greater Hinggan mountains. These two regions are mostly inhabited by minority nationalities. The Qinghai-Tibet plateau is a vast area in the west and south west of China. It covers 27 per cent of China's total land. Such a geographical environment has formed an enclosed region lacking communication with other regions and therefore has become an undeveloped area. The towering height and large area of the Qinghai-Tibet plateau has also limited emigration of residents to the lower region (east and south-east) where the major part of Chinese culture has developed. The arid zone also has an undeveloped background in the history of Chinese civilisation. Apart from these two geographical zones, the area of the cradle of Chinese civilisation can be further divided in two (see Figure 10.3).

Owing to the favourable climatic and physical conditions for agriculture, the early civilised area possesses 95 per cent of China's arable land and population. This area is divided into northern and southern zones with a clear boundary running between them. The Qiling mountains and Huai River are regarded as the dividing line. The division of the cradle of Chinese culture into Northern and Southern China Plain, together with the semi-arid zone and the arid zone, has thus divided China geographically into four zones. The areas covered by the four zones are listed below:

1. Qinghai-Tibet Plateau (Semi-arid zone) consists of : i) the Yaluzangbujiang Basin, ii) Chaidamu Basin, iii) Qilian Mts. iv) the region around the source of the Yellow River, and v) Hengduan Mts.
2. Tarim-Jungger Basin-and-Inner Mongolia Plateau (Arid zone) consists of : i) the Talimu Basin, ii) Tianshan Mts. iii) Tulufan Basin, iv) Zhuenger Basin, v) Altay Mts. vi) Corridor to the West of the Yellow River, vii) Inner Mongolian Steppe, viii) Ordos Plateau.
3. Northern China Plain consists of : i) Guanzhong Basin, ii) Loess Plateau, iii) Hebei Plains, iv) Shangdong Peninsula, v) Rehe Mts. vi) Plains of the Liao River, vii) Songnen Plains, viii) Hinggan Mts. ix) Lowland of the Three Rivers, x) Changbai Mts.
4. Southern China Plain consists of : i) Yunnan-Guizhou Plateau, ii) Sichuan Basin, iii) Qinling Mts. iv) Plains of the Lower Yangtze River, v) Yangtze Delta, vi) Jiangnan Mts. vii) Mts area along the south-east coast, viii) Nanling Mts. and the area to its south, ix) Pearl River Delta.

There is existing a close relationship between the formation and the evolution of the main styles (i.e., courtyard, stilt and cave) of Chinese vernacular dwellings and the influences of the climate, the geography, materials and construction techniques of China. Evidence and positive research can be observed from historical literary records and architectural studies related to vernacular dwellings in China. It may

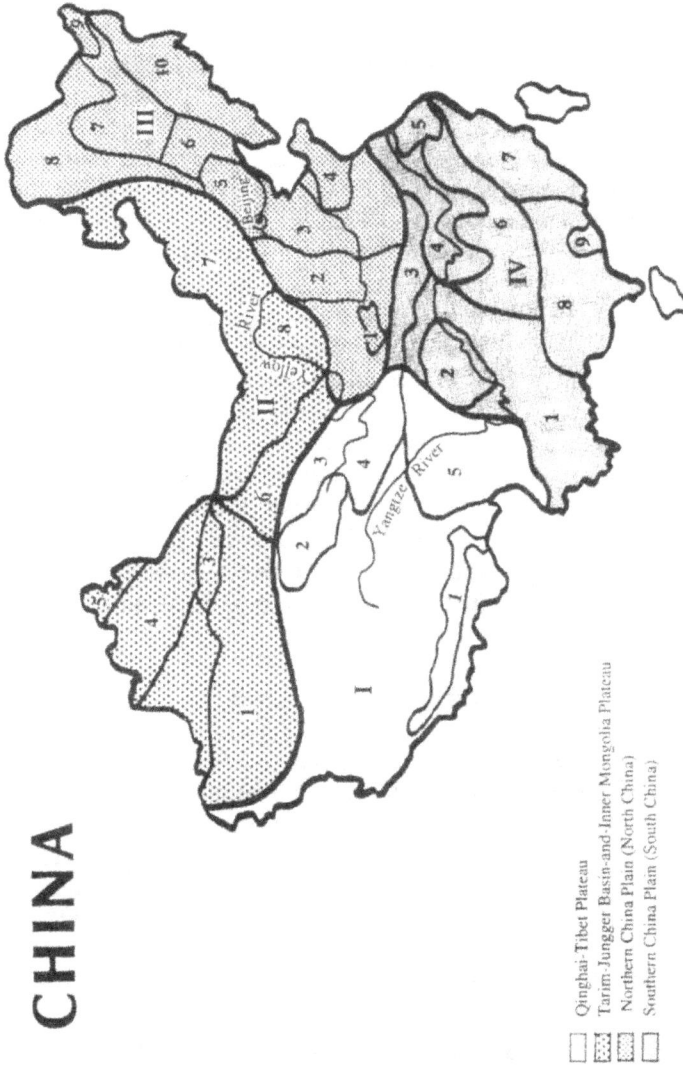

CHINA

Qinghai-Tibet Plateau
Tarim-Jungger Basin-and-Inner Mongolia Plateau
Northern China Plain (North China)
Southern China Plain (South China)

Figure 10.3   Geographical regions of China
Source: Qin (1993) and Chen (1981)

be assumed that natural conditions such as climate, geography, land form and materials, are the primary factors determining the early styles of local dwellings. Meanwhile, social, political, aesthetic and religious concepts also dictate the growth of form and the development of style. Analysis will be provided next.

The origin and distribution of the three main styles of Chinese vernacular dwellings

Achievements in research of archaeology and anthropology have demonstrated that cave dwellings and 'nest' dwellings on trees were two types of primitive houses in Chinese architectural history. Earliest evidence has been found in remains of the Old Stone Age (8000 B.C.) and in Hemudu culture in the New Stone Age (6000 B.C.). As the study of the archaeologist Yang Hongxun revealed in 1980, it was noted that the caves and nests were the rudimentary antecedent forms of Chinese derivative buildings. In the former, the inhabitants who lived in the Loessial areas of the middle reaches of the Yellow River created the cave dwellings. In the latter the root of the nest dwellings can be tracked to the regions of the marshy and wooded lower reaches of the Yangtze River, and its evolution from natural 'nest house' to artificial stilt dwelling had been completed in the central plain in South China (Shan, 1992, p.112; Yang, 1980).

The distribution of the two main kinds of primitive dwellings in China has been divided by the Yangtze River. Almost all the cave dwellings were formed on the north side of Yangtze River, while the stilt dwellings were formed on the south side. As Shan Deqi wrote:

> A comprehensive analysis related to the location of existing vernacular dwellings with their different timber structural systems – 'pillar and beam' (*tailiang*) framing system observed in north side of Yangtze River and 'pillar and transverse tie beam' (*chuandou*) framing system in south side of Yangtze River, and both were found in archaeological remains, all of which could provide support for the division of cave dwellings in North and stilt dwellings in South.

(Shan, 1992, p.127)

The earliest record of the different styles of vernacular dwellings in North and South of China was outlined in *Natural Science Chronicles* Vol. 3. by Zhang Hua in the Jin Dynasty (Jin Dynasty A.D. 265-316), and he pointed out 'cave dwellings in northern areas and stilt dwellings in southern area, the causes of these formations are to prevent from cold and heat stroke separately'.

The building material for stilt dwellings (from natural house to artificial one) mainly was wood or bamboo. The wood and bamboo were used as the material of the strut frame and enclosure walls. The wooden or bamboo framework functions to support the roof, and those walls in such a building serve principally to enclose or screen. They form nonload-bearing walls structure which is not strikingly different from standard post-and-lintel systems used in the West. In contrast, soil was the main building material for the cave dwelling (from natural house to raw earth building). The raw earth wall took the functions of skeletons and enclosure system, creating load-bearing wall structures. The load-bearing wall was common in buildings made of tamped earth and also in those of adobe and kiln brick. In the evolutionary process of the two sorts of primitive dwellings, the stilt dwelling fell gradually down towards ground and the cave dwelling rose gradually on ground. At the same time, wood and earth, the two main kinds of building materials, have been combined in one building with their individual characters. Based on that combination, a new kind of style dwelling – **courtyard house** appeared on ground with the composite structure of wood and earth (Shan, 1992, p.129; see Figure 10.4). Therefore the **courtyard dwelling**, **stilt dwelling** and **cave dwelling**, although indicating different levels of development, represent three main traditional vernacular dwellings. These three styles of local dwellings were developed, improved and handed down from generation to generation. Up to now they are still used by common people among various nationalities in China.

From archaeological remains the pillar and transverse tie beam (*chuandou*) structural houses were mainly found in the southern areas of China in recent decades, and the pillar and beam (*tailiang*) structure in north parts of China were used. These provided further a basis for Chinese architectural historians and archaeologists to verify the hypothesis and the analysis of the distribution and development of the primitive dwellings.

The pillar and beam (*tailiang*) structural system is depicted in the final part of the hypothetical sequence for the development of the cave dwellings. It evolves from a horizontal cave through a vertical pocket pit to a semi-subterranean covered pit and finally to a single room completely above the ground. The pillar and beam (*tailiang*) structure has been found in the mature form of courtyard dwellings on the north side of Yangtze River.

In contrast, the pillar and transverse tie beam (*chuandou*) system is viewed by archaeologist Yang Hongxun (Yang, 1980) as the consequence of the evolutionary outcome of the nest dwelling. The nest began as a roofed platform held within a single tree and evolved to a free-standing building on pillars and finally left the tree. It is nevertheless supported by treelike poles above the ground. The pillar and transverse tie beam (*chuandou*) structure is still widely used today on the south side of Yangtze River (see Figure 10.4).

According to their research results, some Chinese architectural historians and archaeologists argue that the pillar and beam (*tailiang*) structural system was formed in North China and the pillar and transverse tie beam (*chuandou*) system was born in South China. Both are the precursors of the basic Chinese wooden framework which is a significant characteristic of traditional Chinese architecture.

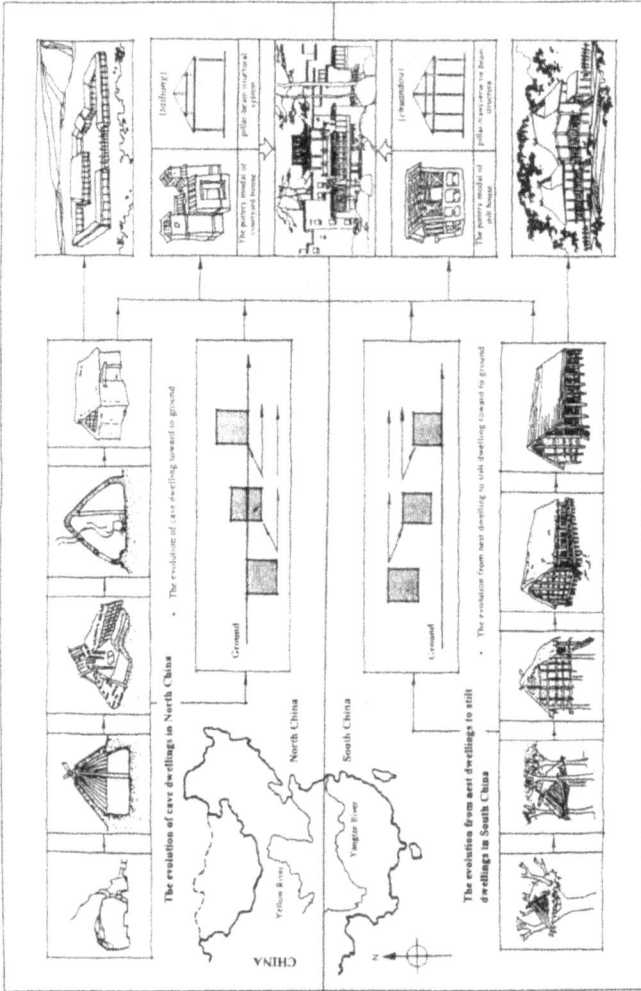

Figure 10.4   Hypothetical development of early dwellings in China

Next the principal physical and climatic factors which affect the housing forms in distinctive geographical areas are examined. Situated in the Northern Hemisphere, the Chinese mainland is to the east of Europe and on the west coast of the Pacific Ocean. Such a geographical position makes monsoon circulation easy to take shape. As a result, China is one of the few regions in the world where a strong monsoon climate can be observed. The way and the direction the wind blows changes periodically according to the different seasons of the year.

During the winter and early spring, most areas in China are subject to a cold wind from the north (the strong wind from the north and north-east or north-west). The winter temperature can fall to minus 10°C. The summer temperature, however, rises often beyond 30°C through most the region. This always happens in Loess area and desert zone. These areas are located along the middle and lower reaches of the Yellow River, where the largest group of Chinese nationals, the Han people, were first scattered. The howling wind roars down from Siberia across the plains and carries yellow dust that darkens the sky and obscures everything. People often have to wear masks to cover their entire faces and heads. As a practical solution, the cave dwellings and the form of courtyard house compounds, with high enclosure walls on four sides, were developed to cope with the extremes of the brutally harsh climate (Cheng, 1994, p.16; see Figure 10.5).

In the summer, the regions along the Chinese south-east coastal areas are frequently struck by typhoons produced from tropical cyclones in the western part of the North Pacific Ocean, and by tropical monsoons from south-east and south-west in the Indian Ocean. The tropical monsoons from south-east and south-west bring abundant vapour above the Pacific and the Indian Oceans. This has formed a climate with high temperatures and a lot of rain (Cheng, 1994, p.17; see Figure 10.6). The southern tropical windstorms and the floods destroy plants and houses and kill people every year in the areas on the southern side of Yangtze river. There are also many wild animals, snakes and injurious insects in these humid and rainy regions. Under such severe conditions stilt dwellings with their raised platforms were built on hillsides with flanked hills to the right and left of the housing sites. Such stilt houses with their housing sites provided ideal refuge and protection from typhoons, floods and wild animals. Its raised platform also provided a flow of agreeable breeze in a hot humid environment (see Figure 10.7). This style of stilt dwelling with the Chinese cultural tradition has been widely adopted throughout South East Asia and the Pacific regions (Sumet, 1983).

The popularisation of courtyard houses in China

When the Qin Kingdom conquered South China in 214 BC, advanced culture and technology were introduced from North China to the South. It led to a great amalgamation of the different cultures between southern and northern areas and between majority and minority nationalities. In the field of architecture, elements

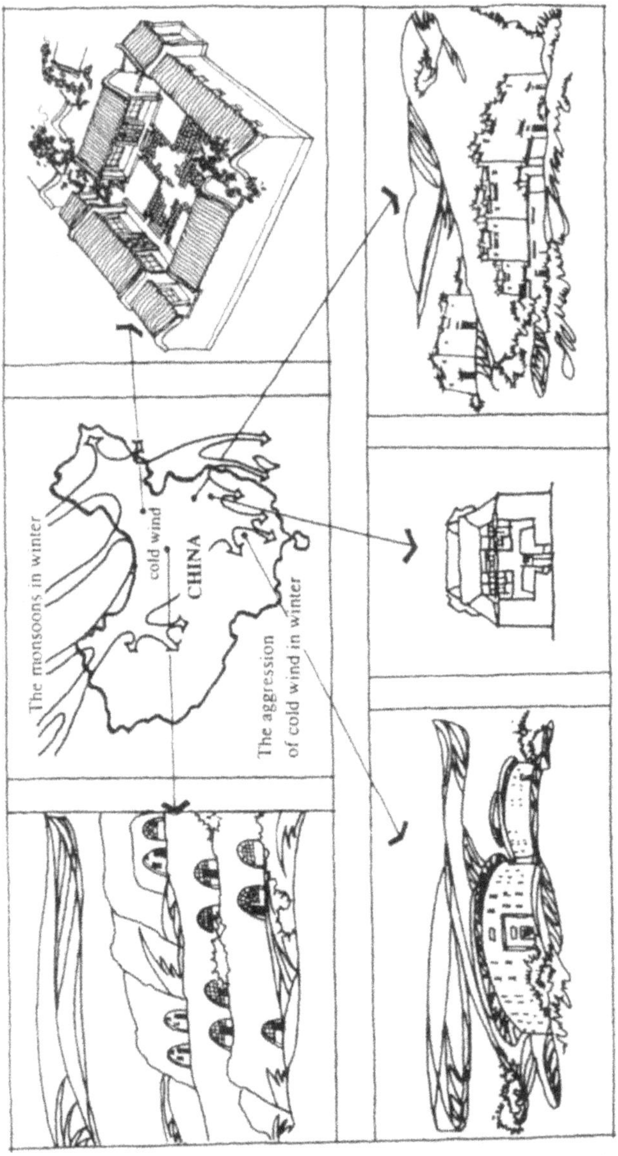

Figure 10.5

The cave dwelling and the courtyard house compounds with high enclosure walls shaped by the natural environment in China

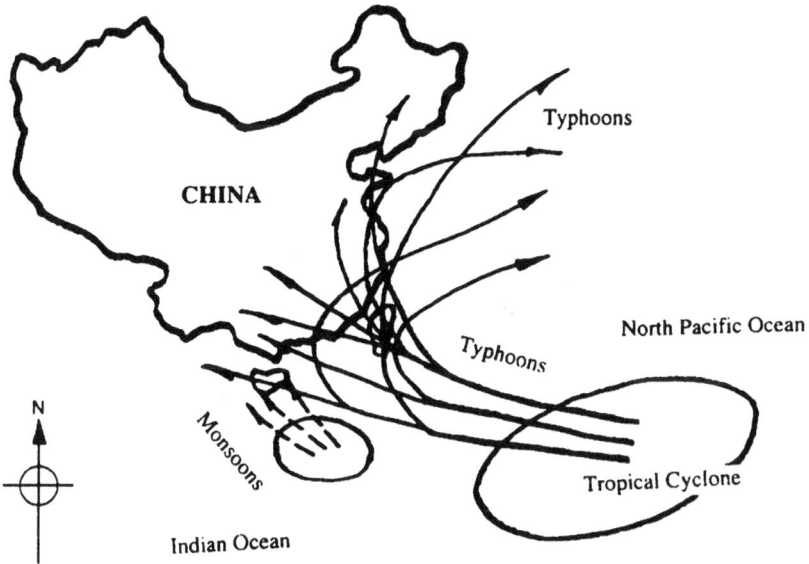

Figure 10.6   The aggression of tropical cyclone in summer in China
Source: Cheng (1994, p.17)

of roof and the principles of the spatial arrangements of courtyard dwellings, as well as other components of the northern architectural style, were introduced and combined with the local dwelling style. Those stilt dwelling forms in developed areas of South China experienced some major changes. In some cases, the earlier forms in the evolution of stilt dwellings were drastically modified and transformed into new forms of local courtyard houses or different styles of stilt dwellings. In the course of Chinese history, such combination of various cultures has taken place several times. This led the advanced style of courtyard dwelling to spread widely in different parts of China and also improved the amalgamation of the varied local dwellings. This is the main reason why the style of the courtyard house became very popular in China.

In addition, the wooden structure and the wooden enveloped stilt buildings have changed their images through time. In developed coastal and riverine areas, cities and towns grew up quickly with high population density and increase of cultivated land. The forest resources were reduced quickly. Hence, the style of the stilt houses which used wood as the only material became inappropriate. In order to adapt to the changing ecological environment, there was a need for the local dwellings (characterised by their pillar and transverse tie beam, or *chuandou*) to transform into new forms of courtyard houses. The transformed courtyard houses

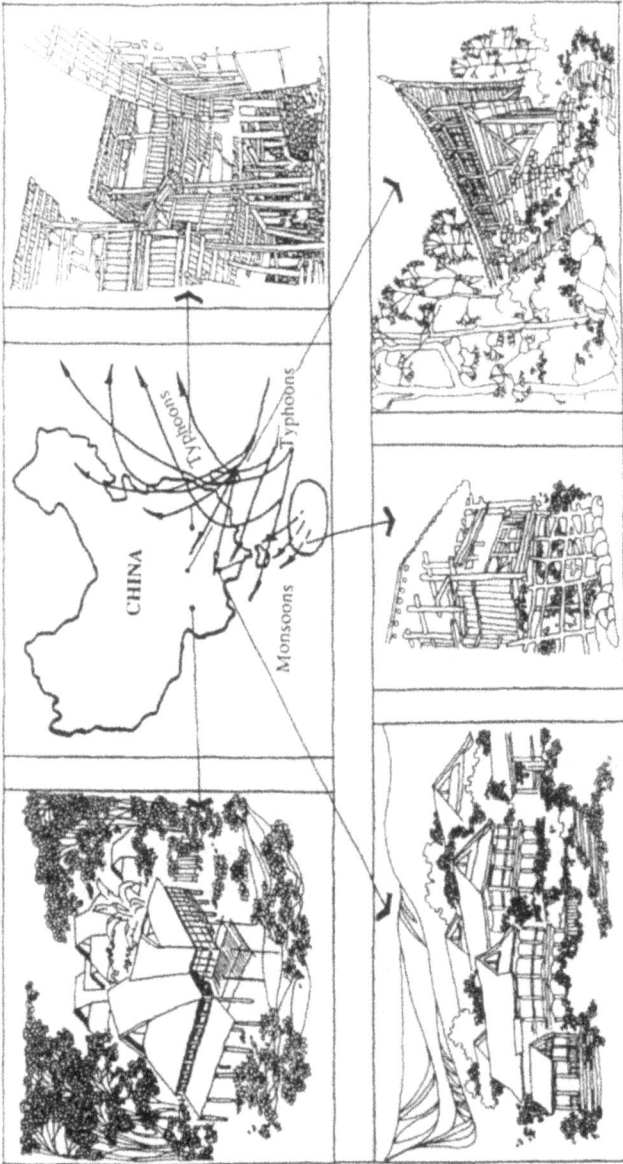

Figure 10.7 The examples of the stilt dwellings raised above the ground on poles found in South China

normally consisted of a timber frame structure and nonload-bearing adobe or kiln brick walls, instead of wooden walls, with a tiled roof (see Figure 10.8).

The later developed compact courtyard houses in South China were characterised by their high building density, two or three-storey surrounding buildings and very narrow courtyards with wide corridors in front of all rooms. All these were made to adapt to their climatic conditions and were mainly based on local people's practical needs in daily life. In particular, the forms of the compact courtyard houses in southern areas were more effective than stilt dwellings in coping with the attacks of frequent typhoons and floods. The high walls or buildings surrounding their narrow courtyards also performed the function of preventing the sun's rays from hitting the courtyards and drawing warm air from the rooms below. Now the style of stilt dwellings can only be found in remote mountains districts and the boundary of south-west area and south area in South China where minority nationalities live.

Cave dwellings still exist in Loess plateau of north-western China, principally in the provinces of Gansu, Shaanxi, Shanxi and Henan. The inhabitants living in the caves now number about 45 million. In the ochre Loessial uplands, the annual rainfall is generally less than 500 millimetres. The natural environment is very dry and denuded, covered often by a thick mantle of yellow earth 10 to 100 metres deep. Local houses traditionally have been dug into the soil, which cost only a quarter of surface dwellings. The soil is an abundantly available resource and makes, at relatively low cost, a dwelling warm in winter and cool in summer.

Cliff side cave, and sunken courtyard cave, have been two general types of traditional Loessial dwellings. The sunken courtyard cave has been a popular house form in the Loess plateau. A large square or rectangular pit exceeds 100 square meters in size to form a sunken courtyard. With side walls often exceeding nine meters in depth, the sunken courtyard provides surfaces into which caves can be excavated. The courtyard serves as an important outdoor living space whenever the weather permits, and is also a secure walled compound to keep chickens, draft animals and pigs. In recent years, it has been reported that there are a few cases of transforming original cliff side caves into a sunken courtyard houses by inhabitants themselves. In these cases, the living conditions of old cliff side caves have been improved by the excavation of a central pit. The traditional disposition of rooms in typical courtyard house has been respected and utilised in order to accommodate all domestic needs in an orderly way (see Figure 10.9).

The sunken cave, however, is damp in the summer, poor in ventilation and, because of the difficulty in courtyard drainage, is not safe against flood. Recognising the positive and negative features of cave dwellings, some peasants in recent years have built supplementary surface dwellings of adobe bricks or tamped earth near their cliff side caves to form a courtyard with enclosed walls. Inside the caves, the warm environment is assured during the winter with the use of stove and *kang* bed. The surface dwelling provides an alternative sleeping and eating

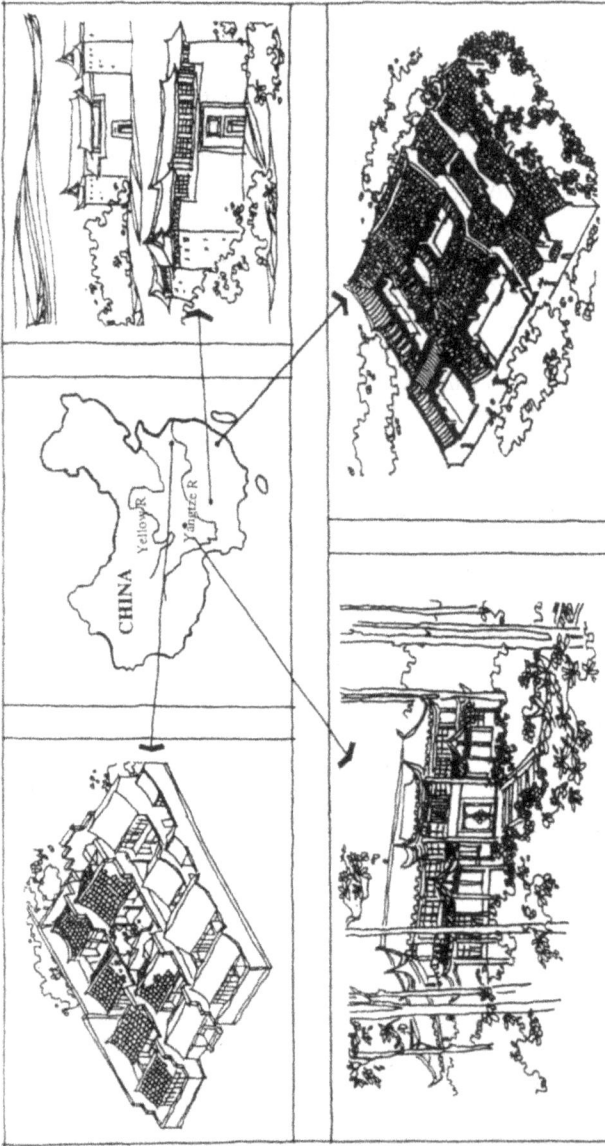

Figure 10.8   The examples of the transformed courtyard houses which combined the characteristics of local stilt dwellings in South China

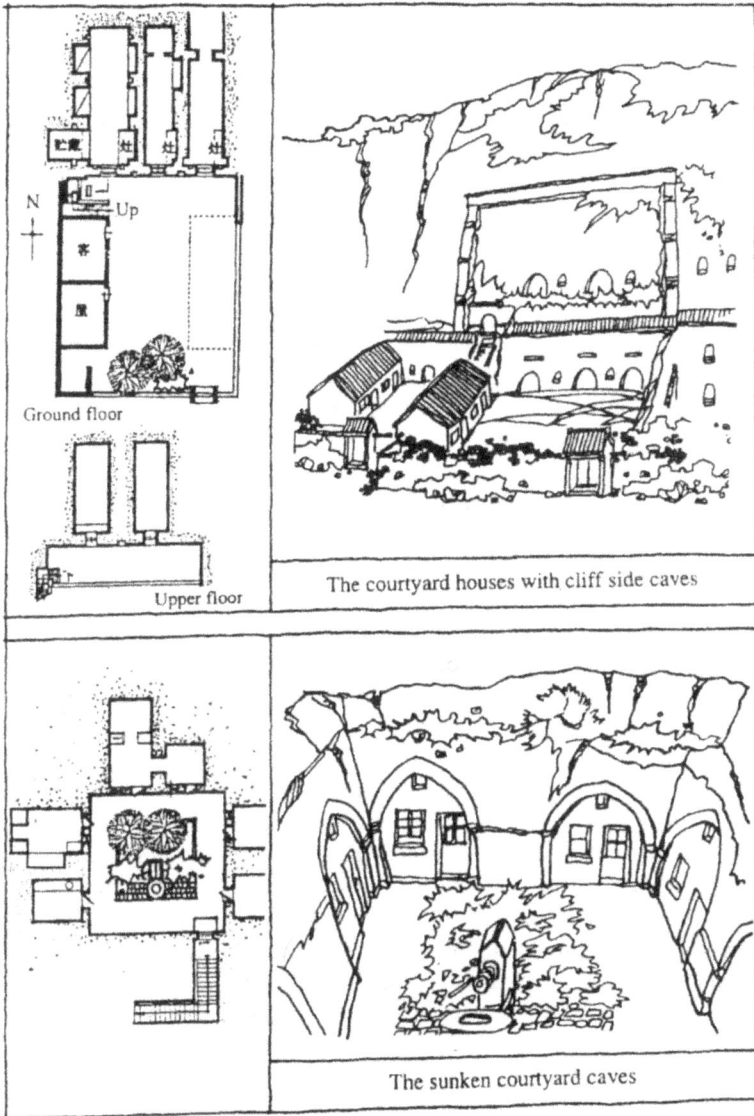

The courtyard houses with cliff side caves

The sunken courtyard caves

Figure 10.9   Examples of the transformed courtyard houses which combine
with cliff side caves, and the sunken courtyard caves in north-
western China

environment during the summer to take the advantage of good ventilation. The courtyard house mixed together with caves has become a trend in the Loessial uplands. This could imply that the caves will be gradually obsolete, and may be replaced by courtyard houses on the ground at least.

Courtyard housing tradition with the influences of the specific Chinese traditional society

Generally speaking, the courtyard house has been typical of housing patterns for over one thousand years in China. The typical housing form was used by the majority of the population from north to south. It is believed that the courtyard house once had more advanced elements in building materials, structural techniques, spatial organisation and carrying on the traditional socio-cultural context than any other forms of dwellings (Shan, 1992, p.118). To some degree, it can be regarded as an 'ideal model' in the transformation of successive dynasties in an agricultural society.

The walled-off compound with its own courtyards inside takes on a special introverted quality. The seclusion of the courtyard, separated from the outside world, is an important feature of Chinese architecture. From the imperial palaces left by the past dynasties down to the dwellings of the common people, this feature has remained to date. This architectural tradition of enhancing a small introverted world by the building ensemble can be explained by the social conditions of Chinese political history. The course of historical development in China has not remained static, but has been full of changes politically, socially and culturally. More than 20 dynasties have come and gone over the past 2000 years. Invasions of 'barbarous or semi-civilised tribes' swept through now and then to disturb the established order. In addition, internal dissension and factional strife broke out periodically. Under these conditions, people tend to withdraw themselves, becoming entrenched within the safe barriers of the inner life against outward misfortunes. Their happiness depends entirely upon the safety in their own inward state. Thus the communistic character of the family system and the inward feeling of withdrawal from the outside world did not only stimulate the people to construct physical boundaries as defences against outside forces, but also retain the enclosed form of courtyard compound without any essential changes for several centuries.

The forms and the characteristics of the three main styles of Chinese vernacular dwellings

According to the local dwelling classification discussed above, the evolutionary relationship between the main styles of traditional vernacular dwellings, their distributions and their characteristics are listed in the following chart and tables. Two maps of China's traditional district divisions and present administrative divisions are also used to illustrate the district distribution of traditional vernacular dwellings (see Chart 10.1, Tables 10.2 – 10.4, and Figure 10.10).

The courtyard house as typical domestic dwelling in China

The typical spatial organisation of courtyard houses in China

A courtyard house is a residential compound in rectangular shape and symmetrical layout. The enclosed courtyard, as the centre of the house compound, is surrounded by buildings on four (or sometimes three) sides. The buildings are linked up by corridors and combined with the surrounding walls and an entrance gate. These form the basic characteristics of a courtyard compound. Though built in different scales and sizes, all courtyard houses are composed by the same basic unit with five major components as follows:

- *Zhengfang* – main building,
- *Xiangfang* – wing buildings,
- *Weiqiang* – surrounding wall,
- *Damen* – entrance gate, and
- *Tingyuan* – courtyard.

A large courtyard house (such as the residence of a prince) may contain up to nine units. The major units are located at the centre and side units at the left and right. If a unit in a courtyard house has buildings on four sides, the unit is named *Siheyuan* - 'four-in-one courtyard'. Sometimes a unit has no building to the south of the courtyard, and such a unit is known as the *Sanheyuan* - 'three-in-one courtyard' (see Figures 10.11 and 10.12). In most rural areas in China, the farmers' houses normally have one basic unit with its courtyard surrounded by buildings on three sides. In urban areas, the most common courtyard housing form generally has one basic unit with one front unit, sometimes with one more unit behind the basic unit (see Figure 10.13).

The courtyard house with two or more units is generally divided into *Neizhai* - the inner quarter - and *Waizhai* - the outer quarter. This is achieved by a separating wall built along the southern end of the wing buildings on the east and west sides, thus the courtyard is divided into two parts - inside the wall is the inner quarter and outside is the outer quarter. In a medium or large-scale courtyard house, there are always three parts: core quarter, inner quarter and outer quarter. The core quarter is located behind the inner quarter. The outer quarter, the inner

• The courtyard dwellings:

No	Title	District distribution & nationality	Climate	Land forms	Characters of plan and spatial arrangement		Main characters of the dwelling form		Main material, structure and colour
1	Typical courtyard dwelling	Jing, Ji, Jin and Liao in mid North China. Han, Man, Hui nationality	Cold, dry with not enough sunshine	Plain	Regular & symmetrical plan with a central north-south axis and front & inner closed and cohesive courtyard spaces.		Double-pitch roof, Chinese gabled roof, cylindrical tile		*Tailiang* (pillar and beam) framing system; brick or earth walls; grey wall and grey tiled roof
2	Rural courtyard dwelling	Shandong in the south-east of North China & rural areas and towns in North China.	Dry & cold	Plain and hilly land	Irregular symmetrical plan with a central north-south axis. Main building & Wing building on one side with wall form a courtyard		Double-pitch roof, Chinese gabled roof, mud-thatching roof		The timber beams raised on the brick or stone load-bearing walls, main colour is loess.
3	Heavenly well dwelling	East coastal area and south-west area in South China. Han, Bai, Naxi.	Humid, rainy with long sunshine	Plain	Regular symmetrical plan with closed small courtyards (formed by buildings on four sides or three side with a wall to south.		Double-pitch roof, fire-sealing gable, cylindrical tile, ridge raising to both side.		A combined structure of *tailiang* (pillar and beam) and *chuandou* (pillar & traverse tie beam); brick wall and grey tiled roof
4	*Hueizhou heavenly well dwelling*	Wannan and Gandonghei in the mid central area of South China Han majority nationality	Hot, rainy with long sunshine	Plain and hilly land	Regular, closed and symmetrical plan with opened main hall without front wall connecting small courtyard. Most houses are two storeys		White coating wall with grey tiled roof. Varied combination of step gable & big gate shade.		A combined structure of *tailiang* and *chuandou* framing systems; decorations with most brick and stone carving.
5	*Shancheng courtyard dwelling*	Sichuan in the west area of South China. Han majority nationality	Hot, humid with little sunshine	Plain in mountains	Symmetrical plan with front & inner courtyards. Main building no minor rooms on its either side.		Double-pitch roof, overhung gable-end roof, varied gate shades		*Chuandou* (pillar & traverse tie beam) structure; grey brick wall and grey tile

Table 10.2   The classification, distribution and characteristics of the types of Chinese traditional dwellings: courtyard dwellings

- The courtyard dwellings:

No.	Title	District distribution & nationality	Climate	Land forms	Characters of plan and spatial arrangement		Main characters of the dwelling form		Main material, structure and colour
6	*Minnan* courtyard dwelling	Mindongnan, Yuebei in the south area of South China	Hot with many typhoons	Mountains and hilly land	Regular, closed and symmetrical plan with a central axis and several linked grid shape courtyards formed by surrounding rooms.		Double-pitch roof, fine fire-sealing gable, great ridge raising		*Chuandou* frame with appearance of wooden colour, brick or stone wall with rich decorations.
7	*Hakka* courtyard dwelling	Yuet, Min, Sichuan & Taiwan in the south-east & south-west area of South China. Han majority nationality	Climate typical of the mountainous area along the south-east coast with frequent typhoons, and the Mts. area to the south of China	Mountains	Regular & symmetrical round or rectangular complex compound with a central axis. Houses are built around the courtyard with single row, double row, even three or four row		High & thick rammed earth outer walls as tall as 3-4 storeys. The form is simple & grand with small windows in the outer walls. It is almost all closed for defence		Outside thick rammed earth walls, inside timber structure
8	*Yikeyin* courtyard dwelling	The Kuming of Dian, Wannan, Sichuan, Hunan and Hubei in South China. Han majority nationality	Hot, raining region in south-west area of South China	Mountains and hilly land	Regular & symmetrical plan with a central axis and a heavenly well. The house is almost all two storeys		High outer wall with single or double pitch grey roof. The shape seems Chinese seal.		*Chuandou* (pillar & traverse tie beam) structure with adobe wall, loess colour and grey tiled roof

Table 10.2

The classification, distribution and characteristics of the types of Chinese traditional dwellings: courtyard dwellings (continued)

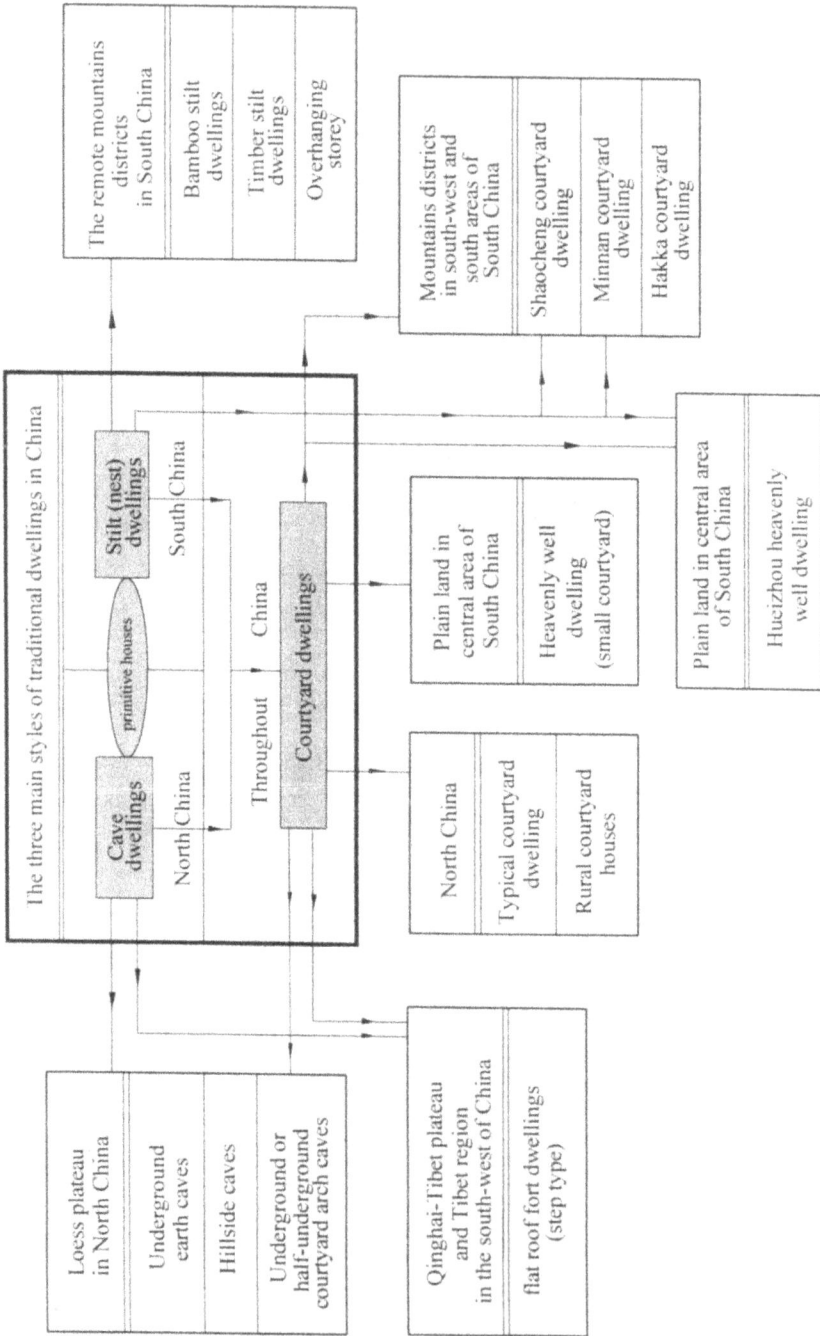

Chart 10.1 The evolutionary relationship between the three main styles of traditional dwellings in China

- The stilt dwellings:

No	Title	District distribution & nationality	Climate	Land forms	Characters of plan and spatial arrangement	Main characters of the dwelling form		Main material structure and colour
1	Bamboo stilt dwelling	Dianxinan in the south-west area of South China. Dai, Jingpo and Jinuu minority ethnic groups	Humid, hot, raining regions in south west area	Plain	It is simple bamboo house with its raised platform on second storey on posts. The plan is spacious and well ventilated with open corridor, stairs & yard	Four pitch Xieshan roof. The form is tall and graceful with solid upper part and void lower part		20-40 bamboo pillars supporting 'pillar & traverse tie beam' frame with bamboo wall & thatched or tiled roof
2	Timber stilt dwelling	Gueibei, Qiandongnan in south & south west areas of South China. Tong, Miao, Zhuang & yao minority ethnic groups	Humid, hot raining regions in south and south west areas	Mountains	The plan is multi-roomed with a big main hall & an open stove. The platform is on second or third storey on posts. The spaces beneath platform is used for many purposes but above platform is for living	Double-pitch, big Chinese overhang gable end roof often with big eaves on gable. The form is complete, simple with orderly even spacing surroundings		Timber 'pillar & traverse tie beam' frame with wooden board wall and tiled roof or bark roof
3	Overhanging storey	Ermei, Chongqing in south-west area & a region of river in hilly land in Zedong of south-east area Han majority nationality	Humid, hot raining regions with many typhoons in south-west area & coastal districts in south-east area	Mountains and hilly land	The plan is flexible, arranged according to different land-forms. It is built on slopes and has various types which built according to different forms of the slope. It often has overhanging storey	Double-pitch, Chinese overhang gable end roof with big eaves.		Timber 'pillar & traverse tie beam' frame with wooden or bamboo knitted earth layer wall and small grey tiled or bark roof

Table 10.3 **The classification, distribution and characteristics of the types of Chinese traditional dwellings: stilt dwellings**

- The cave dwellings:

No	Title	District distribution & nationality	Climate	Land forms	Characters of plan and spatial arrangement		Main characters of the dwelling form		Main material structure and colour
1	Sunken courtyard cave	Yu, Jin, Shan and Gan in loess plateau in North-west of China. Han majority nationality	Dry and cold with yellow dust storms in winter and early spring	Plain in loess plateau	The cave rooms along the four sides of a square hole dug into the ground, which forms a courtyard cave dwelling. An open earth stair along the one side of the hole stretch down into the house from the ground		Arch doors and windows, single-line-carved walls. The form seems solid and simple.		Earth-arch structure and loess colour
2	Cliff side cave			Precipice in loess plateau	The caves along the lower side of precipice. The interior of the cave plan extend deep into inside cliff with simple construction.				
3	Flat roof fort dwelling	Qinghai-Tibet plateau & Tibet region in the South-west of China	Cold, high-mountainous area, dry with short time sunshine & great range of daily temperature	Plateau, mountains	The plan is square with a sky well in the centre surrounded by the enclosure building on four sides. Open enclosure corridor start from second storey.		The outer wall is thick and made of piled stones with trapezium windows. The defensive form seems castle in Europe, it is simple and vigorous.		Stone wall, timber frame with earth covered flat roof

Table 10.4 The classification, distribution and characteristics of the types of Chinese traditional dwellings: cave dwellings

The present administrative divisions of China

22. Sichuan Prov.
23. Guizhou Prov.
24. Yunnan Prov.
25. Tibet Aut. Reg.
26. Shaanxi Prov.
27. Gansu Prov.
28. Qinghai Hui Aut Reg
29. Ningxia Hui Aut Reg
30. Xinjiang Uygur Aut Reg
31. Taiwan Prov.

12. Anhui Prov.
13. Fujian Prov.
14. Jiangxi Prov.
15. Shandong Prov.
16. Henan Prov.
17. Hubei Prov.
18. Hunan Prov.
19. Guangdong Prov.
20. Guangxi Zhuang Aut Reg
21. Hainan Prov

1. Beijing Munic.
2. Tianjin Munic.
3. Hebei Prov.
4. Shanxi Prov.
5. Inner Mongolia
6. Liaoning Prov.
7. Jilin Prov.
8. Heilongjiang Prov.
9. Shanhai Munic.
10. Jiangsu Prov.
11. Zhejiang Prov.

The traditional district divisions of China

Figure 10.10   Two maps of China's traditional district divisions and present administrative divisions

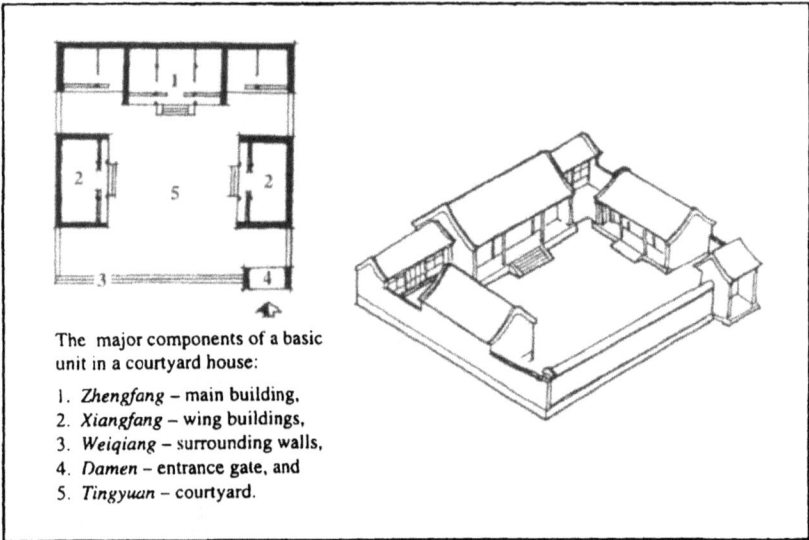

The major components of a basic unit in a courtyard house:

1. *Zhengfang* – main building,
2. *Xiangfang* – wing buildings,
3. *Weiqiang* – surrounding walls,
4. *Damen* – entrance gate, and
5. *Tingyuan* – courtyard.

Figure 10.11   A 'three-in-one courtyard' house formed by one basic unit

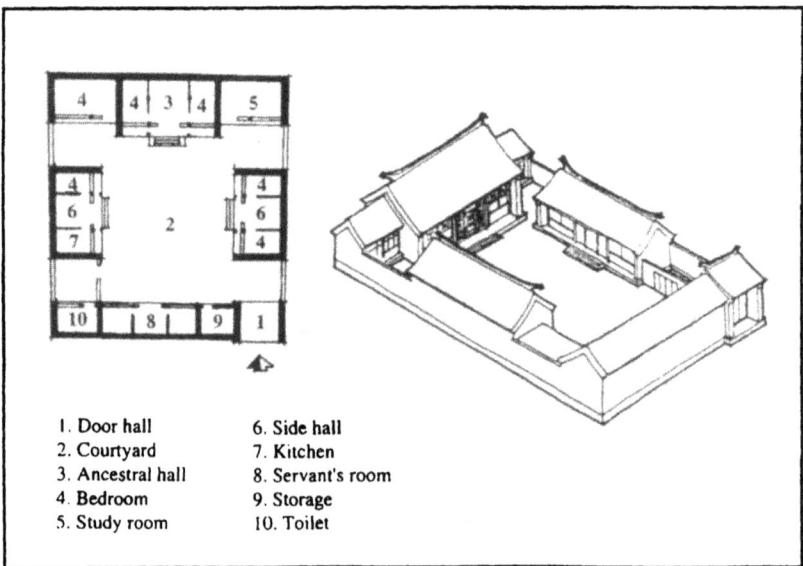

1. Door hall
2. Courtyard
3. Ancestral hall
4. Bedroom
5. Study room
6. Side hall
7. Kitchen
8. Servant's room
9. Storage
10. Toilet

Figure 10.12   A 'four-in-one courtyard' house formed by one basic unit

1. Door hall
2. Front courtyard
3. Inner courtyard
4. Ancestral hall
5. Sitting hall
6. Bedroom
7. Side hall
8. Servant's room
9. Guest room
10. Kitchen
11. Storage
12. Toilet

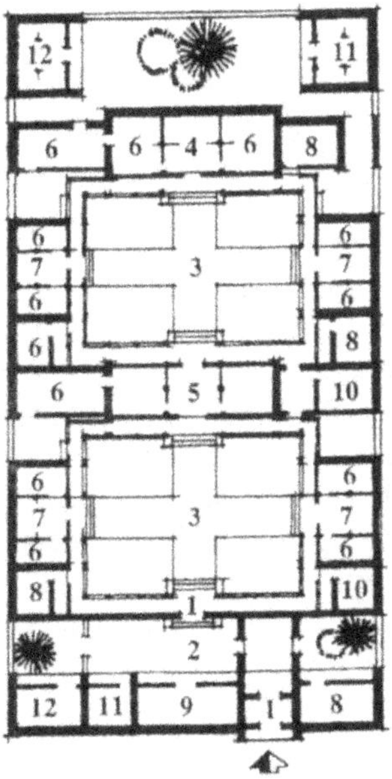

Figure 10.13   A typical courtyard house in Beijing

quarter and the core quarter are made in sequence along a central axis on the north-south direction according to the Chinese hierarchical order system.

In a courtyard compound, the main building and the inner courtyard are the two most important parts. The main building is composed of three rooms in a small-scale house, five to seven rooms in a medium or large-scale house. The central part of the main building contains the principal rooms. The principal rooms, consisting of ancestral hall and 'next rooms' - the rooms next to the ancestral hall on either side, have the highest roof and largest size in the entire compound, while smaller and lower rooms are attached to either side of the principal rooms. Since these minor rooms look like ears on both sides of a face, they are given the name *Erfang* - ear rooms. The main building is usually elevated on a tamped earth foundation with higher base and steps.

Symbolically the ancestral hall is the focus of the family and the centre of the house. Physically it possesses the largest room with a southern exposure for getting sufficient sunshine during the day time, which indicates the ancestor hall is in the most important position in the compound. The ancestral hall has multi-functions in the Chinese house. Similar to a living room, it can be used for:

- Ancestral worship and sacrificial ceremonies during annual festival days;
- Ceremonies such as weddings, funerals, the naming of a new-born baby and coming of age at 20 which are all related to ancestral worship;
- Family formal gatherings and sometimes receiving relatives and guests;
- Dining after the previously mentioned large ceremonies; and
- Displaying objects of art.

In the feudal society, the allocation of rooms to different members in a family was subject to the regulations about the order between older and youngster members and between superiors and inferiors. The 'next rooms' were mostly bedrooms for the older generation who had superior positions in the family. Under the system of polygamy, the eastern room was the bedroom of the wife while the western one was given to the concubine, since the East was taken as the superior direction. Only the ancestral hall in principal rooms had a door leading to the outside. The two bedrooms flanking the ancestral hall could be entered only from the ancestral hall. Ear rooms on either side of the principal rooms led to the outside or to the principal rooms. They were made into bedrooms or studies.

On the east and west sides of the courtyard house, the buildings have three rooms respectively with doors facing inwards to the courtyard. These are called *Xiangfang* – wing buildings. The wing buildings were for the younger generation or for children. The centre room was a living room, and the two on either side were bedrooms. The room on the southern side could be used as a kitchen or bed-room. If the space of the courtyard allowed, *Erfang* may have been attached to the southern ends of *Xiangfang* on both sides of the courtyard.

Opposite the main building is an inner entrance gate named *Chuihuamen* – inner entrance gate. The corridors are built linking the main building, wing buildings and *Chuihuamen*. All buildings in the courtyard possess front corridors under the eaves and are linked up all together by the corridors which end at the *Chuihuamen*. These corridors not only provide passages, but also enrich the layers and spaces of the inner courtyard house. The building facing the main building on the south wall, adjacent to the street, is called *Daozuofang* – reversed building.

The reversed building was the least important and usually occupied by servants or used for guest rooms and storage. The guests could not live in the same courtyard as the family members because guests were considered outsiders. The last row of building was often established in medium or large-scaled courtyard houses. It was mainly for unmarried girls or maid servants.

The inner courtyard is another important part in a house. The enclosed space is the soul of the house compound and gives a place for the unity of the family. In many houses in South China, the size of the courtyard is usually small. Such a house fits the demand of southern climate, but lacks ideal ventilation and day-lighting.

The courtyard has the following functions:

- Many houses in both North and South China have no windows on the outer wall. All windows open to the courtyard. As a result, natural lighting and ventilation depend heavily on the courtyard.
- The courtyard is a playground for children and a resting place for adults.
- Various trees and flowers can be planted, and fish-bowls or potted landscapes can be placed in the courtyard.
- The worship of the god of Heaven and the god of Earth during annual festivals takes place in the courtyard.
- Different household chores such as the washing and drying of clothes, washing food, etc., take place in the courtyard.
- It provides passageways to any other rooms in the house.

From these functions, it can be seen that the courtyard is the outcome of the specific lifestyle in the traditional Chinese society.

In fact in South China and North China, different patterns of the courtyard dwelling could be found. Although these various patterns share similar basic characteristics, differences do exist. The following two sub-sections will examine a selection of the distinct types of courtyard dwellings found in the twentieth century. Through the study of different courtyard house patterns in South and North China, the influence of different natural conditions upon the formation of different house patterns will be clearly seen.

The subtropical and tropical courtyard houses in South China

Most of South China is situated in the subtropical zone, whereas some parts are located in the tropical zone. The traditional subtropical and tropical courtyard house forms in South China are characterised by the compact courtyard dwellings with small courtyards, and thus known as 'heavenly well dwellings' and constitute a logical development of the combination of two types of earlier-developed dwelling forms. One is called stilt dwelling and the other is called original courtyard house. This latter type can be traced back to the earlier pattern of the courtyard house in North China. The combined courtyard houses chose the timber structural technique of the stilt dwellings in South China. The framing structure of the stilt dwelling is a system of pillar and transverse tie beam (*chuandou*), which could adapt to complex hilly land forms by supporting the house lifted above the ground by pillars. Because of its unique structure, the lower part of the stilt dwelling is open, permitting the circulation of air. This makes the stilt dwelling suitable for a tropical humid climate (see Figure 10.7). Such timber structures were widely adopted in the subtropical and tropical courtyard houses throughout South China.

At the same time, as the origin of the standard northern building technique, the pillar and beam (*tailiang*) structural system was also widely used in southern courtyard dwellings by immigrant groups of Han people and their descendants from North China since the period when the Qin kingdom overpowered South China in 214 B.C. The basic principle of the spatial arrangement of the subtropical and tropical courtyard houses was mainly based on that of the typical courtyard house in North China. The employment of the tile roof and the use of brick or stone nonload-bearing walls were also borrowed from the house form in North China (see Figures 10.8 and 10.14).

In the central area of South China, such as Anhui and Zhejiang, the courtyard houses are small in layout. They are two-storied buildings with enclosed high walls. Windows are seldom found in the outer walls. The function of the solemn-looking high wall is for security and defence as well as for protection from fire. Once inside the wall, the typical dwelling gives a vivid appearance with a symmetrical layout, a defined axis and hierarchical but integrated arrangement of the house. This is very similar to the style of the northern courtyard house found in cities such as Beijing.

In Figure 10.14, House 1 has only one basic unit, that is a 'four-in-one courtyard'. An ancestral hall and two side-halls to the west and the east of courtyard could all open to the courtyard with movable doors and partitions. A back-hall is placed behind ancestral hall. The courtyard, representing a sixth of the total area in the whole compound, is small in comparison with those in the north where a courtyard may exceed a third of the whole courtyard house (see Figure 10.13). Because of its small size, sunlight is often restricted from entering the rooms. This, however, is

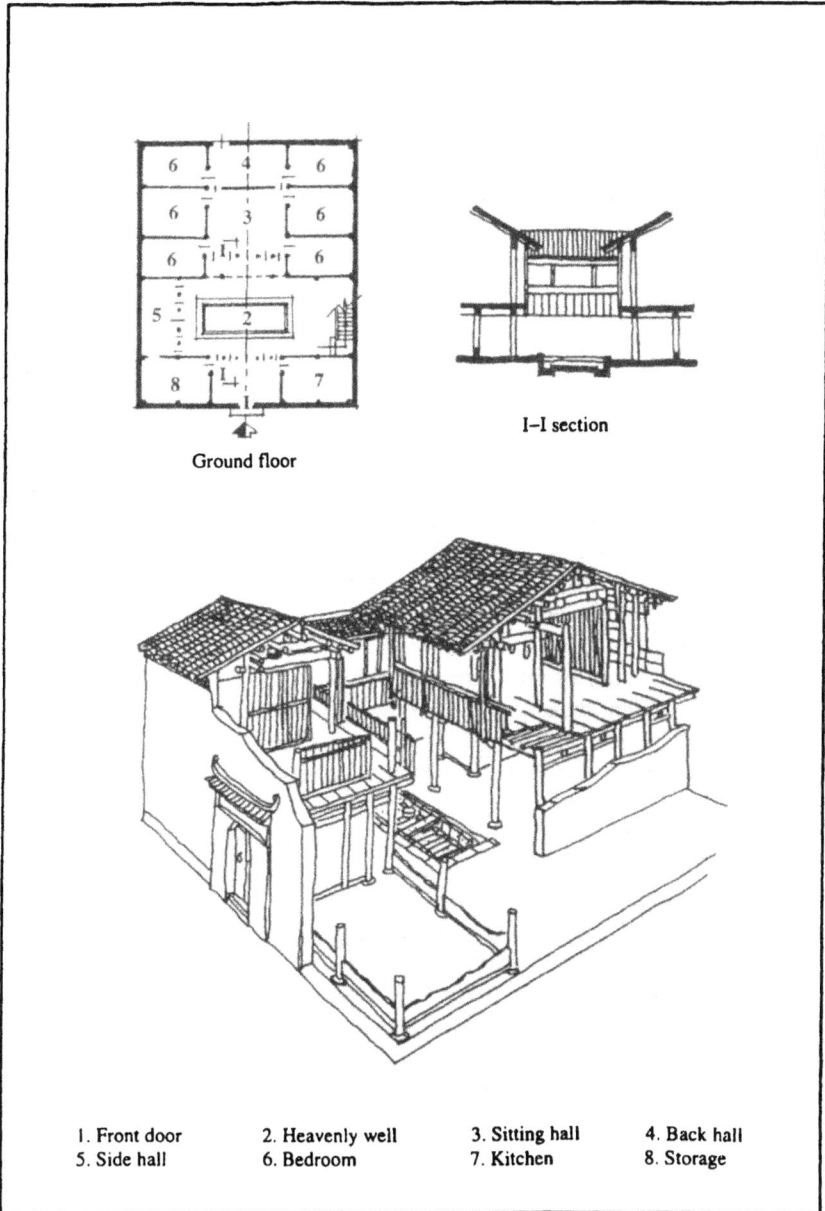

Ground floor

I–I section

| 1. Front door | 2. Heavenly well | 3. Sitting hall | 4. Back hall |
| 5. Side hall | 6. Bedroom | 7. Kitchen | 8. Storage |

Figure 10.14   House 1 - a typical compact courtyard house in Anhui province
Source: Liu (1957, p.90)

circumvented by adding substantial roof overhangs. Since the size of the courtyard in the southern courtyard house is small, this kind of house is usually called 'heavenly well' (meaning small courtyard) dwelling.

The *Yikeyin* courtyard house is another example of traditional subtropical courtyard house form in South China. Since its plan looks like a typical Chinese seal (*Yikeyin* in Chinese), it is given the name the *Yikeyin* courtyard house. It can be found in the provinces of Yunnan, Sichuan, Hunan, Hubei and southern Anhui (Liu, 1930). In House 2, the two-storied buildings have an ancestral hall on the second level above the sitting hall. In this house, the spatial arrangement shows that all the facilities (including the ancestral hall, bedrooms and storage rooms) have been moved to the second storey of this single-unit house (see Figure 10.15). The ground floor has a sitting hall and two bedrooms, whereas the side buildings are usually used as kitchen, stables and pigsty. The two stairways are located between the main building and the side buildings.

The *Yikeyin* house form can adapt to many climatic environments. For example, in Yunnan province, which is located at a high altitude in the windswept Yunnan Kueizhou Plateau, the form of the *Yikeyin* house has been widely adopted as common dwellings to cope with the local harsh natural conditions. The dwelling consists of two-storied buildings to protect the house and small courtyard from frequent dust storms in the province (Liu, 1979). A study of the *Yikeyin* courtyard house in south-eastern Anhui has examined the relation between the plan of the dwellings and the climate of this warm and hilly area (Zhang and et al., 1957). In the hilly lands, frequent thunderstorms throughout the whole year bring numerous floods to these areas. The forms of common dwellings on the hillside are characterised by two-storied buildings surrounding a set of small courtyards while the ground floor is without windows and back doors. The small courtyards generally have a rectangular stone pool dug into the ground to prevent flooding by collecting rain water from the courtyard and from the roofs. There are no drainpipes from the roofs. The rain water held in the pools could then pass through drainage outlets to the outside. The small courtyards are combined with halls. The only boundary between the courtyard and hall is a change of level, as no doors or windows are used to separate the two. They are completely open to each other, so it is convenient to use the courtyard on a fine day and is easy to move into the hall when the weather is rainy.

If economic conditions allow, some small houses can be renovated and enlarged. But the *Yikeyin* courtyard house normally does not exceed two units. Houses 3 and 4 are both examples of the enlarged *Yikeyin* courtyard house form (see Figure 10.16). House 3 is a two-storied building. The plan is a combination of two 'three-in-one courtyard' with one being placed behind the other. House 4 joins the two-storey 'three-in-one courtyard' with a reversed 'three-in one courtyard', forming an H-shape with only one lateral main building. They all share common features with the small-scale *Yikeyin* house.

云南"一棵印"民居

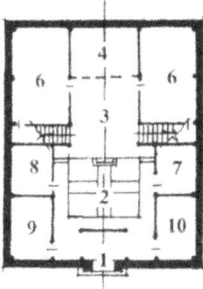

Ground floor

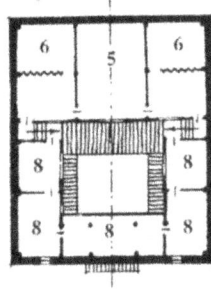

Upper floor

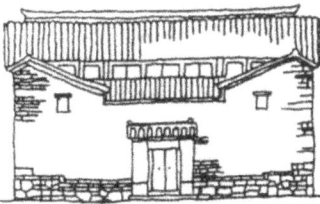

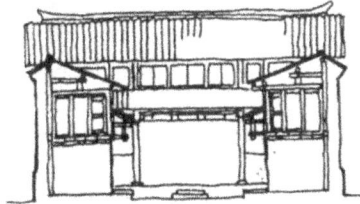

1. Front door	2. Heavenly well	3. Sitting hall	4. Back hall
5. Ancestral hall	6. Bedroom	7. Kitchen	8. Storage
9. Stable	10. Pigsty		

Figure 10.15   House 2 - *Yikeyin* courtyard house, Kuenming, in Yannan province

Source: Liu (1957, p.101)

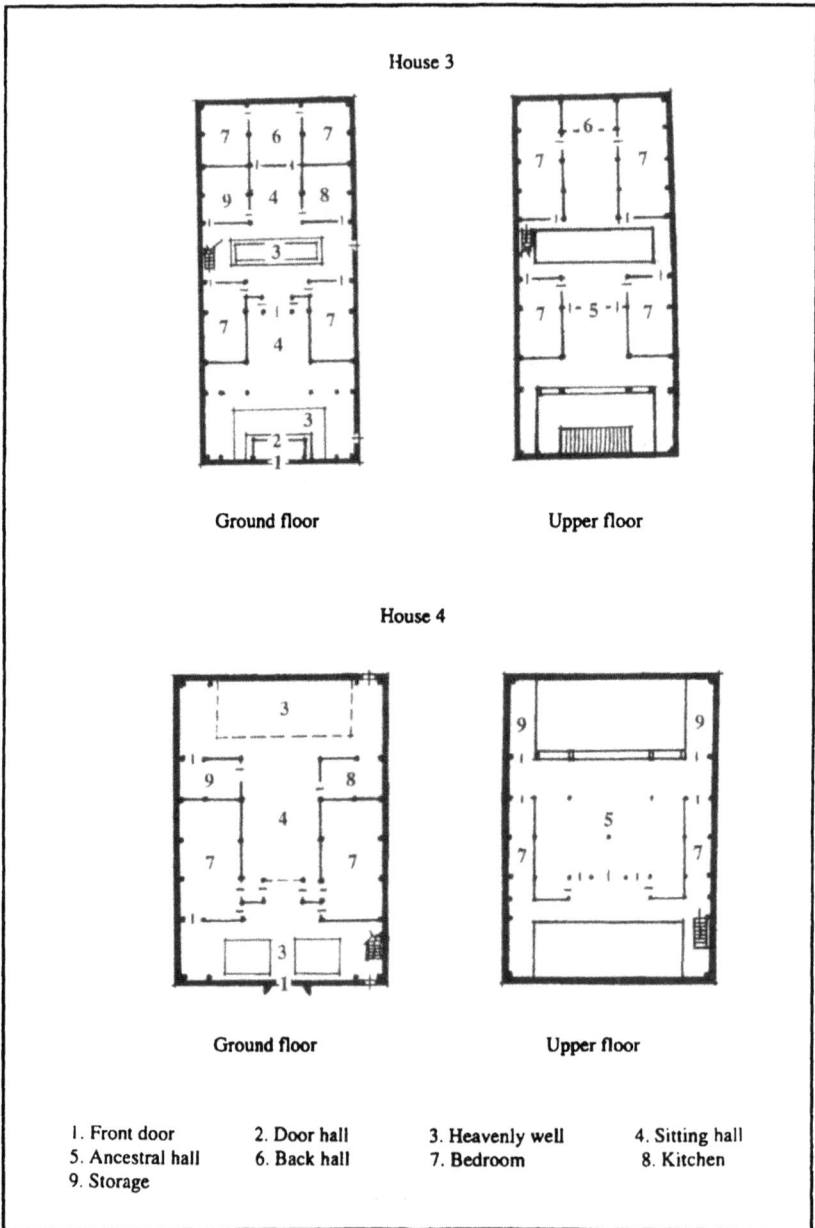

House 3

Ground floor   Upper floor

House 4

Ground floor   Upper floor

1. Front door	2. Door hall	3. Heavenly well	4. Sitting hall
5. Ancestral hall	6. Back hall	7. Bedroom	8. Kitchen
9. Storage			

Figure 10.16   Houses 3 and 4 in Anhui province
Source: *The Architect* (No.9, p.151 and p.157)

In places where communities were defined by clan groupings, enclosed large compact courtyard house complexes were developed. A large compound contains at least two units on a central axis. Sometimes protecting building groups are attached to the main compound on both sides to form a large compact complex for joint families. This housing form can be found in the provinces of Zhejiang, Fujian, Guangdong and Taiwan. House 5 is an example of the large compact courtyard house in Zhejiang province of the south-east coastal area of South China. This compound is mainly single-storied buildings and has three groups. Located at the centre of the whole compound, the main group consists of two 'four-in-one courtyard' with the last row of the buildings being two-storey. At the end of front hall an ancestral hall with an inner courtyard in front of the ancestral hall is placed in the central position of the entire compound. Beyond the central hall a two-storied back hall with a small courtyard stands in front. Other two groups are attached to the main group on both sides. Each side group consists of two complete basic units of 'three-in-one courtyard' (see Figure 10.17).

In remote mountainous areas of South China, large compact courtyard house complexes with high enclosed walls exist even today. The high walled compound is regarded as a symbol of the need for protection where bandits were common in the past. As a 'functional' element in the layout of the dwellings in remote areas, the walls have been retained even today even though the need is much less pronounced than in the past. House 6 is another example of the large compact courtyard house complex in Zhejiang province. The complex is two-storied buildings and consists of three groups. The main group consists of two 'four-in-one courtyard' and is located at the centre of the whole complex. The main group has two south-north main passage-ways on both sides of the main halls to avoid passing through the main halls when entering or leaving the house. Other two groups are placed in parallel with the main group known as protecting building. As side buildings each has its own main passage-way leading to the outside. In the complex, other passages running from east to west connected the three groups, leading from the outermost building on one side to the one on the other side. These longitudinal and latitudinal passages formed a circulated interaction network in the complex (see Figure 10.18).

From the examples of the traditional subtropical and tropical courtyard houses, the following common characteristics can be found.

- Two-storey houses with high fire-sealing gable walls rising above double sloped roofs are common throughout South China
- High walls enveloping small and narrow courtyards provide restricted exposure and better shading for the surrounding rooms.
- The doors and partitions of all main halls facing courtyards could be totally removed allowing an unobstructed flow of air from the front to the rear of the house along the central axis.

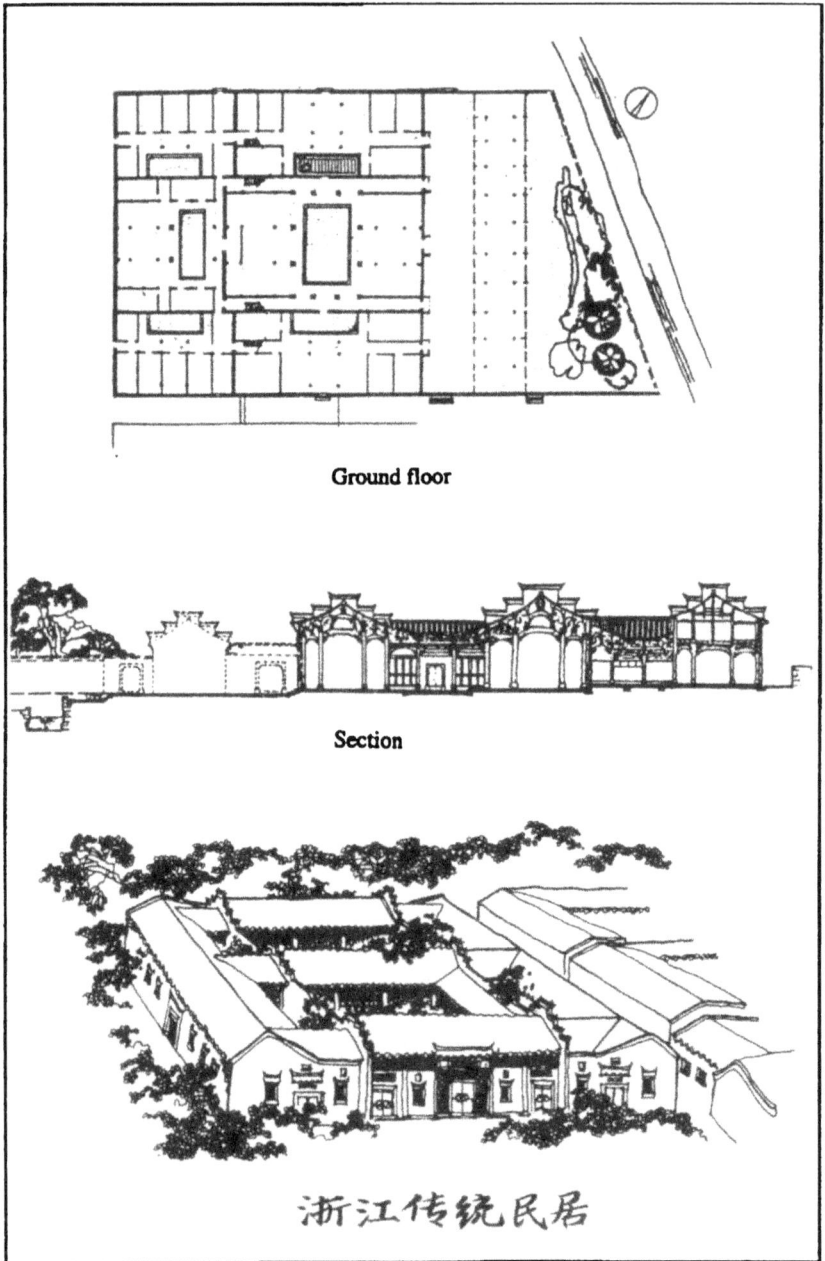

Ground floor

Section

浙江传统民居

Figure 10.17   House 5 - a traditional dwelling of Yiwu in Jhejiang province
Source: Li and Yu (1990, p.61)

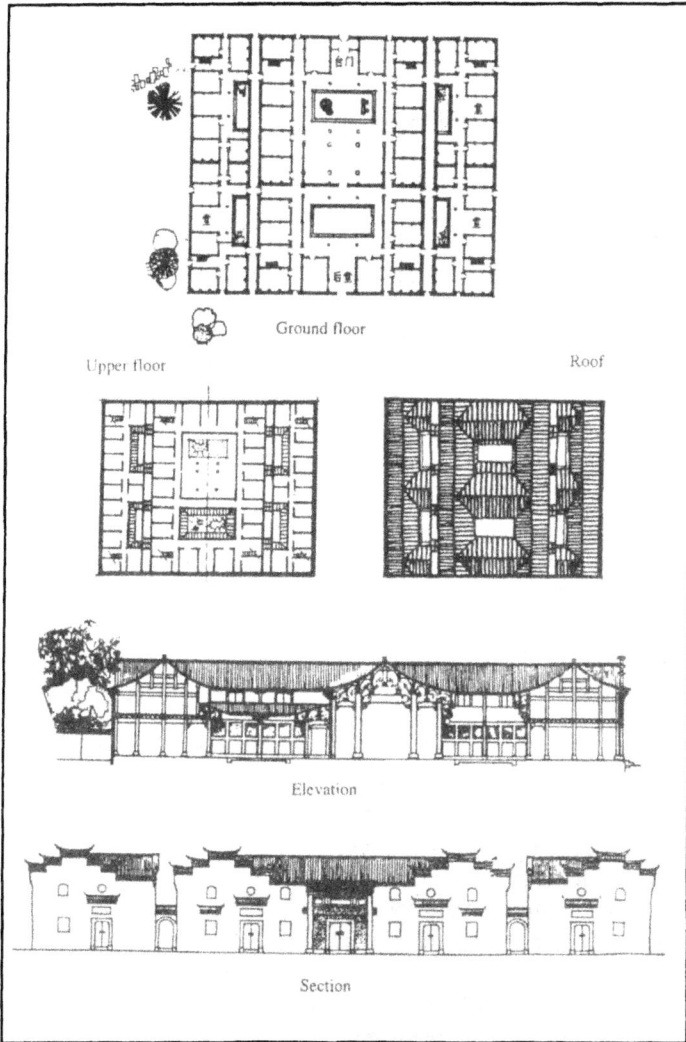

Ground floor

Upper floor

Roof

Elevation

Section

Figure 10.18   House 6 - a large compact courtyard house complex in Zhejiang province

Source: Yang (1990, p.49)

- The exterior facade of south facing dwellings of various sizes presents whitewashed walls with only limited openings.
- A basic symmetry exists on both sides of the south-north central axis.

The patterns of courtyard houses in North China

The patterns of courtyard houses in Beijing are regarded as major forms of residences in the city. This is not only in the case of Beijing but also in many other parts of North China. This could be explained by the fact that the natural conditions in North China were similar, and the influence of the imperial capital was powerful in the northern areas. As a major residential form, the courtyard house compounds of Beijing have existed in the city for over 800 years. In the thirteenth century, with the conquest of China by Mongols and the founding of the Yuan Dynasty (1279-1368 A.D.), the Mongols, a nomadic ethnic group from the north of China, established their capital in Beijing. The emperor of Yuan ordered two Han scholars, Liu Binzhong and Guo Shoujing, to take charge of the planning and the construction of the new capital. These two planners relied upon ancient Han traditional city planning principles to build the city. With grand-scale construction projects started at that time, the courtyard houses, being a representative of housing patterns for over 1,000 years in China, began to appear simultaneously with the palaces and offices in the city. Through the construction and reconstruction of the next two dynasties of Ming (1368-1644 A.D.) and Qing (1644-1911 A.D.), the patterns of the courtyard house compounds had been eventually fixed.

The courtyard house of Beijing was influenced by its closeness to the imperial court and its demands for strict social codes and official rituals. The layout and the spatial organisation of the house were subject to the social and family hierarchical order. The size of the house, the dimension, the decoration and even the colour of the tile were all restricted by the rank and status of the householder. Because of its symbolic function, the pattern of the courtyard houses in Beijing has been regarded as an example of an 'ideal form' and was copied into other areas around Beijing. In these areas the social conditions such as family organisation, customs, beliefs and way of life were strongly influenced by that of the imperial capital; the natural conditions of climate and land forms were also similar to that of Beijing. Hence, the patterns of Beijing courtyard houses became very popular forms over a long period of time in North China. The typical pattern and spatial organisation of Beijing courtyard houses have been discussed earlier in this chapter.

In south-west areas of North China (the birthplace of ancient Chinese civilisation), there remain a few integrated ancient cities. For instance, in the old city in Pingyao County, the city wall, the general layout and road networks inside city have been preserved intact. There is a large number of preserved traditional dwellings which are in harmony with the environment of the city. The local dwellings, like the traditional courtyard houses in Beijing, are all in regular forms of the courtyard houses. However, a distinctive style to be noticed in most of the main buildings in Pingyao dwellings is that they are built of brick vaulting caves with a *Fengshuilou* on the upper floor. While the wing buildings are in single-pitched roofs.

House 7 consists of two basic 'three-in-one courtyard' units with the reversed one placed in front of the other. A door-hall (a covered entrance area resembling a pavilion) connects the first and the second units and crosses the separating wall in the centre (see Figure 10.19). The first unit served as the service area with a servant's room, storage, a fuel room and guest rooms. The second unit, the central part, was the family residential area. The main hall in the middle of main building in the second unit combined the two functions of the ancestral hall and the sitting hall, where the ancestors of the family were worshipped and guests were received.

In each bedroom on either side of the main hall or flanking the side hall in the wing building, there is a *Kang* - a heatable brick or adobe bed taking over a third of the room area along the window. On top of the stove, the *Kang* is set up beside the gable wall in the bed-room in order to heat the room in winter and to dry the damp in summer. The roof of the main building is paved with bricks to provide a sunning terrace and an area to enjoy the cool in the summer evening. One or two outdoor stairs lead up the terrace. The terrace is enclosed by a higher parapet and a *Fengshuilou* (one room house with double-pitched roof) is usually set up on the terrace according to *Feng-shui* theories (Song, 1992).

The front gate of the courtyard house often combines with reversed rooms to the south-east or the middle of front building according to the theory of *Feng-shui* (see Figure 10.19). If the entrance way has to be built in some other place because of the restrictions of roads or land forms, a symbolic entrance way needs to be built in the recommended place to bring luck and safety to the family. In House 8, the front gate is built to north-east side of the house compound, and the entrance way is rearranged to form a second entrance to ensure good fortune (see Figure 10.20; Song, 1992, p.83). Walking through the gate, one would face a screen wall on the gable wall of the main building. On the left along the entrance way, there is a pair of screen walls with caved niches for both the village god and door god facing each other on opposite walls. A *Paifang*, a memorial archway, stands on the passage. Since the width of a house site is limited to three or five rooms, the wing buildings and the reversed building usually do not exceed the width of main building. The plan layout of the local dwelling is therefore made narrow and long.

Comparatively speaking, a complete space sequence from entrance to main caves in a Pingyao dwelling is more or less the same as the courtyard house of Beijing. However, the Pingyyao dwelling has its own features. First of all the scale and form of courtyard are very special. With the deepening of courtyard space, the courtyard become narrower and narrower from entrance to main building, while the height of wing buildings on two sides of the courtyard is increased gradually.

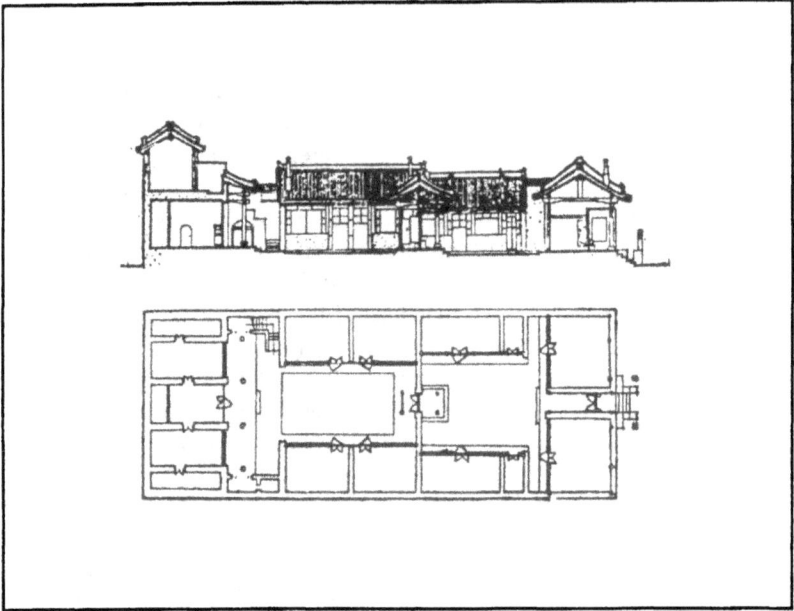

Figure 10.19   House 7 in Pingyao county, Shanxi province
Source: Song (1992, p.81)

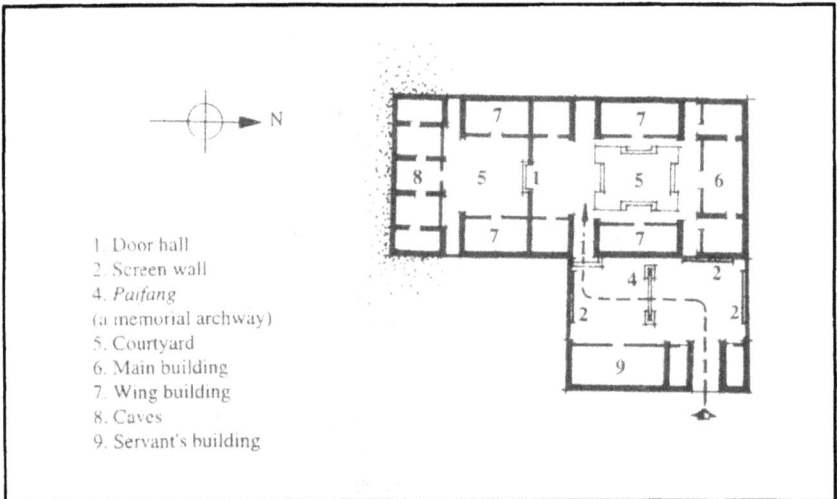

1. Door hall
2. Screen wall
4. *Paifang*
   (a memorial archway)
5. Courtyard
6. Main building
7. Wing building
8. Caves
9. Servant's building

Figure 10.20   House 8 in Pingyao county, Shanxi province
Source: Song (1992, p.83)

This makes the space more cohesive and closed. The roofs of the wing buildings in the local dwellings are almost all single-pitched roofs leaning towards the courtyard; the reversed building and even the main building (if not caves) have the same roof style as well. The single-pitched roofs lean and overhang deeply towards the courtyard, which enhance the effect of the cohesive and closed space of interior courtyard and outer appearances. Therefore, residential dwellings in the west part of North China have their unique characteristics when compared to the Beijing's courtyard houses.

Socio-cultural meaning in the traditional Chinese courtyard houses

Ancient Chinese philosophy

It is a commonplace in China, of two thousand years standing now, that the whole Chinese philosophy is divided into two parts: Daoism and Confucianism. Daoism represents the philosophy in its original purity. Daoism holds that the *Dao* (way) gives free rein to nature. There being no overriding element, all things develop in their own way as their natures dictated. The basic fundamental value of Daoism favoured common people. For instance, the poise and inner calm that may be derived from the attitude of contemplative Daoism elevates a man who holds it above the struggling mass of other harried men, and may even give a psychological advantage in dealing with them. Different from Daoism, Confucianism contributes to norms of social behaviour. The moral philosophy of Confucianism could offer intellectual support to those people who cannot find it in Daoism when they think themselves in association and communication with others. Because both Daoism and Confucianism relate to different aspects of life, most Chinese people may be holding one philosophical attitude one day and the other the next or even holding both attitudes at the same time. Many Chinese feel that every 'Chinese soul' is really half Confucian and half Daoist (McNaughton, 1974). Such 'Chinese soul' is also embodied in Chinese architecture.

The integration of the philosophy and the traditional courtyard houses

The basic Chinese philosophical ideas such as the cosmological and metaphysical concepts of *Yin-Yang*, *Five Elements* and *Qi* (vital breath) emerged as early as the beginning of Zhou Dynasty (1122-221 B.C.). In Chinese history, the Zhou Dynasty was divided into two stages: West Zhou (1122-771 B.C.) and East Zhou (771-221 B.C.). Since the early East Zhou, the whole dynasty was split up into seven states, beginning with a period which saw a great change and cultural boom in ancient Chinese society. This time has been called by Chinese historians the age of 'contention of one hundred schools of thought'. Many of ancient philosophical concepts were developed separately into doctrines of literati school and became state orthodoxy in each kingdom.

In the two following dynasties, Qin (221-206 B.C.) and Han (206 B.C.-A.D. 220), the ancient Chinese philosophy was raised to a higher level than before. Both the Qin and the Han Dynasties were periods of imperial unification. The 'unification' implies that not only the separate states were united, the different schools of philosophical ideology were also integrated. In addition, different symbols and metrology systems of the individual states began to combine to form a new and unified system after Qin. During the Han Dynasty, both Confucianism and Daoism became mature and dominant ancient ideological systems. They complemented each other and largely influenced the culture, philosophy, and aesthetic thought of the Chinese.

At the same time, practical experience of house construction was accumulated and a basic courtyard house form was gradually accepted as a general dwelling style for common residents (Liu, 1932, p.129). This was demonstrated by the existing models of houses made of pottery and by drawings on tiles, bricks and stones unearthed from Han tombs. The philosophy and housing principles had developed separately following different streams and now they began to merge, that is, traditional philosophy and house design began to exert influence on each other.

On the one hand, the philosophical ideology provided theoretical guidance for house building practice. On the other, the builders tried to express the ideology through the design of houses. As a result, the form and spatial organisation of the houses specifically reflected the features to which the ideology approached. Owing to the integration of the philosophical ideology and house building, previous building experiences began to accumulate and formed a unified system. Under such historical conditions, courtyard houses began to be widely accepted all over the unified country.

The physical design and spatial organisation of the traditional Chinese courtyard houses are deeply rooted in the ancient Chinese philosophy, either Daoism or Confucianism, or both. But Daoism and Confucianism influenced Chinese architecture differently. Daoist stressed a harmony between buildings and their environments, finding architectural expression in beautifully sited buildings and romantic ensembles, and developing artificial landscapes and ideal man-made environments. The qualities of Confucian architectonics, on the other hand, emphasised the importance of ethical criteria, liturgical and hierarchical orders, axis and symmetry to control spatial organisations (Needham, 1971). In other words, the emphasis of Daoism was on the holistic and harmonious relationship between man and nature, laying the basis on the Chinese view of nature, whereas Confucianism dealt with the connection between man and his society, giving birth to the code of ethics.

When those ancient ideologies became government doctrine and went along with the ruling power, however, the meaning of the forms and special arrangements of the formal houses were interpreted to express the ideology of the ruling class and to emphasise a rigidly hierarchical order of the feudalistic family and society. Those construction principles of the formal houses were used as immutable guidance which had to be observed for political purposes. Therefore the housing regulations in traditional dwellings were also regarded widely as a reflection of political rules.

The courtyard house as a microcosmic model

The concept of cosmology in traditional China

The cosmology of ancient Chinese culture was the main emphasis in Daoism. Since the dawn of history in China, man has been accustomed to consider the cosmic aspect of nature. The cosmological beliefs reflected the ancient Chinese view of an ideal world. For a long time, the ideal model drove the Chinese traditional societies[1] to make an effort to improve the quality of the environment for human life. Just as the concept of paradise or utopia may be different in every society, the desirable quality of built environments was quite different as well.

The Chinese cosmology was formed by the basic components of *Yin-Yang* (the two fundamental forces in the universe), the *Five Elements* (of which all things are composed) and the *Qi* (vital breath or energy). The application of the philosophy of the *Yin-Yang*, the *Five Elements* and the *Qi* can be found in all fields of life including religion, politics and pseudo-scientific teachings. Since the Han Dynasty, the concept of cosmology has been firmly established as the main part of the essence of Chinese philosophical thinking. The origin of *Yin-Yang* and the *Five Elements* could be found in the desire of the ancient Chinese to categorise all life and objects in the universe, and to simplify the complex phenomena they encountered in their daily life. Moreover, they attempted to analyse the main components and find common elements and principles in all forms of life and all inanimate objects. The answers to their questions were found in the all-dominating principles of *Yin-Yang* and the *Five Elements*.

The School of Yin-Yang The universe of the ancient Chinese was naturalistic with its characteristics of regularity. Nature was seen to operate through the interplay between the two elements of pairs of matters, such as light and darkness, heat and cold, male and female, activity and passivity, and so forth. The ancient Chinese used the *Yang* to represent the first of each pair and *Yin* to present the second of each pair. The *Yang* and *Yin* were not in absolute and permanent opposition to each other. They might be described as definable phases in a ceaseless flow of change: when the sun goes the moon comes; when the moon goes the sun comes. The sun and moon give way to each other and their brightness is produced. *Yin-Yang* was defined as the endless source of all life force in the universe. The most basic idea in Chinese cosmology was that the interaction of *Yin* and *Yang* produced all things in the universe. Neither *Yin* nor *Yang* alone could produce life. It was believed that living creatures were surrounded by *Yin* and enveloped by *Yang*, and only the harmony of these two forces could bring harmony to the lives of all living creatures. The two forces were always considered equally important in Chinese thought: a balance between them ensured happiness, health and an orderly world.

The relationship between *Yin* and *Yang* can be demonstrated by a geometrical figure (See Figure 10.21). It was a symbol of an amazing intuition of traditional Chinese philosophers that balance was fundamental to the nature of things and to the very existence of the universe. It appears that all matter may have a counterpart in anti-matter, and all beings consist of an infinitude of interactions. Balance is in the nature of things and every imbalance tends to form a new balance.

Figure 10.21   Chinese *Yin-Yang* symbol

The School of Five Elements In the material world, there was inevitably an infinite variety of phenomena beyond explanation. Chinese philosophers by late Zhou times (1122-221 B.C.) had overcome this confusion by classifying all things into the so-called irreducible five elements. The 'Five Elements' consisted of wood, fire, earth, metal and water. Through the interaction of *Yin* and *Yang*, matter became differentiated into the 'Five Elements'. These in turn interacted to produce the great variety of existing things, all of which were therefore related to one of the elements, or represented different combinations of them. As a consequence of the principle of constant transformation embodied in the *Yin-Yang* theory, the concept of the primary elements focused on their ceaselessly interacting, transforming, and replacing each other.

In the theory of the 'Five Elements', there were two types of orders, the Mutual Production Order and the Mutual Conquest Order. They were related to all aspects of Chinese life which existed in the Han times. The two orders were concerned with the prophecy and divination of human affairs, and were bequeathed to all later ages (Needham, 1971, p.285). The theory of the Mutual Production Order was to a certain extent based on the following natural laws.

- Wood produces Fire, as the friction caused by the drilling stick causes wood to burn.
- Fire produces Earth, as wood can be burnt to ashes which in turn becomes earth; therefore Fire is said to produce Earth.
- Earth produces Metal, as ores are found in the stones on mountains, which are formed from the accumulation of earth. Therefore Earth produces Metal.
- Metal produces Water, as metal liquefies when it is melted, therefore Metal is said to produce Water.
- Water produces wood, as trees depend on water for their growth and survival.

These principles of the Mutual Production Order can be illustrated in an interdependent production cycle, as shown in Figure 10.22.

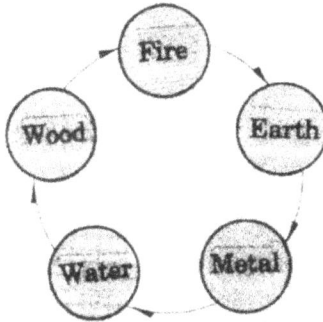

Figure 10.22   The Mutual Production Order of *Five Elements*

The second order is the Mutual Conquest Order. This order describes the series in which each element is said to conquer the next: Water, Fire, Metal, Wood, Earth. The order is based on a logical sequence of ideas that has its basis in common scientific knowledge: the fact that elements do harm to one another derives from the nature of the universe. In an abstract sense, the concentrated element is said to be able to conquer the element which is diffused. In particular, the Mutual Conquest Order can be described as follows.

- Wood conquers Earth, because the former can loosen or excavate the later.
- Metal conquers Wood, because metal can cut or carve wood.
- Fire conquers Metal, because fire can melt or even vaporise metal.
- Water conquers Fire, because water can extinguish fire.
- Earth conquers Water, because earth can dam and contain water.

This sequence is shown in Figure 10.23.

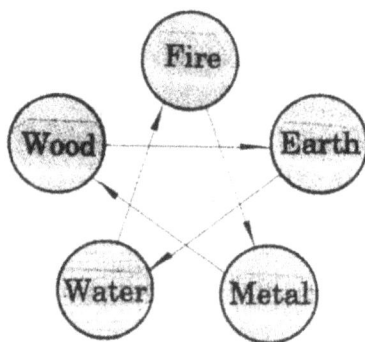

Figure 10.23   The Mutual Conquest Order of *Five Elements*

The 'Five Elements' and the two orders were considered important in forming the background to traditional Chinese philosophy and speculation, and also important in forming a fundamental part in the Chinese cosmology. They were put forward by ancient Chinese scholars as an explanation for the course of natural law and would apply in human affairs. The 'Five Elements' and the two orders were therefore useful for prediction, laying the basis in foretelling fortune or misfortune in social life. In this way, the Chinese developed a striking method of determining how man balanced with nature. In fact, even people themselves were categorised into one of the 'Five Elements' according to their time and date of birth, which was strongly emphasised in order to search for a proper residential environment.

The concept of Qi In order to understand the rhythm of nature (whose harmony was necessary in order to achieve cosmic order), the Chinese developed a complete explanatory system which was based on the concept of *Qi*. Any discussion on the cosmology of Chinese houses must therefore include this vital concept of *Qi*, or the 'breath of life'. The concept of *Qi* originated during the period of Han Dynasty (206 B.C.-A.D. 220). It was a supplement of the earlier developed *Yin-Yang* theory. The *Yin-Yang* concept was extended and specified by the concept of *Qi*, and *Qi* was a medium through which *Yin-Yang* acted on the universe. The Chinese at that time observed the process of growth and decline exemplified by the birth and death of all life in the universe as brought on by the different winds of the four seasons in an endless cycle. At the same time, the continuous flow of the life-giving water in rivers and streams was considered to be powered by a certain force of nature. By connecting the power behind movement of the winds and waters into a single force, the Chinese arrived at the concept of the invisible breath of life (*Qi*), which was believed to be the cause of all change in the universe.

The basic principles of the concept of *Qi* can be summarised as follows:

- The Chinese considered the universe as a container pervaded by *Qi*. Han Nan-Zi said: 'The Great Beginning produced an empty extensiveness and this empty extensiveness produced the cosmos. The cosmos produced the primal fluid *Qi* which had its limits' (Fung, 1931, p.396). If the universe is regarded as a container, the imagined sides of this container are the boundary limiting *Qi*'s movement.
- The *Qi* underwent periodical phases of dispersion and condensation. In the stage of dispersion, *Qi* was invisible and intangible. With the condensation of *Qi* the world came into being. Again *Qi* began to disperse and it would revert to its former state. Therefore in Chinese minds, there was an intimate connection between the condensation of *Qi* and the existence of all beings. *Qi* was the essential element which gave life to all beings through its condensation, while its dispersion resulted in death (Fung, 1931, p.484).
- *Qi* can be categorised into *Yin Qi* and *Yang Qi*. *Yang Qi* was known as heavenly *Qi* and *Yin Qi* as earthly *Qi*. The balance between *Yang Qi* and *Yin Qi* ensured an orderly world. In his *Religious System of China,* De Groot (1897, p.948) wrote: 'when heavenly (*Yang*) *Qi* descends and earthly (*Yin*) *Qi* ascends, *Yin* and *Yang* unite, ten thousand things will be engendered. If heavenly *Qi* does not descend and earthly *Qi* does not ascend, *Yin* and Yang cannot be blended and the ten thousand things do not develop.'
- Life depends on *Qi*. Dong Zhongshu, a scholar of West Han (A.D. 24-220), explained the concept of *Qi* through a metaphor that man's existence in the universe like a fish's attachment to water: 'Within the universe there exists the *Qi* of the *Yin-Yang*. Men are constantly immersed in it just as fish are constantly immersed in water. The difference between *Qi* and water is that the turbulence of the latter is visible, whereas that of the former is invisible.'

The concept of Qi has its prevailing impact on many aspects and subjects. However, it is not intended here to discuss the influence of *Qi* on the development of ancient Chinese sciences and philosophy. In the context of traditional Chinese architecture, the analysis will focus on how the *Qi* has influenced the search of an ideal site and the construction of an ideal house.

The courtyard house as a microcosm of the universe

Feng-shui Theory The Chinese did not build houses only for dwelling's sake, but also for expressing an abstract notion – a proper place between heaven and earth in which people dwelled. A prevailing concept which existed in the traditional period was that man, living under the domination of nature, best ensured his security and felicity by conforming and adapting himself to the influences of the universe. *Feng-shui* theory, a Chinese concept of living environment, was an application of traditional Chinese cosmology in Daoist philosophy to housing in practice. It was concerned with the relationship among man, house and universe in an attempt to integrate people, their activities and nature. During the imperial epoch of China from 221 B.C. until A.D. 1911, *Feng-shui* played an ever important role in providing builders with theoretical guidance and helping inhabitants to identify a good living environment to build their ideal home. It encompassed an array of patterns and symbols to assist in the selection of proper sites for dwellings, palaces, cities, graves and even roads, all aiming at identifying a proper residential space, and seeking happiness, wealth and longevity.

Basic to *Feng-shui* was the notion that human alterations of the landscape did not simply occupy empty space. Rather, building sites were viewed as great certain properties which influence, even control, the fortunes of those who intrude upon the site. As explained by Maurice Freedman (1969):

> When a man puts up a building he inserts something into the landscape and between him and his neighbours. It follows that risks attend his enterprise and he must take precautions. The physical universe is alive with forces that, on the one side, can be shaped and brought to bear on a dwelling and those who live in it, and, on the other side, can by oversight or mismanagement be made to react disastrously. In principle, every act of construction disturbs a complex system made up of nature and society, and it must be made to produce a new balance of forces lest evil follows.

A set of books about *Feng-shui* theory had been drawn since the early Han Dynasty. But, many valuable works have been lost because of destruction from old dynasties to new ones. *The Canon of Dwellings* ascribed to Wang Wei of the fifth century (Needham, 1971) in *Imperial Encyclopaedia* is considered to be the oldest book available about *Feng-shui*. It contains the principles of constructing an ideal living environment. This book had been widely referred to by *Feng-shui* finders and craftsmen in the traditional period. Other important *Feng-shui* books were *Ten*

Books of Yang Zhai, Three Aspects of Yang Zhai and *Yang Zhai and People*[2]. Here *Zhai* means the dwelling places, *Yang* indicates the alive and *Yin* indicates the dead. In fact, the *Feng-shui* theory contained two parts, one part dealing with the housing theory for the living and the other for the dead, hence the houses for the living are known as *Yang Zhai* and 'houses' for the dead are called *Yin Zhai* (i.e. the graves). Although *Yin* and *Yang* were seen as equally important theoretically, the living is more emphasised. Therefore, the books related to the *Yang Zhai* were generally more important than *Yin Zhai* books. These books formed a literary basis of *Feng-shui*. By relying on cosmology and following a popular set of practices in the *Feng-shui* theory, the Chinese strongly believed that they could dwell in the most suitable and favourable residential environment for their families.

The model of an ideal residential site in accordance with Feng-shui

Under the specific social condition, the most important subject in the *Feng-shui* theory is the search for a proper building site. In the opening chapter in *Ten Books of Yang Zhai*, the importance of choosing a proper residential site for the living is strongly emphasised:

> The most important part of a dwelling site is the existence of surrounding mountains and rivers through which *Qi* flows. This exerts great influence on the locality, which in turn is crucial in influencing people's fate. If the surrounding formation is malefic, even a perfect inner shape of the house will not enable its inhabitants to reach the stage of total luck. Therefore, the outer surrounding of the house is of vital importance and should be first taken into consideration.
>
> *(Ten books of Yang Zhai*, 1911, p.2).

It was stated in *Feng-shui* theory that an auspicious site was defined through its visible landscape features. Those five elements of wood, fire, metal, water and earth were entitled to represent the different shapes of local landscape features (see Figure 10.24). Before selecting a building site, the shapes and the features of the landscape should be analysed. As a *Feng-shui* manual dictated:

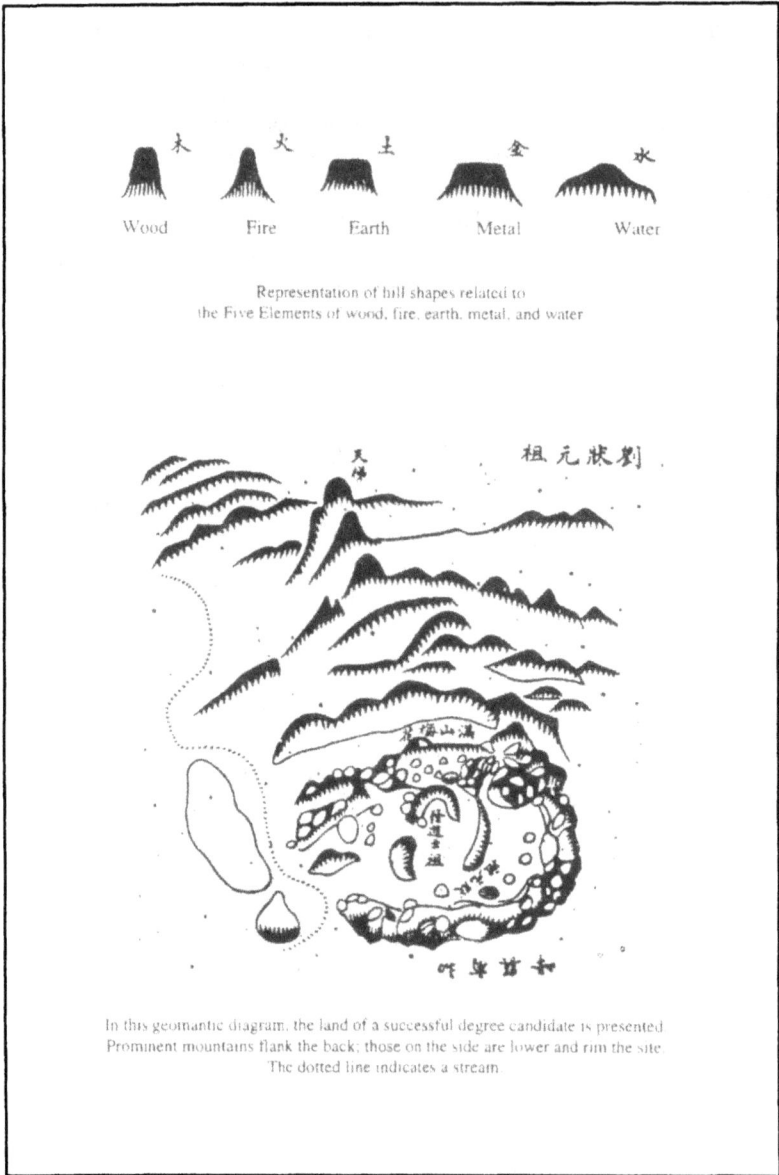

Figure 10.24   The notion of 'ideal site' in *Feng-shui*
Source: Knapp (1986, p.111)

On a rock hill you must take an earthy site; on an earth hill you must take a rocky site. Where it is confined, take an open place; where it is open, take a confined space. On a prominence, take the flat; where it is flat, take the prominent. Where strong comes, take weak; where weak comes, take strong. Where there are many hills, emphasise water; where there is much water, emphasise hills.

(Xingxiang, 1957, p.63)

The characteristics of a most desirable site in *Feng-shui* theory can be modelled as follows:

- The layout of an auspicious site should be shaped by an ideal formation of mountains or hills. In the shape of embrace, main mountain stood to the rear of site with the altitude higher than the chain of hills on the right and left sides of the site. The front of the site (south) was open. The shape of the enclosure site was considered as an ideal container of *Qi*. It also looks like a crook of the elbow in a curved arm, to provide protection from inclement weather or an enemy.
- The lie of the land should be gently sloping and, if possible, there should be a river or valley nearby to allow surface water to drain easily, preventing the site from unhealthy dampness and flooding. This requirement can be satisfied when the inner part of the site (closed by mountain) is higher than the ground at the entrance of the site. The innermost point on the central north-south axis is regarded as being the best location on which to build the house.
- A winding road in front of the house is more desirable than a straight one. This is because i) the strong external winds from the front cannot disperse the lively *Qi* of the internal site and ii) the evil things cannot easily enter through the curved or bent road. Therefore no straight roads or passages should lead directly to a site of dwelling.

Based on the above three main points, the illustrations of the ideal site model can be visualised in Figure 10.25.

In *Feng-shui* theory, mountains are a metaphor for nature and therefore receive prominent attention. The Chinese believed that mountains or hills were conveyors of *Qi* and symbolised the veins and arteries of nature. The ideal site protected on three sides by mountains or hills was able to retain its lively *Qi* and was the ideal blend of *Yang Qi* and *Yin Qi*. The interaction of *Yin Qi* and *Yang Qi* was believed responsible for the quality of a residence. Every site itself provided the *Yin* (earthly) *Qi*, while the amount of *Yang* (heavenly) *Qi* which entered the residence was dependent on the shape and orientation of the site. When *Yang Qi* blended with *Yin Qi*, the result strongly influenced the lives of the inhabitants. Therefore,

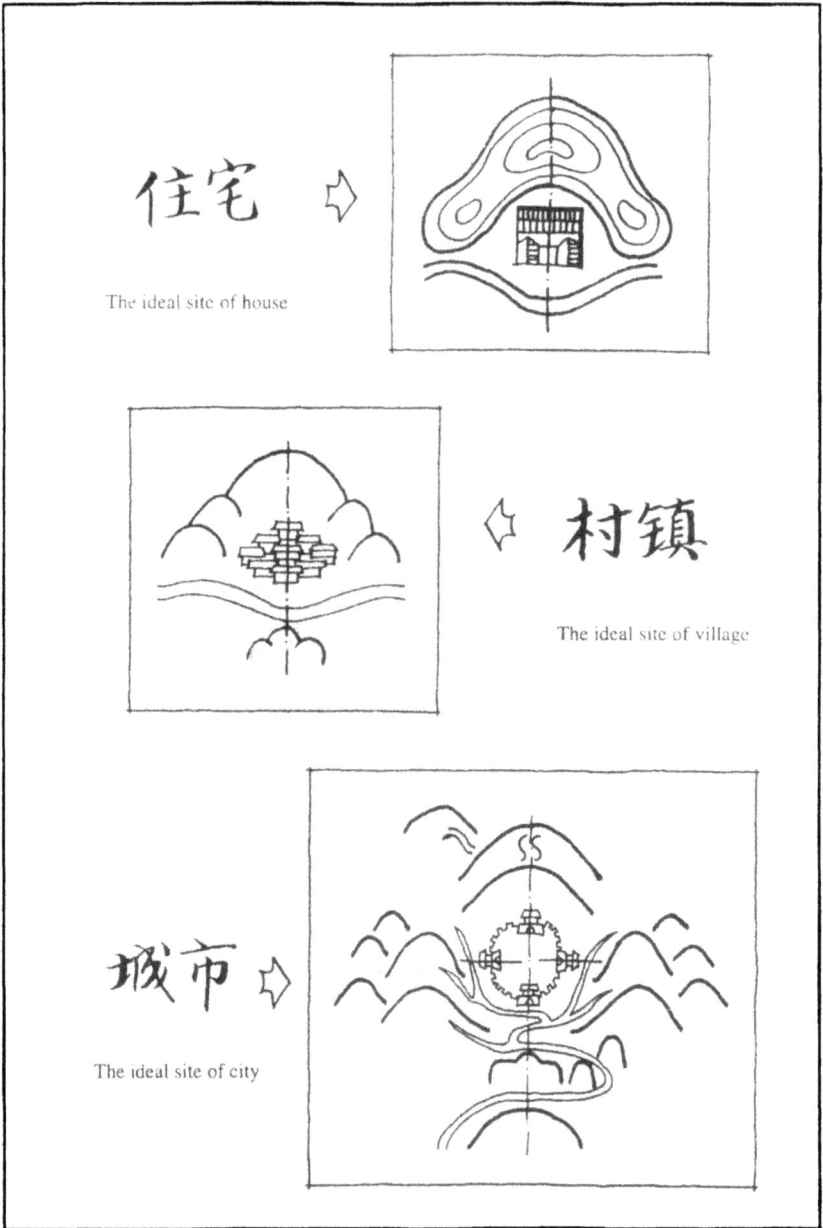

住宅 ⇨
The ideal site of house

⇦ 村镇
The ideal site of village

城市 ⇨
The ideal site of city

Figure 10.25 The ideal sites of house, village and city in *Feng-shui* theory

.he house should be placed at a location which would receive the right amount of both *Yang Qi* and *Yin Qi*; too much of one or the other would be maleficent.

In plain areas, main streams and their tributaries can also enclose a site and convey *Qi* to the site in the same manner as the mountain ranges. This idealisation of the natural environment can be seen from the biological point of view. The mountain range or main stream can be compared to the powerful trunk of a tree, through which nourishment (*Qi*) is sent to the end of the branches for flowers to blossom. If the pistil of the flower is the ideal residential site, then the foothills or small streams enclosing it can be regarded as the petals of the flower, protecting the pistil from the harsh winds (Cheng, 1994). In the same manner as the flower needs the sun to blossom, the site needs the addition of *Qi* to be able to flourish.

In fact, those requirements of ideal site were practical considerations which underlaid the ritualised behaviour of *Feng-shui*. A south-facing slope that is protected on the northern side by a set of interlocking mountain ranges provides a building site open to the sun throughout the year and protected in winter from the cold winds characteristic of China's climate. Such as 'sitting north and facing south' has been obligatory for Chinese dwellings, especially in the northern and central areas of China. The orientation of the house may be seen as a device for obtaining the best advantage of sun and wind. Because the sun is regular in its path across the sky, the axial arrangement of a house controls the degree to which the sun's ray is seasonally captured or evaded. These natural conditions can be fine-tuned by adding the overhanging eaves which block the extra heat from the summer sun (at a high altitude) and permit the entrance of sunlight from low altitude in winter.

The pattern of the courtyard house as a microcosm applied in practice

The ancient Chinese endeavoured to make their living environment as a miniature of an ideal world. The 'ideal world' was defined as a world of harmonious cosmos. Chinese people strongly believed that harmony was a fundamental principle of the world order, and a harmonious cosmos can give vitality to all creatures including humans. Since the Han Dynasty (206 B.C.-A.D. 220), Chinese cosmology was drawn up as an idealised structure of the universe in the minds of the people. They regarded Heaven and Earth as a macrocosm, and man's living environment, including the state, the city, the dwelling, and even the human body as a microcosm, a reflection of the macrocosm. They strongly believed that the analogy existed between the macrocosm and the microcosm with the reflection of one in the other[3]. As a reflection of cosmic geometry, the model of the ideal site in *Feng-shui* theory was made as a practical version of the ideal pattern of the universe which was formed out of the collective knowledge and beliefs of intellectuals in their search for explanations of the universe. The basic pattern of the universe and its many practical versions were widely applied and continuously reinforced in planning the ideal construction of the state, cities and houses to adapt different environments. Paul Wheatly has analysed the Chinese thinking and said: 'the pre-established harmony of the Chinese universe was achieved when all beings spontaneously followed the internal necessities of their own nature' (Wheatly, 1971).

In reality, however, it is usually difficult to obtain such an ideal site as suggested by the *Feng-shui* theory. Firstly, in a rural environment very rare sites can exactly match the requirements for the ideal site. Secondly, the rise of urbanisation made it even more difficult to find such natural ideal sites in towns and cities. Therefore, *Feng-shui* theory basically provided an ideal site model derived from the cosmology, and set the guidelines for a desirable living environment. In order to obtain the desirable living environment, the evolved form of courtyard house compounds has been selected as a symbolic ideal model and as also a microcosm. As can be seen clearly in the diagrams (see Figures 10.12 and 10.13), the courtyard is surrounded by lineal rooms, corridors and walls. The ancestor hall, the most important room of the house, is situated at the northern end of the courtyard along its central axis. The main entrance to the courtyard is placed on the side opposite the ancestral hall; it is also seen as the entrance for heavenly *Qi*. The courtyard in front of the main hall, corresponding to the open space surrounded by the hills or mountains in the ideal site, is believed to be the space where lively *Qi* accumulates. In this way, the house fulfils the functions of containing lively *Qi* in the same way as the ideal site in *Feng-shui* (see Figure 10.26).

The cosmological order through interactions and balance between the *Yin* and *Yang* and among the 'Five Elements' had been applied to generate the philosophical planning ideas of the courtyard house. In a courtyard house, the building and the courtyard represented respectively the solid and the void, or, the positive and the negative, the pair resembling the element of *Yang* and *Yin*. The balance and harmony of the *Yin* and the *Yang* forces were carefully employed into the plan and the spatial organisations of the courtyard house in order to achieve an ideal house, i.e. a secure and permanent place for the inhabitants.

The general form of a courtyard house had a combination of several buildings surrounding a courtyard on four (or sometimes three) sides, enclosed walls, corridors and gates. It was so designed as to provide a container for *Qi*, a concept coming from the imitation of the universe. In the history of Chinese traditional architecture, the development of the traditional courtyard dwellings was continuously influenced and guided by the *Feng-shui* theory. Some housing features strongly reflected the expression of Chinese philosophy. The general characteristics of Chinese traditional houses can be summarised as follows:

- A house was a combination of several single buildings surrounding a courtyard on four (or sometime three) sides, with enclosed walls, corridors

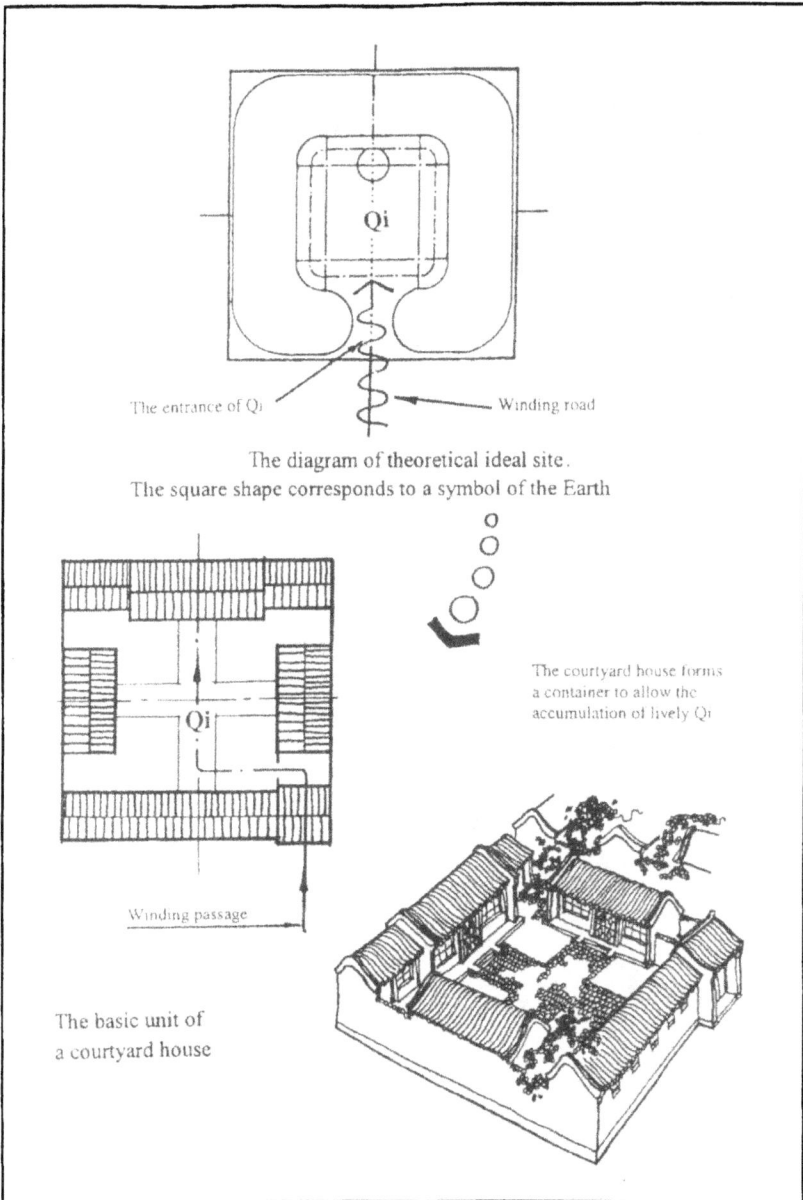

The diagram of theoretical ideal site.
The square shape corresponds to a symbol of the Earth

The courtyard house forms
a container to allow the
accumulation of lively Qi

The basic unit of
a courtyard house

Figure 10.26   Examples of courtyard houses with their features as the reflection of a microcosm

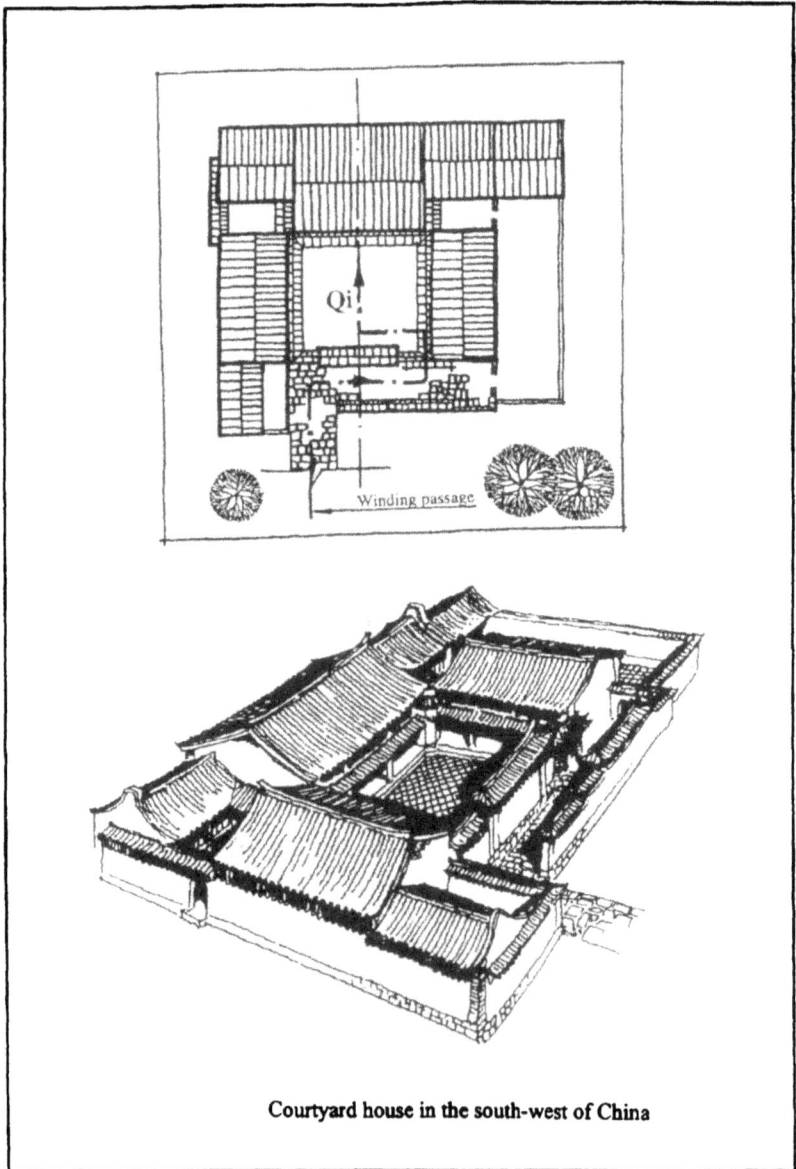

Courtyard house in the south-west of China

Figure 10.26   Examples of courtyard houses with their features as the reflection of a microcosm (continued)

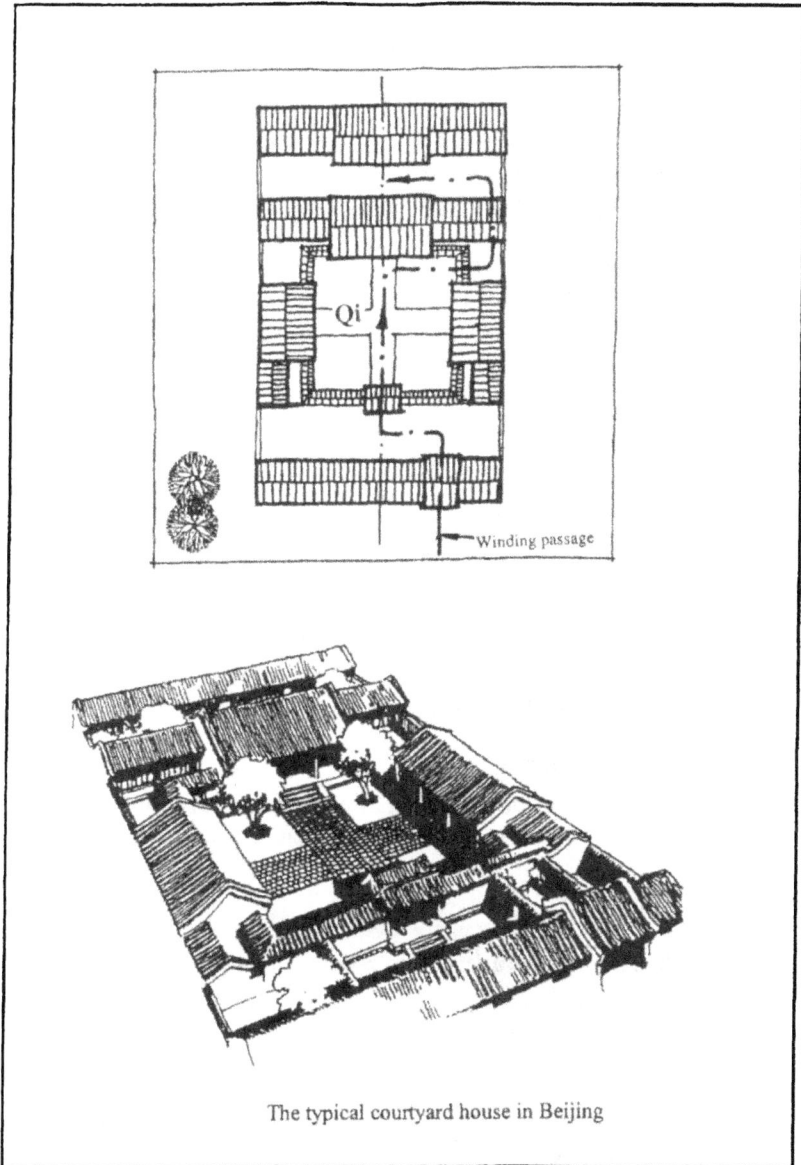

The typical courtyard house in Beijing

Figure 10.26   Examples of courtyard houses with their features as the reflection of a microcosm (continued)

and gate, forming a set of individual and separated courtyard units in one compound.

- A single building was rarely used to be an individual house. The plan of those single buildings in a housing compound had a high degree of stylisation.
- The courtyard (the enclosed space) was the soul of a house compound. It provided a place for the unity of the family. As an expression of cosmic geometry, a courtyard was usually laid out in the form of a four-side shape, generally a square.
- The architectural styles were reflected by the different combinations of single buildings, corridors and walls with their shaped courtyards.
- The layout of the courtyard house was a symmetrical plan following cardinal orientations along a north-south axis. The most important building of a house was located at the northern end of the central axis.

As a recreated model, the layout of the courtyard house and its spatial organisation were given a lot of cultural implications through symbolic interpretation. From the view of *Feng-shui*, a basic courtyard unit was not only a house for dwelling, but also a structured vision of the universe and an ideal container of *Qi*, as a reflection of the cosmos of Heaven and Earth. The squared courtyard, the important feature of traditional Chinese architecture, was seen as the soul of an enclosed group of buildings. A square is a simple, geometric plan, but in the minds of the Chinese, a square also corresponded to a cosmic symbolic representation because they believed that the 'sky is round and land is square'. This ideal form conforms to the Chinese people's 'close to the earth' idea, or the belief that when man is close to the earth, health will prevail. The ancient book *Zhou Li* described that the square-shaped ideal house form was an expression of cosmic geometry, reflecting the rule that all made under heaven should live in a structure that was a replica and a symbol of the earth.

The courtyard house with its functions in religious rituals

The traditional courtyard houses and old family rituals

In traditional Chinese eyes the ancestral hall and the courtyard were the essence of a dwelling. They were seen as the unifying power of the family because they enabled rituals to be carried out. The principal elements of traditional Chinese dwelling have their roots in the worshipping rituals in ancient time. In the dawn of Chinese civilisation, religious worship had been widely accepted. People believed that the universe was filled with gods (such as the heaven god and the earth god) and the spirits of ancestors. The powers from these gods and spirits could be appeased by man's worship and sacrifices. The people's serious attitude toward worshipping divinities and spirits can be seen in the passage from *Rites Records*[4]. 'The people of Shang Dynasty (1600-1066 B.C.) respected their gods; the chief led his people to pay sacrifice to gods and spirits before performing rites'. From the writings inscribed on oracle bones, it was found that the Shang people lived in a world of religious wishes and fears. The god they honoured most was *Di* (a super ruler in heaven), who was believed to control the annual harvest in autumn and military affairs. Spirits from people's ancestors could bring luck or harm to their descendants. Various rites took place for the gods and spirits to assure the security of families and the state, and to prevent future calamity. In many such rituals, ancestral worship and worship of nature played a crucial role in the living and dwelling of the ancient Chinese people.

Archaeological findings in Banpo village in Shanxi province of China have provided some proof. In the plan of the tribe settlement in prehistoric China, smaller houses allocated to the tribe members were situated in concentric circles around and all their doors faced a large house which was located in the centre of the settlement. These smaller houses were either excavated dwellings in the ground or semi-excavated dwellings with a roof constructed above the ground. In both the excavated and semi-excavated dwellings, a square entrance was flanked by two walls and a cooking pit at the centre of the dwelling was surrounded by columns supporting the roof (see Figures 10.27 and 10.28). A small hole in the roof directly above the pit opened to the sky and provided for ventilation. Some Chinese architectural historians have explained that the ventilating hole in the house also had the function for the worship of gods and ancestors by drifting of the smoke of wishes to the sky (Liu, 1981).

The large house was built above ground and mainly fulfilled social functions. Apart from being the residence of the tribe leader, it also provided living quarters for tribe members who could not work independently, such as the old, the sick and the children. The large house was also a meeting place for important events such as religious ceremonies (Yen, 1981). The building itself was constructed with better materials and was more complicated in structure than all the other small houses. A cooking pit in the ground was surrounded by a terrace of 10 cm above the ground. When the pit was used to communicate with the gods during worship ceremonies, sacrifices were placed on the terrace. In this manner, the large house fulfilled both ritual and residential functions and symbolised the centre of the tribe (Yang, 1983).

The above evidence indicated that since the earliest stage of Chinese architectural history, a house was a place where residents were able to communicate with their gods and spirits of ancestors through rituals. The house had not only provided people with a residence, but also with a place of protection for their gods and family ancestral spirits. Each dwelling had both residential and worship functions.

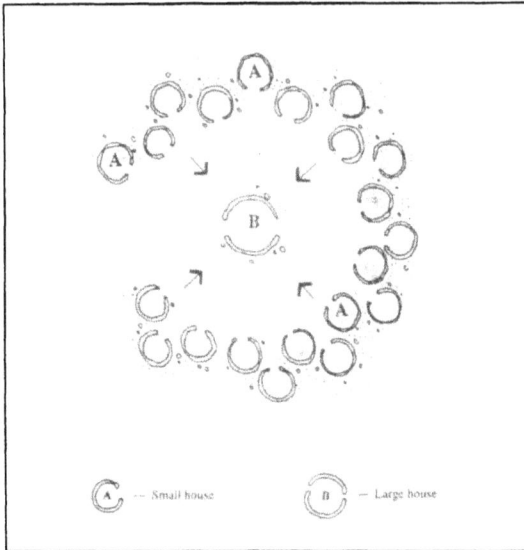

Figure 10.27   The plan of a tribe settlement with its centripetal pattern in prehistoric China
Source: Li (1985, p.140)

Figure 10.28   The reconstruction of a small house in a tribe settlement in Banpo village, Shanxi province
Source: Li (1985, p.83)

In the tribe settlement, there was a spatial core in its physical centre. The spatial core was surrounded and faced by common dwellings in a concentric circle. A large house for the leaders was located at the centre of the settlement with good quality building materials, symbolising the power of leaders and the spiritual centre of the settlement. The emphasis on the importance of central space as the soul of a group of buildings had existed even in the beginning of Chinese housing practices. This design approach conformed with the Chinese customs of the central importance of the family and the requirement for the family rituals. As a result, this approach has been widely used in housing planning and housing construction. It has also been a main design technique in the spatial organisations of traditional Chinese architecture (see Figures 10.27 and 10.29).

The importance of the family worship led to the centrality of such a worshipping place in the home. By West Zhou (1122-771 B.C.) the domestic house still contained a fire pit inside the house. The function of the fire pit was two-fold, one for cooking, the other for worshipping. As the hole in the roof opened to the sky, sacrifices were placed in the fire pit directly underneath, fulfilling the requirements for both cook and worship. This place of worship was known as *Zhong liu*. According to Chen Xiangtao (Qing Dynasty, A.D. 1644-1911) a relationship existed between the *Zhong Liu* and the development of Chinese house in the ancient times. He argued that when the houses were excavated dwellings, an opening was made in the roof, usually in the centre. The function was for ventilation, natural lighting and worship purposes. Due to the opened hole in the roof, rain flowed into the house through the opening, leading to the name of *Zhong Liu* which means 'central drip'. With the development of houses above the ground, the *Zhong Liu* gradually evolved to take the shape of *Yan Liu* which means 'the dripping of water from the eaves'. This means that the roofs of the buildings on the four sides of a central opening slanted toward the centre so that rainwater would flow into the opening called *Yan Liu*. It was deduced by some architectural archaeologists that the origin of the courtyard in traditional houses was the *Zhong Liu* in excavated dwellings which was developed into the *Yan Liu* and then into a central courtyard. The common characteristics of all three elements, *Zhong Liu*, *Yan Liu* and the central courtyard of a courtyard house, were their openings to the sky so as to allow the drifting of message smoke to the gods of heaven, penetration of sunlight, and a pit in the ground for worshipping.

As housing construction and spatial organisation were developed by the late Zhou period (Zhou Dynasty, 1122-221 B.C.), the worship area in a house was divided into two ceremonial spaces: the ancestral hall and the courtyard. The ancestral hall was built indoors for ancestor worship, and the courtyard was open to the sky for the worship of heaven and earth gods. Consequently, a clear spatial division appeared in the house. The division manifested into a front and a back section. The front was used for the worship of ancestors and the back for living. According to the study of Li Yunhe (1985), the house form with front hall and rear rooms

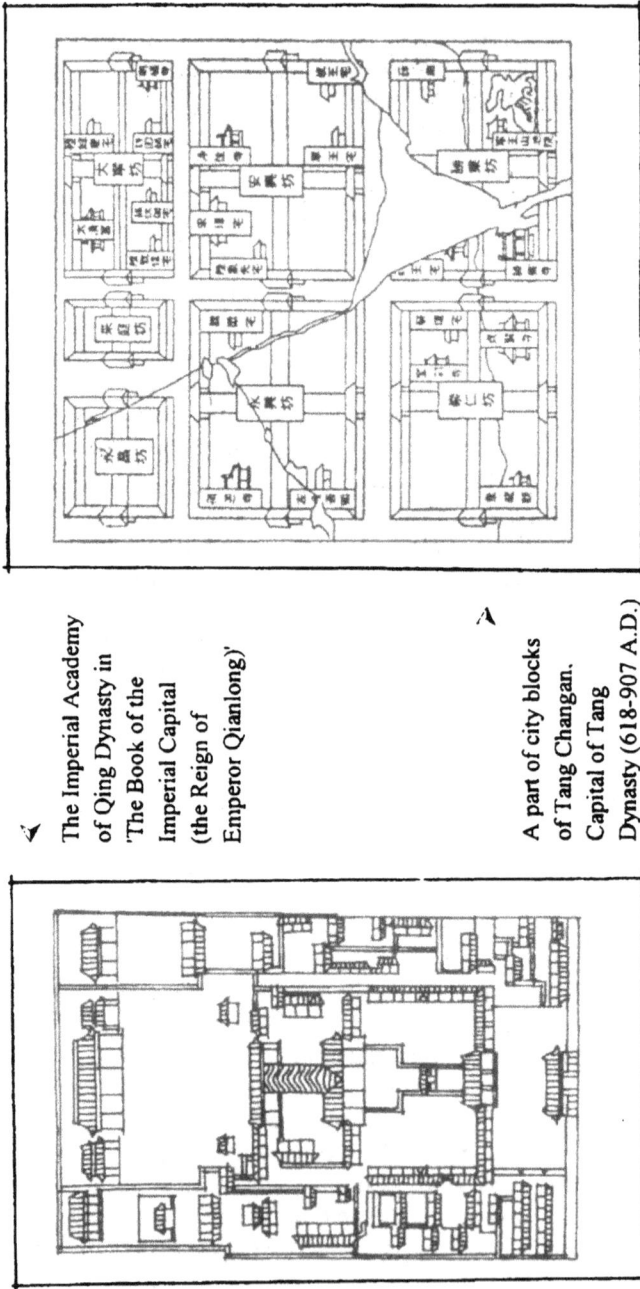

The Imperial Academy
of Qing Dynasty in
'The Book of the
Imperial Capital
(the Reign of
Emperor Qianlong)'

A part of city blocks
of Tang Changan.
Capital of Tang
Dynasty (618-907 A.D.)

Figure 10.29   The examples of traditional building groups with their centripetal planning patterns, which was the main design technique in the planning of Chinese traditional architecture

have become most common and popular housing type since later Zhou period (Li, 1985; see Figure 10.30). The front hall had a worship altar, which was used as a family religion for the worship of the ancestors' spirits. The rear rooms provided living areas for residential purposes .

The central importance of the family had been a specific characteristic of Chinese traditional society (Thompson, 1989); and the function of the ancestral worship had been certainly a specific distinguishing characteristic of the traditional family. This relationship made Chinese religion more a family matter than an individual choice. In view of the central place of ancestor worship in Chinese culture, family religion was basic; individual and communal religion were secondary. The emphasis on the family religious power led to the importance of the ancestral hall and the courtyard inside a dwelling. For these reasons the functions of the ancestral hall and the courtyard as related to family religious rituals will be investigated next.

Ancestor worship and ancestral hall

The Chinese people believed that the deceased superiors possessed even more spiritual power than they had possessed in life. Their spiritual power could control the life of their descendants. That was, they were able to intercede with heaven and earth gods to send blessings or calamities to the surviving family members. Therefore, the pleasing of their ancestors and the subjecting of the will of heaven and earth through rituals which took place in ancestral halls and courtyards were important events in the family. According to the work of Laurence G. Thompson (1989), the function of the Chinese ancestor worship in a traditional family can be seen in the following aspects:

- Ancestor worship demonstrated the continuing love and remembrance of their descendants. Their ancestors would send down to them the sorts of happiness, official position, wealth, sons, love of virtue, long life, and a peaceful death.
- Ancestor worship was confined to the kinship group. It played an indispensable role in reinforcing the cohesion of family and lineage.
- In the light of the family system and its hierarchical structure, original relationships can be retained in full force despite the death of a senior.

When people's beliefs and values were reflected in the arrangement or design of their residences, they regarded their ancestral hall as a temple in the house in which ancestral spirits dwelled. The ancestral hall, therefore, received more attention than other buildings in the house. It was built at a central place on north-south ritual way with better materials, highest roof and biggest size, expressing a

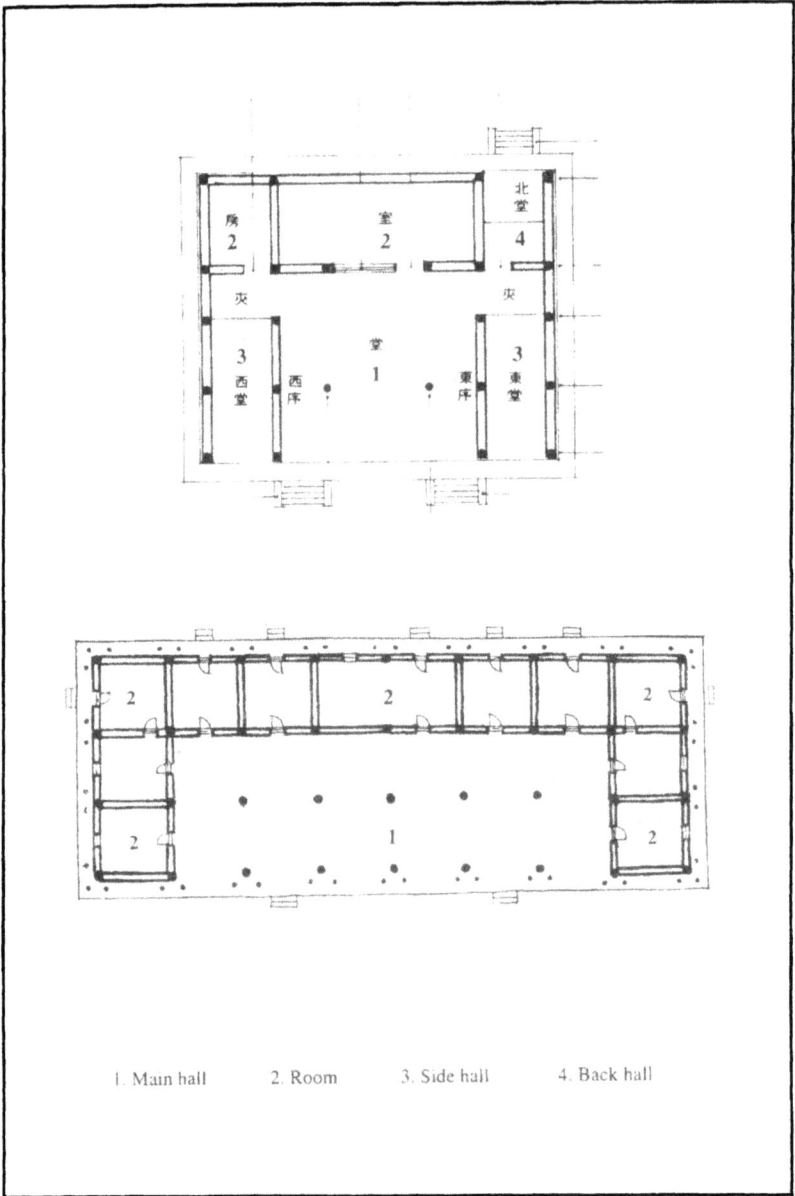

1. Main hall   2. Room   3. Side hall   4. Back hall

Figure 10.30   **A popular house form with front hall and rear rooms, which appeared in the late Zhou Dynasty (1122-221 BC)**

Source: Li (1985, p.84)

focal point of the house. The ancestral hall commonly contained a high, long table upon which were arranged in an orthodox order, ancestral tablets. Ancestors were placed on the right stage and their gods on the left stage, the left position being of higher rank than the right. On the wall behind, a large portrait of a deity and a pair of couplets were hung. Periodic offerings of food and incense related to prescribed ritual underscored the centrality of the room.

The ancestral hall was a ceremonial place in the courtyard house. The ritual of worship in the ancestral hall was performed by all members of the family. Here, also, family members paid their respects to the elders in the morning, on their birthdays and during Chinese new year days and religious holidays. It was also a place for family celebrations and a social place for weddings, funerals and seasonal festivals. Moral codes and family ritual were observed during these ceremonies, and proper behaviour was also learned here. It can be seen that the ancestral hall was treated as a 'family church' where the ancestor's position was intensified in the family hierarchy. It is also an important feature of the traditional courtyard house in China. As Thompson (1989) has noted, the ancestral hall is basic to Chinese traditional houses because it moulded Chinese society into its traditional form, in which the interests, responsibilities, and loyalties tended to be focused inward to the family and lineage rather than outward to the public realm.

Worship of heaven and earth gods and the courtyard in the traditional house

In traditional times, the worship of heaven and earth gods was one part of the religious expressions of the family. Those heaven and earth gods were humanised by Chinese popular religion. For instance, the supreme god in heaven was known as *Di* in the Shang Dynasty, while the Zhou Dynasty named him *Tian* (Huang, 1982, p.359). As the highest of all heavenly gods, the role of *Di* corresponded to that of the king of the state, while the gods of the four directions of east, south, west and north were entitled as his officials. *Di* was seen as controlling man's life in the following ways:

- He observed man's deeds and made judgement. He also encouraged and rewarded virtue and punished evil.
- He had the authority to grant leadership to the most capable successor and remove power from those unqualified.
- To show his displeasure, his warnings to man came as natural disaster or man-made calamity (Huang, 1982, p.360).

The earth god was a popular deity found everywhere in China. Every tiny residential area, even every home, had its own earth god. The humbleness of his shrines was an indication of his closeness to the people and was most intimately involved in people's lives. As Thompson (1989, p.66) wrote : 'The people appeal to them for everything which affects their lives. All births and deaths are reported to them..... They are thought especially to protect their worshipers against mildew, locusts, and caterpillars. As the people believe a faithful heart will gain their favour, and bring a rich harvest, they are continually found in worship before their shrines....' The little images of the earth god were found in almost every household. They were usually kept on the floor of courtyards as close to the earth as possible, protecting the house and its inmates.

A passage in the *Li Ji* (The Records of Rites) describes the worship of the heaven and earth gods in early times: 'The people of the Shang and Zhou Dynasties burned piles of timber on an earth mound so that the smoke could carry their wishes up to the gods of heaven. By the same token, sacrifices to the earth gods were buried in pits in the ground so that the earth gods would be able to receive them'. The worship of heaven and earth gods normally took place at the same location within an enclosed and protected area. Such ceremony performed in the courtyard that was frequently mentioned in an ancient book of *The Book of Odes*.

As mentioned previously, the Chinese ancient residence was regarded as a place where people were able to communicate with their gods and the spirits of their ancestors through rituals. Every dwelling had the dual function of residence and worship. This religious practice in a Chinese family was handed down from generation to generation for thousands of years. An open space named *Zhong Liu* (central drip) was only a hole in the roof of the house in tribal settlement, which was used by the inhabitants for the worship of gods and ancestors. As the development of housing spatial organisation, the worship area was separated from one area at the centre of house into two ceremonial spaces: one was the ancestral hall indoors; the other was the courtyard (*Yan Liu*) in front of the ancestral hall for the worship of the heaven and earth gods. These two worship spaces, being regarded as a focal point of the house, formed an entire ceremonial area for the religious rituals of the family.

Meanwhile, as literary records indicate, the worship of heaven and earth gods was performed in open space since the dawn of Chinese civilisation, the courtyard located at the centre of house was regarded as an orthodox pattern. With the emphasis on the religious rites in family, the position of the courtyard in traditional dwellings was also strengthened. Being the focal point of a house compound, the courtyard, an enclosed space open to sky, represents the soul and heart of the house, integrating the interior and exterior of the house into one.

The courtyard house with the influences of Confucianism

The influences of Confucianism in Chinese society

Confucius (551-479 B.C.) is the most important philosopher in Chinese history. He is one of the ancient scholars who greatly influenced Chinese society and ideology, and made tremendous contributions to the development of Chinese civilisation. In Western Han (206 B.C.-23 A.D.) Confucianism became the orthodox philosophy and retained this position up until the present century. For more than two thousand years, Confucian philosophy has played a principal part in the formation of the most basic social and political structures of traditional China. In addition, the influences of Confucian philosophy spread far and wide to some other Asian countries, such as Japan and Korea. Even in this century the name of Confucius is still invoked in ideological struggles by some conservatives and by some of the most radical, who seek by means of varying interpretations to show that Confucius favoured their views (Fung, 1934).

Confucius was born in the Warring States (770-221 B.C.) at the end of Zhou Dynasty; that was a time when imperial rule was breaking down. The feudal lords acknowledged only nominal allegiance to the king. There was very little law and order save what each man could enforce by his own right arm, his armed followers, or his powers of intrigue. Even the greatest noble could not be sure that he would not be ruined and perhaps assassinated. The position of the common people was tragic. Whoever won the wars, the losers were the common people. Even when there was peace they had no security, for they had no right. They were virtual pawns of the aristocrats, whose principal interests had come to be hunting for power, engaging in wars and living extravagant lives. To pay for these pastimes they taxed the people beyond what they could bear, and suppressed all protest ruthlessly.

To Confucius these conditions seemed intolerable, and he resolved to devote his life to trying to right them. He was a great admirer of the Duke of Zhou who initiated the Zhou Dynasty and looked upon himself as a transmitter of early Zhou culture, rather than as an innovator. He taught a moral philosophy with man as the centrepiece. In order to meet his moral responsibility, he believed that a man must think for himself. This belief led Confucius to place as much emphasis on thinking as on learning. The central concept of his philosophy was that an ideal man was one whose character embodied the virtue of benevolence and whose acts were in accordance with rites and rightness. He talked to others about the way in which the world might be made a better place to live in. Gradually he gathered about himself a group of young men to study and to spread his doctrines, and so he became known as a teacher. Yet for Confucius it was not enough to be a teacher. He wanted to direct the government of a state and to see the world of which he dreamed come to life under his hand. But none of his chief ambitions had been fulfilled. After his death, as his teachings were handed down from one generation of disciples to another, the Confucian group gradually grew in size and influence.

For Confucius, as for the whole of the Chinese tradition, politics is only an extension of morals. Provided that the ruler is benevolent, the government will naturally work towards the good of the people; and the populace will be loyal and obedient. With the virtue of benevolence, the state will naturally grow towards order and eternal peace. In his opinion a ruler's success should be measured by his ability, not to amass wealth and power for himself, but to bring about the welfare and happiness of his people. This political concept remained and made Confucianism popular with the common people whose life became difficult under the consecutive wars and oppressions.

From the period of the sixth emperor Wu in the Han dynasty, the governments became more acceptable to the Confucians. The thought of Confucius was given interpretations by the Confucians based on their views and requirements of the time. Confucian doctrine was exercised as a guiding ideology and to justify their rule in government. From this time the doctrine was changed and elaborated to go along with the ruler's views. Confucius was made a powerful statesman and was converted to totalitarianism. Most effective of all, the government put totalitarian sentiments into his mouth as a supporter of unlimited imperial authority. This is why on the one hand the influence of Confucianism has dominated all aspects of Chinese life for nearly two thousand years and on the other, why Confucius is criticised for having been too much interested in the orderly arrangement of affairs and laid down precise rules for human beings to follow in their conduct and their thinking. The strict doctrine which had persisted for many centuries in feudal society is attacked and ridiculed by contemporary radicals.

Ethics, a system of moral principles, was emphasised by the feudal rulers. It played a great role in Chinese family and society. In the term *Lun-Li* or ethics, the character denotes the principles of the behaviour of human relationships and hierarchical organisation. *Lun-Li* was conceived by Confucius as the proper conduct of every member of the society when communicating with others. The accepted doctrine of the hierarchical organisation differentiated between sexes, seniority, generations, patriarchy, and thereby produced a definite rank for each person in the family and society. These moral principles were recorded in three early Chinese classics of the Zhou Dynasty, *Zhou-Li* (*Zhou Rites*), *Yi-Li* (*The Rituals*) and *Li-Ji* (*Rites Recording*). They became law and constitution, and were used in helping the emperor to rule.

House as a symbol of family reflecting the structure of Chinese society

From the sociological point of view, the family is considered as a basic cell in the organism of the monolithic society. It has been noted by philosophers and social scientists that 'society is a structure made up by families, and peculiarities of a given society can be described by outlining its family relations' (Goode, 1965, p.1). Among all civilisations, Chinese culture probably attached more importance to family values than any other cultures did. As families formed the most important social group, the family system, therefore, was deduced into a social system. Lin Yutang, the famous Chinese writer and sociologist, observed the function of Chinese families as follows: 'The family system is the root of Chinese society from which all Chinese social characteristics derive... The family system and the village system, which is the family raised to a higher exponent, account for all there is to explain in the Chinese social life' (Lin, 1989, p.169). Eighty-seven years ago, Johnson examined the reasons for the stability and long-lastingness of the social system in China and provided an explanation: 'The essential units of social and political organisation were the same – it was not the individual but the family. Thus public institutions, schools, guilds, and even the government in China sprang from the family, and therefore explanations for their particular characteristics can be found in it' (Johnston, 1910, p.135).

The main forces of the influence of the family can be traced back to the early stage of Chinese imperial epoch. Since the beginning of the Han Dynasty, Confucian ideology became state orthodoxy. Under the influence of Confucian ideology, the Chinese traditional family system was once regarded as one of the outstanding models for the patriarchal system in the world. It stressed the importance of the family as the basic social unit. This pattern has persisted in contemporary China (Lang, 1968, p.331). The family is *Jia* in Chinese: the *Jia* and house are synonymous in Chinese. This is expressed by Jone K. C. Liu: 'The image of the family and its physical domain and sociality is fully expressed and defined in the design of the Chinese house' (Liu, 1980, p.257).

In the traditional Chinese society, a large and extended family with its physical and social dimension was an ideal type of its family system. A large house to the Chinese mind acted as an important symbol of the family's social identity and strength. It was also a symbol of family hierarchy which was fulfilled through housing spatial organisation. For a majority of Chinese people, the most desirable way of life was in the image of the large extended family – 'five generations living under one roof'[5]. Such household might have as many as two to three hundred people. A large and extended family was also an economic unit where money and land were held in common and administered by the head of the family. The consumption of each individual member and his family largely depended on his contribution to the family income.

Han Baode and Hong Wenxian laid stress on a traditional family as a whole and indicated:

Chinese family was featured in the lack of individuality to the unique characteristics of their living spaces. In the long run, the flexibility of the size of the living unit (or family), which could consist of a couples as the smallest unit or include all lineal relations, servants and some collateral relations as in a joint family, led to the absence of egoism in family members and the placing of the family as a whole before the individual. They emphasised the whole family as a group in a compound, regardless of its size, while the privacy of the individual and his personal territory were of little importance.

(Han and Hong, 1973, p. 21)

When China entered the modern era early this century, the old Chinese family system has been criticised as the negation of individualism. It was believed that the excessive development of such a family system controlled a man and entirely dominated his behaviour; personal independence was severely restrained.

Fei Xiaotong (1948, p.41) tried to explore the reason why the individual was not the essential unit of the Chinese social organisation. His argument was that in Confucian philosophy, 'the Chinese saw a direct transition from the family, Jia-family, to the state, as successive stages of human organisation, and an individual person was only meant to be a part of the family. Without the family structure as the uniting power working internally among family members, the state would not have peace'. This statement coincides with the old sayings: 'when every family is in order, the state will be in peace' or 'put the family on order and rule the state in peace'. The hierarchical organisation of the Chinese family came mainly from Confucian social and family ideology. The older generation enjoyed higher respect from the younger ones, and the head of the family was the father of the oldest generation. Ancestor worship and filial piety was claimed by Confucianism to be the main virtue in the Chinese family institution, and strong parental authority was imposed over their children. The role of the younger generation on the family was often negligible. Women played a secondary role to men; one of their duties was the absolute obedience to the man i.e. father, husband and son. Thus women did not have any right or official voice in the family councils (Lang, 1968, p.332).

The family has played an important role in influencing the Chinese society. It has become literally an institution and control of the way of life. When the power of the family as a social image became strong, a member of the family could only see it through his relationship with the society. The family activities took precedence over individual actions. Each individual's life and fate were arranged, and became part of the overall social and economic network. Marriage, skills, careers were a family concern, and so were the daily activities of eating, thinking, entertaining, grief and sorrow, happiness and gaiety. They were all related to the family, the family events and the family action. Thus the much admired family system in feudal society survived through many changes and turmoil in Chinese history. But it usually belonged to the richer families who owned property in common and worked together in the family enterprise under the head of the family. The poor families were often excluded, for they lacked the manpower and commodities to sustain a certain level of wealth or surplus food to support a large family, and to maintain a large family structure in which to live together.

Although the extended family was the most desirable life pattern for China, it was, in fact, a backward culture in a modern world. With a series of political and social movements striving for democracy and Western ideas bringing forth the changes of social, economic structure and political organisation, great changes occurred in family structure with a move towards the smaller or nuclear family. With greater social mobility and economic freedom, the role of the individual, the position of women and youth greatly improved. The small, nuclear family is the model of China today. But, the basic value and life style of the Chinese traditional family still remain especially in rural areas.

Stylisation and continuity in Chinese architecture

The Chinese concept of family studied above would give a perspective for understanding the unique characteristics of the Chinese living environment in traditional times. In this section, the Chinese traditional architecture influenced by their social values is discussed. It is attempted to explore the reasons, from a socio-cultural point of view, why the stylisation in different types of building groups had dominated Chinese architecture over one thousand years.

If we skim through the books related to Chinese traditional buildings, it can be found that uniformity of spatial organisation and building forms exist in most different types of building groups (see Figure 10.31). Nearly all types of traditional Chinese architecture have the same composition in their plans. Each plan had a fixed location for the dwelling, which was usually placed at the rear of a building group. The front section used to be a court of justice (in a government office), shop (in commercial buildings), or ceremony hall (in religious temples). Even a palace used to be divided into two major areas: the administrative offices of the central government in the front and the residence of the royal household in the back (Li, 1985, p.81). It could be seen that traditional Chinese buildings normally have two separate realms, the front part being public area for working, and the rear part containing private and residential areas. Every compound has these two parts with its high enclosed walls, each part consisting of several buildings facing around a courtyard.

Wherever the group of traditional buildings exists, there are walled-off compounds. The physical wall can be seen as the first element of stylisation in the traditional Chinese architecture. The strong visible boundary has been regarded as a symbol of the traditional culture. It was considered as a carrier of the spirits of patriarchal system based on Confucian philosophy. With the emphasis on physical boundary, family life and any activities in compound can be separated from both the street and neighbours. But inside the wall, there was little concern with

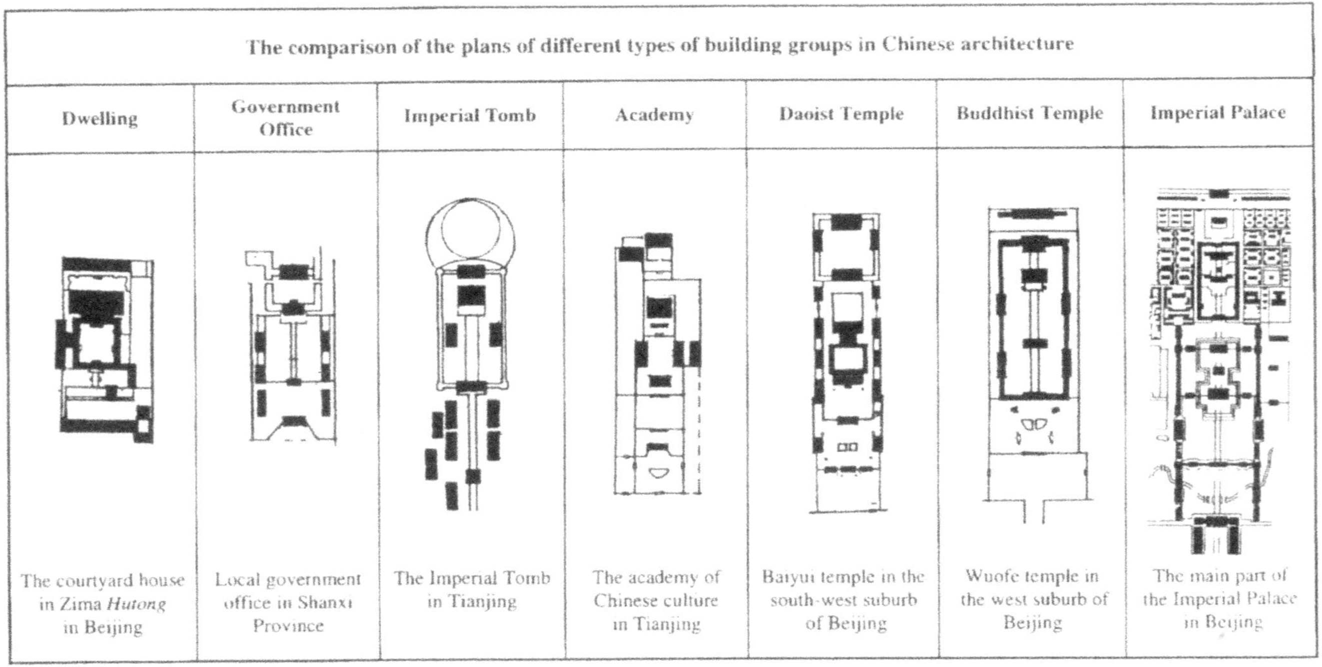

The comparison of the plans of different types of building groups in Chinese architecture

Dwelling	Government Office	Imperial Tomb	Academy	Daoist Temple	Buddhist Temple	Imperial Palace
The courtyard house in Zima *Hutong* in Beijing	Local government office in Shanxi Province	The Imperial Tomb in Tianjing	The academy of Chinese culture in Tianjing	Baiyun temple in the south-west suburb of Beijing	Wuofe temple in the west suburb of Beijing	The main part of the Imperial Palace in Beijing

Figure 10.31 **Stylisation in the spatial organisation of different types of building groups in Chinese architecture**
Source: Li (1985, p.78)

privacy: family members could hear one another and the house could be seen through. It was believed that the wall had carried on the functions of protecting the privileged position of the patriarch in the traditional family and creating a situation to stifle the differing opinions from the members under their position or people outside the wall. In modern China, especially during the period of the Great Proletarian Cultural Revolution (1966-76), the symbol of the wall in traditional architecture was often criticised as a backwardness of the old feudal society.

In his study on the classification of building functions in China, Chuta Ito provided the following observation:

> No matter what the function of the architecture may be, the forms of their plans and elevation were all similar and without much variation. All the plans of different types of building groups show a similar character: the most important building is located transversely on the central axis and in front of it; a courtyard is flanked on the left and right side by symmetrically placed lineal rooms connected by corridors or galleries.
>
> (Chuta, 1941)

Chuta Ito believed that this symmetrical arrangement of space should be attributed to the 'preference of symmetrical balance' of the Chinese people, which led to the continuous utilisation of a balanced plan for thousands of years. But if the whole explanation for the consistency in using a certain form lay in a people's aesthetic preference for a particular geometrical pattern, then this preference could easily have changed during such a long period of time and allowed other forms to take over. If, on the other hand, the symmetrical pattern and the walled-off compound symbolised an ideal form that Chinese aspired to reproduce, then it can explain why the arrangement remained nearly unchanged for over one thousand years.

In his work on Chinese architecture and urban planning, Li Yunhe proposes a view towards explaining why the stylisation in different types of building groups had dominated Chinese architecture for a long time. According to his description, a 'standardised design' and an 'all-purpose principle' were followed by most of the house builders in China. They used a plan which was capable of adjusting to any function the building might have. He suggests that the 'standardised design' was widely accepted and spread in Chinese traditional time. It was applied to buildings, vehicles, garments, ritual vessels, etc., where the same principle was strictly followed. Taking garments as an example, he shows that the same principle was suited for all situations through its flexibility. It was not necessary to make clothes of different styles for the different social classes. All garments had the same cut, but the difference between them lay in the material, the colour and the embroidered pattern of each piece of clothing. A certain colour or pattern could only be worn by people from a specific social rank, and people's clothing directly reflected their social status. The same principle applied in architecture. The same planning pattern was used for different types of building groups (Li, 1985).

The traditional houses, for instance, were built mostly in a standard fashion. The social rank of those who dwelt within can be seen through the colour of the tiles on the roof, housing size with the number of rooms and its decorations. Yellow roof was the imperial colour and only the emperor's residences could have yellow-tiled roofs, but princes and the highest officials could use glazed green tiles for their roofs. Ordinary city folks had to be content with unglazed grey tiles. Civil service rank would determine how many 'bays' (Chinese building was measured in bays, or the spaces between columns) and columns an official was allowed to build. No matter how rich they were, no Chinese courtier would ever have dared to create their house to match those of the princes. Private wealth would have been put into fine art collections and the creation of gardens rather than the building of palatial mansions to rival those of the emperor.

For a long time, the stylisation existed in different types of building groups and dominated Chinese architecture. There may be many evidences and reasons for the explanation. To sum up, the stylisation and continuity in traditional Chinese architecture were a reflection of the specific Chinese socio-cultural traditions. The traditional Chinese architecture was more than a practical building system. The concept of the Chinese architectural design was closely linked with ideas of real and ideal social order, which was clearly based upon Confucian philosophy. The standard model, the orderly and harmonious hierarchy of class and seniority, the concept of 'sky does not change, so everything does not change', the feudalistic system grown from and adapted to the sky – all these expressed a permanence which controlled Chinese thinking, and brought about the seemingly unchanged, unique Chinese architectural style.

The spatial arrangement of the courtyard houses as an expression of Chinese family hierarchy

In Chinese cultural tradition, social and ethical norms strongly reflected a highly rigid hierarchical order among human relationships. Reed Gillingham has explained: 'A hierarchy of human relationships that is man to elders, man to ancestors and man to family' (Gillingham, et al., 1971, p.107). As the physical product of a social production, the form of house was a clear response to the social nature. The spatial organisation of courtyard houses with its axial and symmetrical layout expressed the social and family hierarchy which derived from the teachings of Confucius. The Chinese believed that only by following the moral code of Confucianism was it possible to preserve family and social order.

The Chinese hierarchical order system

China has been a traditional society in which antiquity and older generations were highly respected and revered. For example, in the pre-historical period, Xia Dynasty was believed to have been an age of peace and order[6]. During that time, the throne was abdicated in favour of the most qualified successor and the land was allocated to common people according to *Well Field System*[7]. This period was regarded by Confucius as having the best political system and as an ideal model for the imperial society. During his lifetime, Confucius emphasised this through his political activities and teachings. Because of the influence of Confucius and his efforts, people gradually began to idealise this period. This led to the reverence for antiquity.

Qin Yaoqi pointed out:

> The Chinese value system was strongly oriented to the past. The mode of thinking was revering antiquity and the idea of respecting elders. This was inseparably connected with the ethical and agricultural society of China. In this society, the older generation was regarded as the instructors of the younger and was seen as the embodiment of wisdom and experience handed down through the generations.
>
> (Qin, 1978, pp.50-51)

Life in the agricultural society was stable and held little change, so that most of what the younger generation would encounter in life had already been experienced by the older members of the society. Confucians laid great stress on the authority of elders and set up principles about individual conduct and the hierarchical order. All these became moral norms and the most important rule in the feudal society. People's conduct was strictly in accordance with the relationships between members of different generations or ranks (such as between father and son, mother and daughter-in-law, elder and younger brother etc.) and everyone should strictly follow the moral norm and rule.

There were many moral codes in the hierarchy of the family. The highest was the obedience, that is, to obey the elders – grandfather, father, followed by the eldest son. The hierarchical order gave each individual a definite status in the family or society and also defined the person's relationships to all other individuals who may (or may not) be of the same family or social rank. This family order would be ensured only when everyone knew his place and acted in accordance with his position. Different behaviour was required when dealing with others depending on the intimacy of the relationship between them and depending on different situations and places. The system of the hierarchical order was intensified through the teachings of Confucius, which was described by Nelson Wu: 'Educated from childhood in etiquette, the ancient Chinese learned to be at the right place, at the right time and to follow the right path. According to the moral code, people were given their own position and responsibility, and this laid the basis for an orderly family and for eternal peace.' (Wu, 1963).

The spatial arrangement of the courtyard house reflected the formal, rigid and hierarchical nature of the family structure

In traditional courtyard compound, a house in medium or large-scale was normally divided into three quarters: the core quarter, the inner quarter and the outer quarter. The three quarters were not treated equally and hence they were of different sizes with different locations and decorations according to their importance in one compound. Therefore, the hierarchy of the family can be reflected by the structure of the house (see Figure 10.32). In the plan of the house, further division was sometimes necessary. The inner quarter was subdivided into personal residential area and joint living area. The outer quarter contained a service area and a supplementary area. The distribution of the different quarters in the house or the allocation of the buildings and the rooms to different family members was subject to the regulations on the hierarchical order based on the status and position of the inhabitants.

The core quarter The core quarter was the most important and the most private area in a courtyard compound. To demonstrate its importance, the ancestral hall was located in the core quarter on a north-south axis. The most honoured building was also built in this area to provide accommodation for the senior generation. Since the senior generation were the most respected and honoured members of the family, they were not involved with trivial matters of everyday life. But they did attend important occasions such as the younger member's marriage or the division of property. In fact, the core quarter was a place for the retired senior generation to enjoy the fruit of their past work. Being the deepest section in a courtyard compound, the core quarter excludes outsiders and is kept away from the noisy street. Its main characteristics were seclusion and tranquillity.

  Early each morning, the younger generations would come to the core area to pay their respects to the elder generation and to listen to their advice and admonitions. Children were forbidden to play or to make noise here. During festivities or memorial ceremonies, the most important rituals would take place in this area: family members would worship their ancestors in the ancestral hall one by one or together. The worship of heaven and earth gods was held in the courtyard in front of the ancestral hall. Generally speaking, the core quarter was the focus of the family and the super-area for the members possessing high position in a family.

The inner quarter The inner quarter was a major living space consisting of personal residential area and joint living area for ordinary family members. The

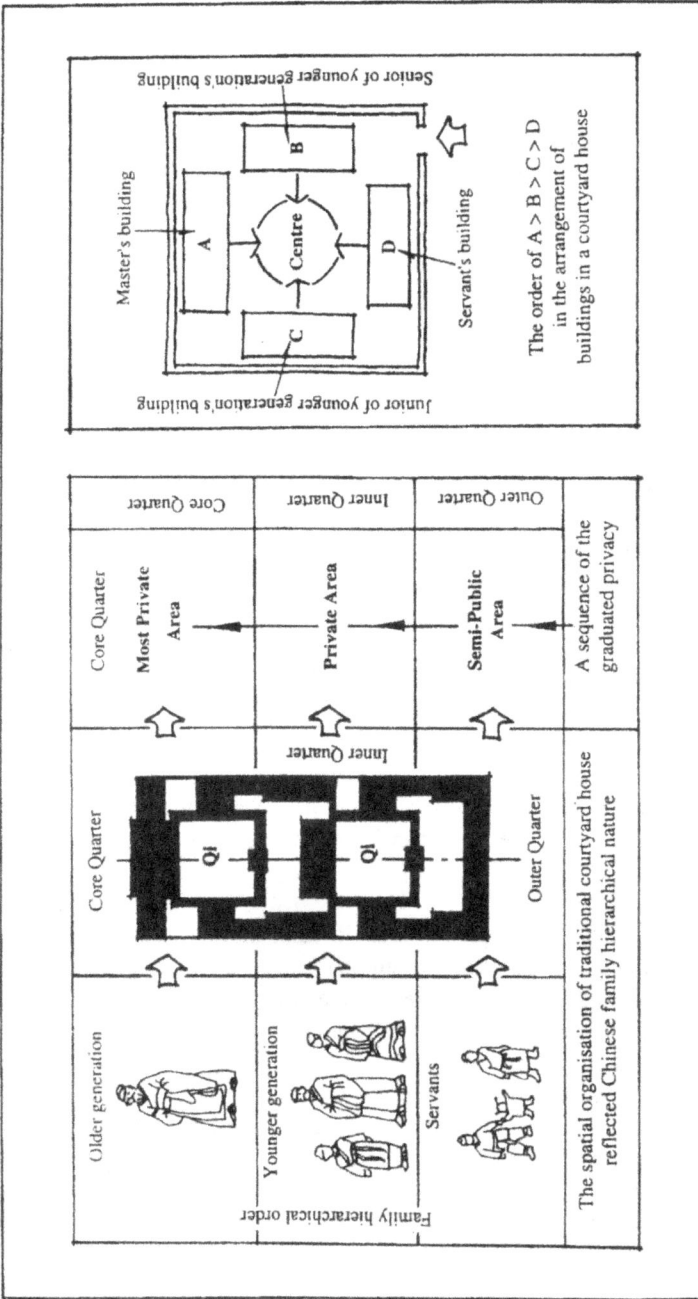

Figure 10.32 The typical traditional courtyard compound in a medium-scale with three quarters: the core quarter, the inner quarter and the outer quarter

inner quarter involved three or four lineal buildings around the central courtyard on each side. The building for the householder was located perpendicularly on the central axis to the north. It had a sitting hall, bedrooms and study rooms. As a principal building, it possessed the highest roof and largest size in the quarter. The householder of the inner quarter can be compared to an executive, taking charge of all family affairs and dealing with external affairs. Hence his private rooms were always placed next to the sitting room on both sides, making it convenient for him to meet guests. The buildings facing the courtyard to the east and west were for younger generations and children. According to the hierarchical order system, the East was taken as the superior direction to the West, and the ranks of those on the eastern side was higher than those on the western side. Following this rule, the senior of younger generation occupied the building on eastern side, the building to the west was given to the younger ones. The size of the inner quarter was decided by the size of the family but also dependent on its wealth and the social position of the householder. For most families the inner area usually had one unit, but for larger sized families, the inner quarters had two or three units.

The normal organisation of space and the arrangement of buildings in the courtyard house strongly reflected the ideology of the hierarchical order. In order to symbolise the authority, the honoured buildings were located strictly on the central axis with a symmetrical arrangement. These important buildings included the ancestral hall and the rooms for the older generation both beneath one roof, and the sitting hall with its flanked rooms for the household, sometimes with a door hall. The building with the ancestral hall had the highest roof and largest size in the whole compound. Generally speaking, the height of the buildings in the courtyard was determined by the status of their inhabitants: the higher the status the higher the roof. Consequently, it gave the appearance of the courtyard house that the front and side buildings were lower than the back and central buildings. As shown in Figure 10.32, the importance of the buildings in each quarter followed the order A > B > C > D.

The outer quarter   The outer quarter was located in the front area of the compound. It included service area and supplementary area open to all family members, servants and guests. This area had a door hall, rooms for porters, servants and guests, and storage rooms with front courtyard. These servants were responsible for all household duties. According to the living function, the service area was usually located between the inner quarter of the masters and the public area outside the family walls. Without their master's instructions, the general servants were not allowed to enter the inner areas. Just as the high walls and gates separating the outside public area from the house compound, the service area was clearly separated from the master's areas by walls and gates. There was another group of servants who lived close to their master's bedroom in the inner areas to tend to his daily needs.

When a normal guest visited the family, he was accommodated with lodging in the outer quarter. Fixed rules in the treatment of guests also stated that the guests could not live in the same courtyard as the family members. As guests were considered outsiders, guest rooms were located in the service area, not in the inner area. During the daytime, guests were invited into the sitting room in the inner area, but at night they returned to the guest rooms outside of the inner area. Exceptions were only made for higher-rank guests who could rest in the inner quarter.

In general, the form of courtyard houses usually had a basic symmetry with a central axis on north-south direction. The balanced spatial organisation with a sequence of alternation between buildings and yards was an important consideration in the design of houses. This implied 'an architectural spatial encoding of the hierarchical order in family structure' (Chua, 1978, p.10). The form of the houses was a clear response to the Chinese family hierarchical nature. The centre of a compound was the symbol of authority in the family, and it enabled the family to install the head of the family at a precise space in the house. The emplacement of the head at the symbolic centre with the subordinates submitted to the left and right was a standardised arrangement on every formal ritual occasion when the head of family and his subordinates were both present. The spatial arrangement of courtyard houses provided a series of graduated privacy stages from the public to the semi-public and to the private, then to most private (see Figure 10.32). Nelson Wu has thus commented: 'The graduated privacy is achieved through a sequence of yard, gateway and step to frame, to block, to penetrate, and to lead to the next anticipated space. This ushering a guest would indeed be a time-consuming matter, because the passing of each gateway is a penetration into new depths of some one's privacy' (Wu, 1963, p.32). This symmetrical layout and spatial organisation provided a clear and interpretative reading to the 'idealised' family image in the symbolic structure of the hierarchical order.

Continuity and development of traditional courtyard houses

Since the break down of over 2,000 years of the enduring structure of traditional China in 1911, a series of wars and revolutions, and the introduction of Western modern forms of economic and political organisation brought rapid changes in society (both in ideology and in reality). The wave of upheaval of society, together with the constraints of economy, the decline of traditional Chinese ideology, and the alteration of traditional evaluation, imposed destructive impacts on the development of the traditional courtyard houses. Due to some inappropriate policies after 1949 (the establishment of the Peoples' Republic of China), most traditional houses faced deteriorating changes. The values of the form of traditional courtyard houses, their traditional cultural artefacts and decoration were largely neglected. From 1949 up to now, several families shared one courtyard house and the so-called multi-household courtyard compound has been a major dwelling form in China.

The economic reform of China (1978) implemented over the last 18 years has brought a high level of prosperity to China. The speed of urban construction during this period exceeded that of any period since the foundation of the People's Republic of China in 1949. However, as fashionable high-rise buildings were put up, the old existing quarters were severely ignored, and their condition deteriorated through time.

Since 1990, some new housing designs and experimental projects have been initiated in Beijing in response to the urgent need to deal with the large scale redevelopment of the increasingly dilapidated old residential quarters. This has represented a leading effort to probe the possibility of new courtyard house systems. Some new types of courtyard houses have been explored as an attempt to balance the housing shortage and the social inheritance. The construction principles of the traditional courtyard houses are being utilised to set up the new courtyard house system. In practice, the key aim of these new housing designs for the old housing quarters is to achieve a high building density and a better living environment, subject to the strict regulations governing building heights and floor area ratios. A straightforward task is to re-house the existing population in overcrowded old housing quarters and to protect the horizontal planning features of the traditional Beijing.

In the scheme of redeveloping old dilapidated quarters, many concerns of conforming to the traditional residential environments have been emphasised at the planning level. The strategy is to continue to use the original road system, keeping the pattern of the traditional urban fabric structure as one way of integrating the conservation of urban organic order which is embedded in its physical environment. For instance, the rebuilding of the residential community of *Xiaohouchang* is built on the basis of the above the planning idea and the strategy. This site lies close to the site of the west wall of the Old City. Historically this area was the poorest residential quarter of low-income people. After rebuilding, the old roads and main lanes in the site have been retained and widened. Some blocked lanes are opened up, forming a major road structure for the new community being rebuilt on the same site (see Figure 10.33). In the designer's mind, the utilisation of old streets and roads is the linkage between the new residential environment and the traditional urban tissue.

The reconstruction of *Ju'er Hutong* neighbourhood is a further illustration of the planning strategy. This project has been set as a successful example among the pilot experimental redevelopment projects of dilapidated housing quarters in Beijing. The site of the *Ju'er Hutong* neighbourhood is located to the north of the Old City centre, one block away from the south-north central axis of the city. The

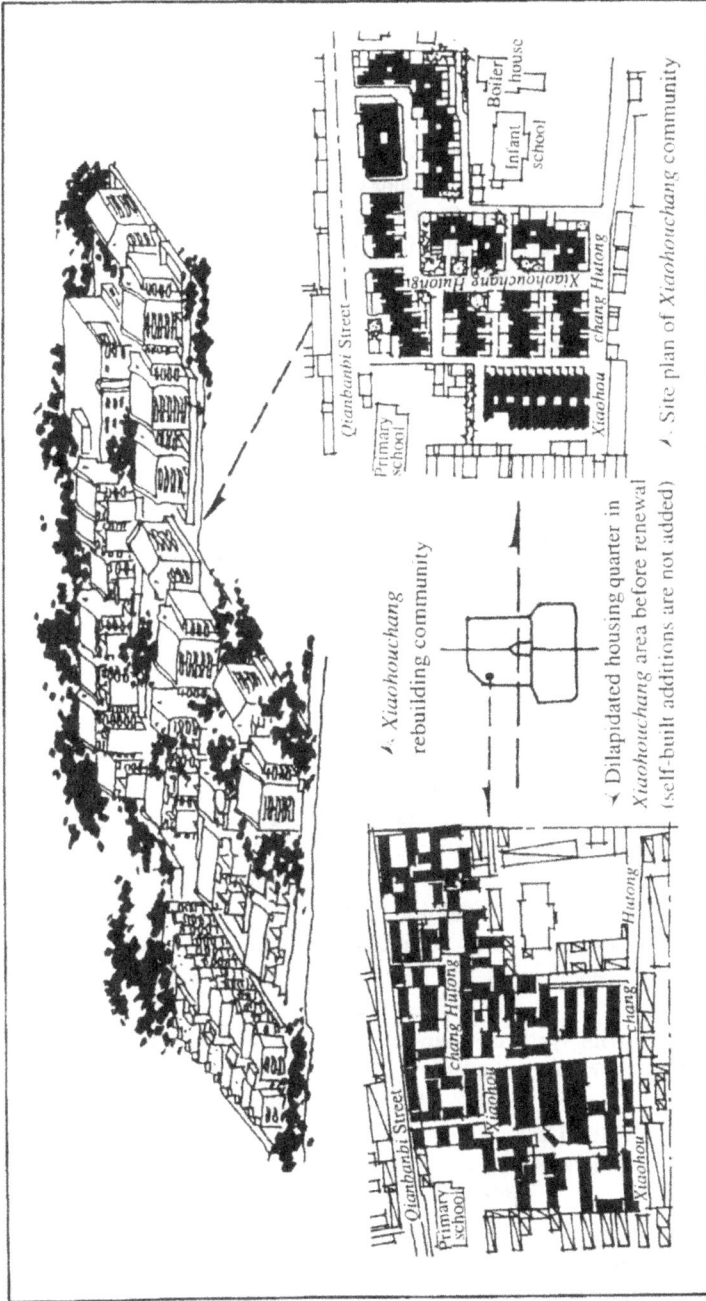

Figure 10.33   The site plan of *Xiaohouchang* rebuilding community
Source: Huang and Lu (1991, p.3)

old dilapidated neighbourhoods consisted of a number of old single-storey courtyard compounds of different qualities. The general approach of the *Ju'er Hutong* project was to combine the preservation, renovation and rebuilding of the old courtyard compounds in a single project (see Figure 10.34).

In order to replace the worst courtyard compounds, the exploration of a new courtyard compound system has been emphasised. The housing pattern of traditional courtyard compound is utilised and enlarged in order to set a basic new courtyard compound unit and to form a central feature of neighbourhood community. At the neighbourhood planning level, a basic courtyard compound unit is designed. As a basic model, it can be expanded, repeated and detached to form either an independent neighbourhood compound or groups of neighbourhood compounds (see Figures 10.35 and 10.36). Their flexible sizes could fit any available plot as a plug-in courtyard compound (Wu, 1991a).

Recently, some new courtyard housing projects have been completed. Here, the traditional design technique in the arrangement and layout of groups of buildings and the characteristics of traditional housing types have been utilised (see Figure 10.37). Many efforts are made in order to achieve the fine-grained mix of contemporary housing design, modern technological systems and traditional Chinese architectural design principles. A transformation from the traditional single-household courtyard housing form to a contemporary multi-household courtyard housing form is in progress in China.

Conclusions

A variety of Chinese vernacular dwelling forms have existed in the diverse natural environments in a nation of 9,560,900 square kilometres since very early times. All these forms can be classified into three types: stilt dwellings, cave dwellings and courtyard houses. Built largely of earth and wood, Chinese houses utilise local materials and draw on a building tradition. Following social and technological developments and in order to adapt to a changed ecological environment, the courtyard house has been selected and developed as an 'ideal form' throughout China.

This chapter begins with synthetic analysis of various factors responsible for the formation and development of the courtyard houses which represent the main stream of traditional Chinese houses. The factors identified include the specific climatic system, the natural environment, the social and political conditions, and cultural/philosophical beliefs. Having been accepted as an 'ideal model' of Chinese dwellings over several ancient dynasties, the courtyard houses have embodied the attempt of Chinese people to identify the relationship between the environment and themselves. In addition to the basic need to shelter themselves and their possessions from outside disturbances, courtyard houses performed

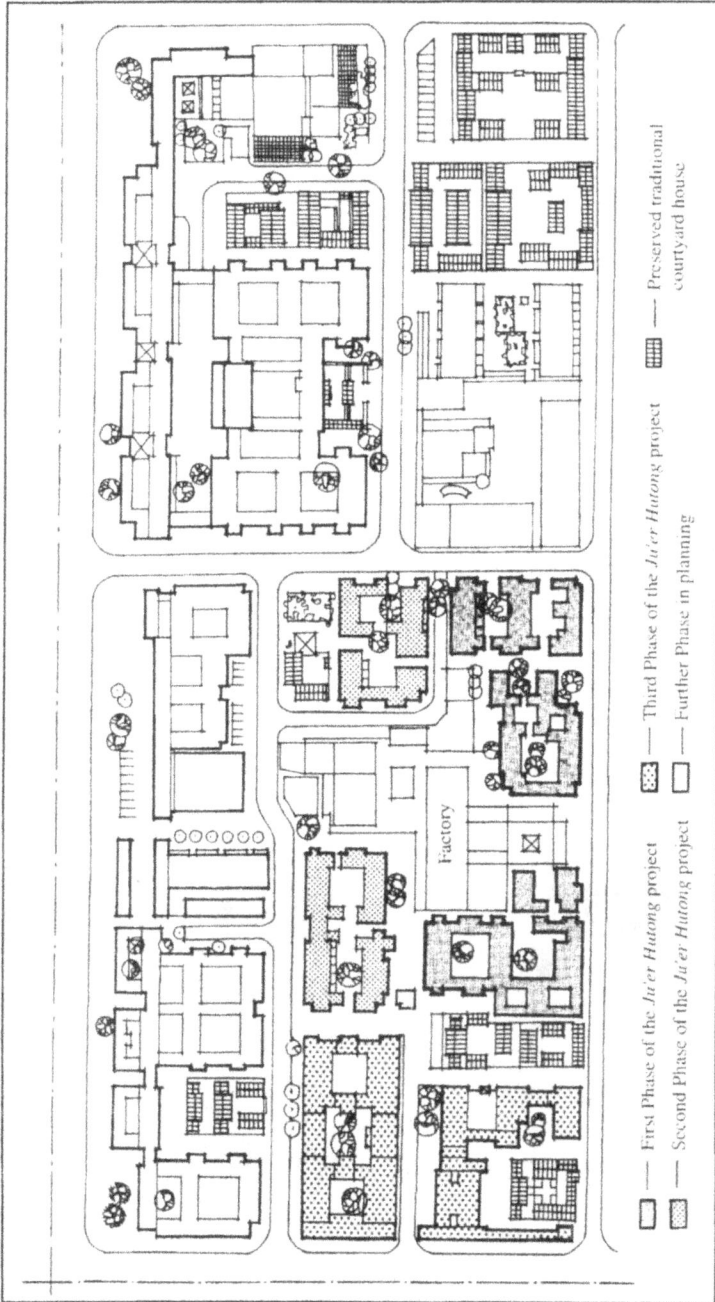

Figure 10.34   Site plan of the entire *Ju'er Hutong* project
Source: Wu (1994, pp.15-16)

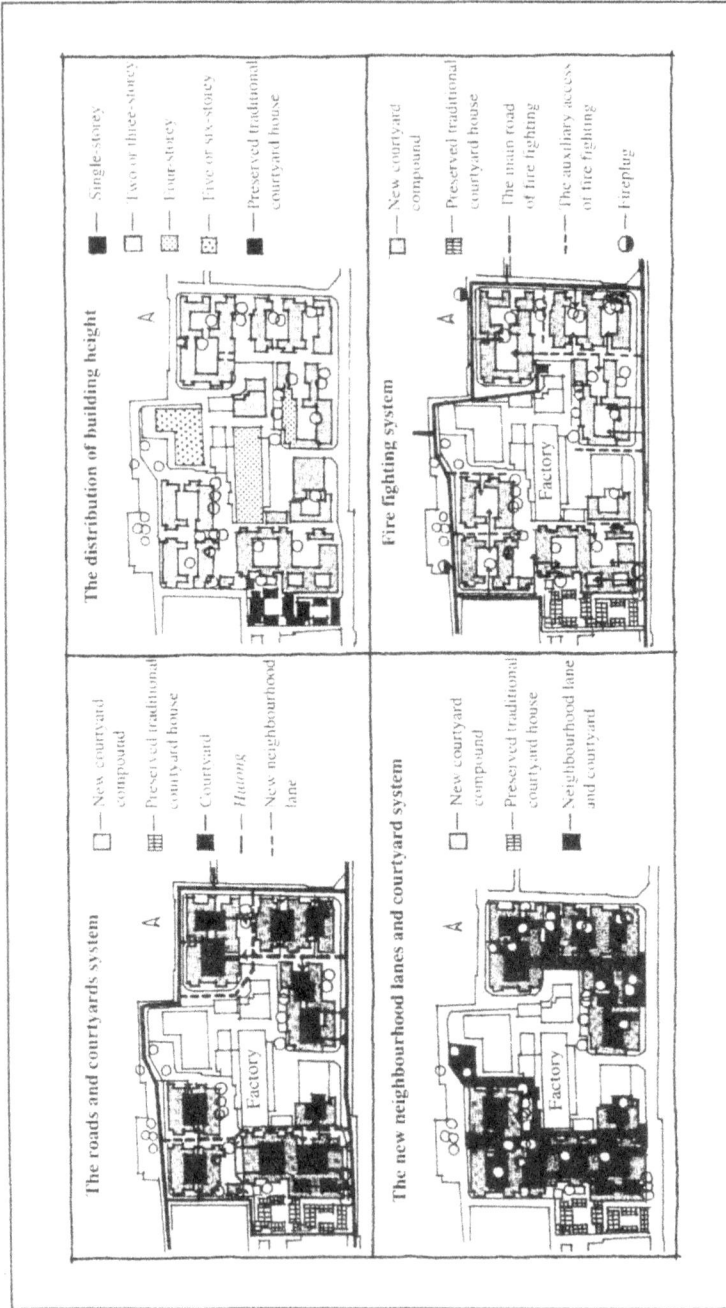

Figure 10.35 **New courtyard compounds in the first and second phases of the *Ju'er Hutong* project**
Source: Wu (1994, pp.15-16)

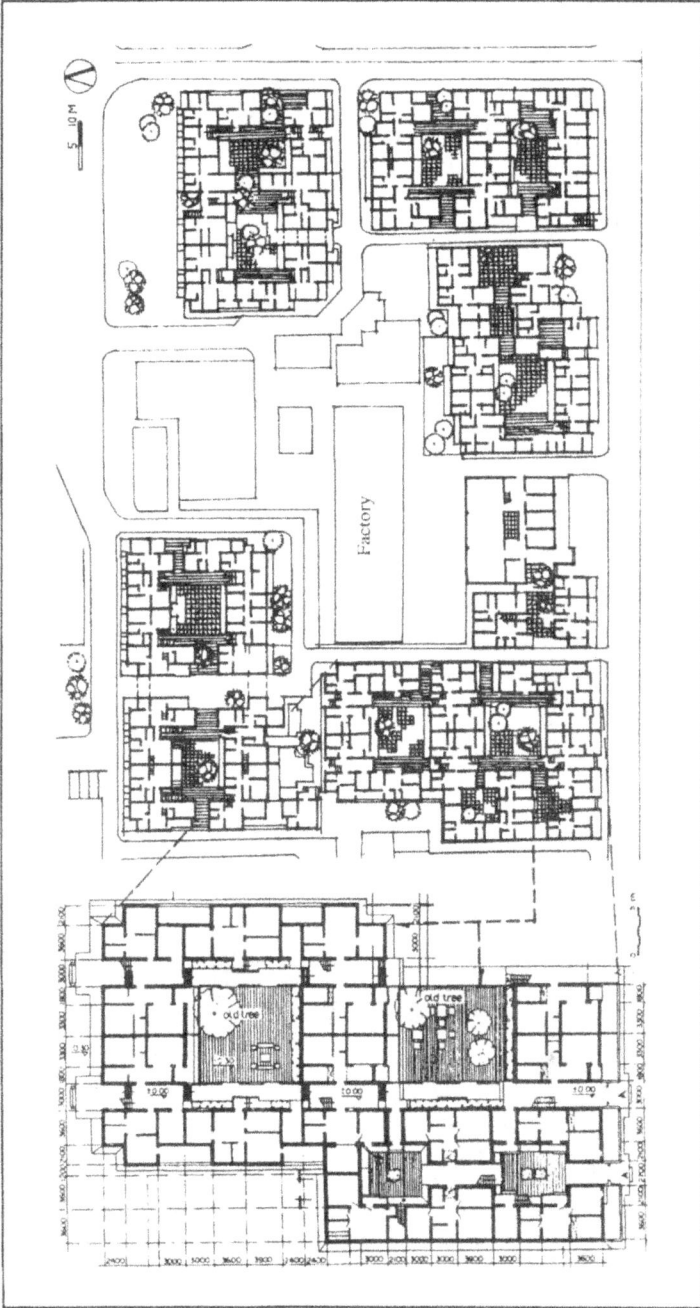

Figure 10.36 **The plan of the new courtyard compounds in the *Ju'er Hutong* project**
Source: Yuan and Zou (1993)

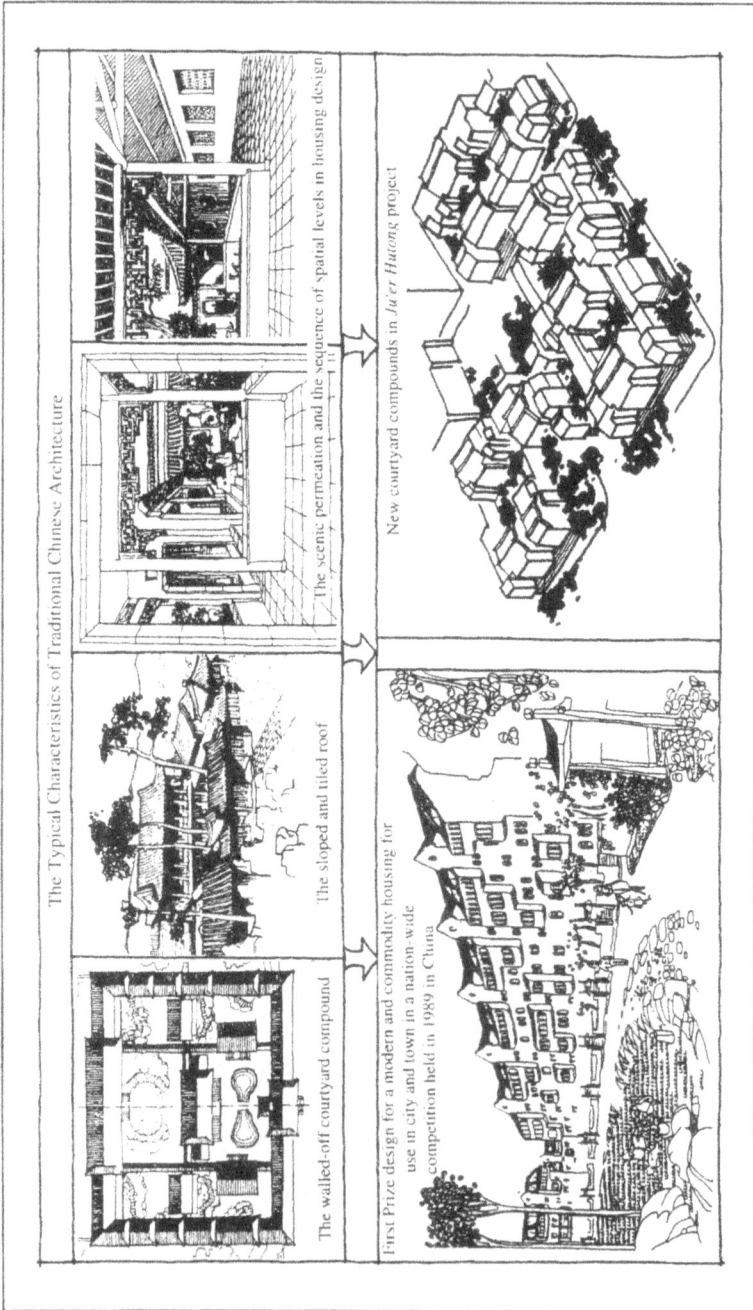

Figure 10.37   The symbolisation of traditional courtyard house style on modern houses

two important functions: to stress social identity and status of the inhabitants with the social and family hierarchy, and to enhance harmony between the man, the house and the nature.

In this century, periodic wars and political turbulence have imposed a devastating impact on the healthy development of the courtyard houses. However, being deeply rooted in the long historical stream of the social, cultural and ideological context, courtyard houses with their major traditional features have remained. The only exception is that some changes have been, are being and are to be made to the old style of the courtyard houses, which are the reflection of social and cultural changes.

Notes

1   The traditional societies in China lasted over 2,000 years from the Han Dynasty (206 B.C.-A.D. 220) until the end of the Qing Dynasty (1644-1911 A.D.).

2   These books were reprinted at the beginning of this century, *Ten Books of Yang Zhai* and *Three Aspects of Yang Zhai*, Shanghai: Shuyentang Press, 1911. *Yang Zhai and People,* Shanghai: Chiangtung Press, 1911.

3   Ancient Chinese books which briefly addressed this subject include: Shu, M.K. *The Hidden Emptiness.* Shao, Y. *Polttical Theories of the Emperor.* Tai, S. *The Great Plan of the Emperor.*

4   In the beginning of the foundation of Zhou Dynasty (1066 - 771 B.C.), the earlier regulations, social orders and life styles of various states before the Zhou Dynasty were modified. The historical experiences were accumulated and supplementarily revised. Based on that, new regulations and social standards were set up and were named *Rites.* The compiled *Rites* by Zhou scholars became one of earliest and the most important classical literary records in Chinese history. The *Rites* included the following three parts: i) *Zhou Rites* which were records of administrative works and regulations in Zhou government. ii) *The Rituals* which included all the rituals reflecting the codes of conduct in people's relationships, and, iii) *Rites Record* which was a collection of academic papers related to rites. The three volumes put together are called *Three Rituals.* *Three Rituals* formed the earliest literary basis of Chinese traditional rites.

5   A common Chinese saying, it refers to a large and happy family with many children, grandchildren, and great grandchildren.

6   Xia Dynasty (2357-2200 B.C.) from a legend of ancient China. Yao and Shun were two legendary sage kings in that period.

7   The *Well-Field System* was a system of land division in the Zhou Dynasty under which a 900-mu plot (each mu = 733.5 square yards) was divided into nine portions like the character (well), with the eight outlying portions

separately cultivated and owned by eight families, who jointly cultivated the central portion belonging to the state. See Qin Qingfang, *The Origin and Development of the Well-Field System* in *the Journal of the Study of History*, No. 4, Beijing, 1965.

Bibliography

Chen, C. (1981), *A historical and cultural atlas of China*, Haia Shobo: Tokyo.
Cheng, J. (1994), *Feng-shui and architecture*, Science and Technique Publishing House: Jiangxi. In Chinese.
Chua, B. (1978), *Adjusting religious practices to different house forms in Singapore*, Unpublished paper thesis, National University of Singapore.
Chuta, I. (1941), *Peculiarities of Chinese architecture*, Academy of Oriental Culture: Tokyo. Chapter 3.
De Groot, J.J.M. (1897), *The religious system of China*, Vol. 3, Book 1,
Fei, X. (1948), 'Rural China', Guan Cha Press: Shanghai, pp.38-44.
Freedman, M. (1969), 'Geomancy', *Proceedings: Royal Anthropological Institute of Great Britain and Ireland*, Royal Anthropological Institute: London, pp.5-15.
Fung, Y. (1931), 'Huainan Zi', *A history of Chinese philosophy*, Vol. 1, Chapter 15, Shen Chou Publishing Co.: Shanghai. In Chinese.
Fung, Y. (1934), *A history of Chinese philosophy*, Vol. 2, Commercial Press: Shanghai. In Chinese.
Gillingham, R., and et al. (1971), *A survey of traditional architecture in Taiwan*, Centre for Housing and Urban Research, Tunghai University: Taiwan.
Goode, W. (1965), *The family*, Prentice-Hall Inc.: Englewood Cliffs, NJ.
Gullestad, M. (1993), 'Home decoration as popular culture', *Gendered anthropology*, Routledge: London, pp.128-161.
Han, B., and Hong, W. (1973), *Banqiao Lin Family Compound: The survey, study and restoration*, Donghai University: Taizhong.
Huang, D. (1982), 'Ceremonies in Chinese history', in Tai, L. (ed) *New treatise on Chinese culture*, Vol. 1.
Huang, H and Lu Kemeng (1991), 'The Reports of Old and Dilapidated housing renewals in residential development and planning in Beijing', *Architectural Journal*, No. 9107, pp.2-12. In Chinese.
Johnston, R.F. (1910), *Lion and dragon in northern China*, Dutton: New York.
Knapp, Ronald G. (1986), *China's Traditional Rural Architecture*, University of Hawaii press, Honolulu, USA.
Lang, O. (1968), *Chinese family and society*, Archon Books: New York.
Li Min and Yu Baiquan (1990), 'Traditional Chinese dwellings in Yiwu, Zhejiang', *Architectural Journal*, No. 9005, pp.59-61. In Chinese.
Li, Y. (1985), *Cathay's idea-design theory of Chinese classical architecture*, Chinese Architectural Industry Publishing House: Beijing. In Chinese.
Lin, Y. (1989), *My country and my people*, Wen Hua: Beijing. In Chinese.

Liu, C. (1981), 'Two aspects of early Zhou architecture.' *Bulletin of Architecture*, Vol. 4, pp.20-22. In Chinese.

Liu, D. (1932), 'Notes on houses of both Han Dynasty.' *Journal of the Social for Research in Chinese Architecture*, Vol. 3, No. 3, In Chinese.

Liu, J.K.C. (1980), *Housing transformation: A study of family life and built form in Taiwan*, Dissertation thesis, University of California: Berkeley.

Liu, Z. (1930), '*Yikeyin* houses in Kunming, Yunnan.' *Journal of the Society for Research in Chinese Architecture*, Vol. 7, No. 1, In Chinese.

Liu, Z. (1957), *Chinese Architectural Types and Structural Forms*, Beijing: Chinese Architectural Industry Publishing House. In Chinese.

Liu, Z. (1979), 'Picture and illustration album of ancient buildings in Dongpei village near Kunming.' *Collection of Scientific and Technical History*, Vol. 2, In Chinese.

McNaughton, W. (1974), 'Confucianism and Taoism', *The Confucian vision*, University of Michigan Press: Michigan. In the Introduction.

Needham, J. (1971), 'Physics and physical technology', *Science and civilisation in China*, Vol. 4, Cambridge University Press: Cambridge, UK.

Oliver, P. (1987), *Dwellings: The house across the World*, Phaidon Press: Oxford.

Qin, S. (1993), 'Geography of China', *China*, New Star: Beijing.

Qin, Y. (1978), *From tradition to present*, Shini Bao Cultural Publishing House: Taipei. In Chinese.

Shan, D. (1992), *Human being with their living environments: A study on traditional local dwellings*, Tsinghua University Press: Beijing. In Chinese.

Song, K. (1992), 'A simple analysis of Yangzhai Xiangfa', in Wang, Q. (ed) *Research of Feng-shui theory*, Tianjing University Publishing House: Tianjing, pp.70-88. In Chinese.

Sumet, J. (1983), 'Case Study 4 - Thailand. House on stilts, pointer to South East cultural origin', *Architecture and Identity, Regional Seminar in the series Exploring Architecture in Islamic Cultures*, Singapore,

Ten books of Yang Zhai. (1911), *Ten books of Yang Zhai*, Shuyentang: Shanghai. Reprinted in 1911.

Thompson, L.G. (1989), *Chinese religion: An introduction*, Wadsworth Publishing Company: Belmont.

Wheatly, P. (1971), *The pivot of the four quarters: A preliminary inquiry into the origins and character of the ancient Chinese city*, Aldine: Chicago.

Wu, L. (1991a), 'Innovative approaches for the future: The redevelopment of dilapidated housing quarters in Beijing.' *Architectural Journal*, Vol. 9102, pp.7-13. In Chinese.

Wu, L. (1991b), 'Rehabilitation in Beijing.' *Habitat International*, Vol. 15, No. 3, pp.51-66.

Wu, L. (ed) (1994), *Beijing Ju'er Hutong new courtyard housing experiment*, Institute of Architectural and Urban Studies, Tsinghua University: Beijing.

Wu, N. (1963), *Chinese and Indian architecture*, Prentice Hall Int.: London. Chapter 4.

Xingxiang, S. (1957), *Feng-shui*, Shanghai Xingxiang: Shanghai.

Yang, H. (1980), 'The development of early architecture in China', *Corpus of architectural history and theory*, pp.112-135. In Chinese.

Yang, Q. (1983), 'Traditional farmhouse form in Kuanzhong, Shanxi Province', *Collected essays on the history of Chinese architecture*, Vol. 2. In Chinese.

Yang, Q. (1990), 'Traditional dwellings in Yiwu, Zhejiang', *Architectural Journal*, No. 9001, pp.46-51. In Chinese.

Yuan Bin and Zou Huyin (1993), 'The Rational and the Creative Design: Comment on the New Courtyard Houses of Ju'er Hutong Project', *International Architecture*, No. 9303, pp.65-67. Chinese Journal.

Yen, W. (1981), 'Study of social structure based on early village settlements in Jiang Zai', *Archaeology and cultural relics*. In Chinese.

Zhang, Z., and et al. (1957), *Ming Dynasty house in Huizhou*, Chinese Architectural Industry Publishing House: Beijing. In Chinese.

Section IV
Case study from South America

11 Balancing capacity with vulnerability:

Dwelling on unstable land, Caqueta, Lima, Peru

DAVID SANDERSON

Introduction

This chapter seeks to identify and discuss the conditions faced by families living in some of the most vulnerable areas of Lima, Peru, and to highlight some of the strategies that are employed to mitigate the risks faced. Like many of South America's major cities, Lima continues to experience rapid and unplanned urbanisation, with consequent strains on transport, infrastructure and shelter. Yet, an often neglected point relates to the vulnerability of migrants forced to live on the poorest quality land.

The chapter focuses on *barrio* Primero De Mayo[1], a community living on the site of a former rubbish dump in Caqueta, one of Lima's densest and poorest areas. The original invaders colonised the site in the early 1950s when all other available land was taken. Today, the area of about 3,000 residences with semi-legal ownership inhabit a neighbourhood of roads and buildings, none of which lasts for long: whilst the land continues to consolidate due to the poor quality ground, buildings continue to sink. The view is one of broken, cracking buildings, some completely sunk with roofs at ground level.

The area is one of a mixture of **vulnerability** and **capacity**: whilst buildings subside, needing to be rebuilt on average every three to four years, people continue to move into the area; and whilst many of the services in the area require constant attention, the *barrio's* location near to the city centre assures a continuing local economy. Finally, the trade-offs between access to income (positive) and current quality of living (negative) leads the local community to want to stay, despite governmental plans to establish a park in place of the neighbourhood.

315

Caqueta

Caqueta, located near to the commercial centre of Lima, grew dramatically during Peru's economic stagnation of 1985-90 with the rapid growth of informal markets providing cheap food and goods for the city. Street traders, or *ambulantes,* sprang up in almost every street as low priced foods attracted visitors from all over Lima. Today, the area is characterised by congestion: a surfeit of street traders crowd most main streets and public spaces, producing large amounts of garbage which the irregular garbage removal services do not cope with. Caqueta accomodates an estimated residential population of about 15,500, living in just over 3,000 formal and informal dwellings. Shelter ranges from unconsolidated 'illegal' wooden shacks found within the densest of the markets, to tenured adobe constructed houses and four to five-storey buildings of concrete frame/brick infilled and rendered.

Barrio Primero de Mayo

The visitor to *barrio* Primero de Mayo is firstly faced with the difference in height from the surrounding neighbourhood; the *barrio*, sited on the top of the garbage tip, now consolidated with earth and rubble, is approximately three metres higher than its neighbouring settlements.

The first settlers invaded what was one of Lima's major garbage tips in the early 1950s. The location of the tip, and the fact that it was the only vacant space of a good size left so close to the city centre led the invaders to colonise the tip for themselves. The land continued to be covered by the invaders with layers of earth and rubble placed over the rubbish. Large scale invasions followed until political pressure was such that provisional land ownership was granted. Today, the current association is striving to formalise ownership, although governmental authorities have not yet granted this.

Unsurprisingly the key problem for the area is the very poor quality of the land. The garbage beneath the top layer goes down for an estimated 15 meters. The unstable land results in a continual sinking of buildings into the ground as the garbage compacts under their weight.

History of Barrio Primero de Mayo[2]

Points made in an interview given by a resident of Primero de Mayo:

- About 40 years ago the area was a tip and each family that occupied the area levelled their floor with rubble; it could not be levelled to the neighbouring *barrio.*
- The families that came to live in the area were from Rimac and the provinces.

- The most important thing to happen was the connection of water and drainage.
- The neighbourhood has a communal centre, a health centre and three public eating places (restaurants).
- The organisation had fallen into disrepute because of the leaders who continue to ask for money and who do nothing with it. The most active have been the oldest residents.
- The majority work as street traders in Caqueta, Plaza de Union and Plaza 2 de Mayo, which are close to the neighbourhood.

Plate 11.1   Primero de Mayo. Note the drop at the end of the road to the neighbouring *barrio*

It is something of an irony that as the usual process of building and infrastructure consolidation and improvement has occurred, as in other parts of Lima, the process has in fact contributed to a worsening of overall conditions. When initially colonised a piece of land for each invader would have been demarcated and a flimsy wooden shack built which would have done little to affect the land. However, as consolidation took place and timber was gradually replaced by concrete, brick and adobe, buildings have sunk and cracked.

Poor land as increasing vulnerability

Because of the poor quality of the land, the condition of the buildings and infrastructure in *barrio* Primero de Mayo has served to increase community and individual vulnerability to a greater degree than in the neighbouring *barrios* in several key ways:

Building failure

As well as the 'slow sink' of buildings, the *barrio's* population is at risk of death and injury from sudden building collapse. Compounded by Lima's location within a seismically active zone - Lima ranks as the second highest area of seismic activity in Peru - the prognosis is for an area that is likely to experience a high degree of destruction when the next earthquake occurs. In one building visited during research, a municipal hall, a recent, minor tremor had caused two cracks, approximately five centimetres in width, in the concrete floor and brick walls.

Plate 11.2   A typical building in the neighbourhood. Buildings are constantly being rebuilt, one report being once every three to four years

Some time was spent discussing problems of construction with local builders. All were aware of the poor quality land in the area. The better builders tended to reinforce their concrete well to try to minimise cracking; others, however, hardly made any reinforcements. Some, in addition, did not use lintels, preferring instead to rely on the (insufficient) integrity of window and wall frames.

Raft foundations, whilst known about, were considered too expensive for everyday housing to implement - the cost of the additional flooring materials required over traditional foundations makes them unaffordable to local dwellers. For some buildings, however, sufficient funds are available. One church visited was built on a raft foundation, which whilst preventing cracking, allowed the building to subside uniformly to one side by several degrees.

Consideration of other forms of foundation is currently not an economic option: in the mid 1980s a study by the Rimac Municipality[3] concluded that pile foundations of over 15 metres - deep enough to reach the stable land past the rubbish - would be required to give adequate strength to buildings in the neighbourhood. Clearly this is not a viable solution for a low-income settlement.

The predominant building material used for floors and first storey roofs is concrete, whilst walls tend to be build using reinforced concrete frames with brick infill. Whilst lightweight bricks are in evidence and appear to be used frequently, the concrete used makes for heavy construction, particularly at roof level. Other lighter weight options such as tile are available within Lima; however, tile does not allow flexibility for the future building of successive storeys when resources allow - a key activity as families grow and also in terms of consolidating/increasing investments.

Builders were, in addition, not using timber - an alternative, lighter weight construction material - as a long term building solution for upper storeys. This may be accounted for by the relatively high cost of wood due to its local scarcity (Lima is located within the desert coastal strip of Peru).

Damage to livelihoods and the perpetuation of poverty

A crucial long term detriment to the community lies in the continual erosion in livelihoods that the neighbourhood causes. Buildings in the *barrio* require constant maintenance and modification often (and sometimes quite literally) just to stand still. Many buildings appear to be in a continuous state of reconstruction: the pervading sense in the neighbourhood is one of a continual building site, some in a state of complete renovation whilst others are being rebuilt, re-cemented or extended.

The condition of the land and buildings serves to intensify poverty within the area. In neighbouring settlements of a similar age, there is evidence of ongoing improvement: good infrastructure of concreted roads, street lighting; rendered and painted houses, most of which are two stories or more, some with balconies;

(relatively) well maintained buildings. Primero de Mayo in contrast is much less developed: the roads remain unconcreted and only a few buildings are over one-storey in height. Some houses have collapsed completely and are in ruin, whilst others wait with piles of bricks outside, ready to be rebuilt. In addition, a few of the first storey dwellings have the early stages of increase on their flat roofs: wooden structures already inhabited. It may be these too await to be consolidated, although a good mitigation measure against further sinking (that is, one that reduces a future negative consequence) would be to keep the structure as it is, so reducing excessive weight.

Damage to services

During research, individuals interviewed pointed to a key problem being the maintenance of water and sewerage pipes resulting from the poor ground. Sewerage and water pipes were laid in 1986 and completed in 1988. According to local residents, problems of leaking began almost straight away. A frequent problem lies in the cracking of underground pipes, often caused by large vehicles driving over unconcreted roads - residents believe this is a major factor in increasing the sinking of the buildings. When damage occurs the municipalities are slow to remedy the problem.

Ownership and official interventions[4]

A key issue increasing vulnerability of the *barrio* relates to the seeming confusion over whether the neighbourhood is informal (that is, has no legal right) or formal (with full legal ownership). Community leaders, unsurprisingly, are adamant they have full ownership; *Defensa Civil* (INDESI), the national authority with responsibility for natural hazards, is clear that they do not have full ownership and want to relocate them, by force if necessary. The community points to a form of semi-ownership which was granted to them by a mayor over 20 years ago.

Evidence of some acceptance of legalisation by the authorities is also evident, through the provision of services, including street lighting (although poor quality) and water and sewerage pipes. The community is also still there, 40 years after first invasion.

The view of INDESI, however, is that the community should not be where it currently is. The current masterplan developed by INDESI for the area shows the neighbourhood as parkland, with all buildings, services and people removed. The plan is for residents to be relocated to Ventanilla, a district on the edge of Lima where new facilities (schools, houses, etc.) are being developed.

Ventanilla, however, is far from the centre of Lima and is considerably less developed with fewer amenities than in Caqueta. Crucially, it would be bad for employment: many of those living in Primero de Mayo work in the centre of the city or in the Caqueta markets; travel to and from the centre each day from Ventanilla would be time consuming and expensive.

The community had been offered relocation to another site within Lima in the early 1970s following an earthquake in which Caqueta's infrastructure and buildings were damaged. They refused, however, since the location being offered was even further away from central Lima than where they currently were in Caqueta. During interviews older residents stated that with their present knowledge of how their neighbourhood has failed to improve they wish they had made the move then. It is too late now though because the land they had been offered has been colonised by others.

Research findings

The following information presents some of the findings of the research carried out in the community as part of a European Union funded project to identify and take action to reduce risk. The project was implemented by the Oxford Centre for Disaster Studies (OCDS) with the Peruvian NGO, *el Instito Para la Democracia Local* (IPADEL). The information presented was gathered by door to door questionnaires, observation and the gathering of 'life stories', and is intended to give a picture of some of the physical and social aspects of Primero de Mayo.

Interviews with residents

The following comprise key points from interviews with two residents. The first being an original invader of Primero de Mayo; the second a former leader of the *barrio*.

Snra Primitiva Uriba At the time of the original invasion of the land, Snra Primitiva Uriba was a teenager.

- Primitiva arrived from Huancayo thinking moving to the capital would be good; the reality, however, was different.
- The settlement of this neighbourhood started in 1951; before the invasion, they lived as squatters in a line of vehicles and did not have anywhere to go. However, they got to hear news about this new settlement (Primero de Mayo). They were still young and were supported by adults who had a large piece of land; an older lady carried out the legalities within the invasion leadership because she had documents.
- They formed the first community committee with Jerardo Avila and constructed the first shacks; afterwards they constructed houses of adobe

and used water from the river and drainage systems, which was bad smelling, to make the mud blocks.
- The person who planned the settlement was the leader.
- The wife did the work because the husband worked as a loader of cement in the north cone of the city.
- Previously, in the community centre they had parties and had collections in order to get a school and teachers. A very important thing was the help of the Jesuit priest who constructed the church and managed to acquire electricity in 1955.

The former leader of Primero de Mayo

- He started the Primero de Mayo settlement in 1951 and was from Huancayo.
- They worked as labourers in public service and as independent workers/bricklayers.
- The place was the first land fill over a municipal dump in Lima; immediately before the invasion it was being used to raise pigs. The guardian of the land was called Pedro Maldonado.
- In the time of President General Odria (1950) the site was settled. The site was illegally invaded and formed the first *barriada*, Cercado de Lima. The process was peaceful and started with 100 families, growing to 500, when it received official recognition being called a workers' neighbourhood (*barrio obrero*).
- The neighbourhood was a lot more peaceful in its beginning, 150 families each with an allotment of 200 by 200 metres. Now there are 650 families and the allotments have been sub-divided. Those who remain are the children; little has changed.
- The river previously was very deep; it has gradually diminished because of the rubbish that is continuously thrown into it.
- The part that is most hazardous within this locality is the road in which the telephone is situated. There are 15 metres of rubbish and the floor has sunk two metres because of the installation of water and drainage. The houses continue to crack because of the land.
- The houses, when repaired, last only three to four years.
- In the 1970 earthquake, many of the adobe houses collapsed as did the banks of the river.
- The land is not fully registered; only provisional title has been granted and only the houses 25 metres in from the ravine have any title. This documentation is from the time of Orrego.
- The communal organisation, until 1970, counted on good participation, union organisation and they worked under a common order.

• *Defensa Civil* in this zone has done nothing in the management of the ravine and there is not the support that is talked about at the national level.

Table 11.1   Summary of vulnerabilities and capacities, Primero de Mayo

Vulnerabilities	Capacities
Site	
former rubbish tip - very poor quality land.	good location: close to Caqueta market and city centre - access to income.
Structural (buildings)	
consolidated concrete frame and brick infill buildings. Some two/three stories with many cracking and sinking. Unstable land accentuates tremors to increase severe building damage and collapse.	consolidated housing; local skills and knowledge to mitigate effects of poor land (e.g. strengthened foundations, usage of lightweight bricks).
Layout, services and infrastructure	
poor electrical connections lead to fires; frequent flooding from overflowing pipes; pipes frequently crack due to weak ground (especially when traffic drives on roads over services).	layout in blocks with space for access of emergency services, e.g. for fire engines; lighting, water and sewerage supplied; roads being upgraded; infrastructure enhances sense of permanency.
Political	
threat of removal because of poor land by authorities.	high profile area: issues and problems known in Lima.
Community	
forced relocation; delinquency: drugs and crime.	very strong community organisation; existing community groups; site is many years old; grass roots commitment to betterment; acceptance by community leaders of problems.

Plate 11.3   A dwelling affected by land sinking

Door to door survey

A door to door survey was made of the buildings at the intersection of five roads within Primero de Mayo. The research team of OCDS and IPADEL staff went door to door seeking information on the number of residents and the length of time that they had lived in the dwellings. In addition, a visual survey was made of the construction of the dwellings.

Plate 11.5 **A builder demonstrates shuttering for building part of a concrete frame**

Plate 11.4 **A builder on site**

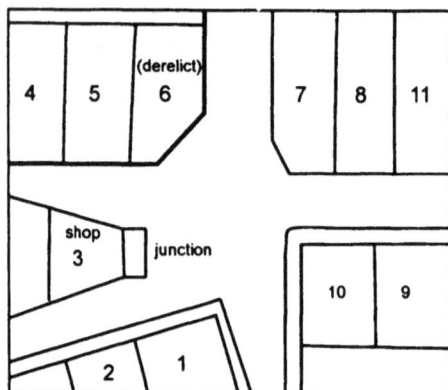

Figure 11.1 Sketch plan of central intersection, Primero de Mayo

Household survey findings

Table 11.2 details the findings relating to the plan shown in Figure 11.1 (the house number refers to the houses visited by members of the research team).

  The community is well established. All but House 2 have been resident for well over 20 years; House 2 has remained in the family - their parents have handed it on. This longevity of residence reinforces two points:

1. The perceived value by the residents in staying in the area.
2. The ability of residents to cope with their circumstances, mostly by rebuilding properties as they subside.

Table 11.2   Household survey findings

House number	Family name	No. of adults	No. of children	No. with work	No. of years in property
1	Martinez Anigama	3	3	2	35
2	Ward Rojas	2	1	2	3
	Yanez	2	1	2	1
	Otero Pinillos	2	0	1	2
	Ward Florian	2	2	1	2
3	Flores	9	3	5	45
5	Bustamante Olano	5	1	1	25
7	Fortunato Usquiano	3	1	3	44
8	Morales Accedo	4	2	1	45
10	- Derelict -				
11	Aguirre	5	3	3	22

Construction materials of walls

Table 11.3 indicates a consolidated ground floor with progressively less finish and permanency to building materials on successive storeys above. Brick walls are used at ground floor level for all but one of the houses, with concrete frames for most. The use of render at ground floor level indicates the effort made to improve the finish of buildings. None of the buildings surveyed had rendered upper storeys since they were relatively new constructions.

All second-storey additions were built in wood. This follows the pattern of building in 'temporary' materials first with a view to later consolidation in brick and concrete, as funds allow.

Table 11.3   Construction materials used in walls

house number	Ground Floor				First Floor				Second Floor	
	brick	adobe	reinforced concrete	render	brick	adobe	wood	reinforced concrete	matting	wood
1	●	●		●	●			●	●	●
2	●	●	●	●	●			●	●	●
3	●	●	●	●	●			●		●
4	●	●	●	●	●	●		●	●	●
5	●	●	●	●	●	●		●	●	●
6	d	e	r	e	l	i	c	t		
7	●		●							●
8	●		●	●			●			●
9	●			●	●			●		●
10										
11	●		●	●				●		●

Conclusions

Primero de Mayo is an area that, more than any other of its neighbours, continues to trade-off its vulnerabilities against its capacities. In this balance, three general points might be made:

Bottom-up over top-down.

A key vulnerability to *barrio* Primero de Mayo (possibly even the greatest) has been the lack of meeting between the top-down approach of governmental bodies, such as INDESI, and the bottom-up activities of the community themselves. The *barrio* has flourished in spite of overwhelming problems including poor land, shortage of resources and official opposition. Whilst the community has continued to maintain the neighbourhood, the governmental (INDESI) approach has been one of adhering to its aim of creating a park in place of the neighbourhood at great cost and at great loss of the investments that have continued for over 40 years, and of using forced relocation if necessary.

The nature of illegality.

Illegality is not necessarily an obstacle for community improvement. Conventional wisdom has it that informal settlements do not invest in individual and neighbourhood improvements until ownership (legality) has been obtained. Yet within *barrio* Primero de Mayo (and elsewhere within Caqueta) neighbourhood organisations have lived and improved areas with semi-legality. The illustration of *barrio* Primero de Mayo is one of fudged ownership - the community has a half promise from a previous mayor that the land is theirs. For the community this has been enough to underpin the consolidation of the area and for them to argue their full ownership and rights to remain.

Perception of risk is outweighed by livelihood considerations

The neighbourhood was offered relocation before, and continues to be offered improved living conditions. Yet, it does not accept, due, primarily (if not solely) to the advantages of the location providing access to incomes. The view is one of 'hardship now for a better future'. This occurs even in spite of the continual drain on resources through continual rebuilding - and the ultimate damaging effect on livelihoods - that living in the *barrio* brings.

Notes

1 Information for this chapter was gathered as part of a European Union funded project which sought to identify risks within Caqueta and to implement community based risk reduction measures. The project was implemented by the Oxford Centre for Disaster Studies (OCDS) in association with the Peruvian NGO, *Instituto Para La Democracia Local* (IPADEL). Research presented in this project was gathered as part of this project; the author acknowledges the work of Luccio Cortez and Liliana Miranda (IPADEL) and Cormac Davey (formerly of OCDS). The project is described in Sanderson, *Reducing Urban Risk as a Tool for Urban Improvement* in *Environment and Urbanization*, Vol 9, Number 1, pp.251-261.
2 Interview with residents, October 1995.
3 Miranda, CIUDAD, 1996; in conversation.
4 Official interventions within the area are described in Sanderson, 'Building Bridges to Reduce Risk', in *Reconstruction after Disaster: Issues and Practices*, (1997) A. Awotona (ed), Ashgate, pp. 148-165.

Index

For Product Safety Concerns and Information please contact our EU
representative GPSR@taylorandfrancis.com
Taylor & Francis Verlag GmbH, Kaufingerstraße 24, 80331 München, Germany

www.ingramcontent.com/pod-product-compliance
Lightning Source LLC
Chambersburg PA
CBHW031436210326
41599CB00046B/4160